INTEGRATING MODERATELY AND SEVERELY HANDICAPPED LEARNERS

INTEGRATING MODERATELY AND SEVERELY HANDICAPPED LEARNERS

Strategies that Work

Edited By

MICHAEL P. BRADY and PHILIP L. GUNTER

With Linda Parnell, Technical Editor
A Foreword by Roger J. Blue

A Project of

The Association for Retarded Citizens-Tennessee

CHARLES C THOMAS • PUBLISHER
Springfield • Illinois • U.S.A.

Published and Distributed Throughout the World by

CHARLES C THOMAS • PUBLISHER
2600 South First Street
Springfield, Illinois 62717

© *1985 by* CHARLES C THOMAS • PUBLISHER

ISBN 0-398-05127-5
Library of Congress Catalog Card Number: 85-4726

With THOMAS BOOKS *careful attention is given to all details of manufacturing and design. It is the Publisher's desire to present books that are satisfactory as to their physical qualities and artistic possibilities and appropriate for their particular use.* THOMAS BOOKS *will be true to those laws of quality that assure a good name and good will.*

Printed in the United States of America
SC-R-3

Library of Congress Cataloging in Publication Data

Main entry under title:

Integrating moderately and severely handicapped learners.

"A project of the Association for Retarded Citizens-Tennessee."
Bibliography: p.
Includes index.
1. Mentally handicapped—Services for—United States—
Addresses, essays, lectures. 2. Mentally handicapped—
Rehabilitation—United States—Addresses, essays,
lectures. 3. Mentally handicapped—Education—United
States—Addresses, essays, lectures. 4. Mainstreaming
in education—United States—Addresses, essays, lectures.
I. Brady, Michael P. II. Gunter, Philip L.
III. Association for Retarded Citizens-Tennessee.

HV3006.A4I56   1985   362.3'8'0973   85-4726
ISBN 0-398-05127-5

DEDICATION

This book and the work that led to its development was strongly influenced by a great many people. To the many contributors in this book who so willingly (if not promptly) gave their energies, we thank you. To Dick Shores, Jim Fox, Floyd Dennis, Paul Alberto, Luanna Meyer, Toshi Hirabayashi, Camille Almy, Cecil Sells, Sealii Epenesa, and so many others who so competently shaped our skills and values, we thank you. To our loved ones and colleagues who endured us as we developed this book, we thank you. And finally, to Jeff, Troy, Simi, Sabrina, Norvin, Steve, and other students who taught us about education and so much more, we thank you.

FOREWORD

After suffering generations of degrading custodial care, the 1950s ushered in America's first real attempt to relate to the human value of people who are considered to be mentally retarded. Two major turning points occurred during the 1950s and 1960s. They were: (a) the establishment of what is now the Association for Retarded Citizens of the United States as a citizen and consumer advocacy organization and (b) federal legislation established by the late President John F. Kennedy.

Since that time, tremendous changes have occurred to alter the lives of our nation's retarded citizens. The national goal has been to provide ways for retarded citizens to be integrated into society as productive, contributing members. Institutional care is gradually being replaced by community integration. Education, training, equality, and human rights are spotlight issues.

The struggle for change has not been without growing pains. Many of the concepts applied to normalization have been implemented through trial and error. As a result, much of the research became obsolete and discarded before implementation of it provided any real value, while other potentially valuable research has not reached practitioners' hands. A confusion of philosophies still exists as a direct result of establishing program models without a solid data base. Untranslated research adds to the conflict of philosophies on institutionalization and leaves the service provider, the family, and the retarded citizen in a state of confusion and frustration. The service provider today is presented with a myriad of material, research, training models, and textbook information, much of which is not useful for teaching practical daily skills.

In this book, Michael Brady and Phil Gunter have compiled a practical guide, translating technical research into workable reality. By selecting the respective works of some of the nation's most recognized authorities, they have captured the concept of integration of moderately and severely handicapped citizens into the mainstream of their communities. Any service provider will be able to draw working knowledge from this book that will enable them to provide better services for their mentally retarded clients or students. In addition to the information offered in this book, a real value lies in the style in which it is written. Any parent, teacher, vocational educator, or classroom aide will find it extremely useful in their relationship with a retarded citizen.

Finally, on behalf of the ARC–TN, I extend a warm thank you to the editors and authors of this book. All have donated their efforts so that the proceeds of book sales will go to the ARC–TN for our continued work advocating for retarded citizens. Your professional advocacy is greatly appreciated.

Roger J. Blue
Association for Retarded Citizens — Tennessee

INTRODUCTION

This book is about integrating persons who are moderately or severely handicapped into a wide range of normalized community environments and activities. Questions such as, "Who can be integrated?" or "Does integration work?" are not examined in this book. Rather, information in each chapter is directed toward a more positive and practical question posed by Wilcox and Sailor (1980): "How can we make integration efforts successful?" We are pleased with the broad range of pragmatic responses that the chapter authors have contributed to further efforts toward integration.

Progressive Inclusion

The evolution of educational services for handicapped persons in America has been called a trend of "progressive inclusion" (Reynolds & Birch, 1982). The systematic efforts to include handicapped persons in the mainstream of society "is a consequence of litigation, legislation, and an increased public awareness of the rights of handicapped persons to live and learn in integrated community environments...with rare exception, the literature indicates that integration is both proper and overdue" (Johnson & Meyer chapter in this text). It is becoming increasingly apparent that the doctrine of automatic segregation of moderately and severely handicapped people in American society is being replaced with the emerging trend to integrate each individual into as many aspects of society as possible.

In communities across the nation, a wide range of alternatives are becoming available to integrate moderately and severely handicapped individuals into normalized community services (Taylor, 1982). Efforts are being made to provide educational services to all handicapped individuals and to train teachers based on students' service needs rather than categorical labels, medical descriptions, or other administrative conveniences (Brady, Conroy, & Langford, 1984). In research projects, demonstration centers, group homes, schools, neighborhoods, and job sites, educators and human service planners are seeking and providing more effective ways of integrating moderately and severely handicapped persons into various aspects of American society. The strategies provided by the authors in this book, and the work carried on by colleagues across the nation, represent a positive approach to the integration of people with moderate and severe disabilities.

A Difficult Task

Providing comprehensive, functional, age appropriate, integrated, community based services is undoubtedly a difficult task. The furor over the current effort to shift funding priorities from institutions to community based programs is evidence that change is a slow process. It is unfortunate that social and physical segregation has become the standard to be challenged. Educators have had to argue why handicapped students *should be* educated in neighborhood schools. Rehabilitation personnel have had to argue why others *should be* given access to work. Agency planners have had to argue why people with disabilities *should be* allowed to live in typical, neighborhood communities. Too seldom have we questioned why any person should be *removed* from the mainstream of society, solely on the basis of his/her impairment. In short, segregation has been the rule; integration has been the exception.

Unfortunately, a difficult task has been made more difficult by the necessity to promote the *re-entry* of many people *back* into society. However, the difficulty of a task does not lessen its importance. We are pleased to note that assistance is coming from many quarters. Recently, the Office of Special Education and Rehabilitation Services of the U.S. Department of Education announced a shift in priority from the review of current regulations to the provision of technical assistance and implementation incentives (Will, 1983). Such an emphasis will do much to further the efforts discussed by the many authors in this book, described by Taylor (1982), or implemented quietly in scores of communities.

Investigating Practical Approaches

Both editors of this book have, at various times, been involved with services for moderately and severely handicapped persons in building, local, or state education agency roles, as researchers or research assistants, as inservice and preservice teacher educators, and throughout our professional careers, as students. As service providers, we have been astutely aware that the philosophical bases for integration, while crucial for setting societal and organizational goals, did not provide practitioners with the assistance necessary for carrying out an integration mandate. And while many researchers and practitioners have begun to search for empirically-supported strategies, literally hundreds of questions remain. Educational researchers only recently have begun examining many aspects of integration that professionals have taken for granted (cf. Fredericks chapter in this text).

Our own research has been directed toward generalization tactics for social skills development (Brady, Shores, Gunter, McEvoy, & Fox, in press; Fox, Gunter, Brady, Bambara, Spiegel-McGill, & Shores, 1984; Gunter, Brady, Shores, & Fox, 1984), the reduction of stigmatizing stereotypic behaviors (Gunter, Brady, Shores, Fox, Owen, & Goldzweig, 1984; Gunter, Fox, McEvoy, Shores, & Denny, 1984), and social validation technology (Gunter, Brady, Shores, Fox, Owen, & Goldzweig, 1984; Gunter, Fox, McEvoy, Shores, & Denny, 1984). Additionally, we have investigated legal administrative aspects of integration, Brady & Gunter, in press-a) and examined legal protections for teachers of severely handicapped students (Brady & Dennis, 1984). We have promoted effective strategies for curriculum improvement in rural areas (Brady & Gunter, in press-b), and conceptualized planning strategies for school-based integration efforts (Brady, McEvoy, Gunter, Shores, & Fox, in press). These experiences have made us aware of the many questions regarding services for persons with significant handicaps. We have, however, resigned ourselves to the fact that many of our efforts may never reach practitioners (Gunter & Brady, 1984). Therefore, in addition to our future research efforts, we will continue to be involved in the development and validation of dissemination and advocacy activities on behalf of moderately and severely handicapped individuals.

The Future

This book, then, is the culmination of the efforts of both researchers and practitioners. All have presented a range of useful strategies representing the research and development efforts of many leading professionals. All have contributed their work to the Association for Retarded Citizens of Tennessee (ARC–TN). This form of advocacy will assist the ARC–TN to seek improved, comprehensive services and will provide practitioners with valuable programming strategies. We encourage practitioners responsible for planning and implementing services for moderately and severely handicapped individuals to access these strategies, discuss the ideas, and continue to strive for better services.

REFERENCES

Brady, M. P., Conroy, M., & Langford, C. A. Current issues and practices affecting the development of noncategorical programs for students and teachers. *Teacher Education and Special Education*, 1984, 7(1), 20–26.

Brady, M. P., & Dennis, H. F. Integrating severely handicapped learners: Potential teacher liability in community based programs. *Remedial and Special Education*, 1984, 5(5), 29–36.

Brady, M. P., & Gunter, P. Educating severely handicapped students: Legal issues in integrated community based programs. *Executive Educator,* in press-a.

Brady, M. P., & Gunter, P. IEP managers: A model for special education inservice training in rural school systems. *The Rural Educator,* in press-b.

Brady, M. P., McEvoy, M., Gunter, P., Shores, R. E., & Fox, J. J. Considerations for socially integrated school environments for severely handicapped students. *Education and Training of the Mentally Retarded,* in press.

Brady, M. P., Shores, R. E., Gunter, P., McEvoy, M., & Fox, J. J. Generalization of a severely handicapped adolescent's social interaction behavior via multiple peers in a classroom setting. *Journal of the Association for Persons with Severe Handicaps,* in press.

Fox, J. J., Gunter, P., Brady, M. P., Bambara, L., Spiegel-McGill, P., & Shores, R. E. Using multiple peer exemplars to develop generalized social responding of an autistic girl. In R. E. Rutherford & C. M. Nelson (Eds.), *Monograph on severe behavioral disorders of children and youth,* Vol. 7. Reston, VA: Council for Exceptional Children, 1984.

Fredericks, H. Research needs: Educational, community based, social, and policy. In M. P. Brady & P. Gunter (Eds.), *Integrating moderately and severely handicapped learners: Strategies that work.* Springfield, IL: Charles C Thomas (this text).

Gunter, P., & Brady, M. P. Increasing the practitioner's utilization of research: A dilemma in regular and special education. *Education,* 1984. *105*(1), 92–98.

Gunter, P., Brady, M. P., Shores, R. E., & Fox, J. J. Multiple peer training: Tactics for generalization of social skills in severely handicapped children. Manuscript in preparation.

Gunter, P., Brady, M. P., Shores, R. E., Fox, J. J., Owen, S., & Goldzweig, I. The reduction of aberrant vocalizations with auditory feedback and resulting collateral behavior change of two autistic boys. *Behavior Disorders,* 1984, *9*(4), 254–263.

Gunter, P., Fox, J. J., McEvoy, M., Shores, R. E., & Denny, R. K. An empirical and social validation of response covariation in the reduction of aberrant behavior of an autistic boy. Manuscript in preparation, 1984.

Johnson, R. E., & Meyer, L. Program design and research to normalize peer interactions. In M. P. Brady & P. Gunter (Eds.), *Integrating moderately and severely handicapped learners: Strategies that work.* Springfield, IL: Charles C Thomas (this text).

Reynolds, M., & Birch, J. *Teaching exceptional children in all America's schools.* Reston, VA: Council for Exceptional Children, 1982.

Taylor, S. J. From segregation to integration: Strategies for integrating severely handicapped students in normal school and community settings. *Journal of the Association for the Severely Handicapped,* 1982, *7*(3), 42–49.

Wilcox, B., & Sailor, W. Service delivery issues: Integrated educational systems. In B. Wilcox & R. York (Eds.), *Quality education for the severely handicapped: The federal investment.* Washington, DC: U.S. Department of Education, 1980.

Will, M. *Life, liberty, and the pursuit of employment opportunity: Goals for Americans who experience severely handicapping conditions.* Keynote address presented at the 10th Annual Conference of The Association for Persons with Severe Handicaps, San Francisco, November, 1983.

ACKNOWLEDGMENTS

A number of people were instrumental in developing this book. Pam MacQuarrie labored for hours with the manuscript. She did a terrific job! Teeny Jones helped throughout the project with the multitude of details that are part of efforts such as these. The staff of the ARC and Peabody/Vanderbilt's Special Education Department helped in numerous ways. We thank you all.

CONTENTS

INTEGRATING MODERATELY AND
SEVERELY HANDICAPPED LEARNERS

Section I
FOUNDATIONS FOR
ADMINISTRATIVE STRATEGIES

CHAPTER 1

OUR SON: THE ENDLESS SEARCH FOR HELP

AURELIA T. SCHAWLOW AND ARTHUR L. SCHAWLOW

Our son was born on March 21, 1956. That was about two weeks later than expected, and more than two feet of snow had fallen in New Jersey over the preceding weekend. There were some anxious hours, but eventually the snow did end and roads were cleared in time for the trip to the hospital. The birth was long and difficult, and was complicated by a deep transverse arrest that the doctor, busy with another patient, overlooked for several hours. But our son was so beautiful and lively; our first child! We named him Arthur (after his father and paternal grandfather) Keith. We have always called him Artie.

At the time, Art was a research physicist at Bell Telephone Laboratories in Murray Hill, New Jersey, and Aurelia was choir director of the First Baptist Church in Morristown. We had a new house in Madison, and Artie was the center of our life. Before long, he was joined by two sisters, Helen, born in July, 1957, and Edith, born in November, 1959. Artie seemed to us a perfect baby, ahead of the books' predictions in physical development like turning over, sitting up, standing and walking. Yet, if we had been more experienced parents, we might have known that he was neither as demanding nor as responsive as most children. He was quick to learn things by himself, but not at all easy to teach.

Around the age of one, he began to say a few words, but then he stopped. He gradually became more withdrawn and often seemed content to amuse himself by listening to music or playing with toys.

Becoming concerned, we began what was to become an endless search for help. An old friend, a distinguished European-born neurologist, told us that our son had "a mathematician's personality" and would eventually start to talk. At that time, New Jersey had no medical school. Even though we lived in an affluent suburban area, there were few specialists familiar with the more unusual childhood conditions. We did find a pediatric neurologist

*The Schawlows are parents of an autistic son. *Arthur Schawlow* received his Ph.D. from the University of Toronto. He currently is Professor of Physics at Stanford University. He received a Nobel prize in Physics in 1981 for his contributions to the development of laser spectroscopy. *Aurelia Shawlow* received her M.A. from Columbia and is a musician, singer, and choral conductor.

who, although extremely busy, eventually did examine our son. She decided
that he had petit mal epilepsy and prescribed a drug for that. Almost
immediately, it was apparent to us that the drug was not helping, and that
he was becoming even more withdrawn. Moreover, he became incontinent,
so that he was no longer "acceptable" in a nursery school. In addition, there
were occasional episodes when his face would suddenly turn purple, and he
would have a far away look. We tried to get the doctor to see what was
happening, but we could not even get our telephone calls returned much of
the time. This was the first of several times that doctors blithely prescribed
drugs and then refused to recognize harmful effects that were immediately
evident to us. Another such incident occurred when Artie was about seven
years old. A neurologist prescribed heavy doses of an amphetamine. We
begged him to monitor the effects closely, but it was the same story. Perhaps
he felt we must give the drug enough time to act. We think that he was
looking for some kind of anomalous reaction of the drug, but it was quickly
and painfully evident that the drug was doing just what amphetamines
usually do. Artie lost his appetite, and would only eat a very few things. His
stereotypic behavior became even more persistent. Then, too, he was awake
until 1:00 a.m. night after night.

The Search for Services

By 1961, when he was five years old, it was apparent that there was no help
to be had for him in our area of New Jersey, not even an appropriate school
or day care program. Thus, when Art received an offer of a professorship
from Stanford University, and we learned that parents there had set up a
school for children like Artie, we decided to move. One of Art's colleagues
in the physics department had a daughter who was similarly withdrawn and
nonverbal, and his wife had been a leader in establishing the school.

The first year at Stanford was a good year for Artie, and the school
seemed to be something he enjoyed. But then the director of the school left
for a better position, and things did not go well for our son under her
replacement. Artie was not willing to participate in the group activities and
would wander off by himself more often. We sought help from neurologists,
which led us to the amphetamine incident recounted earlier, and from
psychiatrists. The psychiatrists, although they would probably not be classed
strictly as psychoanalysts, were influenced by that school of thought. Their
approach was just to try to get us, the parents, to search our souls to find
what terrible things we were doing wrong. Not only is this approach useless,
but it is also destructive, because it makes the parents less, rather than more,
able to cope with the difficult behavior of the autistic child. Also, that
approach immediately puts a gap between the parent and psychiatrist. If the

psychiatrist insists on treating the parents as his patients, he cannot work with them to help the child who is, after all, the person who needs help.

By the time Artie was eight years old, it was apparent that we could not provide the teaching and companionship of other children that he needed. The public schools had nothing at all for him in those days. But we did find a residential setting, Clearwater Ranch Children's Home, which seemed as if it could provide a good environment for him in a rural area. We placed Artie in the home and visited him there weekly. He came home for occasional visits. After a year or so, he was moved to the Clearwater Ranch Town House, in the small town of Cloverdale. There were six boys in the house, and it was run by a wonderful lady, Mrs. Grace Turner. She had spotted Artie at the ranch and asked for him because he had reminded her of a boy who had started to talk while in her house. Artie learned many things there and those were, on the whole, good years for him in which he gradually became less withdrawn. He did not really talk satisfactorily then, but he sometimes said phrases or sentences. Artie became able to do a number of household chores and took pleasure in performing them.

However, at adolescence, several things took a turn for the worse. Mrs. Turner was not able to continue with the Town House. Artie grew big enough so that he frightened some of the teenage girls who worked on the staff. Even though at that time he never harmed staff or other residents, the staff became particularly nervous when he began to have occasional tantrums. Eventually, they decided that Artie was too big to manage, and we had to find another place for him.

We found another ranch and he moved there. He was immersed in a larger group and apparently did not get enough individual attention because he became more isolated and withdrawn. When he began tearing up clothes and sheets, this home decided that they could not manage him. However, he still had never attacked nor hit anybody.

Hospitals and Teachers

In desperation, we put Artie into a state hospital. It was in a convenient location, 17 miles from our home, and had spacious grounds. We were told about their various programs and workshops, and it looked like a reasonable choice. Besides, we had no alternatives, because there were then few group homes for autistic adolescents and adults.

The hospital proved to be far worse than we feared initially. Somehow, the classes never materialized, or would get cancelled after one or two sessions because the person in charge was needed elsewhere, or for some other reason, or for no reason. Worse than that, the hospital relied on massive doses of antipsychotic drugs of the phenothiazine group (e.g.,

Mellaril or Thorazine) for behavior control. They insisted on drugging Artie until he looked like a zombie. I don't think they had any idea of Artie's abilities; under those drugs he looked and acted really stupid and half asleep. The wards were quite chaotic with a lot of boys who would frequently hit others. We brought him home for visits almost every weekend in order to take him swimming, but under the drugs, it was difficult to teach him.

We continually argued with the doctors and with the hospital authorities to reduce or eliminate the drugs. We were never told that the drugs were good for Artie, but rather that the staff wanted them, or that he needed a tranquilizer for such a violent environment. Not only did the drugs affect his behavior, but physical side effects became evident. Thorazine made his skin very sensitive to sunburn, and it was constantly irritated. Mellaril made it nearly impossible for him to swallow. He still has a habit of holding saliva in his mouth that originated when Mellaril prevented him from swallowing.

Eventually, we learned of the very great danger of tardive dyskinesia, an irreversible condition that often follows prolonged treatment with these drugs. Sometimes the authorities would yield a bit to our entreaties and reduce the drugs; but if they had any trouble with his behavior, a higher dose would again be administered. His behavior did become rougher, a matter of sheer survival in that environment. At last, we found a newspaper report of a court decision that drugs could not be given to patients without their consent. When we showed that to the director of the hospital, her staff studied it and told us that we could not speak for Artie on that because we were not his guardians. We then went to the expense of getting a court order of limited conservatorship which specifically set forth our right to control his medical treatment. The hospital administration was furious, and tried several times to get rid of us and Artie. But somehow, once the drugs were gone, we found in Artie a warm and loving person, who clearly wanted attention and was open to learning. What a contrast from the remote and unreachable child we had known.

We, of course, wanted Artie out of the hospital. We tried several times keeping him at home for extended periods. However, we could not find any appropriate program for him in our community, and it was too much for us to supervise him all day, every day. Since we couldn't manage to keep him occupied at home, we tried seeing what a teacher might be able to do at the hospital. A teacher who had some experience as a sign language instructor, but was working on a college degree to acquire credentials, began visiting Artie at the hospital to try teaching him sign language. It was part of the plan from the beginning that signing might also help him to relax enough to produce some speech. She started with food words like candy, cookie, and apple. The correct sign, or an approximation, was rewarded by a bit of that delicacy. Somewhat to our surprise, he was happy to sit and work for an hour or so at a time on various signs. Although it did not seem easy for him, he did learn a number of signs including those for some articles of clothing and some familiar objects, and he made sounds with some of them. Most striking was the word "bed" which he would say clearly while making that sign. Sometimes surprising things came out, like "peanut butter." Apparently, the effort of making the sign helped to overcome his inhibition against speech. But neither then nor subsequently has he been in a situation where he could really use those signs for communication, and so he rarely does.

What really seemed important was that he had acquired a taste for working at a table with a teacher for extended periods. While he was still working on the signs, we were able to hire an inspired teacher, Mrs. Joanne Glass, who began to work on recognizing letters, words, and simple arithmetic. Progress was exciting, but after a few months, she moved to a better job which did not leave time for working with our son. We hired students who kept up the human contact but did not have the skills to make much progress.

Learning and the Surprise of Technology

Meanwhile, we continued to visit our son every week, and we kept up these visits even later when he moved to a residential home 65 miles away. In many ways, this house and the accompanying day program were great improvements over the hospital; however, the emphasis was on controlling behavior and, as far as we could tell, they did not take seriously the possibility of academic learning. Many of these things we did on our visits were not academic either, but we did use letter cards every week. He learned to recognize letter shapes by inserting them into the cards from which they had been stamped. Each time he inserted one, we would repeat the name of the letter and usually the word which accompanied it on the card (e.g., "L for lion"). However, we only began to realize what he had learned when we bought a Texas Instruments Touch and Tell™. This device produces a synthesized voice that asks things like "Where is the red letter Q?" or "Can you find the small letter X?" Correct answers are given by pressing the appropriate letter on the device and are rewarded by a few notes of a tune and by the voice saying cheerily, "You found the small letter X." After a slightly timid start, it was soon evident that Artie knew all of the letters of the alphabet by name, upper, and lower case. He also had no difficulty when the synthesized voice asked him to "Show me the letter for king," or some other word. Artie had learned the alphabet.

So he knew the alphabet, but how much did he really know about words? There are various packages of Word Lotto available with cards which bear pictures of familiar objects and their names, such as "umbrella" or "shoe."

He could easily pick out any card asked for by name and match it with the right picture on the large card. Aurelia then printed the words on the backs of the small cards and asked him for the cards by name. The first week he succeeded in identifying the six cards presented to him and the next week, 12 more. By then it was apparent that he could recognize any card she presented and was not just memorizing them at that time.

Next, Aurelia tried reading a beginning level story book with him. It was a simple version of the old story about the three bears. Then she told him, "I taught myself to read by underlining words whenever I could find them. Let's see if you can find the word 'bear' and underline it." He was able to do that right away, and it was soon apparent that he could recognize any word, not just a list of words that he had been taught. He really had developed the idea of how to read.

But how could he communicate what he was thinking? We were given a most exciting clue during our trip to Stockholm in December 1981. There we met Dr. Karin Stensland Junker, who is a renowned authority on autism and author of the book *Child in the Glass Ball.* This book is about her own autistic daughter. Dr. Junker told us that a young man, 24 years old, had been brought to her office a few months earlier. He appeared very withdrawn and typically autistic, and sat seeming not to notice what was going on around him. Yet he had learned to communicate by using a calculator-like device that printed out words on a paper tape. For instance, she asked him, "May I have some of your tapes?" He replied (in Swedish), "No." "Why not?" she asked. "Because it's no good when the sun shines" he said. The device uses a thermal printer, and the tapes fade when exposed to sunlight. Mats, as his family called the young man, understood that the tapes faded; now, at last, he could express it. How marvelous! Just imagine how frustrated he must have felt when he could not express his thoughts at all.

We found out some months later that this device is a Canon Communicator™, which is sold in this country for about $600 by Telesensory Systems near our home in Palo Alto. We bought one, but our son would only type words if we guided his hand and mostly seemed to want to bang the keys randomly. Meanwhile, we were trying some of the other things described earlier. We got the address of the Swedish boy's parents and eventually received a letter telling how they had taught their son to read and type. We were excited because we found many similarities between what they had done and what we were trying.

The Epson HX-20™ portable microcomputer became available late in 1982, with a full-size keyboard, a liquid crystal display, and a small printer. We wrote a program for this computer which would present either single letters or words on the screen with a series of dashes underneath, like:

Viola Rönnlund
Vikingsvägen 26
S-175 61 Järfälla
Sweden

17-02 1983

Mr. A. Schawlow
Stanford University
Stanford, California 94305
U S A

Dear Mr. Schawlow,
Thank you for your letter of October of last year and I apologize
for the delay in replying. It has taken a while to compile everything and then to get it translated to English. I hope it will be
of help to you.

Here are some notes on Mats and how he learned to read and write
with the aid of a typewriter and later to use his communicator.
Mats's sister, who is a teacher, and I, his mother, started to
teach Mats a kind of unit reading. That was as early as 1967. We
were only able to teach him during his summer vacations and every
second or third week when he came home to see us.

We tried to make him point at pictures representing words which
belonged to phrases he was to read later. We asked him about each
picture and he seemed to understand us and pointed at the right
pictures.

The next step was to give him words. First he combined two-
letter, and then three-letter words with the pictures. For the
most part, he managed to match the right words with the pictures.

Mats lived at home between 1970 and 1975 and we continued the
way we had started - combining words with pictures. Gradually,
he managed to put longer words, five-letter words, six-letter
words, to the right pictures. We proceeded with short phrases,
e.g., "The child is playing," "The rabbit is eating," and
these he managed to place with the correct pictures.

After this, Mats started making words from letters. I showed
pictures of, for example, a girl, a boy, an animal, a house, a
car, or a rose. We had mixed the letters and he chose the right
ones to spell out the word suitable to the picture. We kept this
up for about a year. Then he started spelling out two-word phrases.
These phrases were gradually increased to five words.

Some time later, we started reading books. I read aloud and Mats
followed each line with his finger. After a couple of pages, we
stopped and I asked him to show me where a certain sentence

appeared in the text. At about this time, I encouraged Mats to
practice writing the letters of the alphabet by hand.

Later on we started practicing with an electric typewriter. Mats
tried to answer questions from a book for children in second and
third grade (8-9 year olds). The questions were, for example, "A
lemon is not sweet but _ _ _ _." Mats had to type out the missing
word on the typewriter. Another simple example was to answer a
question such as, "this animal you get milk from.' In most cases,
he managed to type the correct answer.

We continued the reading - now going one step further - both of
us reading quietly to ourselves. After having read three or four
pages, I asked who the passage was about and what sort of actions
were being carried out. He progressed very well and his spelling
was remarkably good considering he had not been practicing difficult words. We continued with this type of reading and are doing
so at present. By now we have read a great number of books. Nowa-
days he uses his communicator to answer our questions. The
advantage is that he can always carry the communicator he got
three years ago.

Mats has typed several letters to friends and relatives on his
electric typewriter. However, I have always to dictate these letters or nothing would be done - he finds it difficult to take the
initiative himself. He can also write by hand and he has written
some letters in this way, though I must hold my hand lightly on
his. Right now I am trying to make him write by hand without any
support. Every now and then it works.

When it comes to reading and writing, we are hoping that he will
start asking us questions. We feel that this would be a great step
in our mutual contact and communication. We so much want him to
take an interest in the world around him instead of turning inward
into himself, but we do not know how to help him in this matter.

These are some of the methods we have used with Mats and for
the most part, we have had very encouraging results. I do hope
our efforts can be of help to you and that you will keep in contact with us and let us know if you have any success. We wish you
all the good fortune and patience when helping your son.

                    Kind regards

(signed)   Viola and Magnus Rönnlund

B O O K

The program was written to ensure that nothing was entered if he hit several keys at the same time. He had to hit the right key, and no others. Artie could bang at the keys all he wanted, but nothing would happen unless he hit the right letter, first B and then O, O, and K. Each time a correct letter was entered, the computer would emit a brief tone. After the word was finished, the computer would play four notes of music and print the word on the little printer. This worked and Artie enjoyed it. although he still wanted a parent's hand on his to guide him. Sometimes, he would do nearly all of the guiding by himself, but he would rarely do it alone. Later, we wrote another program that displayed and printed larger characters, up to seven on a line rather than the twenty of the computer's regular character set. This was an improvement. but he still wanted a hand on his.

Right now, Artie's primary problem seems to be motivation. He has not seemed to realize that he can communicate with words. We are working on that now. Instead of emphasizing the typing, we are getting him to point at YES or NO or to circle the desired word. He is beginning also to use a communication board to pick out which of his activities, or which food, he wants by pointing to a word on a board. We learned in Orlando, Florida, last year about one teenage autistic boy whose behavior improved dramatically when he was given a communication board to describe his moods. When he came to school, he could point out whether he felt sick, angry, or tired. A communication board is quick and direct, but the range of choices is necessarily limited. However, it does seem to be working for Artie and gives him a verbal way to tell us some things. We hope that his success with it will soon carry over into answering questions by typing a word. Then we will return to the Canon Communicator™ which he can carry with him and which might eventually be used to express any thought.

To teach him to type, we have used the Epson microcomputer, (although it is far from ideal) because we had to use a portable computer. Since he is in the state hospital, which is thoroughly chaotic, we can not set up and use a regular computer. It would, we think, be better to have a large, brightly colored display. We expect that he will move to a group home shortly, and we will be able to experiment a little there with a home computer (e.g., the Texas Instruments 99/4A™) for which programs for preschool and beginning reading are available. The Texas Instrument computer has a voice synthesizer which should be useful. It can talk as well as display words on the screen.

Artie's Future

Clearly, we are very much in the middle of our attempts to help our son learn to communicate. Already he has learned much, as we have learned much about what he knows and can do. He learns quickly at times and does not require endless repetition. His attention span is not short, and he will work at a task for a long time if he wants to and feels it is worthwhile. On the other hand, he becomes easily frustrated and we need to plan things so that he can quickly succeed at each new step. Anything that helps communicate his thoughts and feelings will help to reduce the frustration that he must feel so often.

Adults normally expect to keep learning new things throughout their lives. For instance, Art began to learn about microcomputers when he was 56 years old. Unfortunately, too often we *assume* severe limitations on the learning potential of developmentally disabled adults. As a result of our experiences with Artie, we believe that in many cases, the only reason they do not learn is that nobody tries to teach them. We are excited that our son is not at all too old to learn and is making progress. He wants to learn and enjoys it. How far he will get we do not know. We are learning something new every week about what he knows and how to get him to reveal it. We are still learning new approaches from other parents and from teachers and hope for more in the future.

The spark is there. Can we learn to fan it into flame, will it grow by itself, or will it fade away again?

Postscript

This chapter, to this point, was finished and submitted in August, 1983. We ended with a question; that question now has an answer. Since September, Artie has been communicating fluently with the Canon Communicator™. He seems able to type out anything he is motivated to communicate, with good spelling and sentence structure. It seems hard to believe, but it has happened.

In mid-August, we began consulting with a speech pathologist, Ms. Brendan Webster. She devised some simple board systems which guaranteed Artie immediate feedback if he communicated by pointing to the word for an activity, material, or snack. He learned that communication by printed word got results. He also learned to use a Texas Instruments VOCAID™ as a talking communication board. Although his vocabulary is limited, he has learned to pair phrases to develop sentences (e.g., "I would like . . . to be left alone.").

Then we reintroduced the keyboard and asked him to type out the word to which he had just pointed. It became clear that he could switch back and forth from the typewriter keyboard to the alphabetically-arranged Canon Communicator™ with no problems at all. Again, using only the choices from his communication boards, we ensured that he got whatever he typed. We still did not know whether he could type the words without copying from the communication boards.

In September we took him out for his usual outing and ended up at an ice cream store. He has often waved his arm upward in a gesture indicating that he wanted something in a particular direction. This time, he waved in the direction of a shoe store. We told him, "Come out to the car, get the machine, and tell us what you want." Then he took the communicator, and typed "SHOES." We were delighted, and took him in the store and bought him new shoes.

Two days later, Aurelia visited him on the hospital grounds. Instead of using the communication board to choose activities and materials, he typed his choices without copying. At the end of the visit, she said, "Tell me where you would like to go now." He typed, "GO TO MCDONALDS." She then asked, "What would you like to eat there?" and he answered, "HAMBURGER." She asked, "Would you like ice cream?" and he replied by typing, "ICE CREAM." "What would you like to drink?" she asked, and he replied "COKE." He got each item and then he asked for "PIZZA WHEEL" (a nearby pizza parlor), and "SAUSAGE PIZZA." After that he wanted, and received, steak and salad from another nearby place. It was getting late, and time for his mother to go home, but Artie typed, "STAY YOUR TIME WITH ME."

Then he typed, not once but three times, "I WANT TO GO HOME." Although that was not a convenient time for a home visit, she could not deny him and so he came home. It became apparent that he really hated the hospital and was deathly afraid of returning. Fortunately, a few weeks later, we were at last able to complete arrangements for him to move to an excellent new group home. During his three weeks at home, he communicated by typing every day. He now has a surprisingly large vocabulary, quite good spelling, and good grammar.

So far, Artie communicates mainly with his mother, and primarily about matters that interest him but are not too deeply emotional. However, he has told us that he has been able to read "SINCE I WAS TEN," and that he had not shown it before because it was "TOO HARD." His mother asked, "How is it that you can do it now?" He gave her a sweet smile and typed "I LOVE YOU."

After a few hours in the new group home, he typed "I LIKE IT HERE." He is beginning to communicate with the staff members there, and we hope that before long, he will do it without anyone's hand on his. So far, he wants the reassurance and occasional guidance of a familiar hand.

From these experiences, we are even more convinced that our son does not need endless repetitions to acquire a new skill. He needs, rather, to understand what is wanted and to gain confidence that he can do it. Usually this requires finding easy steps and motivation. Given those, progress is rapid.

Most of all, we have learned that he knows much more than he has been able to communicate and that he can learn more. We are more than ever convinced that the main reason many autistic adults appear unable to learn is because so few people try to reach them and to teach them.

CHAPTER 2

PRINCIPLES FOR
INTEGRATED COMMUNITY PROGRAMMING

DOUGLAS P. BIKLEN AND SUSAN B. FOSTER

The making of integrated, community based programs for moderately and severely handicapped persons demands planning. Ironically, it also requires us to reject many of the traditional, "boiler plate planning solutions." For example, planners frequently conceptualize solutions to problems such as nonservice and poor service in terms of concepts such as "comprehensiveness," "continuum of services," "continuity of services," and "economics of scale." Yet these concepts do not adequately capture either the solutions or the problems posed by the question "How can we make integrated, community based programs work?" The problems have not been merely a failure to articulate a *comprehensive* array of services. Indeed, the problem has been to select appropriate services. The problem has not been one of filling in gaps in an otherwise sound system of services. Rather, the problem has been one of needing to almost entirely supplant an ineffective and indeed destructive system, namely total institutions. The problem has not been one of discovering and maximizing economies of scale but of deciding what is a human scale.

We can not even think about applying basic planning principles (e.g., comprehensiveness, needs analyses, continua of treatment) until we identify and agree upon some larger, guiding moral principles. We need these larger principles to inform our day-to-day planning endeavors. To accomplish this, we pursue three tasks for this chapter. We will examine (a) the predominant models of services which have characterized community residential services for developmentally disabled persons, and (b) the key principles of

---

Douglas Biklen is the Director of the Division of Special Education and Rehabilitation at Syracuse University. He received his Ph.D. from Syracuse in 1973. Dr. Biklen has long been known for his personal and professional commitment to community based, integrated services for persons with handicaps. He has been the Director of the Center on Human Policy and has numerous publications involving political and social aspects of segregation.

Susan Bannerman Foster completed her Ph.D. in Special Education at Syracuse University. She has held administrative and advocacy positions for various agencies serving severely handicapped persons. Dr. Foster's research and publications include studies of state-run institutions and communication in a neonatal unit.

normalization and least restrictive alternative (LRA), which must guide community services development. (The term Least Restrictive Environment [LRE] is a more particular application of the LRA concept.) Once we have articulated these principles, we can then accomplish a third task, (c) to outline the administrative and programmatic principles which can be used successfully to make integration work.

Predominant Service Models

The call for community based services for developmentally disabled consumers has been met in a variety of ways. Generally, these services fall into one of three categories: (a) development of community systems as extensions of institutions (i.e., "total institutions" as defined by Goffman, [1961]), (b) ad hoc community services development, and (c) community based programs developed through a systemic planning process. This section includes a brief description of these three models of service development, concluding with a discussion of the long-term implications of each model.

Community Services as an Extension of the Institution

The development of community services as extensions of institutions is not new. Some of the earliest attempts to support mentally retarded people in the community occurred in the 1920s and 30s when it became clear that the "feebleminded" (as mentally retarded people were then called) were not the menace to society they had been thought.[1] Leaders in the field of mental retardation began to urge adaptation of some of the progressive reform measures being used in the fields of mental illness, criminal justice, and social welfare.[2] These reforms emphasized community services and included traveling clinics from state mental hospitals, foster care, residential colonies, and parole. Since the institution was the predominent treatment model at that time, reformers designed the community services around the institutions, as "extensions" of the existing system. They believed that institutional and community based program could co-exist within the same service continuum, and that both were necessary components of individualized treatment programs.

While these early services may not seem community based as we define the term today, they nonetheless were the forerunners of many currently popular practices. For example, Vaux (1935) described a program in which 32 "mentally defective adults" from the Newark State School were placed into 14 family care homes. Today, the placement of developmentally disabled people in the care of someone who has been licensed and hired by the state to provide residential services in his or her own home is common.

Although participation as a family or foster care provider is voluntary and the residential setting private, the service is coordinated and funded by the state, most often through the same administrative structure as the state institutional system.

Similarly, colony and parole programs were the forerunners of state operated group homes and "community status" release programs, in which the resident is released from the institution but remains a client on the institution books. Often described in institution reports as a "social rehabilitation" program, the colony served as a kind of "half-way" house between institution and community. For example, Bernstein's (1920) description of the colony plan at the Rome State Custodial Asylum included "girls' colonies," in which women were placed in older homes in the city and "trained" for parole as factory workers or live-in domestics in private homes, and "boys' colonies," or farms, where men were "trained" for parole as workers on local farms.[3]

Today, these training programs would be considered peonage. However, the colony model developed into what would be described today as group homes. States most often are divided into catchment areas, or regions, each of which includes an institution as a major component, if not centerpiece. of service delivery. Within these systems, the state operated community residences are run through and by the same administrative network in charge of the state institutions. Generally, the community programs reflect an effort on the part of the state to fill gaps in services which have not been addressed by the private sector, or to provide community living opportunities to institutionalized people excluded from existing programs because they are defined as difficult to serve. In either case, the result is often a community program which functions as an extension of the local institution.[4]

Parole was the legal mechanism by which a resident moved from the institution or colony to the community. Parole was not the same as discharge, since a resident on parole remained under the control and supervision of the institution and could be returned to the institution at any time. Similarly, current practices such as the state of New York's release to "community status" perpetuates the legal process through which a resident can be released from the institution to a community program (e.g., a group home or parental care), but remain on the institution books as under the care and protection of the state. This practice enables the state to retain a significant amount of fiscal and clinical responsibility for and control over the individual. Additionally, return of the individual to the institution is facilitated should the need arise.

There are several potential advantages to community programs run through state agencies. First, many states are mandated by their state legislatures to provide services for all developmentally disabled persons. No one can be excluded because their needs are complex or their level of disability severe. Unfortunately, when this mandate is fulfilled within systems lacking sufficient community alternatives, the result is often institutionalization, particularly for clients with severe or multiple disabilities.

Second, the centralized and highly coordinated nature of state administrative structures increases the potential for extensive planning within these systems. However, the continued use (even growth) of institutions is testimony to the failure of most state systems to utilize this potential as a means of achieving deinstitutionalization.

The potential advantages of state systems are usually outweighed by the disadvantages inherent in systems in which community based residential programs are extensions of public institutions. First, community programs developed by the state and administered through local institutions generally are defined as part of a continuum of services in which the institution plays an important role. The institution may be a "last resort" within this continuum, but nonetheless remains within the range of viable residential options. In short, the institution retains a significant, if not central role within the system. The following quotes illustrate ways in which this role has been envisioned, both historically and currently, by leaders in the field. In both cases, the institution is described as playing a central role within the larger state system.

> It is seen that in this program (of increased community services) the institution plays a wholly different part from that which it did in the early stages of work amongst the feebleminded. It can be seen that the institution now forms a way-station on life's highway for the feebleminded into which enter raw material of the crudest type and out of which go into the community well-trained persons fitted to take a resonable share of life's burdens and to assume the part of decent, law-abiding citizens. The institution is the keynote to any and every program for properly handling the problem of feeblemindedness. Around it must revolve all other state machinery. The dominant note, it will be seen, of the state institution is becoming less and less custodial and more and more medical and educational. There is less and less the atmosphere of the poorhouse and more that of the hospital and training school (Anderson, 1921, p. 369).

> If the community is capable of providing primary services and programs required by retarded persons, what will be the future role of a residential facility (institution)? It can be summarized in one word—specialization. It is anticipated that most residential facilities will function as regional centers, offering specialized short-term, intensive treatment programs; specialized extended care and developmental training for severely and profoundly retarded, multiply handicapped persons; and specialized back-up and consultancy services (Scheerenberger, 1974, p. 5).

While in theory institutions could maintain a contained or specialized role within a larger system including community based services, in practice the institution tends to dominate the system. The Progressive reform measures in mental health and criminal justice during the early decades of this century provide a compelling illustration of this point. In an effort to individualize treatment, reformers advocated the development of a range of community based services in addition to the already established institutional system. They believed that this could be accomplished through the institutions, and that institution administrators would assist in the implementation of the new programs (Rothman, 1980).

However, their hopes proved false. Either the administrators and other institution professionals did not believe in the value of community programs or were unwilling to invest their time, money, or staff in the development of programs which they felt would undermine the existing system. As a result, Progressive reforms rarely had the funding or professional support to become effective. The community programs that were implemented became "arms" of the institution, facilitating the achievement of the institution's goals, including the screening and even recruitment of candidates for institutionalization (Rothman, 1980; Wolfensberger, 1975). The belief that institutional and community programs could co-exist within the same administrative framework led to the demise of the community services via their subordination to the institutions. As the reform measures failed, the institutions swelled in size and increased the scope of their authority. The result was a period of steady institutional expansion (Rothman, 1980; Wolfensberger, 1975).

Today, most state systems include the institution as a viable residential service alternative. If history repeats itself, the community programs within these systems are doomed to be overshadowed by the institutional model. The conflict of interest inherent in systems in which the same administration is required to run institutions and develop community based alternatives, combined with fiscal disincentives to deinstitutionalization (i.e., the failure of funds to follow clients from institution to community; the construction of new institutions which must then be filled in order to repay the construction loans) has perpetuated the use of institutions as viable residential options within a continuum of services. The definition and implementation of community programs as extensions of the institution embody as well as promote these patterns of service.

More ominous still, there is evidence from some states to suggest that when state operated group homes and institutions are included within the same continuum of services, the community placements may be "way stations" which facilitate the admission of clients to the institution as well as their release into the community. For example, in her study of the process by which clients living in the community were admitted to a state institution, Foster (1983) found that admission to a state operated group or family care home was an important step in the client's institutionalization. While this step reflects the institution's attempt to forestall admissions by utilizing available community resources, it also reflects the joint administration of these programs and the symbiotic relationship which can develop under these conditions between state operated community homes and public institutions. Moreover, the paucity of residential support systems, whether institutional or community based, insures that any available placements will be constantly utilized.

Ad Hoc Community Services Development

This category refers to the development of services by scattered, uncoordinated groups, resulting in an ad hoc pattern of residential programs. Advocacy groups such as the Association for Retarded Citizens (ARC), and other private coporations have been largely responsible for the ad hoc development of community programs.

Initially, private interest groups, corporations, and organizations restricted their role to that of advocating for developmentally disabled people and lobbying for increased and improved services (e.g., institutional reform and the development of community based services). However, these reforms and services were often slow to appear. To stimulate their development by the public sector and to provide essential services to developmentally disabled people and their families, these private advocacy groups and organizations began to develop their own services, moving from an advocacy role to one of direct service provider. In some cases, these programs were funded solely through private donations and fund raising campaigns. Most often, however, these corporations have been supported through public sources, including state and federal funding mechanisms.

There are several long-term implications of ad hoc services. While the state maintains some control and direction via funding allocations, these programs are administered by the private sector and are less likely to become extensions of institutions than are the state operated programs which include institutions within their service continuum. In addition, small private programs developed by local groups are more likely to encourage consumer participation as well as involvement with the surrounding community. Further, ad hoc private service development may yield a greater variety of types of services.

On the other hand, the small, private agency does not have a legal responsibility to serve all developmentally disabled consumers, and is therefore likely to develop services tailored to a single consumer group (e.g.. people with cerebral palsy, autism, mental retardation, etc.) or a single program model. This uncoordinated and fragmented pattern of program development is exclusionary, even discriminatory, since clients who cannot meet the specific criteria for admission will not be served. Moreover, clients who do receive services may find themselves without a program as their needs change (e.g., a private agency operating a program for children does not provide services for clients over age 21). The result is that many developmentally disabled consumers become lost in a maze of referrals. shuffled from agency to agency, or worse still, excluded from all available community programs and so are forced to apply for admission to an institution. In short, the ad hoc development of community programs often leaves the consumer without real choices, a condition within which the decision to institutionalize is a "false choice" forced on consumers and their families as a result of the lack of appropriate community alternatives.

A related implication of ad hoc service development is that these programs are difficult to monitor unless the service provider requests and pays for independent evaluation. The result is that private programs often vary widely in quality of programming. Moreover, the potential for client abuse and misuse of funds increases when services are not coordinated and monitored. The problems throughout the nursing home industry illustrate graphically the dangers inherent in a service system which relies solely on the good will and honesty of individual service providers (cf. Mendelson. 1974). This is not to minimize the potential for abuse in large, centrally coordinated programs such as institutions. In fact, institutions and ad hoc services represent opposite extremes, each with their own potential problems.

Third, it is difficult, if not impossible, to plan for the future when services are uncoordinated. The result is a self-perpetuating pattern in which individual providers create single, one-shot programs in an effort to fill gaps in services, only to discover yet another unserved group of consumers. Services developed ad hoc are like an old roof; every time one leak is patched. another appears. (Examples of ad hoc developed services are presented in the chapter by Anderson in this text).

Finally, when advocacy groups such as parent associations become direct service providers, it is difficult for them to continue to fulfill their role as advocates. Time, money, and energy once devoted exclusively to advocacy now must be divided. Moreover, there is an inherent conflict of interest when those providing services are also required to monitor services. Ideally, advocacy groups should not provide any services to consumers. Their role should be restricted to protecting the rights of the consumer and to assuring that appropriate resources are available. The trend toward direct service provision on the part of advocacy groups may lead to a compromised advocacy system, or worse, to a situation in which advocacy activities are nonexistent.

Community Based Systems Developed Through A Systemic Planning Process

Systemically planned services can be developed and sponsored on a public, private, or quasi-public basis. By "systemic," we mean that the community services are designed to meet the individual needs of *all* developmentally disabled clients, thus making recourse to institutionalization unnecessary. By "planned," we mean that the services are developed with specific goals in mind, such as the inclusion of all developmentally disabled consumers, flexible models, and the potential for the system to grow and change with the needs of the consumer. Systemic services do not just happen; they must be planned.

The Eastern Nebraska Community Office of Retardation (ENCOR) (Lensink, 1976) and Macomb-Oakland Regional Center (MORC) (Park, 1978) are two examples of community based program models that have been developed through a systemic planning process. Both models incorporate elements of public, as well as private models. For example, MORC is a state agency which develops, coordinates, and monitors a wide range of community programs. Most are individually administered by private agencies. In addition, MORC assists these programs with staff training and planning. The result is a system which includes the advantages of a large, centrally coordinated system with the independence and flexibility of small, private programs (see Parks. 1978 for a more detailed description of MORC).

Similarly, ENCOR is a quasi-public corporation which is funded and partially administered by the state, but which retains much of the administrative structure of a private corporation (e.g., a governing board and advisory committee which involves citizen groups). The result is a system which enjoys the scope and authority afforded a state agency while retaining the identity and responsiveness to consumer needs inherent in private programs (see Lensink, 1976 for a further description of ENCOR).

Both of these systems are relatively new, ENCOR since 1969 and MORC since 1970. In both, consumers and professionals joined to make a major commitment to the provision of community services in the community and the prevention of institutionalization. In fact, the institution is not recognized as a viable service alternative in either system.[5]

In each system, services were planned to include all developmentally disabled consumers, and to insure enough program flexibility to allow for future service additions and modifications. As a result, they have been able to recognize and overcome challenges and roadblocks that might have proven insurmountable in other, less flexible systems.

There are several long-term implications of systems that are developed through a systemic planning process. First, these systems are best suited to the provision of community alternatives for all developmentally disabled people (and therefore to total deinstitutionalization) since they, by definition, offer a wide range of programs tailored to the specific needs of consumers. Second, planned programs such as ENCOR and MORC are flexible; that is, they are designed in a manner which facilitates adaptation to the changing needs of consumers. Third, these programs are durable, in that they are likely to last over time and so provide their clients with continuity as well as variety of service. Fourth, it is easier to maintain standards of program quality within planned, centrally coordinated systems. Finally, systems which incorporate elements of public and private programs are more likely to encourage consumer participation and the involvement of local communities, both of which are essential to the development of responsive and lasting community services.

The advantages of planned, systemic community services provide the blueprint for deinstitutionalization. In the following sections, we will examine the legal, moral, administrative, and program principles which underlay the systematic development of community services.

Guiding Principles

Normalization Principle

In 1959, Bank-Mikkelson, then head of mental retardation services for Denmark, spoke of permitting retarded people opportunities to live in as normal a fashion as possible. He called this the *normalization principle*. A decade later, Nirje elaborated on the concept: "making available to the mentally retarded patterns and conditions of everyday life which are as close as possible to the norms and patterns of the mainstream of society" Kugel & Wolfensberger, 1969, p. 181). In the early 1970s, Nirje spoke often of the central value of normalization for the field of retardation. One of his favorite examples grew out of a conference held in Scandanavia at which retarded people were asked to suggest policy changes that might affect their lives. Their requests were consistent with the normalization principle. People asked not to be given special preference in receiving housing referrals (there were housing shortages then as there are now in Sweden). They asked that when taken into town, they preferred not to be taken in large groups, but in small groups of two or three. They asked that as adults they not be sent to special camps only for retarded people, but that they have opportunities to take their vacations in the regular vacation resorts of Europe as nonretarded people do. And so it went, each claim supporting the quality of life that people labeled retarded sought for themselves.

In the United States, the normalization principle took hold almost as soon as Nirje and Bank-Mikkelson's words were heard. Ironically, the Scandanavians had developed the concept in reaction to what they had observed in America's colossal error in building institutions as the centerpiece of human services for people with retardation. The concept of normalization was immediately popularized by Blatt, Dybwad, Wolfensberger, Nirje, and others (Kugel & Wolfensberger, 1969). In 1972, the Canadian National Institute of Mental Retardation published what is now regarded as the seminal work on the principle of normalization, *The Principle of Normalization in Human Services.* Wolfensberger defined the concept more broadly than others, making it a principle that could be applied to a variety of fields, including mental retardation, mental illness, and physical disabilities: "utilization of means which are as culturally normative as possible, in order to establish and/or maintain personal behaviors and characteristics which are as culturally normative as possible" (Wolfensberger, 1972, p. 28).

Unlike many of the perspectives associated with services to people classified as retarded, the principle of normalization does not limit the social planner or policymaker to an examination of individuals and their characteristics. So much of the literature on disabled people focuses on the abilities of limitations or individuals or categories of individuals. The normalization principle, on the other hand, places an emphasis on the environment in which people live their lives. It forces us to examine the social demands upon people, e.g., the isolating and stigmatizing effects of placing people in large remote institutions. It questions the prudence of educating disabled adults to engage in makework or children's play activities. It suggests that policies which treat disabled people in unusual ways are immediately suspect. It allows us to see that much of what has been done for retarded people has confirmed their differentness and precluded their integration into the mainstream organizations of society.

Least Restrictive Alternative

The ideological principle of normalization is further enhanced by recent legal developments with respect to the delivery of human services, particularly in light of the newly developed legal concept of *least restrictive alternative* (LRA). In September 1970, Alabama cut the mental health budget for that state, forcing cutbacks in staffing of the Bryce State Hospital. That measure led to litigation by the employees who charged that minimum standards of safety and treatment could not be maintained with the available employees. In August of 1971, the case was expanded to include residents of the other mental hospitals in the state and of the Partlow State School, the state institution for retarded persons (Wyatt v. Stickney, 1972). Finally, in April 1972, after several interim orders in which Judge Johnson compelled the state to increase staffing and bring the buildings into compliance with minimum standards of safety and health, the Judge ordered a final set of minimum standards for treatment of the institutionalized residents. These provisions included prohibition of institutional peonage, physical standards for the buildings, minimum staffing requirements, nutritional standards, individualized evaluations and habilitation plans for each resident, guaranteed transition services for those leaving the institutions, certain measures to create a safe and supportive psychological environment, and, perhaps most important, the requirement that all residents be given *the right to the least restrictive setting necessary for habilitation*. In short, the principle of least restrictive alternative was to become a legal equivalent for normalization.

The LRA principle has become a popular, if controversial, concept in human services, particularly in the areas of education and residential services. Yet, its origins are in the U.S. Constitution and in corporate law. The first court case in which the concept surfaced involved a milk producing company and the city of Madison, Wisconsin (Dean Milk v. Madison, 1951). In that case, the city of Madison passed an ordinance forbidding the sale of milk in Madison by milk producing companies located more than 25 miles away. The city's interest was to protect the citizenry against spoiled milk. Yet, in so doing, the city intruded on the interests of milk producers located beyond the 25 mile limit. The effect was devastating to those producers. The Court held the city ordinance unconstitutional and ordered the city to find a *less drastic* means (e.g., inspection) of protecting the citizenry from spoiled milk.

Nine years later, in a case involving teachers' rights of association, the Court drew a similar conclusion (Shelton v. Tucker, 1960). The Court struck down an Arkansas law requiring teachers to identify the organizations to which they belonged. The Court ruled that "even though the governmental purpose be legitimate and substantial, that purpose cannot be pursued by means that broadly stifle personal liberties when the end can be more narrowly achieved." In its basic form, the concept holds that *the state may puruse its legitimate interests, but it must do so in a manner that least intrudes upon or stifles individual rights.* Hence, the connection of LRA to freedom.

This principle of least restriction or least intrusion derives from the Constitution. Under the Constitution, government must always balance various interests and rights, with an eye to protecting the rights of the people. Further, the Constitution holds that the life, liberty, and property rights to which citizens have equal access under law, may not be infringed upon or denied without affording them due process of law. Put simply, if the state intends to abridge their basic rights, people must have an opportunity to be heard and, presumably, competing rights and interests must be balanced. Put in the context of community services, if the state's interest is to protect or serve the developmentally disabled person (by providing residential, recreational, vocational, and similar programs) it must do so in a manner that does not necessarily abridge the person's liberty.

It is a short step from these constitutionally based conceptualizations of LRA to their application in human services. As we have noted, forced segregation carries with it the possibility that people may find their rights of travel, liberty, and association abridged. In the area of education, for example, one court (PARC v. Pennsylvania, 1972) stated:

> It is the Commonwealth's obligation to place each mentally retarded child in a free, public program of education and training appropriate to the child's capacity, within the context of presumption that, among the alternative programs of education and training required by statute to be available, placement in a regular public school class is preferable to placement in special public school classes which is preferable to placement in any other type of program of education and training.

Later, in Mills v. Board of Education (1972), a federal judge in the District of Columbia ruled that the LRA principle applied to all handicapped children, not just to those who were retarded. It is important to note that in both cases, the Court did not question the state's interest in providing appropriate educational services. It only questioned the locus of such services, holding that children's location in or in proximity to the mainstream of education should be intruded upon only to the extent necessary.

Application of the LRA concept to commitment and deinstitutionalization cases follows the same line of reasoning. In Lake v. Cameron (1966), Covington v. Harris (1969), Dixon v. Attorney General (1971), Jackson v. Indiana (1972) and a host of other cases, the court has ruled that the State may commit people to institutions if the persons are found to be dangerous or in need of treatment, but that the state must use the least drastic means of responding to an individual's needs. This was essentially the court's view in Youngberg v. Romeo (1982), if more narrowly stated. Specifically, the Court found that institutionalized retarded persons are entitled by their liberty interests protected under the Due Process clause of the Fourteenth Amendment to *reasonably* safe conditions of confinement, freedom from unreasonable restraint, and minimally adequate training as "may be reasonably required by these interests." In other words, if professionals deem that treatment programs are needed in order to keep people from undue restraint (i.e., greater restriction) then such treatment must be provided. In essence, the overall pattern of court decisions with respect to LRA has found that a state may not, as a matter of course, take away people's liberty simply because they are disabled.

The case of Wyatt v. Stickney (1972) provides a statement of the Court's position with respect to residential placement and LRA. Judge Johnson ordered: "No person shall be admitted to the institution unless a prior determination shall have been made that residence in the institution is the least restrictive habilitation setting feasible for that person." The Judge then outlined his plan for more integrated services, not unlike the education services noted in PARC v. Pennsylvania (1972). He called for retarded persons to be placed, as much as possible, from more to less structured situations, from larger to smaller facilities, from congregate to more individual residences, and from separate institutional settings to more integrated community residences.

As the case law spelling out LRA has developed, it has become increasingly clear that the concept, like so many constitutional principles, is a dynamic one. That is, LRA does not allow for a template approach to imposing human service models. Rather, it suggests that options or alternatives must be explored, that people's needs must be addressed individually, that simple path or monolithic approaches to service delivery are suspect and potentially unconstitutional if they deprive people of individual rights. Thus, it is not surprising that courts have been unwilling to accept state claims that "alternatives do not exist" as sufficient reason to allow for continued violation of individuals' rights. The courts have called upon the states to ensure, to the greatest extent possible, that individual rights are protected. In Morales v. Turman (1974), a case involving an institution for so-called emotionally disturbed and delinquent children, the Court ruled:

> This procedure (applying the principle of LRA) is hollow if there are, in fact, no alternatives to institutionalization. The state may not circumvent the Constitution by simply refusing to create any alternatives to incarceration; it must act affirmatively to foster such alternatives as now exist only in rudimentary form, and to build new programs suited to the needs of the hundreds of its children that do not need institutional care (e.g., group homes, half-way houses, home placements with close supervision).

Similarly, in the Willowbrook case (N.Y.S.A.R.C. v. Carey, 1976), the Court rejected the state's claim that LRA meant least restrictive alternative "available."

Despite the rather clear evolution of the LRA principle from its constitutional origins to its application in litigation, statutes, and professional practice, two questions are frequently posed with regard to LRA. First, if it is true, as we suggest, that LRA is a concept that will be perpetually redefined as technologies for serving people and as our conception of freedom and liberty change, is it not impossible to tie LRA to specific service types?

Frequently, the concept of LRA has been articulated programmatically as a cascade from the most restrictive types of service (i.e., the institution) to the least restrictive (i.e., mainstream independent living) ones. However, the concept of LRA does not automatically legitimize the institution. If all retarded people can benefit from some form of community based living arrangement, then is the institution not removed from the continuum of least restrictive placements?

In terms of its place in the Constitution and in litigation, LRA becomes an operable concept only when state interests come into conflict with individual interests. Without state intrusion, the concept has no legal meaning. But, the concept of LRA *has* infused a variety of state and federal statutes and regulations as well as professional language. *Thus, the concept has become a framework through which professionals and lay audiences alike are creating and evaluating human services.* Predictably, as the context becomes more popular, or at least more frequently used, it also becomes vulnerable to being wrongly defined. Just as "dumping" of mentally ill and retarded persons into communities has been regarded by some as "deinstitutionalization," it is not surprising that LRA has been interpreted as doing nothing, as inaction. Yet, clearly that was not the Courts' intent in spelling out the LRA concept. It was not a license for inaction but protection against wrong action. LRA is not a philosophy of "do-nothingness." Quite to the contrary the concept provides a mechanism for balancing competing interests without unjustly abridging individual rights. In the context of human services, LRA has provided a means to balance service with relative degrees of individual freedom. To call that do-nothingness is to miss the point entirely.

Decisions about what constitutes the optimal or best possible treatment for a person classified as mentally retarded are made in the context of existing human service systems and ideologies. That is, we are rarely "free" to make service programs or individual habilitation plans in the exact manner of our liking; hence, the banality of such phrases as "it's another catch 22," "the funding patterns won't allow us to do what we know is best," and "they (the clients) keep falling between the cracks." All individual and local decisions are in some measure shaped by the larger systems within which they are made. In a capitalistic society, for example, the rich have more choices than the poor in terms of the human services available to them. Similarly, on a less global level, a choice of birth control methods, whether for disabled or nondisabled family members, certainly would be influenced by forces which transcend the individual (e.g., available technologies, religious and other cultural standards, laws, cost, and accessibility). In the same vein, implementation of the LRA concept will reflect the context in which such decisions are made.

A few examples of how the systems context can influence the application and interpretation of LRA may prove helpful here. Take, for instance, the state system that provides only one service mode to meet a particular need (e.g., employment, vocational training, education, birth control). If a state's vocational training and employment plan for retarded persons provides the single option of a sheltered workshop, then program planners, families, and retarded persons will find it exceptionally difficult to fulfill their commitment to the LRA principle. Whatever their feelings or clinical judgments about the most appropriate way to meet an LRA standard, the prevailing reality will render their best intentions impotent. For years, in the area of residential services, most states provided only two options outside the natural home. These included family care (usually reserved for a few mildly disabled adults) and large state run institutions. To cite the words of one leading critic of institutions:

> Our institutions have been Procrustean. It did not matter who or what the resident was, whether young or old, whether borderline or profoundly retarded; whether physically handicapped or physically sound; whether deaf or blind; whether rural or urban; whether from the local town or from 500 miles away; whether well-behaved or ill-behaved. We took them all, by the thousands, 5,000 to 6,000 in some institutions. We had all the answers in one place, using the same facilities, the same personnel, the same attitudes, and largely the same treatment. And if our guest did not fit, we made him fit! (Wolfensberger, 1975, p. 69)

Similarly, states that have propagated intermediate, district-level schools for retarded persons may find that this administratively efficacious service model poses a fundamental contradiction to the principle of LRA. Such systems have, for the purposes of administrative efficiency and presumed economies of scale, created large centralized schools serving disabled students only. In fact, such segregated school systems are now the objects of desegregation litigation in Missouri, Ohio, and elsewhere.

To the extent that service systems follow the financial structures which turn ideology and philosophy into programmatic reality, we may find LRA concerns entangled in a web of bureaucratically imposed limitations. This "economic imperative" is typified by most states which provide residential services primarily or solely in state facilities or state institutions. State residential facilities often are financed through the issuance of bonds. The bond holders must be repaid their investment and interest over 20–30 years. Consequently, states will have a self-interest in maintaining the enrollments of the facilities in order to keep federal reimbursements flowing; these third party payments can be used to offset the bond debt. Hence, while states may desire to implement an ideology of normalization and least restrictive alternatives, they initially find this to be an economically disastrous course, as they are saddled with newly constructed residential centers. Presumably, even if the economic incentives were less compelling, the mere existence of large bureaucracies, human service worker unions, and large, physical plants, would make deinstitutionalization difficult. That is, large institutions and their various constituencies may be incapable of unbiased implementation of the LRA principle.

Thus far, we have noted the potentially frustrating effects of single mode systems and economic imperatives on the exercise of an LRA principle. The other potentially serious barrier to LRA is the conflict which sometimes exists between specialized separate disability related service systems and generic service systems. Undoubtedly, implementation of LRA will have explosive repercussions as it becomes clear that many existing separate programs for the disabled, including schools, residential facilities, recreational programs, and medical services, even public housing perhaps, may violate the LRA principle. Service systems organized along disability lines may limit the movement of individuals from specialized services to generic ones and from one specialized service to another.[6]

Administrative and Programmatic Principles

The principle of normalization and LRA serve as general guiding principles in the development of all services for disabled consumers. In the following sections, we will describe more specific principles, or conditions, under which normalization and LRA can best be implemented. These conditions are divided into "administrative" and "programmatic" principles. Administrative principles include those specific strategies which form the structural design of community services. Programmatic principles are the "meat," or heart of the service, guiding day-to-day practice. It is important to stress the interactive quality of these concepts; no single principle will be successful unless it is used in concert with the others.

Administrative Principles

Separation of institutional and community based services. As noted earlier, community programs which are developed through existing institutions, or which include institutions within their continuum of services, are likely to be overshadowed and eventually subordinated to the institutional model. Moreover, if all retarded people can benefit from community based residential services as suggested by a wealth of research (Biklen, 1979) and court decisions, then the inclusion of institutions within a continuum of services may violate the rights of retarded citizens to treatment in the least restrictive setting. Certainly the principle of normalization suggests total abandonment of institutionalization as a form of effective and moral treatment. If institutional placement is legally, morally, and clinically indefensible, then community based programs must be developed separate from institutional systems in order to remain independent of and resistant to institutional influence and administrative control.

The development of community programs through private agencies is one example of how the separation of community from institutionally based services might be accomplished. However, as we will discuss later, this must occur in a planned fashion. In the case of state operated systems which often administer community based and institutional programs through a single agency, it is also important to discover ways of maintaining clear separation of community from institutional functions. For example, a state can minimize the impact of its institutional system on emerging community services by defining catchment areas which exclude existing institutions, refusing to build new institutions where they currently do not exist, contracting for community services with private agencies rather than developing state operated programs, and administering state operated programs in cooperation with local advocacy and consumer groups.

Community based services must be available unconditionally to all developmentally disabled people. This principle, often described as "zero reject," is absolutely essential to the development of a truly alternative system to institutions. As long as community programs exclude clients on the basis of disability, age, or any criteria, institutions will have a clientele. Phrases such as "comprehensive continuum of services" are meaningless to those who fall outside the boundaries of the continuum. If the first administrative principle is to design a service continuum which excludes the institution as a viable source of treatment, the second is to insure that there will be a place for all developmentally disabled people *within* the continuum.

In order for services to fulfill the zero reject principle, they must meet three specific conditions: variety, flexibility, and durability. First, the system must provide a wide variety of services in order to insure that programs will be available to meet the individual needs of every disabled consumer. This includes services for severely handicapped clients and clients with multiple disabilities. Without sufficient variety, programs will be forced to restrict admissions. Almost invariably, the people excluded under these conditions are those who are seen as the most difficult or troublesome to serve, e.g., persons with profound and multiple disabilities, particularly those who are medically involved.

Second, the service must be flexible. In order to maintain a policy of zero reject, service systems must expect that consumers' needs will change and be ready to respond accordingly. As noted by the authors of the 1978 MORC Report to the President, "there will never be a complete service system. Something will always be lacking. There will never be enough varieties in residences" (U.S.D.H.E.W., 1978, p. 3). Without flexibility, even the most varied and comprehensive system will eventually become exclusionary, and consumers will be forced to either leave the system or submit to inappropriate or ineffective services and treatment.

Third, community based services must be durable. That is, if they are to maintain a zero reject policy over time, they must endure. System administrators should insure that their services will be available to all consumers who need them not only in the present, but in 10, 20, even 50 years. Parents of developmentally disabled people often seek institutional over community placement because they believe that the community program will not last, and they do not want their son or daughter shuffled from one community service to another, only to end up in the institution after all else has failed. Community based service systems must be as durable as the institutions they are trying to replace, both for security to clients and their families and to fulfill their obligations to provide unconditional service to all consumers.

Services must plan for regular, internal, and external evaluation. In order to provide high quality programming which is responsive to consumers' needs, services must include a wide range of internal and external evaluation procedures in the design and administration of their programs. Examples of internal evaluation mechanisms include the regular solicitation of feedback from clients and families (both formally and informally), grievance procedures, and routine reviews of individual programs by a team of staff and clients. Internal evaluations are useful sources of regular feedback on daily issues as well as larger administrative concerns. They provide a record of the daily "health" of the program. The drawback to internal evaluations is that they are not always objective reflections of what is happening; staff and clients sometimes do not have enough distance from the program to evaluate it accurately.

External evaluation procedures are essential to insure continued program quality and as a safeguard against ineffective or incomplete internal evaluations. External evaluation mechanisms include monitoring via citizen advocacy or consumer groups, watchdog committees, and the hiring of external consultants to evaluate the service. While some external evaluations are limited to specific parts of the service or take only a broad look at the program, others offer a comprehensive and detailed assessment of every aspect of the system (cf. Wolfensberger & Glenn, 1975a, b for one example). The advantage of external assessments is that they are free of the conflict of interest inherent in most internal evaluation procedures. However, unless external evaluations are mandated by funding requirements or litigation, they remain optional, and feedback from them can easily be ignored. While we do not recommend that service planners become so pre-occupied with program evaluation that they create a bureaucratic maze of assessment mechanisms, we do strongly encourage the inclusion of both periodic and ongoing internal and external assessment procedures in the development of services.

The value of consumer involvement. While consumer involvement may seem implicit in every point made so far, we believe that it is so fundamental to the development of quality community services that it requires separate consideration. Community based programs which do not involve consumers in their development, implementation, and evaluation may be durable, but they are unlikely to be effective in promoting individual growth or providing responsible support to developmentally disabled consumers and their families.

Historically, the value of consumer input in human services has been underestimated, even ignored completely. Professional expertise was believed necessary to even the most basic and simple decisions in every area of human activity (Bledstein, 1976). In those cases involving individuals who had already been labeled "incompetent," professional control seemed even more justifiable and extended to a role not unlike that of parent or guardian (Rothman, 1980).

Under these conditions, consumer involvement in community programs is often restricted to a token parent or client on an advisory board, or to client response questionnaires which are filled out without being read or given serious consideration. For consumer input to have impact, it must be contributed from a point of authority and equality. This does not mean that services should be controlled and managed solely by consumers. Rather, the opinions of consumers should be considered equally with those of professionals when program decisions are made.

There are a variety of ways to involve consumers in services, all of which are predicated on a genuine commitment to the value of consumer opinion and expertise. Given this commitment, consumers and their families should be included as expert consultants and authorities in the planning and implementation of community services through functional and powerful advisory boards, as staff trainers, and as monitors of program quality. Consumers can provide valuable input in the design of program curricula and in the identification of program strengths and weaknesses. They may also target areas for future service development. Most important, consumers represent the perspective of service recipient, and as such are an important source of information about whether or not the service is achieving its goals. The opinions and recommendations of clients and their families should always be given serious consideration.

There must be fiscal incentives to develop and use community based services. Economics is a major factor in the success or failure of community based services. There are not enough funds to support both institutions and community programs; it must be one or the other. Thus far, institutions have retained the lion's share of funds, to the detriment of community based alternatives.

In many cases, the fiscal structures are a disincentive to deinstitutionalization. For example, institutions in New York State are 100% funded, while in the case of community residences, the county is required to provide 25% of the cost. It is therefore not uncommon for group homes and other kinds of community based residences to meet resistance at the county level.

A second example involves funding for family care programs. While few would dispute that developmentally disabled children are better off with their natural families, funding and access to professional resources often encourage out-of-home placements. In New York, natural parents are not eligible to become family care providers (and thereby receive a daily stipend to assist in the care of their disabled child) until the child reaches age 18. Moreover, in a recent study of formerly institutionalized persons who had returned to community placements, 15% of the natural family providers interviewed said they found professional services (e.g., counseling, physical or speech therapy, special transportation) too expensive, compared with only 5% of the family care providers. While many natural families still received these services, the study concluded that "natural families are offered the least financial and social support by the institution and its community services staff" (*Deinstitutionalization of Mentally Retarded Persons in New York State*, 1980, p. 73).

We recommend that the distribution of economic and professional resources be consistent with the principles of normalization and least restrictive alternative. That is, the more normative and less restrictive settings should receive the greater allocation of resources. Under this system, clients living with friends or their natural families would receive the greatest support, and institutions the least support. Only when we begin to "put our money where our mouth is" will we begin to realize our goals of quality community based services for all.

Community based service systems must be planned. The conditions in administrative principles described here do not happen automatically. In fact, the natural tendency is in the opposite direction. Community services continue to be developed through or around existing institutional networks. Very few community based residential systems have made or fulfilled a policy of zero reject. Internal evaluations tend to be sporadic and myopic. Planned or invited external assessments are rare, and the suggestions generated through them are seldom given the serious attention they deserve. While consumer participation has increased dramatically in the last 20 years, it is too often treated as a privilege rather than a right, and as a marginal rather than central activity. Funding mechanisms continue to favor institutions over community alternatives.

In order for community service systems to meet these conditions, they must be developed through a careful planning process. The key word here is "process." Planning must not be restricted to the initial steps required to set up the system; it must be integrated into the routine working of the system so that it is a part of every decision made. For example, the long-term implications of single versus multiple source funding must be considered before funding decisions are made. Single source funding mechanisms are usually less complex and require less attention to red tape, but they are often more vulnerable to economic cutbacks and may increase the potential for compromised services. Services funded through a variety of sources, on the other hand, often can be maintained even when one or more sources are withdrawn.

The planning process is a vital function of the system; when it slows, the system becomes sluggish. When it stops, services begin to atrophy. Systems which fail to incorporate strong planning components into their administrative and programmatic structures will eventually find their goals subverted and their programs without a coherent structure or direction.

Planning should be an important part of all aspects of a community service system. In this section, we have examined the basic administrative principles which underly the development of comprehensive, responsive community systems. In the final section, we will describe programmatic principles which guide the day-to-day aspects of services, and which also require careful and continuous planning on the part of program administrators and staff.

Programmatic Principles

Functional programming. People who live in community residences, whether in supportive apartments, group homes, foster and family placement or some similar setting usually need assistance in learning independent living skills. Ironically, much of the programming we see in community residences does not focus on functional life skills. Residents may be learning such things as bead sorting, cutting and pasting, and coloring. These are not functional skills; they do not help a person live more independently. By "functional programming" we mean a structured program of skills that a person can use to gain greater access to the wide variety of environments encountered within a daily routine. Functional skills include domestic living, vocational, personal hygiene, social and recreational, and the full range of other skills necessary for daily living. In addition, it is important that the method of instruction be functional. That is, people need opportunities to learn to use real washing machines and dryers, not imitation ones; to use zippers on coats, trousers, and jackets, not zippers on specifically prepared pieces of cloth; to prepare actual foods which they and their friends or associates will eat for a meal. In other words, functional programming succeeds best when it is presented in naturally occurring contexts.

Community referenced instruction. Functional programming focuses on a broad range of skill areas, each of which can be designed to meet the daily living needs of the person for whom it is intended. Community referenced instruction is a corollary of functional programming. It is important for program staff to examine the community in which people with developmental disabilities will be living to discover many of the goals for programming. For example, there is little purpose in teaching bus riding skills to people who live in a community that has no buses, teaching bolt sorting in a region that has no machine factories, or teaching microwave cookery to people who do not have microwave ovens. The principle of community referenced instruction calls on staff to survey their community in terms of relevant vocational opportunities, community living skills, and social/recreational experiences. For example, staff in a community residence should walk around the neighborhood to secure information about crosswalks, street lights, neighbors with whom to converse, large supermarkets or small convenience stores, areas with lots of traffic or just a little, parks in which to play or rest, and so forth. If it is quite likely that people will have opportunities to use fast food outlets, then it would be appropriate to train for those experiences. For example, some people would need to learn how to make their food selections known. Others may need to learn how to handle money. Still others may need to develop skills in restaurant behavior. The purpose of community referenced instruction is to make life in the community more enhancing, easier, and more enjoyable. (The reader is referred to Freagon et al. in this book for further examples.)

Individualization. Many publishing companies and service agencies have developed standardized curricula for teaching basic living skills such as cooking, hygiene, mobility, and social interaction. While some of these curricula may prove useful as a starting point for program staff, most such curricula do not adequately focus on the individual needs of the people for whom they are intended. If we adhere to functional and community referenced programming principles, it becomes obvious that pre-developed curricula will not be sufficiently individualized either to the person or to the immediate community. We may, for example, have a standardized curriculum for teaching people how to shop in a large grocery store (e.g., teaching people to locate a shopping cart, to move a cart down the right side of an aisle, to match products with pictures of products, to find eggs near milk), but we will have to individualize to the extent that every store has some different characteristics in terms of how it is organized, check-out procedures, and personnel. Also, each person learning grocery shopping comes to the task with different abilities. We must individualize for each of these factors.

Natural environment. To the extent possible, it is always preferable to teach independent living skills in natural environments. That is, we can best teach domestic living in people's homes. We can best teach restaurant behavior in a restaurant. The advantage of using natural environments is that we present people with the kinds of situations that they will encounter repeatedly, and we present them in their full complexity. We may need to "break down" the activities or skills into behaviorally distinct steps. Yet, to the extent that we can offer them in natural environments, we help bridge the age old problem of generalization.

Integrated programming. Living in the community is no guarantee of integration. One of the criticisms waged against deinstitutionalization has been that people may end up "institutionalized" in community programs (Bercovici, 1981). That is, they may still lead relatively routinized, dehumanizing, segregated lives. They may not be afforded opportunities to partake of the community and thereby to be part of the community. For many people, integration will occur only with affirmative support for integration. Specifically, we can foster integration by making it an inherent aspect of programming. We can involve nondisabled people in restaurant training. We can enlist neighbors to help with and be present during mobility training or recreational outings such as bowling or going to a movie. Integration occurs when people have opportunities to participate in the activities and events of integrated groups such as churches, clubs, and neighborhoods. For children and youth this may mean opportunities to participate in sporting activities for nondisabled as well as disabled people. It may mean attending integrated schools. It may mean doing things with or for other families in the neighborhood. The opportunities for integration are literally limitless, yet to achieve them, staff must consciously pursue them.

Natural cues. When we teach people certain tasks or skills, we usually provide them with didactic instruction. We present material in a logical sequence. We provide cues and directions. We correct errors. We praise success. Yet such a didactic approach, in which the student's success depends largely on instructions and prompts provided by the teacher, often does not yield independence. It is important, therefore, to help people learn to identify natural cues in their environments. Through natural cues, rather than teacher initiated prompts, a person can become more independent of programming staff. Take, for example, grocery shopping. If people learn that where they see a box of crackers, they are also likely to find cookies or where they see fruit they will probably find vegetables, then they will be able to shop more independently. Similarly, if people learn to associate the sound of car engines with subsequent car movement, they will have discovered a principle important to pedestrian safety. As we develop independent living curricula, we must identify those natural cues in the environment which can replace a teacher's didactic cues.

Age appropriate services. It was not too long ago that few people in the professions of special education and rehabilitation questioned practices of serving people with developmental disabilities under one roof, irrespective of age. It was not uncommon to find treatment centers serving preschoolers and adults in the very same rooms. Public schools often operated special schools for students with disabilities, ranging in age from 5 to 21. Moreover, program activities often were geared to a young population even if provided to older age groups. Thus, secondary students could be seen doing cut-outs and coloring that traditionally seemed appropriate for elementary-aged students. And few in our profession questioned such practices. Now, however, we generally agree that program content, grouping for programs, and program location should be designed to ensure that each is as age appropriate as possible. While adults with severe retardation may not be capable of certain activities usually associated with adult living (e.g., driving a car, reading novels, working on a computer), they may be able to engage in activities which are more adult than child oriented. For example, in social/recreational programming, it would be appropriate to participate in folksinging, but not in singing children's songs; it would be appropriate to have a birthday party, but not with children's birthday hats and games; it would be appropriate to browse through a *National Geographic* magazine, but not through a *Sesame Street* book.

Criterion of the next environment. Earlier, we discussed the concepts of functional programming and community referenced programming. Both principles aid in the development of services which will help people become increasingly independent throughout their lives in the community. By applying the criterion of the next environment to the design of functional, community referenced programs we further focus on people's futures. The concept asks us to determine those criteria on which people whom we serve will be evaluated or those factors which will determine people's success in future settings. For example, if a person will need to travel through a community in order to succeed in a pending community residence, then that becomes a criterion for the current training program. Similarly, if a person will need to attend to a task for a half hour at a time without a break in order to succeed in a vocational program, then that can become a criterion for current programming.

Continuity of programming. More typically than not, people with disabilities have few choices for program options. They face a "take it or leave it" choice. People move to a new program when they become too old for the first, when they are perceived as troublesome, or when they are in need of "a change." In such situations almost any change is seen as possibly beneficial. Only occasionally do people actually move because another program option is judged more appropriate or a logical next step. In this context of ad hoc program transfers, people not only lack program choices, they usually do not enjoy any real continuity or development from one program to another. Since programs often are operated by different agencies, under different legislative mandates, and by professionals with different styles and approaches, people experience extreme disjointedness in their programs and dislocation of their lives. Under such conditions, it is impossible for people to become part of a community, to develop long-term friendships, or to enjoy a sense of belonging.

The advantages of continuity are numerous. People can benefit from past experience when the content of a new program builds on that of a previous one. When people achieve goals they can move to new opportunities; they do not have to endure the insensitivity of being asked to repeat program content that was mastered months, even years earlier. Staff can feel a sense of purpose in helping people move from one program and one set of goals and strategies to another. People can enjoy the right to know, at least in some vague sense, the experiences they are likely to encounter in future programs. By contrast, discontinuity is simply debilitating.

None of this should be taken to suggest that people's lives should be "programmed." Rather, people should have program choices. Ideally, there should be a relationship between programs. But there must also be variety; everyone deserves real choices. For example, several programs may share the goal of promoting domestic living skills, yet they may use radically different instructional approaches, staffing patterns, and program sites. One program might be organized in the form of a token economy while another adheres to natural cues and informal didactic instruction. Each could prove effective for different people.

The most difficult case. The moment that programs set criteria, someone is left out. When each program in a system of services has its own selection or eligibility criteria, it automatically has a basis for negotiating with other services in the system over the people served. In many systems, not everyone receives services. Some do indeed get left out, rejected when they are perceived as not fitting the criteria. Sometimes criteria are used as an excuse to reject someone who is unwanted. But even in an atmosphere of equanimity, as long as each program has its criteria, there is the very real possibility that people will "fall between the cracks."

Some systems develop a service setting for those who do not fit. They create a service or program designed exclusively to take in those rejected by all others. Usually, such a service is an institution, the place of last resort.

The problem with last resort services is that they become symbols of hopelessness. They are the places for people who have no options.

We propose that each community's service system and the majority of programs in it espouse the principle of serving those with the most difficult problems first. This principle has several things to commend it: programs come to view the people served as potential challenges and not as "cream puffs" (those judged easiest to work with) and "hard core" (those hardest to work with). Whether or not people succeed in a program is seen as being determined as much by the program's competence as the person's. So-called difficult clients are not automatically defined as someone else's responsibility and consigned to custodial containment.

Collecting data. Without history there is no optimism. Unless we can look back and see change, progress, and achievement, we have little reason to feel good about the future. Thus it is with programs; those in which staff collect data on how people change in the setting have something to report after a month, year, or years. Reports of progress, however modest, give staff encouragement and a reason to continue. In short, unless we believe change is possible, we will have difficulty working for it.

The following are types of data collection which we have observed in community programs and which have been of obvious value to those who collected it, and often, to others outside of the programs who have wanted some evidence of program effectiveness:

1. Photographs of people in programs, taken in chronological fashion.
2. Behavioral change data which specify the performance of individual people in the setting.
3. Evidence of interaction by people in a community residence with their larger community.
4. Medical and psychological data on people served in programs.
5. Periodic program evaluations (e.g., Program Analysis of Service Systems or PASS).
6. Periodic interviews with staff and people who live in community residences.
7. Staff and resident diaries; diaries of family members.
8. Recording of positive integration experiences by people in community programs.
9. Minutes or notes from group meetings of people in community programs.
10. Comparisons of individual and program performance against stated objectives and goals.

Program dispersal/separation of functions/generic services. Some treatment centers, even some which consider themselves community based programs, pride themselves on the fact that they offer comprehensive services under a single roof or on a single campus. Clearly, such centers mimic the institution; they offer a sheltered environment in which real, prolonged interaction with the mainstream of society is carefully circumscribed. Even those community agencies that seek maximum integration find it difficult at times to maintain integrated services. Zoning battles, public namecalling, and other forms of prejudicial treatment militate against integration. Yet compromise on this issue threatens the very meaning of community programming.

It is not enough for residential programs to exist in the community. The people who live in community residences also need places to socialize, to work, to continue learning, to shop, to get a haircut, and to take care of other matters of daily living. Ideally, they can use the community as their resource. This occurs most naturally when community programs follow three associated principles:

1. Whenever possible, utilize generic services. Regular work settings, medical services, and social gathering places are available for use by people with disabilities. We must assume that the generic services are the services of preference; special services "for the disabled only" should be sought only in those situations where the generic service cannot be appropriately used or *adapted* to meet a person's needs.
2. Programs of like and different nature (e.g., community residences, work stations, social meeting places, school programs) which serve people with disabilities should be dispersed throughout a community. We should not be in the business of manufacturing disability ghettos.
3. Services should be separated by function. It is not normative for people to find all of their needs met in a single setting. People generally go out of the home to work, to get a haircut, to meet friends, to secure medical services and so forth. If such services are provided through human service programs, they can best approximate normal community living if they are organized at different locations throughout the community, with each type of service offered in a different location.

Overcoming handicapism. In each of the principles discussed previously, we have implied a commitment to the concept of normalization. The opposite of normalization is handicapism. We find it manifest in virtually every aspect of community programming and community life. While community program staff and residents cannot hope to expunge all forms of handicapism (e.g., namecalling, pity, hostility) from society, community programs need not contribute to handicapism themselves. The following are major areas in which handicapism must be challenged regularly.

1. Programs should not appeal for public sympathy or support on the basis of pity toward people with disabilities.
2. Programs should expunge demeaning language (e.g., retards, slow ones, childish nicknames for adults), unnecessary labels, and professional treatment jargon to which nondisabled people are not similarly subjected.
3. People in community programs should be treated in accordance with their age as much as possible.
4. Program staff should assume that people in community residences can fully understand what people around them say and do. Practices such as speaking in front of people as if they were not present are clearly dehumanizing.
5. Programs should be committed to utilizing and securing available technology which can improve the life opportunities of people with disabilities; anything less demeans the person with a disability as "not worth the expense."
6. Programs for people with disabilities should be organized in a fiscally responsible, even conservative fashion. The fact that programs receive public support should not be an excuse to inflate costs unnecessarily. Such cost inflation can only generate resentment against people with disabilities.
7. Programs should attempt to encourage self-determination on the part of people living in community settings. This may take the form of people determining the types of community living arrangements into which they move, the manner in which a program operates, program planning, and service evaluation. This practice parallels the administrative principle of a systems level commitment to consumer involvement.
8. Programs should pay careful attention to location and physical plant when choosing a site. In general, programs should be located in appropriate locations (i.e., group homes in residential neighborhoods, job sites in existing community businesses and industrial parks) and in buildings which are well maintained and fit into the neighborhood.
9. Program names and addresses should be as normative and enhancing as possible. For example, a group home should not have a title; the address should be a street and number (i.e., 510 Main Street, not The Main Street Boys' Home).
10. In general, people with different kinds of disabilities should not be grouped together since the negative imagery attached to one group may compound the negative imagery associated with the second group. Instead, disabled people should be grouped with typical people.

For example, it is much more enhancing to serve mentally retarded children in a class with typical children than it is to place them in a separate setting with others who share similar disabilities.

Summary

The development of a true community requires complete rejection of the traditional institutional model and a parallel commitment of professional, technical, and economic resources to a radically different model. In this chapter, we have tried to outline a blueprint for a lasting, comprehensive system of community based services, including guiding administrative, and programmatic principles. Our lists are intended as a general and introductory resource. The reader is encouraged to add to our points, and to use them as a rough map. We hope and intend that they prove useful to everyone engaged in the development of community services, including consumers, their families, and service providers.

NOTES

1. For example, in his later writing Fernald (1919) admitted that his earlier judgements of mentally retarded people had been overly harsh and unfair.
2. Rothman (1980) described the Progressive reforms as follows: "Their principles can be summarized succinctly. Progressives aimed to understand and to cure crime, delinquency, and insanity through a case-by-case approach. From their perspective, the Jacksonian commitment to institutions had been wrong, both for assuming that all deviants were of a single type, the victims of social disorder, and for believing that they could all be rehabilitated with a single program, the well-ordered routine of the asylum. To Progressives, knowledge about and policies toward the deviant had to follow a far more particular bent. The task was to understand the life history of each offender or patient and then to devise a remedy that was specific to the individual . . . Some reformers were environmentalists, locating the roots of the individual's problem in one or another of the wretched conditions of the immigrant ghetto. Others adopted a psychological explanation, looking to the mind-set of the deviant for the causes of maladaption. But whatever the orientation, the two schools agreed that each case had to be analyzed and responded to on its own terms." (p. 5)
3. It is important to note that these farms also served another purpose, namely, to render the institutions self-sufficient.
4. This is not to say that the state is incapable of developing community programs which are not extensions of the institutions. For example, the Macomb-Oakland Regional Center (MORC) is a state program which provides community living alternatives for clients within its catchment area that are not part of a larger institutional model. However, in the case of MORC, the planners

consciously and carefully avoided the building of a large institution within their system, putting their energies instead into the development of community programs. In contrast, most state systems are built around existing institutions. (Ironically, the MORC planners eventually were forced to build a 90-bed institution by the state. It is a further testimony to their commitment to community services that the MORC staff managed to construct the facility as a series of duplex-like housing units for eight clients each, as opposed to the more traditional large ward model.) The MORC system will be discussed in greater detail later in this chapter.

5. There are other regional programs, some of which predate MORC and ENCOR, including programs in Connecticut, Massachusetts, and California. We have chosen MORC and ENCOR because we feel they most clearly exemplify the positive aspects of comprehensive regional systems.

6. For further discussion of the LRA concept, see H. Rutherford Turnbull (Ed.), *The Least Restrictive Alternative: Principles and Practices*, (Washington D.C.: AAMD, 1981). We are indebted to the AAMD Legislative and Social Issues Committee, of which Biklen was a member, for its clarification of the LRA principle. The Committee's background papers provided important background for the above discussion.

REFERENCES

Anderson, V. V. Mental hygiene problems of subnormal children. Part B: In institutions. *Proceedings of the National Conference on Social Work*, 1921, 367–371.

Bercovici, S. Qualitative methods and cultural perspectives in the study of deinstitutionalization. In R. Bruininks, C. E. Meyers, B. Sigford, & K. C. Lakin (Eds.), *Deinstitutionalization and community adjustment of mentally retarded people*. Washington, D.C.: American Association on Mental Deficiency, 1981, 133–144.

Bernstein, C. Colony and extra-institutional care for the feebleminded. *Mental Hygiene*, 4(1), 1920, 1–28.

Biklen, D. The community imperative. *Institutions, Etc.*, 1979, 2(8).

Bledstein, B. *The culture of professionalism: The middle class and the development of higher education in America*. New York: W. W. Norton & Co., 1976.

Covington v. Harris, 419 F.2d 617 D.C. Cir, 1969.

Dean Milk Co. v. Madison, 340 U.S. 349, 1951.

Deinstitutionalization of mentally retarded persons in New York State: Final report, June 30, 1980. Washington, D.C.: U.S. Department of Health, Education, and Welfare, Office of Human Development, Developmental Disabilities Office, 1980.

Dixon v. Attorney General, 325 F. Suppl 966 M.D. Pa., 1971.

Fernald, W. E. A state program for the care of the mentally defective. *Mental Hygiene*, 1919, 566–574.

Foster, S. B. The politics of caring: Case studies of people considered for admission to a public residential facility for the mentally retarded. Syracuse, NY: Syracuse University. Unpublished dissertation, 1983.

Goffman, E. *Asylums: Essays on the social situation of mental patients and other inmates*. Garden City, NJ: Doubleday, 1961.

Jackson v. Indiana. 406 U.S. 715. 1972.

Kugel, R. B., & Wolfensberger, W. (Eds.). *Changing patterns in residential services for the mentally retarded: A President's committee on mental retardation monograph.* Washington, D.C.: President's Committee on Mental Retardation, 1969.

Lake v. Cameron, 364 F. 2d 657, D.C. Cir. 1966.

Lensink, B. ENCOR, Nebraska. In R. Kugel, & A. Shearer (Eds.), *Changing patterns in residential services for the mentally retarded* (rev. ed.). Washington, D.C.: President's Committee on Mental Retardation, 1976, 277–296.

Mendelson, M. *Tender loving greed.* New York: Knopf, 1974.

Mills v. Board of Education, 348 F. Supp. 866 D.D.C., 1972.

Morales v. Turman, 383 F. Supp. 53, 125, ED Texas, 1974.

New York State Association for Retarded Children v. Carey, 393 F. Supp. 715 E.D. NY. 1975.

PARC v. Commonwealth of Pennsylvania, 343 F. Supp, 279, E.D. Pa, 1972.

Parks, J. Placing the 'unplaceable.' *ARISE,* July, 1978, 22–24.

Rothman, D. J. *Conscience and convenience: The asylum and its alternatives in progressive America.* Boston: Little, Brown, & Co., 1980.

Scheerenberger, R. C. Model for deinstitutionalization. *Mental Retardation,* 1974, *12*(6), 3–7.

Shelton v. Tucker, 364 U.S. 479, 1960.

U.S. Department of Health, Education and Welfare. *MR 78 mental retardation: The leading edge. Service programs that work.* A staff report of the President's Committee on Mental Retardation. Washington, DC: Office of Human Development Services, 1978.

Vaux, C. L. Family care of mental defectives. *Journal of Psycho-Asthenics,* 1935, *40*, 168–189.

Wolfensberger, W. *The principle of normalization in human services.* Toronto: National Institute on Mental Retardation, 1972.

Wolfensberger, W. *The origin and nature of our institutional models.* Syracuse, NY: Human Policy Press, 1975.

Wolfensberger, W., & Glenn, L. *Program analysis of service systems: A method for the quantitative evaluation of human services* (3rd ed.), *Vol. I: Handbook. Vol II: Field manual.* Toronto: National Institute on Mental Retardation, 1975. (a)

Wolfensberger, W., & Glenn, L. *Program analysis of services systems (PASS).* Toronto: National Institute on Mental Retardation, 1975. (b)

Wyatt v. Stickney, 344 F. Supp. 387 M.D., AL, 1972.

Youngberg v. Romeo, 102 S. Ct. 2452, 2462, 1982.

CHAPTER 3

PLANNING COMPREHENSIVE
COMMUNITY BASED SERVICES

Daniel D. Anderson

Community based service systems for moderately and severely handi-capped persons are as varied as the communities in which these ser-vices are provided. In most communities we find a confusing combination of public and private agencies. Some community agencies provide a broad range of services, yet specialize in their clientele. For example, private community agencies (e.g., Easter Seal Society or United Cerebral Palsy) may implement health, education, and social service program activities; however, these services may be limited to clients with a specific disabling condition. By contrast, other agencies may provide a limited service, such as vocational rehabilitation counseling, to individuals with a wide range of disabling conditions.

In the past few years, the relative "public-ness" or "private-ness" of agen-cies has become less distinct. Many private agencies provide services under contract to public agencies, thus falling more and more under the influence of the public sector. On the other hand, public agencies have designed and developed more alternative programs to meet the unique needs of special-ized population groups.

Public and private organizations may be organized at the local, regional, state, and national levels. For example, public education is organized and funded at a local, state, and national level. On the average, public education receives about 42%, 50%, and 8% of its funding from local, state, and national governments, respectively (Campbell, Cunningham, Nystrand, & Ustan, 1980). At the local level, there are about 16,000 public educational agencies. Hundreds of regional and cooperative educational agencies exist in the 35 states that utilize such an organizational structure.

At all levels, education agencies are subject to federal laws such as the

*Daniel D. Anderson directs the Hawaii Department of Education's statewide effort in planning compre-hensive services for children and youth who are severely handicapped. He has master's degrees and direct service experience in education and social work. Dan has worked in residential as well as community based programs serving handicapped persons. His work experience also includes planning spcial education programs and providing technical assistance in the U.S. Pacific Island Territories.

Education for All Handicapped Children Act (P.L. 94-142) and the Rehabilitation Act of 1973. Under P.L. 94-142 and Section 504 of the Rehabilitation Act, public educational agencies are required to provide services to school-aged students who are moderately or severely handicapped. And that is only education. The potential combination of public or private, health, education, and social service agencies, at one or many organizational levels, results in an endless number of community service systems.

A Systems Approach

An investigation of individual community service systems is well beyond the scope and intent of this chapter. However, knowledge of your community's service system for moderately and severely handicapped persons is a "must" if you intend to make any positive impact on that system. Failure to understand your community's service system increases the possibility of being caught in a series of "traps" that will prevent you from improving the quality of the services provided to clients.

General systems theory has been found useful in developing an understanding of service systems. The stages of developing knowledge about a system have been described by Carlisle (1981). In general, knowledge of a system is first gained through the identification and description of the system in terms of its environment. Next, understanding is developed through the recognition of the component parts of the system and the interrelationships among those parts. The final stage of knowledge is understanding the interrelationship between system parts in terms of their interdependencies and patterns of order. "The interdependence of elements (parts) that combine to form a whole is the universal means to identify and define a system" (Carlisle, 1981, p. 12).

The concept of "open systems" (Easton, 1965) emphasizes the interdependence of the system and its environment as well as the interdependence of the component parts within political systems. Easton's open system model is helpful in understanding service systems as well. The important concepts in the systems model are "system" (input, process, and output), "environment," and "feedback."

The systems concept and its use as an analytical tool will be valuable to those involved in assessing and improving service delivery. The strength of the systems concept is in its adaptability and applicability. However, a word of caution: there is a corresponding weakness. The use of the systems concept for analysis and planning may lead to overly specific and tedious applications (Keusch, 1981).

System. A system may be defined as the interrelationships among the components of that system: "inputs" (resources, materials); "process" (activities, programs); and, "outputs" (results, accomplishments). In a service system, the "inputs" include the clients or students, staff, materials, equipment, facilities, etc. Activities, programs, and services comprise the system's "processes." And the system "outputs" are the results. For example, students with increased knowledge and skills or increased levels of participation in normal community activities are "outputs" of good community based service systems.

One of the advantages of utilizing a systems model for organizational analysis is the model's ability to focus on various levels of a given system and the relationship between levels. One may use a systems model in the analysis of public education at the district, school, and program level. The model may also be used to analyze a student's individualized educational program (IEP) or an adult's individualized habilitation plan (IHP).

Environment. An advantage of utilizing an open system view in system analysis is that emphasis may be placed on the environment and the forces within the environment that impact upon the system. As an example, in the environment of the school system, one of the important forces that may impact on the process of education is another system, the teachers' union. Other environmental forces influencing a community school system include population, social values, and economic and political conditions.

Focusing on the student, there are any number of forces that must be taken into consideration if we are to accomplish educational objectives or desired outputs. If our objective (*proposed* output) is to increase the participation of the student in normal community activities, then our educational system must place greater emphasis on the environment and provide training in the community (e.g., social communication, bus training, shopping centers, etc.).

Karl Weick (1976) used the term "loosely coupled" to describe the relationship between systems or between sub-systems within a larger system. Loose coupling is a way of describing the differences we may find in two classrooms serving similar students in the same school. Both classrooms may be viewed as equal components from the school system perspective. From a sub-system view, differences may abound. Each class is a unique system in itself. Each class is loosely coupled with the other classrooms, yet is independently influenced by different environmental factors. For example, one teacher may be strongly influenced by professional associations and training. The other teacher may be influenced by the union and community associations outside of the profession. The two teachers may have very different educational philosophies and ideas regarding normalization and the integration of education for individuals who are moderately and severely handicapped.

Feedback. Feedback is the communication link between the system and its environment, and among the parts of the system. As with all aspects of the system, communication is influenced by the environment. To a degree, feedback is an attempt by the system to influence the environment.

Standards

The system planner who is engaged in program evaluation and improvement requires more than a tool for carrying out service system analysis. What is also needed is a standard for comparison. Many specific kinds of human service organizations have established professional or organizational standards, including teacher certification, school accreditation, or other human service standards such as those for rehabilitation facilities (Commission on Accreditation of Rehabilitation Facilities, 1973). Knowledge of acceptable professional or organizational standards is important. The purpose of this section, however, is to provide you with a more general standard for organizational analysis.

Dosher (1978) established such standards by describing the most effective steps in the process of system organization. Persons engaged in planning, be it developing IEPs, IHPs, or agency program plans, will recognize the parallel between Dosher's effective organizational model and the standard planning model as outlined in Figure 1.

Dosher's Effective Organizational Model	Standard Planning Model
	Needs
Purpose (What Will Be Done)	Goals (Outcomes)
Function (How Will It Be Done)	Objectives (Process)
Structure (Relationship)	Resources (Inputs)
Role (Parts Defined)	Activities (Process)
	Evaluation

Figure 3-1. Comparison of Organization and Standard planning models.

Dosher compared the effective approach in the organization of a service system with the differing approaches frequently found in community systems. Her comparison included both public (government) and private systems.

Most would agree that the effective steps in planning and organizing a system begins with a statement of purpose, goal, or desired outcome. Hopefully, that purpose is based on a sound needs assessment. The next step involves a description of function (i.e., process objectives) or a description of how the organization will accomplish its purpose. Given an understanding of what needs to be done, the structure of the system can be developed and described. Developing structure involves the organization of the resources necessary to carry out the system's function. Given the structure, specific roles, activities, and tasks may be defined and described. One role or activity of the system involves evaluation.

For example, an assessment of students may indicate that a high percentage of those students do not demonstrate the skills necessary to function in the local community environment. Information on functional needs and present levels of student performance may be used to help design a community education program for the purpose of assisting students to develop such skills. (One approach to this type of assessment is found in the Mattison and Rosenberg chapter of this text). Given the assessment of need, program purpose or goal statements may be developed. Out of the program goal(s) specific performance objectives may be developed. Methods would be designed based on the proposed objective. The structure and the resources necessary for carrying out the methods would be designed and specific roles and activities for instructional staff described. Program evaluation can be based on the degree to which proposed objectives are obtained.

Unfortunately program planning frequently follows a very different pattern. Very often program structure and service methods are established and in place long before client need and program purpose are clear. This is particularly true when client needs, or our perception of client needs, are changing. We may recognize a new need for community education and be able to develop new statements of purpose and objectives, but we frequently end up having to use the old structure and old methods to accomplish those new objectives.

Not all systems are planned and organized in an effective manner. Many systems that were originally well planned fail to maintain an effective orientation. No matter how clear the original purpose or goal, the organization's external (environmental) and internal (system) forces will change the organization. Without a systematic evaluation of the service organization in relation to client needs and desired standards (objectives and methods) there is no hope in maintaining organizational effectiveness.

Public Systems

As Dosher (1978) suggests, public (government) systems often place greater emphasis on structure and de-emphasize purpose. Through personal experience, many readers may be familiar with public service systems that seem to be far more interested in the maintenance of the structure and stability of the organization than delivering the service.

Some of my work in the past few years has been with small, developing national government systems located in the Pacific Basin. I have frequently found that when need and purpose are unclear, other environmental forces influence organizational decision making. In the new Pacific Island governments, public employment and the structure to support that employment are often more important than any proposed service purposes. Some government agencies adopt organizational models that are frequently inefficient and ineffective in service delivery but effective in public employment and the distribution of government funds (Anderson, 1983; Brady & Anderson, 1983; Hezel, 1982; Nevin, 1977).

Closer to home, Deal and Derr (1980) suggest that the unique nature of public schools must be considered when proposing a system change or system development effort. Some of their observations of American schools supports Dosher's (1978) description of government organizations.

> Schools have diffuse, unclear goals.... The multiplicity of goals makes it difficult for schools to pursue a common direction.... (yet) in reality, schools provide a secure employment system. Teacher unions exert strong influence over teacher salaries and working conditions. Often, negotiated contracts stipulate working conditions which work to the advantage of teachers as employees, not to the educational program of the schools (pp. 98–99).

Schools and other public agencies may begin with a focus on need or purpose, but over the years, as purpose changes and other environmental and system forces grow in strength, the orientation of the system changes. Papagiannis, Klees, and Bickel (1982) believe that school systems have become dedicated to the maintenance of the present structure and system. Papagiannis et al. suggest that: "schools will resist innovation ... radical changes in educational institutions ... or efforts to bring about major changes in instructional methods or organizational structure" (p. 262).

Private System

In the absence of a clear organizational purpose, other factors take precedence. We frequently find that the organizational emphasis in governmental agencies is placed on structure. By contrast, newer community based, private organizations often emphasize role and activities. However, these organizations are equally ineffective in orientation when compared to the more effective approach described by Dosher.

Not long ago, I assisted in the evaluation of a relatively new, privately operated, community based agency. There was a recent change in leadership and the new director felt that it was an opportune time to evaluate program activities. From the new director's point of view, the evaluation was to be focused on the staff, their roles, and activities. Under the previous director, the agency had used a unique outreach model for service delivery to homebased clients. Staff, including the new director, had been trained to use the service model.

As with many new community based agencies, the focus of organization was on the role of the staff rather than the needs of clients. The evaluation found that the service roles (activities) used were not particularly effective in meeting the most pressing client needs. A more comprehensive agency evaluation was requested which addressed all the aspects of the organization including staff activities.

A second evaluation effort was carried out utilizing an open system model. Much time was spent with the staff clarifying relationships within the program: its community environment, purpose, function, structure, and roles. As a result of the second evaluation, client needs were more clearly described in light of the community in which they lived. Program purpose was changed to more closely reflect client needs. Given a clear purpose, agency functions and the organizational structure necessary to carry out those functions were redesigned. Finally, staff roles were redefined. A recent follow-up contact with the agency indicates that staff roles and activities have changed as a result of the systematic evaluation. The director reports that present roles are slightly less efficient but more effective in terms of meeting client needs and fulfilling the purpose of the agency.

New sub-systems of larger established agencies are equally prone to inefficient and ineffective organizational patterns by placing an emphasis on role and function rather than purpose. A few years ago, I visited a new community based special education/vocational education training project. I was impressed with the work (roles and functions) of staff on the project and equally impressed by the skill demonstrated by the students. Being unfamiliar with the community in which the project was located, I asked how the students would use their newly learned skills upon leaving the project. For a moment the question went unanswered. Finally, the project director explained that the skills being taught in the new project were those taught in the community in which she had received her training. Although the student skills were appropriate for the community in which the director was trained, the same skills were inappropriate for the community in which she was now living and working. The project's focus on role and function of staff, as effective as it may have been in developing client skill, was not appropriate when considered in light of the needs of the clients for functioning in their local community environment.

Planning

We all know that there is no sure method for developing or improving a service system. However, there may be a "nearly magical" method for the enhancement of our capabilities to do so. According to Caplow (1976), this magical enhancement can be achieved nine out of ten times by providing an "intelligent emphasis on planning" (p. 202). Caplow explains the direct and indirect advantages of planning. If the planning experience is carried out at "reasonable intervals and in a reasonably democratic spirit, (planning) has all sorts of wonderful side effects" (Caplow, 1976, p. 203). Those side effects are clarifying goals and purpose, bringing functions into alignment. uncovering and resolving structural and operational problems, and opening and intensifying communication.

Caplow also lists the elements of a good plan. Those elements include:

1. Describing, in detail, the current state of the organization (system) and the relevant features of the environment.
2. Analyzing past trends in the system and its environment as a basis for future projections.
3. Dividing the future into successive phases or stages and describing goals for each phase.
4. Estimating the inputs (resources) required to move through the progressive future phases.
5. Estimating environmental conditions required to carry the plan through the progressive future phases.
6. Developing methods to measure plan fulfillment and goal accomplishment.
7. Providing for periodic plan revision in case of overfulfillment, underfulfillment, or unforeseen contingencies.

Planning Orientation: Needs or Resources

The standard or common model for planning was outlined in Figure 1. That model may be utilized in planning a new system or it may be used in conjunction with the suggestions from Caplow (1976) for carrying out a continuous planning cycle. The outlined planning activities include (a) assessing needs, (b) proposing goals or outcomes, (c) developing process objectives, (d) structuring resources (inputs) necessary to carry out activities, (e) accomplishing outcomes, and (f) evaluating both the effort and accomplishment.

Given unlimited resources we, as planners and decision makers, could focus our total attention on the needs of a planning subject. A "needs orientation" to planning is one way of describing such an approach. Public Law 94-142 proposes such an approach in the educational planning for handicapped children. Under P.L. 94-142, IEPs are based on the needs of the student without consideration as to the availability of resources. If the resources necessary to accomplish educational objectives are unavailable, it is the responsibility of the education agency to make those resources available.

Although IEPs for handicapped students should be needs oriented, persons responsible for IEPs often have a resource orientation to planning. That is, plans are based on a perception of the availability of resources. Frequently adjustments are made in developing statements of need or in proposing outcomes (educational objectives) because there is a perceived limit to the available resources.

The use of a resource orientation in planning an IEP results in the student's needs being reassessed in terms of the availability of resources. For example, a physically handicapped student may need to develop specific motor skills. In order to develop those skills, the services of a physical therapist may be required. However, if no therapist is available, the student's educational plan likely will not include objectives and activities that require physical therapy. As a result, the educational plan may not reflect the student's motor development needs.

When plans are too resource oriented, they are not relevant to needs. For example, resource oriented planners of community based services may be overly conservative in their approach to planning and focus on existing segregated programs and policies as a planning base. Educational planning should be needs oriented and focused on the needs that students have for knowledge and skills that enable them to participate in normal community settings.

Resources are not unlimited. When plans are too needs oriented and unrealistic in terms of available resources, the plans cannot be implemented. Educational plans must not be too resource oriented or too needs oriented; both are equally inappropriate. The task of the planner is to find the proper balance between the two orientations of needs and resources.

Public Law 94-142 has assisted educational planners in tipping the balance toward a needs oriented approach with respect to planning IEPs. However, resources are limited and there will likely never be sufficient

resources to meet all needs of every moderately and severely handicapped person. One resource for meeting educational needs that is often
under utilized is the community. We strongly believe that many of the
needs of students, particularly the need to participate in less segregated
and restrictive settings, may be met by more fully utilizing community
resources.

As the planning focus moves from the individual to the group (organization) and community, planners must grapple with ever increasing
discrepancies between needs and resources. The more expansive the planning focus the greater the disparity between needs and resources and the
more important it is for the planner to have a properly balanced orientation.
A balanced orientation maximizes goal attainment as well as the efficient use
of resources.

Planning Traps

As planning becomes more general and community oriented, it becomes
increasingly difficult to balance needs and resources. The paradoxical result
of the planner attempting to be more relevant with respect to the community environment is that planning becomes less client-need oriented and
more resource oriented. The planner is more likely to be caught in "planning
traps."

Traps render the planning less effective by upsetting the balance, by
preventing the planner from developing the proper balance between
the needs of the client(s) and the resources available. I have outlined
four of the most common planning traps which snare the unsuspecting
planner.

Poor planning perspective. The first and perhaps most difficult trap is the
"poor planning perspective." We are caught in this trap when we "do our
own thing" (work in isolation and without a community perspective). When
planning is carried out without a proper perspective of the environment,
the product is likely to end up looking good on the shelf but not likely to
help clients in the community.

Small projects or small private agencies that are role oriented frequently
have narrow or poor perspectives. Often this is due to insufficient resources
to carry out a community oriented needs assessment or to keep abreast of
changing environmental conditions.

Not long ago, I visited three agencies in the same community. All
three agencies served clients with similar disabilities. However, each agency
served a different age group. Thus, each agency was interdependent with

respect to the "flow" of clients through the system. For years clients moved from one agency to the next with little formal communication other than case conferences. Apparently, there had been sufficient stability in the community and in each program to limit communication to individual clients. A need to address planning of the overall service system did not exist.

Two changing environmental factors disrupted the traditional relationships among those agencies. The first was a demographic change; the second change was economic. Combined, these changes would have caused a major disruption in the system of services for severely handicapped persons had cooperative, community oriented planning not begun to take place.

The change in demographics was related to a significant increase in the number of severely handicapped persons in the community. That increase was due, in part, to changes in state policy regarding the prevention of institutionalization. Agency A, serving the youngest age group, and Agency B, the next agency in the client flow, had made adjustments for changing client population. Agency C had not. Because clients remained in Agency B for some time before moving on to Agency C, Agency C had no indication of the degree of change in the client population. Within one year, Agency C was forced to make major programmatic changes which could have been better planned when Agency A had first identified impending changes several years earlier.

The second change, funding cuts, caused problems for all three agencies. As a result of those cuts, Agency A reduced both the number of clients and the quality (frequency) of services. Funding cuts and service reduction by Agency A are expected to have a compound impact on both Agency B and Agency C. Without high quality early intervention programs, the services necessary to meet the needs of clients in Agencies B and C will be more costly. At the same time funds for Agencies B and C have been reduced.

Agencies in the system described above managed to function independently under stable conditions. However, as the forces in the environment changed, the agencies had to respond cooperatively. A changed environment forced the three agencies to recognize their interdependence and develop a broader planning perspective. For a time, the three community agencies were trapped by a poor planning perspective. Their isolated and narrow initial reactions to change were inefficient and ineffective in meeting the needs of clients and the community.

No community agency can be insulated from the forces of change. There is no defense against change other than a pro-active plan in anticipation of change. Planning to avoid the trap of a poor perspective must (a) consider the impact of forces of change (e.g., social, economic, political, policy, and demographic factors), (b) take place in a community context, and (c) utilize an open systems approach.

Nebulous need. The second most common planning trap is "nebulous need." When our purpose is unclear or when we fail to carry out a sound needs assessment, our perception of need becomes nebulous, confused, and vague. When trapped by nebulous needs, there is no defense against the forces of the environment. The purpose of the system is anyone's purpose. The goal of the organization is what anyone wishes it to be. When you are trapped by nebulous need, you and your organization are controlled by the hidden agendas of others.

Examples of organizations with nebulous need have been provided. The school system with diffuse and unclear goals is more subject to influence by external forces (teacher unions, lobby groups, funding variations, special programs, etc.) than the system that has clear goals and purpose. The special education/vocational education project that was unclear with regard to purpose, (to assist students in relation to community functioning) was nebulous in the minds of project staff. The project director supported activities she believed were important based on her past experience. Unfortunately, her past experience was inappropriate for the community she was serving.

There are a number of methods and techniques that may assist program planners. Many needs assessment models and techniques are now available. However, one of the most effective processes is that proposed by Caplow (1976): planning carried out at reasonable intervals and in a democratic spirit. I would emphasize the democratic spirit and add the need to involve clients and other community representatives in the planning process.

Priority paralysis. A sound needs assessment and democratic planning often reveal a large number of pressing needs or problems. Combined, all of the needs are likely to surpass the resources of any one system. Thus, by conducting a sound needs assessment, a system may increase the probability of being caught in the third planning trap, "priority paralysis."

There are many organizations where everything is "top priority." Everything must be "done today." Those organizations are paralyzed, immobilized, or inefficient in meeting needs or accomplishing objectives. Everything is being "worked on" and little is being accomplished. The squeaky wheel often becomes the priority problem and receives the attention. Program staff juggle issues until a particular issue becomes a crisis, thus providing some external direction for priority setting.

Everything cannot be of equal importance. Organizational resources are never sufficient to carry out every activity, accomplish every objective, and meet every need. Planners and decision makers must be able to exercise internal control and set priorities thus enabling the effective distribution of the system's resources.

The organization's statement of purpose or goal should provide direction out of the priority paralysis trap. The organization must also have a leader and a structure for supporting leadership (e.g., communication system). Many have described the kind of characteristics necessary for effective organizational leadership (Campbell, Corbally, & Nystrand, 1983; Likert, 1961; Sergiovanni & Carver, 1980). Whatever else those characteristics might be, one essential characteristic in effective organizational management is the ability to make priority decisions.

Resource rigidity. Related to priority paralysis is the "resource rigidity" trap. Priority paralysis occurs when decision makers fail to prioritize needs and objectives. Resource rigidity occurs when decision makers fail to prioritize the use of resources.

In any system, priorities will be determined no matter what the decision maker's role might be. Priorities may be determined by crisis, as with priority paralysis, or by default when trapped by resource rigidity. In flexible systems, resource utilization decisions are determined by organizational leadership in an efficient and effective manner. In rigid systems, resources are utilized in particular ways because "we have always done it that way."

In the discussion on the needs versus resource orientation to planning, I noted that when sufficient resources are available, needs oriented planning may take place. Additional new resources may be directed to meet the needs; the resource rigidity trap may be avoided.

In some growth organizations (and at times, government planned programs) there is a feeling of unlimited resources. Often, however, new resources are not available to meet new needs. A planner must shift the planning orientation toward the resource oriented approach. If the planner shifts the balance too far, becomes overly resource oriented and insensitive to client needs, then the planner is in the resource rigidity trap. The language of those trapped by resource rigidity is familiar: "We always have done it that way;" "More of the same is better;" and, "For next year's budget, we will just add X% for inflation."

Old ways of using resources should be judged in comparison to new ways. This concept of justifying program function and resource utilization was made popular under the term "zero-based budgeting." Phyrr's book, *Zero-Base Budgeting* (1973), provides useful information on planning and management, and suggests tools to avoid the trap. However, freedom from resource rigidity will not come through the implementation of a new planning concept alone and it is particularly difficult to overcome in government planning. To implement a new program without new resources is a very difficult task. It involves both the process of planning to meet new needs and the task of redistributing old resources. Yet, failure to do so is to accept resource rigidity.

Future

I would like to end on a positive note. Positive change is occurring. Effective community based service systems are developing. New programs are breaking old patterns of resource distribution. In fact, I believe that community based service systems for moderately and severely handicapped individuals are in the forefront of educational, health, and social service system changes as a whole.

Many of those serving severely handicapped individuals have long recognized the failure of the old hierarchical systems (e.g., institutions) to meet human service needs. To meet these needs, new methods have been sought, new service models developed, and new systems designed for delivery. Integrated community based programs are proving to be effective in meeting needs of students, their families, and the community (Brown, Ford, Nisbet, Sweet, Donnellan, & Gruenewald, 1983).

The methods that we are finding useful in meeting the needs of severely handicapped individuals will bring about change in American life. John Naisbitt (1982), in his book *Megatrends*, outlined the forces that are bringing about change in American life. Though more business oriented, Naisbitt identified organizational trends such as "decentralization," "networking," and "multiple-option." Those developments are equally appropriate, perhaps more appropriate, for the delivery of human services.

Decentralization and deinstitutionalization have for some time, been important trends in the delivery of human services. Many communities are developing programs for greater independence in community living. In the deinstitutionalization of services as well as individuals, we have learned the value and necessity of networking. Networking included nontraditional ways of sharing information and resources. Our experience in providing community based services for individuals who are severely handicapped has resulted in much more effective and efficient service system structures. However, as Naisbitt (1982) warns, the old hierarchies remain. The retrenchment of the public bureaucracy will prove to be both a danger and an opportunity for continued development of community based services.

The trend toward multiple-option and participatory democracy described by Naisbitt (1982) has developed in community based service delivery and is evident in the individualized and participatory process of service planning. Such a change has transformed the relationships between the client and the service provider, and has provided direction for change in all human service systems.

Conclusion

"Change occurs when there is a confluence of both changing values and economic necessity, not before" (Naisbitt, 1982, p. 183). We are in a dramatic period of changing values, changing human needs, and changing resources. Community based integrated service systems, though not yet well developed, have the potential to improve the quality of services, the quality of life for moderately and severely handicapped individuals, and to serve as trend setting models for other human service systems.

The present period of change, as with any period of change, provides both dangerous traps and rewarding opportunities. There is no sure method of avoiding the dangers or taking advantage of the opportunities, but there is that nearly magical way of enhancing our capabilities to meet the challenge: intelligent planning.

REFERENCES

Anderson. D. D. *A planning guide for special education personnel preparation in the Pacific Basin.* Honolulu: Pacific Basin Consortium. 1983.

Brady. M. P., & Anderson. D. D. Some issues in the implementation of P.L. 94-142 in the Pacific Basin territories. *Education*, 1983. *103*(3), 259–269.

Brown. L., Ford. A., Nisbet. J., Sweet. M. Donnellan. A., & Gruenewald. L. Opportunities available when severely handicapped students attend chronological age appropriate regular schools. *The Journal of the Association for the Severely Handicapped*, 1983. *8*(1), 16–24.

Campbell. R. F., Corbally. J. E., & Nystrand. R. O. *Introduction to educational administration* (6th ed.). Boston: Allyn & Bacon. Inc., 1983.

Campbell. R. F., Cunningham, L. L., Nystrand. R. O., & Ustan. M. D. *The organization and control of American schools* (4th ed.). Columbus, OH: Charles E. Merrill Publishing Co., 1980.

Caplow. T. *How to run any organization.* Hinsdale. IL: The Dryden Press. 1976.

Carlisle. H. General systems theory, interdependence and organization design. In R. Lippitt & G. Lippitt (Eds.). *System thinking: A resource for organization diagnosis and intervention.* Washington. DC: International Consultants Foundation. 1981.

Commission on Accreditation of Rehabilitation Facilities. *Standards manual for rehabilitation facilities.* Chicago: Author. 1973.

Deal. T. E., & Derr. C. B. Toward a contingency theory of organizational change in education:

Structure. processes. and symbolism. In *Education finance and organization research perspectives for the future.* Washington. DC: The National Institute of Education. 1980.

Dosher, A. W. Technical assistance: A public learning mechanism. In S. Sturgeon. M. L. Tracy. A. Ziegler. R. Neufeld. & R. Wiegerink (Eds.). *Technical assistance: Facilitating change.* Bloomington. IN: Developmental Training Center. University of Indiana. 1978.

Easton, D. *A framework for political analysis.* Englewood Cliffs. NJ: Prentice-Hall. 1965.

Hezel, F. X. *Reflections on Micronesia: Collected papers of Father Francis X. Hezel. S.V.* Working paper series. Honolulu. Hawaii, 1982.

Keusch. R. B. The applications of systems theory. In R. Lippitt & G. Lippitt (Eds.). *Systems thinking: A resource for organization diagnosis and intervention.* Washington. DC: International Consultants Foundation. 1981.

Likert, R. *New patterns of management.* New York: McGraw-Hill. 1961.

Naisbitt, J. *Megatrends.* New York: Warner Books, Inc.. 1982.

Nevin, D. *The American touch in Micronesia.* New York: W. W. Norton. 1977.

Papagiannis. G. P.. Klees. S. J.. & Bickel. R. N. Toward a political economy of education innovation. *Review of Educational Research.* 1982. *52*(2). 245–290.

Phyrr, P. A. *Zero-base budgeting.* New York: Wiley-Interscience. 1973.

Sergiovanni, T. J.. & Carver. F. D. *The new school executive* (2nd ed.). New York: Harper & Row. 1980.

Weick, K. E. Educational organizations as loosely coupled system. *Administrative Science Quarterly.* 1976. *21*. 1–19.

Section II
STRATEGIES FOR SERVICE DELIVERY

CHAPTER 4

EXAMINING AND FOSTERING INTEGRATED SCHOOL EXPERIENCES

SUSAN STAINBACK AND WILLIAM STAINBACK

In growing numbers, special education classes for severely handicapped students are being located in regular neighborhood schools. In addition to the mere physical location of these classes within regular schools, every effort should be made to integrate severely handicapped students into as many regular school activities as possible (Hamre-Nietupski & Nietupski, 1981; Stainback & Stainback, 1982). In other words, severely handicapped students should *not* spend the entire day in the special class environment.

There are many regular school activities (or environments) in which severely handicapped students can participate or at least partially participate. For example, severely handicapped students can participate in the regular lunchroom, hallway, and restroom environments. They also can participate in the regular class environment during many activities such as birthday parties, show-and-tell times, rest time, art, music, and recess (Stainback, Stainback, & Jaben, 1981).

The authors' purpose in this chapter is to examine (a) regular school environments in which severely handicapped students might be integrated, (b) strategies for promoting positive interactions in integrated school

William Stainback is a Professor in the Department of Special Education at the University of Northern Iowa. He received his doctorate from the University of Virginia. His professional experience includes teaching elementary and junior high school children with mild and severe behavioral disabilities. At the University of Northern Iowa, he conducts research and teaches courses on issues and trends in special education. Dr. Stainback has published extensively on the integration of severely handicapped persons. He serves as a consulting editor for several major journals in special education including *Education and Training of the Mentally Retarded* and *Teaching Exceptional Children*. He also has conducted workshops and has made numerous presentations regarding education methods for children who display maladaptive behavior.

Susan Stainback is a Professor in the Department of Special Education at the University of Northern Iowa. She received her doctorate from the University of Virginia. Her research and writings have been widely published. She serves as a consulting editor for several major journals in special education, including *The Journal of the Association for Persons with Severe Handicaps, Behavioral Disorders, Education and Training of the Mentally Retarded,* and *Teaching Exceptional Children*. Before becoming a university professor, she was a classroom teacher of elementary age severely handicapped students. In addition to teaching and conducting research at the University of Northern Iowa, Dr. Stainback has served as a consultant to many agencies and has conducted workshops throughout the United States.

environments, and (c) the training needs of regular class teachers to facilitate participation of severely handicapped students in regular school environments.

Integration Into Regular School Environments

While logically it would not be appropriate for nonhandicapped and severely handicapped students to be integrated during academic and highly competitive tasks, there are numerous ways special and regular class teachers can work together cooperatively to provide integrated school experiences for severely handicapped students. For example, at the elementary school level, regular and special class teachers can help facilitate integration of severely handicapped students with nonhandicapped students by combining their classes during selected activities such as homeroom, art, music, recess, holiday and birthday parties, show-and-tell times, and/or rest periods. There are other ways regular and special class teachers can help facilitate integration. For instance, they can encourage nonhandicapped students to visit the special education classroom(s) to work as tutors and/or simply to spend a little time with a severely handicapped friend. In addition, regular and special class teachers can work together to arrange opportunities for interaction between nonhandicapped and severely handicapped students in the school cafeteria, on the playground, at assembly programs, in the hallways, and/or at the bus loading and unloading zones.

In the remainer of this chapter, the authors describe a checklist to help estimate the degree to which severely handicapped students placed in regular schools are integrated into various regular school environments. Purposes for which school personnel might want to use the checklist, as well as suggested ways of improving a school's score, are also discussed.

The Checklist

The 14 items included in this checklist were determined by analyzing and listing the various environments within a regular school setting in which severely handicapped and nonhandicapped students have been known to participate. Several principals and regular and special class teachers reviewed the list and suggested modifications. Each of the 14 items explores a selected environment such as the playground, lunchroom, hallways, and certain regular class activities (See Figure 1).

The checklist may be used in any elementary or secondary regular school setting in which severely handicapped students receive educational services. Administration of the instrument requires less than 10 minutes. An individual who is intimately familiar with the activities of the severely handi-

Severely Handicapped Integration Checklist

Date _____ Name of School _____
Name and Position of Person Providing Information _____

Directions: After reading each question, put an X under the category that best reflects how many severely handicapped students engage in the specified activity or environment.

Do severely handicapped students:	All (100%)	Most (> than 50% but < than 100%)	Some (approx. 50%)	Few (< than 50% > than 0)	None (0%)
1. ride the same school buses that nonhandicapped students ride?					
2. have their classrooms located throughout a regular school building with classrooms for the nonhandicapped?					
3. attend some school assembly programs with nonhandicapped students? (25% or more)					
4. eat lunch in the school cafeteria during the same time as nonhandicapped students?					
5. eat lunch at the same tables in the school cafeteria with nonhandicapped students?					
6. share recess (or recreational times) with nonhandicapped students?					
7. go on some (25% or more) school field trips with nonhandicapped students?					
8. share special events such as Halloween and Thanksgiving parties or football homecoming celebrations with nonhandicapped students?					
9. share homeroom with nonhandicapped students?					
10. use the same bathroom as nonhandicapped students?					
11. use the school hallways at the same time as nonhandicapped students?					
12. share one or more classes such as art, music, and/or PE with nonhandicapped students?					
13. have their school pictures interspersed with their nonhandicapped peers throughout school publications (e.g., yearbooks, newsletters, or displays)?					
14. share some (25% or more) of the same school jobs and responsibilities as nonhandicapped students (e.g., arranging chairs in the gym for an upcoming assembly program)?					

Score procedures: Determine the score for each question (None = 0; Some = 2; Most = 3; All = 4). Add the individual scores to obtain the total score.

TOTAL SCORE _____

Figure 4-1.

capped students in the school, such as the special teacher or the principal, should provide the data. The accuracy of the information obtained will be directly related to the level of knowledge of that individual.

Response options to each statement included in the checklist are on a 5-point Likert-type scale. These options are designed to reflect various degrees of integration based on the approximate percentage of severely handicapped students integrated in a designated school environment. The options range from *All* (i.e., 100% of the severely handicapped students in the school are integrated in the environment) to *None*, in which 0% are integrated. Each of the possible options receives a point score which is totaled to arrive at a score for a school's integration rating on the overall checklist.

The score for each item is a 4 if *All* (100%) is marked; 3 if *Most* is marked; 2 if *Some* is marked; 1 if *Few* is marked; and 0 if *None* is marked. Possible total scores range from 0 to 56. Although a score of 56 indicates the highest level of integration, the determination of the most appropriate score for any particular school should reflect the needs of the students in that school. Generally, the higher the score, the better the situation in regard to the integration of severely handicapped students within the regular school.

Possible Uses of Checklist

The Severely Handicapped Integration Checklist (SHIC) may be used by a variety of individuals to obtain an objective measure of the "integratedness" of a school in regard to severely handicapped students located in the building. The teacher of the severely handicapped class, for example, could use the checklist to evaluate the degree to which integrated activities are provided for students. Results can yield a clear picture of relatively strong and weak areas of integration, providing guidance for the teacher in subsequent efforts to upgrade the level of integration.

Similarly, the instrument may be useful to other educators. A principal could use the checklist to evaluate an entire school. Consultants to school districts could use it in a systematic evaluation of the schools under their supervision to assist in guiding integration suggestions. State department personnel could use the SHIC to determine state progress in integration activities. The instrument may also be helpful to outside evaluators and researchers as a tool for obtaining an objective measure of the degree of integration within a school. The relative ease, speed, objectivity, and simplicity of scoring the instrument make the SHIC a practical, viable means of collecting useful data.

How to Correct Low Scores on the Checklist

If a school scores low on the SHIC, several steps should be taken. First, determine the environment(s) in which severely handicapped students are *not* integrated. Second, determine *why* integration is not occurring in these environments. Third, find a solution or way of correcting the situation.

If, for example, severely handicapped students are not integrated on buses because nonhandicapped students might ridicule them or treat them in a nonaccepting or cruel manner, then school personnel might attempt to change the attitudes and behaviors of the nonhandicapped students. Similarly, if severely handicapped students are not integrated into a particular class (e.g., art, music, or physical education) because they are so profoundly handicapped that they could not profit from instruction, then school personnel might determine alternative environments or situations where integration *is* feasible. Small groups of nonhandicapped students from a physical education class, for instance, might visit the special class periodically to tutor profoundly handicapped students in rudimentary physical education activities such as gaining motor control of head movements. It should be noted that any such activities should be carried out under the direction of the teacher or other appropriate specialists. The nonhandicapped students might, in the process, learn something about physiology, gain a better understanding of severely handicapped persons, and possibly develop new friendships. Recent research studies have found that well organized and structured interactions between nonhandicapped and severely handicapped students can (a) increase the knowledge of nonhandicapped students about those who are severely handicapped (McHale & Simeonsson, 1980), and (b) improve their attitudes toward severely handicapped students (Voeltz, 1980, 1982). As a result of the individual attention they receive, the severely handicapped students might improve their motor skills as well as profit from the social stimulation.

In conclusion, integrated school experiences can be provided for all severely handicapped students across a variety of school settings. *The specific form or exact nature of the integrated experiences should be individualized according to the age, needs, and capabilities of the student(s) involved.* With planning and cooperation among school personnel, it should be possible for non-handicapped and severely handicapped students to have the opportunity to interact for at least a part of each school day.

Promoting Social Interactions

Interactions between severely handicapped and nonhandicapped students do not always spontaneously occur when opportunities for interactions are provided (Nietupski, Hamre-Nietupski, Stainback, & Stainback, 1984). It may be necessary for teachers to promote or encourage interactions. Thus, the purpose of this section is to delineate and describe three methods teachers could use to promote interactions between severely handicapped and nonhandicapped students: (a) classroom organization, structure and materials; (b) training severely handicapped students in interaction skills; and (c) training nonhandicapped students to interact with severely handicapped students.

Classroom Organization, Structure, and Materials

Hamre-Nietupski (1980) has found that dividing an integrated class into small heterogeneous groups facilitates interactions among students of various developmental levels to a greater degree than attempting to obtain interactions with one or two larger groups. Thus, teachers may want to consider arranging large groups of students in integrated situations into small heterogeneous groups. In addition to organizing the class into small heterogeneous groups, the specific type of small group structure to be used should be carefully considered. Johnson and Johnson (1980) described three group structures that can be used in an integrated classroom situation. These are "cooperation" or positive goal interdependence, "competition" or negative goal interdependence, and "individualistic" learning or no interdependence. In a cooperative group structure, the group as a whole is assigned a common goal and everyone is encouraged to work together to reach the goal. In other words, if the group's goal is to be reached, all students must coordinate their efforts to achieve the goal. Johnson and Johnson (1980) have found that the cooperative group structure produced significantly more positive interactions between handicapped and nonhandicapped students than either the competitive or individualistic group structure.

A third classroom organization factor that has been found to influence interactions are the types of materials, toys, and activities provided. Quilitch and Risley (1973) found that children tend to play alone or together depending on the types of materials and toys available. In their study, for example, during an organized play period when materials such as wagons and balls were available, the children interacted more often as opposed to when materials such as crayons and puzzles were available, which, of course, can more readily be used in isolated play. Stainback, Stainback, and Jaben (1981) have related the implications of these and other similar findings specifically to the severely handicapped. They have advocated the use of social-type materials, toys, and activities that can be used with students across a wide range of abilities to help facilitate interactions between students of varying developmental levels.

Training Severely Handicapped Students

A second approach to promote positive severely handicapped/nonhandicapped student interactions is to focus on enhancing severely handicapped students' socialization skills. The rationale is that if severely handicapped students develop appropriate social skills, nonhandicapped students will tend to interact with them more often. Thus, the discussion presented in this chapter focuses on procedures for training severely handicapped students to engage in direct social interaction behaviors with nonhandicapped students in integrated settings.

Strain and his associates (Strain & Kerr, 1980) have successfully used teacher prompts to elicit interactional behaviors from severely withdrawn, isolated students. Teacher prompts typically involve verbal or gestural motoric prompts directed toward the isolated student(s). In addition to teacher prompting, peers have been recruited to prompt the social behaviors of such students. This technique is referred to as "peer social initiation" (Strain & Kerr, 1980). Recent investigations have indicated the effectiveness of this procedure with elementary age autistic students (Ragland, Kerr, & Strain, 1978). In the peer social initiation procedure, a peer or peers prompt the severely handicapped student(s) to engage in social interactions by making social bids to them. More specifically, in the research by Strain and his associates, selected peers have been trained to make social bids to isolated children, with the purpose of increasing the handicapped students' rate of social responding and social interactions.

Severely handicapped students' social interaction behaviors have been increased through direct reinforcement also. As part of a larger study, Russo and Koegel (1977) investigated a way of improving the social interaction behaviors of an autistic student. They investigated the effects of a behavior modification specialist reinforcing the social interactions of a 5-year-old autistic student. The study was conducted in a regular classroom. The specialist provided the autistic student with token and social reinforcers (first on a continuous, then intermittent schedule) whenever she displayed appropriate social behaviors toward her nonhandicapped peers (such as borrowing a toy and/or sharing candy). After the social interaction behaviors were being maintained at a satisfactory rate, the teacher was trained to administer the intervention strategy. The social behavior of the autistic student was maintained after the intervention was taken over by the teacher.

Training Nonhandicapped Students

A third approach to promote severely handicapped/nonhandicapped student interactions is to directly train nonhandicapped students to interact with severely handicapped students. Recently several professionals have advocated this approach (Hamre-Nietupski, 1980; Stainback & Stainback. 1981a, 1981c). One of the main rationales is that research (Guralnick. 1980) has shown that in integrated free-play situations, at least, nonhandicapped students show a definite preference for interacting with other nonhandicapped students rather than severely handicapped students. Also. some nonhandicapped students have been found to reject and/or to be cruel to handicapped students in integrated situations (Jones, 1972). Therefore. teachers wishing to promote interactions between severely handicapped and nonhandicapped students may need to modify the attitudes and interaction behaviors of the nonhandicapped toward the severely handicapped. As Voeltz (1980) noted:

> If researchers document that nonhandicapped children exhibit an intoler-
> ance for their handicapped peers that includes a willingness to engage in
> overtly cruel behavior, this should posit a challenge to educators rather than
> a limitation. Surely, such behavior of presumably normal children is as
> susceptible to change as the behavior of severely handicapped children. now
> apparently acquiring skills once thought unattainable (p. 463).

Recently, methods and materials have been developed for educating nonhandicapped students about severely handicapped students (see Nietupski. Hamre-Nietupski, Schuetz, & Ockwood, 1980; Stainback & Stainback. 1981a; Voeltz, 1980). Many of these methods go beyond teaching nonhandicapped students about handicapping conditions. The focus is on modifying non-handicapped students' attitudes and behaviors toward severely handicapped students through instructional programs about individual differences and controlled positive experiences with severely handicapped students.

Training Needs of Regular Class Teachers

Because of the integration movement, for the first time in their lives, many regular classroom teachers are coming into direct contact with severely handicapped students. Because many of today's regular class teachers were educated in segregated schools (void of severely handicapped students), many of them have little or no knowledge to guide their responses toward these students. How regular class teachers respond to severely handicapped students could be critical to the success of the integration movement (Hamre-Nietupski & Nietupski, 1981).

The responses of the regular class teacher toward severely handicapped students are critical for a number of reasons. First, nonhandicapped students often model the behaviors of their teachers (Keller & Ribes-Inesta, 1974). Thus, it is important that regular class teachers set a good example in their interactions with severely handicapped students. Second, the support and cooperation of regular class teachers is needed to help maximize the integration of severely handicapped students into regular schools (Stainback, Stainback, & Jaben, 1981). Thus, regular class teachers need training so they can gain the knowledge and understanding required to set a good example for their nonhandicapped students and to work cooperatively with special class teachers to help foster the integration of severely handicapped students into regular schools.

The training needs of regular class teachers have been outlined by Stainback and Stainback (1981b) and are reviewed here. According to the Stainbacks, regular class teachers need answers to at least three basic questions: (a) Who are severely handicapped students? (b) Why are they in regular schools? and (c) What is the regular class teacher's role in the education of severely handicapped students?

Who are severely handicapped students? Basically, what does a regular class teacher need to know about severely handicapped students in order to interact with and provide appropriate guidance for them in the bus loading area, lunchroom, selected regular class activities, and/or on the playground? Due to the paucity of instructional time available to regular education teachers, any information provided should be concise and functional. Information presented should relate directly to what teachers will need to know to work effectively with severely handicapped students on a daily basis (Wilcox, 1977).

Traditional data given teachers (e.g., incidence statistics, chromosomal structural abnormalities, and syndrome characteristics) may not constitute practical use of the short instructional time for clarifying who severely handicapped students are. Technical medical data and terminology is often of little assistance to the teacher when faced with providing guidance and supervision to severely handicapped students (Thomas, 1980). Areas of information that could prove to be helpful include the characteristics of severely handicapped students as (a) students and (b) individuals who may have physical and/or intellectual difficulties that interfere with, yet not necessarily preclude, their participation in many school activities (Brown, Branston-McClean, Baumgart, Vincent, Falvey, & Schroeder, 1979). Definitions of severely handicapped students based on educationally related needs and functions would appear to be the most useful approach for teachers since it is in the educational aspects of the severely handicapped students that teachers are expected to impact most strongly. In other words, for regular class teachers, severely handicapped students should be defined as integral members of the general school population to be approached as individuals rather than as exotic syndromes to be pitied, ignored, and/or feared.

Why are severely handicapped students being integrated into regular school programs? As Reynolds and Birch (1977) stated, "The whole history of education for exceptional children can be told in terms of one steady trend that can be described as progressive inclusion" (p. 22). A brief review of the history of special education should assist regular class teachers in understanding that the current integration movement is not just temporary enthusiasm. Regular class teachers also need to recognize the philosophical and conceptual bases (e.g., normalization principle) for integration of all handicapped students into or as close to the mainstream of society as possible. In addition, regular class teachers should have an awareness of the inherent educational rights of all students. In short, recognition of the philosophical, conceptual, and legal bases behind the integration of severely handicapped students into regular schools should assist regular class teachers in gaining an understanding as to why severely handicapped students are being integrated into regular schools.

Although the basic reasons why severely handicapped students are being integrated into regular schools are philosophical and legal in nature, pedagogical research findings do support integration (e.g., Guralnick, 1981; Rynders, Johnson, Johnson, & Schmidt, 1980; Stainback & Stainback, 1981c; Voeltz, 1980, 1982). Thus, in the preparation of regular class teachers, it is important that they be informed of the research evidence, particularly the evidence related to the benefits of integration to severely handicapped and nonhandicapped students, so they can attempt to capitalize on these benefits in their school settings.

In conclusion, regular class teachers need to understand why severely handicapped students are being integrated into regular schools if their support and cooperation is desired. One way of presenting the reasons would be to review with regular class teachers (a) the history of the integration movement in special education, (b) the philosophical and legal basis for integration, and (c) the research evidence on the benefits of integration to both nonhandicapped and severely handicapped students.

What is the regular class teacher's role? Regular class teachers have a definite role to play in assisting severely handicapped students in becoming integral members of the student body. One basic element in the regular class teacher's role is the need to work cooperatively with special class teachers in preparing the environment to promote optimal integration conditions. This cooperative teacher relationship has been found to be a key factor (Nietupski et al., 1980) in the successful integration of severely handicapped students into regular school programs and activities.

Once a cooperative relationship between regular and special educators has been established, the role of the regular class teacher in the severely handicapped student integration efforts can begin to mature. First, each regular class teacher needs to provide nonhandicapped students with opportunities to interact with severely handicapped students (Stainback & Stainback, 1981a, b). When and how interaction opportunities can be provided should be presented to regular class teachers during their preparation so they have the information needed to make knowledgeable professional decisions about integration activities. For example, regular class teachers should understand that their nonhandicapped students can be provided opportunities to interact with severely handicapped students in a variety of nonteaching situations (e.g., school cafeteria). While, as noted earlier in this chapter, joint class activities in certain academic or highly competitive tasks may not be appropriate, regular class teachers should be aware that there are numerous ways to provide nonhandicapped and severely handicapped students with opportunities to interact.

Regular class teachers need to understand organizational arrangements and procedures to facilitate interactions in situations in which interaction opportunities are provided. Because research has indicated that providing interaction opportunities is not enough (Guralnick, 1980; Porter, Ramsey, Tremblay, Iaccobo, & Crawley, 1978), regular class teachers may be called upon to promote interactions. They should be made aware of how interactions can be fostered by organizing small groups to work on cooperative goals (Rynders et al., 1980) and by encouraging and reinforcing interactions among nonhandicapped and severely handicapped students (Stainback, Stainback, Raschke, & Anderson, 1981).

The final role of the regular class teacher to be discussed here is as the trainer of nonhandicapped students to promote severely handicapped/nonhandicapped student interactions. The regular class teacher should be aware of methods for training nonhandicapped students about severely handicapped students. In their preparation, they should be informed of the methods that have recently been proposed that go beyond (or replace) teaching nonhandicapped students about handicapping conditions (see Stainback & Stainback, 1981b; Taylor, 1982; Voeltz, 1980). These methods focus on teaching nonhandicapped students respect for individual differences and the benefits that can be derived from interactions with persons of different abilities and backgrounds. Thus, one of the regular class teacher's roles might be to instruct nonhandicapped students about human differences as well as about appropriate reactions to human differences that could help foster positive interactions.

Conclusion

Because of the growing national concern for the education of all handicapped children, the Congress of the United States passed P.L. 94–142 in
1975 that mandated free and appropriate education of all handicapped
children in the least restrictive environment (LRE). While this law has been
cited repeatedly to support the rights of mildly handicapped students to be
educated in the LRE, it should be noted that the law also addresses the
rights of severely handicapped students to be educated in the LRE. This
law, The Education of All Handicapped Children Act, provided implementation power and incentive for educators to begin seriously addressing the
needs of severely handicapped students in the most normalized environment possible. Since this legislation, both research findings (Stainback &
Stainback, 1982) and experiences have shown that severely handicapped
students can be successfully provided educational services within regular
community public schools (Hamre-Nietupski & Nietupski, 1981). In addition,
it has been found that both severely handicapped and nonhandicapped
students who share interaction experiences in integrated situations can
benefit educationally and socially (see Stainback & Stainback, 1981c).

Based on experience and research evidence, many professional educators
have recently accepted the position that the least restrictive educational
environment for severely handicapped students is the regular neighborhood public school. This is evidenced in part by the fact that in 1979, The
Association for Persons with Severe Handicaps (TASH) adopted a resolu-
tion calling for the education of severely handicapped students with their
nonhandicapped peers in regular schools.*

REFERENCES

Brown, L., Branston-McClean, M., Baumgart, D., Vincent, L., Falvey, M., & Schroeder, J.
Utilizing the characteristics of current and subsequent least restrictive environments in the
development of curricular content for severely handicapped students. *AAESPH Review.*
1979, *4*, 407–424.

Guralnick, M. Social interactions among preschool children. *Exceptional Children,* 1980, *46*,
248–253.

Guralnick, M. The social behavior of preschool children at different developmental levels:
Effects of group composition. *Journal of Experimental Child Psychology,* 1981, *31*, 115–130.

Hamre-Nietupski, S. *Sensitizing the nonhandicapped persons to severely handicapped students in
regular public school settings.* Paper presented at the Meeting of The Association for the
Severely Handicapped, Los Angeles, 1980.

Hamre-Nietupski, S., & Nietupski, J. Integral involvement of severely handicapped students

---

*Portions of this chapter were adapted from the authors' previous work in *Education and Training of the
Mentally Retarded,* and *Teaching Exceptional Children.* All material reprinted with permission.

within regular public schools. *Journal of the Association for the Severely Handicapped,* 1981, *6,* 30–39.

Johnson, D., & Johnson, B. Integrating handicapped students into the mainstream. *Exceptional Children,* 1980, *47,* 90–98.

Jones, R. L. Labels and stigma in special education. *Exceptional Children,* 1972, *38.* 553–564.

Keller, F., & Ribes-Inesta, E. *Behavior modification.* New York: Academic Press, 1974.

McHale, S. M., & Simeonsson, R. J. Effects of interaction on nonhandicapped children's attitudes toward autistic children. *American Journal of Mental Deficiency,* 1980, *85,* 18–24.

Nietupski, J., Hamre-Nietupski, S., Schuetz, G., & Ockwood, L. (Eds.), *Severely handicapped students in regular schools.* Milwaukee: Milwaukee Public Schools, 1980.

Nietupski, J., Hamre-Nietupski, S., Stainback, S., & Stainback, W. Preparing school systems for longitudinal integration efforts. In N. Certo, N. Haring, & R. York (Eds.), *Public schools integration of severely handicapped students.* Baltimore: Paul H. Brookes, 1984.

Porter, R. H., Ramsey, B., Tremblay, A., Iaccobo, M., & Crawley, S. Social interactions in heterogeneous groups of retarded and normally developing children: An observational study. In G. P. Sackett, & H. C. Haywood (Eds.), *Observing behavior (Vol. 1: Theory and applications in mental retardation).* Baltimore: University Park Press, 1978.

Quilitch, H. R., & Risley, T. R. The effects of play materials on social play. *Journal of Applied Behavior Analysis,* 1973, *6,* 573–578.

Ragland, E. U., Kerr, M. M., & Strain, P. S. Effects of social initiations on the behavior of withdrawn autistic children. *Behavior Modification,* 1978, *2,* 265–578.

Reynolds, M., & Birch, J. *Teaching exceptional children in all America's schools.* Reston, VA: Council for Exceptional Children, 1977.

Russo, D. C., & Koegel, R. L. A method for integrating the autistic child into a normal public school classroom. *Journal of Applied Behavior Analysis,* 1977, *10,* 579–590.

Rynders, J., Johnson, R., Johnson, D., & Schmidt, B. Producing positive interaction among Down Syndrome and nonhandicapped teenagers through cooperative goal structuring. *American Journal of Mental Deficiency,* 1980, *85,* 268–273.

Stainback, S., & Stainback, W. Educating nonhandicapped students about severely handicapped students: A human differences training model. *Education Unlimited,* 1981, *3,* 17–19. (a)

Stainback, W., & Stainback, S. Preparing regular class teachers for the integration of severely handicapped students. *Education and Training of the Mentally Retarded,* 1981, *16,* 188–192. (b)

Stainback, W., & Stainback, S. A review of research on interactions between severely handicapped and nonhandicapped students. *The Journal of the Association for the Severely Handicapped,* 1981, *6,* 23–29. (c)

Stainback, W., & Stainback, S. Social interactions between autistic students and their peers. *Behavioral Disorders,* 1982, *7,* 75–81.

Stainback, W., Stainback, S., & Jaben, R. Providing opportunities for interaction between severely handicapped and nonhandicapped students. *Teaching Exceptional Children,* 1981, *13*(3), 72–75.

Stainback, W., Stainback, S., Raschke, S., & Anderson, R. Three methods for encouraging interactions between severely handicapped and nonhandicapped students. *Education and Training of the Mentally Retarded,* 1981, *16,* 188–192.

Strain, P. S., & Kerr, M. M. Modifying children's social withdrawal: Issues in assessment and clinical intervention. In M. Hersen, R. Eisler, & P. Miller (Eds.), *Progress in behavior modification,* (Vol. 2). New York: Academic Press, 1980.

Taylor, S. From segregation to integration: Strategies for integrating severely handicapped students in normal school and community settings. *The Journal of the Association for the Severely Handicapped,* 1982, *7,* 42–49.

Thomas A. Current trends in preparing teachers of the severely/profoundly handicapped: A conversation with Susan and William Stainback. *Education and Training of the Mentally Retarded,* 1980, *15,* 43–49.

Voeltz, L. M. Children's attitudes toward handicapped peers. *American Journal of Mental Deficiency,* 1980, 84, 455–464.

Voeltz, L. Effects of structured interactions with severely handicapped peers on children's attitudes. *American Journal of Mental Deficiency,* 1982, *86,* 380–390.

Wilcox, B. A competency-based approach to preparing teachers of the severely/profoundly handicapped: Perspective I. In E. Sontag, J. Smith, & N. Certo (Eds.), *Educational programming for the severely/profoundly handicapped.* Reston, VA: Council for Exceptional Children, 1977.

CHAPTER 5*

PROGRAM DESIGN AND RESEARCH
TO NORMALIZE PEER INTERACTIONS

ROBERT E. JOHNSON AND LUANNA MEYER

Interactions among nonhandicapped children in school and community settings can be and are structured by parents, professionals, and community program staff through a variety of episodic special events which the children themselves would be unable to arrange. Extracurricular sports, arts, theater events, community recreation programs, and various social events which adults schedule for children are some examples of such episodic opportunities. Girl Scouts, Boy Scouts, 4-H groups, etc. may continue over extended periods of time, but again they are not readily accessible to the children involved without support and structure from parents and other adults. But if we examine the social lives of most children closely, it is clear that these episodic social interaction and activity enrichment opportunities are only a part of their peer interaction experiences. Children themselves have access to continuous and, across the years, daily play and other leisure experiences with potential friends. Furthermore, these peer interactions increase in quantity and importance as the children mature. By the time they are adults, expectations for them include primary relationships within the peer group and decreased dependency upon parents, teachers, and the various other adults who previously provided support and direction for activities. Sailor (personal communication, 1982) has referred to these interactions between children and the many adults who occupy authority roles in

*Robert E. Johnson is a doctoral student in the Special Education program at the University of Minnesota. He is a research assistant with the Minnesota Consortium Institute for the Education of Severely Handicapped Learners. Research interests include integration, development of social skills in severely handicapped learners, and the effects of interaction between severely handicapped/nonhandicapped peers on the nonhandicapped students.

Luanna Meyer received her Ph.D. from Indiana University in 1976. Currently, she is Associate Professor of Special Education and Rehabilitation at Syracuse University. Prior to Syracuse, she was the Director of the Minnesota Consortium Institute for the Education of Severely Handicapped Learners at the University of Minnesota. She serves as Chairperson of the Executive Committee of The Association for Persons with Severe Handicaps, and as Editor of the Journal of the Association for Persons with Severe Handicaps (JASH). In addition to her work in the area of integration, Dr. Meyer is interested in assessment and evaluation, adaptive alternatives to remediate excess behavior, and interventions to develop social competence in severely handicapped learners.

relationship to those children as "vertical," while interactions within a peer group would be viewed as "horizontal" in nature. Becoming an adult involves an appropriate increase in horizontal relationships; this is true even in the workplace where the adult will still very likely be expected to comply to a vertical relationship with his/her employer. However, an adult also must be successful in a variety of horizontal interactions with co-workers and customers; and, of course, what would one's life be like without the kinds of horizontal relationships which we refer to as acquaintances, friends, and spouse?

In contrast to the opportunities and experiences of nonhandicapped children across the school years, most children with moderate and severe handicapping conditions do not have access to daily and continuous interactions with their peers. Furthermore, those episodic interaction experiences which are structured by parents and professionals (field trips, Special Olympics, classroom birthday parties, etc.) are themselves restricted to relatively homogeneous groups. That is, handicapped children are likely to remain with other similarly handicapped children for most such activities across the lifespan. When less handicapped and nonhandicapped peers are involved in these episodic experiences, their role is most likely to resemble the vertical relationship of a parent or teacher to the handicapped individual. For example, nonhandicapped volunteers keep score and coach handicapped peers in Special Olympics; both children are not involved as participants which would reflect corresponding horizontal roles.

Because of the nature of severe handicapping conditions, children with such disabilities do not have the cognitive, social, and mobility skills to initiate and maintain social interactions with either other handicapped peers or nonhandicapped peers. Additionally, the design of services and environments for handicapped children precludes "normalized" interactions between these children and their nonhandicapped peers throughout the school day, in the neighborhood, and in the community. In most parts of the country, these two groups of children generally are isolated both physically and socially from one another throughout the school years. Even when severely handicapped children attend the same school as their nonhandicapped, same-age peers, they often remain in self-contained special education classrooms throughout the day. They may arrive via separate transportation systems and buses, and enter and leave through a separate entryway which is considered more accessible than the main entrance used by other children. They do not share recess and extracurricular activities with their nonhandicapped peers and may even eat lunch in a special education classroom. More often than not, even their daily schedules will differ; they may arrive at and leave school at different times than do children enrolled in regular education. Finally, programs for severely handicapped children may be centralized even when they are located in regular education buildings, so that most of the handicapped children attending the school come from different neighborhoods than their nonhandicapped peers. As a consequence, the children who receive services in "regular" buildings may be as socially isolated from their nonhandicapped peers as those who attend a segregated, handicapped-only school.

Meyer and Kishi (1984) stressed that physical and social integration must be considered separate issues, and that physical integration should be viewed as only the first step in assuring the social acceptance of handicapped youngsters. Their proposed "Integration Markers" provide an estimate of the degree to which integration actually exists in a particular program. However, the final question which must be addressed is the nature of the social interaction experiences of the children involved. Are the various "reverse mainstreaming," "special friends," and peer tutoring programs which have been promoted by professionals to structure interactions between handicapped and nonhandicapped children appropriate? Such programs are clearly system dependent whenever the children are otherwise isolated from one another and have no opportunity to expand their interactions outside the scheduled episodes (Meyer & Kishi, 1984).

Preparing Children for Integration

The literature on the social acceptance of mildly handicapped students who were mainstreamed into regular classrooms over the past 15 years can be interpreted either negatively or positively. Where neither the child nor the environment were prepared for one another, the data on outcomes are negative; where some intervention effort occured, the data are positive (Gottlieb, 1978, 1981). Johnson, Johnson, and Maruyama (1983) summarized this literature as appearing, at first glance, to be overwhelmingly negative, but they argued that the nature of the integration *context* may be responsible for the past failures. Additional cautions were offered by Asher and Taylor (1981) and Donaldson (1980) in their reviews. Asher and Taylor noted that the negative findings on the integration of mildly handicapped children into regular classes may be a function of asking the wrong questions, i.e., using inappropriate and unduly restrictive dependent measures. Most studies investigating the social status of these students following a mainstream placement inquired whether their nonhandicapped peers would then select them as "best friends." Instead, it would be more appropriate (and normalized) to ask whether they were accepted in comparison to the usual variety of patterns of social interactions among children, of which "best" friendships reflect only one type. Donaldson (1980) argued that where attitudes and behaviors of nonhandicapped children toward their handicapped peers are negative, the task of educators should be to identify existing socialization experiences responsible for those patterns. There may be negative "training" experiences in children's lives which are teaching them to reject and socially isolate persons who are different rather than preparing them to accept individual differences. Whenever attitudes and behaviors are found to be negative, alternative experiences are needed to teach appropriate, positive patterns of interaction (Voeltz, 1984). This view is consistent with the challenge presented by Johnson et al. (1983) in that our generally competitive and/or individualistically achievement-oriented educational system may be directly responsible for negative interactions. They have presented considerable evidence that cooperative learning experiences, which can be equally supportive of academic achievement, will result in more positive peer interactions in heterogeneous grouping arrangements.

There is a rapidly expanding literature on the consequences of exposing nonhandicapped children to information about and contact with severely handicapped children (Voeltz, Johnson, & McQuarter, 1983). This movement toward increased information exchange and contact between non-handicapped persons and persons with severe disabilities is a consequence of litigation, legislation, and an increased public awareness of the rights of handicapped persons to live and learn in integrated community environments (Bruininks & Lakin, in press). With rare exception, the literature indicates that integration is both proper and overdue. Whether or not positive outcomes will occur is a function of our commitment to translating this value into practice and our willingness to expend our resources to insure the quality of this effort (Wilcox & Sailor, 1980). The opportunity to accomplish the integration of severely handicapped individuals into community environments and activities can be guided by the lessons learned in the mainstreaming literature. That is, rather than simply placing severely handicapped children into situations and settings with their nonhandicapped peers and conducting "outcome" or summative evaluations of this effort after-the-fact, we should be asking some rather fundamental program design and strategy questions. Rather than appearing on the scene several years hence with an "I told you so" report *following* integration efforts, researchers and curriculum developers can apply their expertise and experiences to insure that integration is done carefully and constructively from the beginning. Finally, the evaluation which is done should not focus on producing *summative* good vs. bad results; it should follow an interactive model in which information is collected as the program is implemented and is used continuously to refine and revise the activities as information suggests those changes are needed (Cronbach et al., 1980).

The major intent of this chapter, then, is to present the available evidence on the integration program designs that have been proposed and implemented. What are the goals of these integration efforts, and which of these goals are primary? To what extent can each of the integration program designs be considered supportive of normalized peer interactions for the children in those programs. Are there data regarding the kinds of outcomes associated with each of the various peer interaction programs which could be applied to the design of future programs? Before we begin, we should state our bias. The question of integration is not an empirical one. Integration is a value; we accept that value and the challenge to accomplish the return of severely handicapped individuals to community environments. The empirical question is how we can best accomplish the reality of that value-based goal.

Goals of Integration

To evaluate whether or not an integration program is successful, we must measure its accomplishments in relationship to the goals of integration. We could locate five goals or desired outcomes frequently noted in the integration literature:

1. To develop positive attitudes toward handicapped individuals which would facilitate the acceptance of those individuals in various community environments and activities;
2. To provide a social context for the handicapped child to develop various skills (e.g., social, communication, play) which are likely to be facilitated by peer interactions;
3. To provide a social context for the nonhandicapped child which will facilitate the development of additional skills (e.g., social, communication, play) to interact with others who are "different;"
4. To allow for the development of friendships between handicapped and nonhandicapped persons;
5. To normalize the social status of severely handicapped individuals; that is, to provide opportunities to participate in various heterogeneous living, work, and leisure environments which parallel the kinds of opportunities available to nonhandicapped individuals.

In this section, we will review each of these goals and the available information on our achievements in each area.

Attitude Change

One goal of integration has been to change the attitudes of nonhandicapped children in a positive direction. Interestingly enough, the assumption that those attitudes initially are negative may not be accurate. Educators' notions about these attitudes have been based upon sociometric research findings involving mildly handicapped students in mainstream classroom placements.

We have already qualified these past findings and suggested that the past negative interpretations are not completely representative of what actually took place as a result of different mainstream efforts. Thus, Burton and Hirshoren's (1979) extrapolation of this negative interpretation (i.e., if mildly handicapped students were rejected, surely the consequences would be even worse for severely handicapped students) is now outdated. Yet, despite the lack of empirical data, the folklore of inevitable negative consequences (peer cruelty in the form of verbal and physical abuse) is still quite common in many local communities.

In the past few years, investigators have systematically examined the attitudes of nonhandicapped children toward their severely handicapped peers and have found generally positive attitudes prior to and following any interactions (McHale & Simeonsson, 1980; Voeltz, 1980a, 1982). Thus, fears about nonhandicapped children being unaccepting of severely handicapped peers seem to be unfounded. In fact, the evidence suggests that increased contact results in improved attitudes (Brinker, 1982; Voeltz, 1982). There is also evidence that in some cases these attitude improvements may be overly solicitous. That is, nonhandicapped children may report inappropriately and unrealistically positive attitudes toward children with severe handicaps. Voeltz and Brennan (1984) found that although most nonhandicapped children describe their relationship to a severely handicapped playmate in terms which paralleled their relationships to a nonhandicapped best friend, some of the children responded with stereotypical, globally accepting descriptions which could not be considered normalized. The ultimate issue is, of course, whether or not those attitudes have any consequences for what happens to handicapped individuals as they experience increased access to integrated community environments. How are positive attitudes translated into interpersonal interactions? Johnson, Johnson, and Maruyama (1983) reported that some nonhandicapped persons do report ambivalence when initially interacting with handicapped individuals. They cited evidence that overt, verbalized attitudes may be favorable, whereas covert attitudes (and actual behaviors) may be rejecting. They suggested that where initial interactions between handicapped and nonhandicapped people are colored by "over-friendliness" on the part of the nonhandicapped person, the handicapped individual will not be provided with appropriate feedback regarding which social behaviors will be acceptable in such situations. Rather than providing normalized expectations for the behavior of a severely handicapped individual, the consequences of these inappropriate interactions with nonhandicapped peers could become similar to those with the special education teacher who accepts increasing levels of deviance and the overly protective parent who continuously "does for" his or her youngster. The results of each situation would be simply to extend the artificial and nonhabilitative "special" environment to the real world.

Another factor to consider is the possibility of negative consequences for the nonhandicapped child. We would *not* include in this concern any suggestion that it is somehow more important to protect the "mental health" of a nonhandicapped individual who claims to be disturbed by the presence of a severely handicapped individual with physical and cognitive differences. Nonhandicapped persons must learn to tolerate individual differences, whether they are racial, socio-economic, or involve children with severe handicaps. However, it is possible that some models of peer interaction which are proposed as training for integration will have different consequences for the nonhandicapped children involved. Educators, for example, acknowledge the possibility that teachers who work with severely handicapped youngsters may "burn out" after a few years. The consequences may be that they move on to teaching mildly handicapped children, go back to school for a higher degree, or move out of teaching altogether. What would happen, then, to nonhandicapped youngsters who are asked to regularly commit to a peer tutoring or peer interaction program? Will these children maintain their involvement with those particular handicapped peers once the program is over? Will they extend (generalize) those presumably positive attitudes to other handicapped persons across the lifespan and in other environments? Or will they burn out, feeling that they have performed their service and others should do their share?

Closely related to this issue is the possibility that the interactions would actually be stressful for the children involved. This may well be the case where preparation and supervision by teachers is inadequate and the children are ill-equipped for the interactions. If we view any programmatic intrusions into the social world of children as possibly causing stress, then occasionally tapping the attitudes of nonhandicapped children would seem to be an important means of guiding program decisions. For example, it may be that the age of children is a major variable to consider in planning the amount and nature of the interaction educators can expect. A younger student may view the interactions as natural play and be most capable of developing such initial relationships into longitudinal friendships. Older children, experiencing the interactions for the first time in their lives, may approach the interactions as a service or in a "big brother, big sister" manner. Professionals may have preconceived notions of how children *should* respond to the opportunities we provide for them, but we have not done a thorough and careful job of asking the children what they think of our ideas.

Skill Development by the Handicapped Child

There is a growing literature on the acquisition of nonsocial tasks through peer arrangements (cf. Brown & Holvoet, 1982). Efforts to document the acquisition of skills by handicapped children as a function of peer interaction is confounded, however, by a number of difficulties. First, most instruction for severely handicapped students occurred under carefully controlled instructional conditions until recently. In the area of social competence, for example, isolated social behaviors would be trained in highly contrived instructional environments. A severely handicapped learner would be taught to initiate a conventional greeting response (e.g., "Hi") in a school setting in the presence of instructional personnel (Stokes, Baer, & Jackson, 1974). In contrast, Brown and his colleagues have suggested that the criterion of ultimate functioning principle should be reflected in both the goal and process of instruction (Brown, Nietupski, & Hamre-Nietupski, 1976). This approach involves teaching skills which are adaptive for community environments *in* those environments and situations, and there is a rapidly expanding instructional technology detailing the procedural components involved (Brown et al., 1979; Brown et al., 1983; Falvey, Brown, Lyon, Baumgart, & Schroeder, 1980; Ford et al., 1984; Freagon et al., 1983; Wilcox & Bellamy, 1982). Most of this work reflects an *intuitive* call for reform in the way we teach severely handicapped learners, rather than validated alternative instructional strategies. However, two partially validated curricular approaches consistent with these innovations have been field tested (Guess & Helmstetter, in press; Neel et al., 1983). And two instructional packages are available to provide detailed guidelines for teaching social play interaction skills in the context of interactions with nonhandicapped peers, although neither of these is supported with field-test data (Noonan, Hemphill, & Levy, 1983; Meyer, McQuarter, & Kishi, in press). A basic problem, then, is the absence of a validated model which teachers might apply to the development of social and other related skills in social interactions with peers. However, a fundamental *experimental* difficulty in validating these models would be attempting to document those changes which occur as a function of the peer interaction rather than the multitude of other vairables (including teacher instruction) which could be responsible for the change. Of course, that may be the point; whatever is occurring in the context of a peer interaction may be associated with learning opportunities not present in teacher-pupil interactions.

Existing data on the results of instruction in horizontal grouping arrangements involving handicapped-only interactions or interactions with higher functioning handicapped peers is extremely limited but demonstrates that the approach is workable (Gable, Hendrickson, & Strain, 1978; Young & Kerr, 1979). Voeltz and Brennan (1984) provided evidence that nonhandicapped-severely handicapped peer dyads are associated with higher levels of appropriate activity, involvement, and cooperative play in comparison to teacher-student instructional situation dyads. Brinker (1982) reported significantly higher levels of social bids in handicapped-nonhandicapped peer interactions in comparison to handicapped-only interactions. In a study involving moderately handicapped students, Ziegler and Hambleton (1976) reported positive interactions in both handicapped-only and handicapped-nonhandicapped peer dyads, but less aggression and more teaching, interviewing, and comforting/helping were reported in the latter situations. We were unable to locate any other data regarding social skill outcomes.

A final, crucial question involves the empirical and social validity of the social skills which we expect to develop in these peer interaction contexts. Which social skills, acquired in what order, and practiced in which activities will result in increased social competence, and adult adjustment to integrated living, work, and leisure environments? We need to follow these handicapped students into their adult environments to establish the validity of the skills we are teaching them, including the skills we expect to be developed in interactions with peers. Are we ready to accept the possibility that not all nonhandicapped peers will provide appropriate models of particular social skills for their handicapped friends? Our bias is that while we would clearly want to exclude certain kinds of inappropriate experiences from such interactions, part of the integration process must include our willingness to allow handicapped persons normalized access to so-called "deviant" peer activities. This will mean some risk-taking on our part.

Skill Development by the Nonhandicapped Child

There are several issues involved in considering whether or not handicapped children initially have the necessary skills to interact constructively and positively with their handicapped peers. First, are interactions with severely handicapped peers simply an attitudinal issue, or does the "success" of those interactions depend upon whether the nonhandicapped child knows what to do? Voeltz (1982; 1984) has maintained that one reason nonhandicapped children have not spontaneously initiated these positive interactions is because they do not have the necessary skills. That is, they are not familiar with the communication mode utilized by a handicapped child, are not sure what a child with cerebral palsy can do, are unsure whether they should "consequate" negative behaviors, etc. Thus attitude improvements and corresponding behavioral changes would not be dependent upon philosophical ideas; rather they would result from the acquisition of social skills in actual interactions with children who are quite different from their other nonhandicapped peers. There is some evidence that nonhandicapped children describe their interactions with severely handicapped peers as an experience which better prepares them to deal with a variety of individual differences (Voeltz, 1980b). One interesting issue to explore would be to investigate whether nonhandicapped children become more accepting of relatively minor individual differences as a function of participation in interactions with severely handicapped peers. For example, after such interactions, would nonhandicapped children be less likely to socially reject regular classroom peers who previously had been excluded from various activities? Although this possibility appears to have strong face validity, there are no systematic investigations of such possible consequences of integration.

There is considerable evidence that nonhandicapped children can and do acquire the necessary skills to become effective *peer tutors* of their severely handicapped peers. This is true even in programs with no specific training for this role. For example, in one program for high school students, nonhandicapped teenagers were simply instructed to "Go hang out" (Gaylord-Ross & Pitts-Conway, 1984). Other programs indicate an extensive training program to teach nonhandicapped students behavior modification skills (Poorman, 1980), and there is clear evidence that nonhandicapped students function effectively in the tutor role after receiving instruction in how to teach (Fenrick & McDonnell, 1980). Although their program differs from the peer tutoring approach by emphasizing heterogeneous friendships among the children, the "Special Friends" program originally developed in Hawaii focuses upon a structured program to prepare nonhandicapped children for their interactions with severely handicapped peers (Voeltz et al., 1983). These authors maintained that nonhandicapped children require specific instruction in how they can communicate and play with a handicapped friend. They also need an opportunity to ask questions and share experiences with one another and with a knowledgeable adult when they begin these heterogeneous interaction opportunities.

There are many reasons why it might be important to develop a sense of social competence in interactions with severely handicapped peers on the part of nonhandicapped children. As Brown (personal communication, 1982) emphasized, today's nonhandicapped children are tomorrow's employers, parents, and peers of severely handicapped individuals. If we acknowledge that it is unlikely that severely handicapped individuals will be independent, that instead we are attempting to extend the support networks now available to nonhandicapped individuals to include severely handicapped persons, then it is crucial that the community provide assistance to handicapped individuals in a natural and normalized way in a variety of integrated community environments.

Ultimately, whether or not nonhandicapped individuals can and do interact positively with severely handicapped persons may be a function of the quality of the training experiences which are provided to them. It may be important for educators to recognize that the probability of success in such interactions may be a function of the initial structure and support which is provided to the children rather than assuming that nonhandicapped children can handle the interactions without this guidance. Finally, an area which has received little attention thus far has been the level of the social skills exhibited by nonhandicapped peers entering integrated situations. Special educators in particular seem to be prone to the assumption that all nonhandicapped children possess the appropriate social skills to provide a beneficial social interaction experience for a severely handicapped child. Can we identify positive social models for handicapped children and insure that these interactions will be mutually beneficial for the children involved?

Friendships

There is virtually no information on the establishment and maintenance of friendships between nonhandicapped and severely handicapped children. Over the years in work conducted by the second author at the University of Hawaii and in Hawaii's public schools, there have been numerous anecdotal reports by teachers and parents of friendships which initially began through "special friends" programs and continued across several years of school. These reports have included instances of nonhandicapped children taking the initiative (by fifth through seventh grade) of commuting to their severely handicapped "special" friend's home to play after school and during the summer; unfortunately, these reports have not been verified. Clearly, what is now known regarding friendships between children who are nonhandicapped and those who have severe handicaps is confined to direct observations of interactions between these children in the school setting. Voeltz and Brennan (1984) administered a self-report measure (the Friendship Survey) to approximately 150 nonhandicapped children who were asked several questions regarding their experiences with a "best friend" (another nonhandicapped child, though a few children did name their severely handicapped peer), their "special friend" (the severely handicapped child with whom they interacted during the program), and a nurturant figure. If the nonhandicapped children viewed interactions with their special friends as primarily helping in nature, the authors hypothesized that they should respond to the questions in a direction which was a reverse of what they said regarding the person at home who took care of them. Instead, the children described their severely handicapped peers in terms which were more similar to the ways in which they described their "best" friend. To our knowledge, this is the only study which attempted to characterize how children viewed these interactions. The only other information available is an early report, also by the second author, that cites a selective sample of quotes from nonhandicapped children who participated in Special Friends (Voeltz, 1980b). Surely, this area of investigation merits our serious consideration and should receive more systematic attention in the future.

Normalizing the Social Status of Severely Handicapped Individuals

A logical extension of the above issues is what constitutes a friendship. When might heterogeneous social relationships fit into the various natural community environments which do not presently include severely handicapped individuals? Can nonhandicapped individuals include the participation of severely handicapped persons into the numerous events and activities which characterize the real world? Can this be done in a non-extraordinary manner? This is quite different from the once a year Special Olympics or the annual Christmas party sponsored by a local service organization for severely handicapped adults or children. For example, how are nonhandicapped individuals best prepared to perceive that a severely handicapped individual standing at a bus stop needs assistance with finding the correct route, and then to proceed with providing such assistance in a normal and natural way? Again, we are deluged with ideas as to how such normalized behaviors would look in practice, but there is no evidence on how we can achieve such outcomes.

Program Design and Strategies

To what extent can the program design be considered to be supportive of normalized peer interactions for the children involved in integration efforts? In addition, are there data regarding the kinds of outcomes associated with each of the various peer interaction programs, i.e., those which we might judge to be normalized as well as those which we might consider to be different from typical peer interaction patterns in important ways? There may, of course, be different outcomes associated with different program efforts, and we might place different values on these outcomes. One program might be associated with evidence of longitudinal friendships among a small group of students. Another might result in some more minor changes in behavior in *most* students in a school which, while not the same as a friendship, could result in very real and important consequences in various community environments. This might allow severely handicapped children to enjoy increased participation in those environments.

Our review of the existing program models to prepare children for integration revealed three general patterns (or a combination of these): attitude/information. peer tutoring programs, and peer interaction programs.

Attitude/Information

In this approach. the emphasis is upon providing the nonhandicapped child with information about the disabilities of handicapped individuals. Children might be exposed to definitions of particular diagnoses, and a typical outcome measure would be their ability to recall these facts on a knowledge test (e.g.. McHale & Simeonsson, 1980). Or, children might participate in a series of "handicap simulation" experiences (e.g.. walk across a room blindfolded), view movies in which verbal (generally mildly) handicapped children discuss their disabilities and how the community reacts to them, or participate in group discussions about disabilities (e.g., Gottlieb, 1980). Many of these programs appear to be preparatory to intended social contact at some future time; but since children typically continue to attend separate schools throughout the school years, they serve as substitutes for contact. Hence. attitude/information programs may be the only formative school experience affecting how these nonhandicapped individuals will react to handicapped persons throughout their lifespan. It is therefore usually not possible to investigate any behavioral changes as a function of such programs; there are no behaviors to occur. Outcome evaluations thus typically focus upon self-reported attitude measures and knowledge tests (e.g., Siperstein, Bak. & Gottlieb, 1977).

Peer Tutoring Programs

In this approach. the nonhandicapped student is trained to provide instruction to his or her handicapped peer. Although peer tutoring generally originated from the need or desire to provide a more intensive pupil-teacher ratio in classrooms serving handicapped children (e.g., Fenrick & McDonnell, 1980), this approach recently has been proposed as a strategy to prepare nonhandicapped youngsters to accept and positively interact with persons with disabilities (e.g., Kohl, Moses, & Stettner-Eaton, 1984). Outcome measures are most likely to be the extent to which the nonhandicapped student reliably replicated the instructional procedures which s/he had been taught, as well as whether or not the severely handicapped student learned the skills being tutored (Fenrick & McDonnell, 1980).

Peer Interaction Program

In these programs, the emphasis is upon arranging for more normalized. friendship-type peer interactions between nonhandicapped and severely handicapped children who are approximately the same age. The activities in which they would engage during these interactions would parallel those of children's social interaction; they would be restricted to leisure and social play situations and not be extended to include situations in which the nonhandicapped student was clearly helping the handicapped student. Voeltz (1984) maintained that if the intent is to socially integrate severely handicapped individuals into society and various community environments. any program to prepare children for this integration must be contact-oriented and not primarily information-oriented. Information about handi-capping conditions (rather than about the behavioral and communication repertoire of an individual child) may result in stereotypical attitudes and is unlikely to provide socially useful information about what the handi-capped friend is like. We also have suggested that such contact should reflect horizontal relationships and differ in important ways from the more generally available caregiver-child relationship experienced by handicapped children.

What is the information regarding relative outcomes of these program models? Will the vertical structure of a peer tutoring program, for example. eventually interfere with the evolution of more normalized and meaningful. longitudinal social relationships or will it provide an appropriate first experience for heterogeneous groupings of children? We shall return to this issue later.

Teacher Effects

Regardless of which of the three approaches to preparing children for integration occurs, the teacher's role in these efforts is likely to be significant. Since the children involved generally do not attend school in the same classroom, teachers must be willing to at least coordinate their schedules to permit social interactions to occur and to accommodate shared program activities. Teachers establish the ground rules for these interactions, which often begin in the special education room and then expand to the rest of the school environment. Teachers serve as models for attitudes and behavior. That is, teachers model, reinforce, and provide direct instruction in differ-ent interaction styles for children. They also delimit the kinds of activities and materials introduced into the interactions. All of these variables have been shown to have an impact upon the outcomes associated with heteroge-neous grouping arrangements (Johnson, Johnson, & Maruyama, 1983).

To date, there has not been a systematic investigation of the impact of the teacher role on integration and on the quality of interactions between nonhandicapped and severely handicapped children. The Russo and Koegel (1977) study, for example, involved the implementation of a behavior modification package by the regular education teacher which was functionally related to the successful integration of an autistic child into regular kindergarten and first grade classrooms; this study did not focus upon how the teacher might prepare the environment and the nonhandicapped children to include the handicapped youngster. Instead, the focus was upon increasing the instructional management skills of the teacher so that the handicapped child's behavioral gains would not be lost in the transfer from the special to the regular classroom environment. The one exception to this absence of information is the study of the effects of different task structures upon interactions within heterogeneous groups. In particular, Putnam (1983) focused specifically upon variations in the teacher's presentation and supervision of goal structures upon behaviors and attitudes. Since her study involved task structures as well as teacher behavior, her findings will be summarized in the next section.

Most recently, Meyer et al. (1984) investigated the effects of low vs. high levels of teacher intrusion upon the behavior of nonhandicapped and autistic children during dyadic play interactions. The children in this study had already interacted with one another under teacher supervision for nearly a semester. When the study began, the teachers displayed a high level of supervisory "intrusiveness" including verbal cues and praise, modeling and prompting of interaction and play behaviors, and continuous, close physical proximity. Contrasted experimental conditions of high vs. low teacher intrusion resulted in surprisingly few significant differences in behavior. Those differences which did occur favored, for the most part, the low intrusion condition which was associated with higher levels of appropriate and cooperative play. This apparently decreased need for teacher supervision of interactions between these nonhandicapped and severely handicapped elementary aged children followed an intensive and lengthy period of initial teacher instruction and intrusion. Thus a follow-up study by those authors is being conducted to investigate the results for varying initial instructional periods, and another investigation is examining possible differences in children's play behaviors as a function of the specific nature of the teacher instructions.

Task Structure and Activity Effects

Among the variables which might influence the nature of interactions in heterogeneous groups are group size, sex of group members, group structure, and the materials and activity involved. For example, would dyads or triads (with varying participants) be related to differences in interactions such that some arrangements are more favorable than others for social interaction? Will indoor and more passive toy play interactions differ from gross motor recreational activities? Finally, does the process structure of the task make a difference? To date, there are no data regarding these issues with the notable exception of the research on the effects of cooperative goal structures in comparison to individualistic and competitive goal structures (see Johnson, Johnson, & Maruyama, 1983, for a review of this literature).

Johnson and Johnson at the University of Minnesota have spent well over a decade developing an empirical data base to support their contention that the goal structures of school environments do not facilitate the acceptance of the heterogeneous nature of the school population. Until a few years ago, most of their work focused on demonstrating increased interpersonal attraction and social acceptance among students from different racial and cultural groups as a function of cooperative goals structures in school learning experiences. These goal structures were compared to individualistic and competitive goal structures. In the cooperative goal structure, the group learning goal is achieved only if all the members of the heterogeneous group work together, interdependently, to achieve their goal. In the individualistic situation, a student's goal attainment consists of matching and surpassing one's own past performance and is unrelated to what others in the classroom might accomplish. In the competitive learning situation, each student's goal achievements are related to how the other students perform; one student can do well only if others do less well and/or fail. Recently, the Johnsons and their colleagues have extended this work to investigate the effects of cooperative task structures on the social outcomes of heterogeneous groups which include handicapped youngsters. Studies with moderately retarded and severely physically handicapped participants have been done (Johnson, Johnson, DeWeerdt, Lyons, & Zaidman, 1983; Johnson, Rynders, Johnson, Schmidt, & Haider, 1979; Rynders, Johnson, Johnson, & Schmidt, 1980) as well as one study with moderately and severely retarded students (Putnam, 1983). The cooperative goal structure in these studies has involved group science projects and group recreation activities, and the work has been done at both elementary and high school levels.

In general, the evidence is that cooperative groups, in comparison to competitive and individualistic goal structures, result in significantly higher levels of certain positive verbal interaction behaviors between the handicapped and the nonhandicapped participants, and greater interpersonal attraction on sociometric outcome measures. Putnam (1983), whose sample included two severely handicapped students as well as a larger number of moderately handicapped students, extended this work to include an emphasis upon teacher instruction of the cooperative goal structures as a variable. She found that the teacher instructed condition (in which the teacher provided specific examples of cooperative behaviors) produced significantly higher percentages of certain categories of student behavior in comparison to the uninstructed condition (in which the teacher merely instructed the students on the task and evaluation procedures but did not model cooperation). The nonhandicapped students engaged in more cooperative participation with and directed more verbal comments to their handicapped peers, while the handicapped students participated more actively, attended more, and remained closer to their peers in the instructed condition. It would appear, then, that cooperative task structure is a promising program direction for integration efforts, and replications involving severely handicapped students should be the next step.

Contact Role Effects

An unresolved issue which may have a major impact upon integration outcomes is the nature of the contact role which is experienced by severely handicapped and nonhandicapped children who do interact with one another. Programmatic interventions designed to increase interactions between these two groups of children represent either a peer tutoring, a peer interaction program approach, or some combination of each. Each involves socially different role relationships. In the peer tutoring model, the nonhandicapped students are recruited to assist professional staff as tutors for their handicapped peers. These instructional pairings of children may or may not be matched for chronological age. A frequent pattern is to match nonhandicapped children who are older (e.g., high school age) with younger handicapped children. Preparing nonhandicapped children for these programs generally includes information intended to change attitudes and to systematically teach them a set of instructional procedures (e.g., prompting, reinforcing). Nonhandicapped children often will refer to themselves in these programs as volunteers, and the teachers will describe them as "working with" the handicapped students. The preparation of handicapped students for the interaction itself is not usually an issue, as the child is to be instructed in a typical skill sequence much as the teacher would do. However, one measure of the success of such a program would be whether or not the handicapped child continues to make educational progress. Another measure would be the extent to which the nonhandicapped child actually acquires and reliably displays the proper tutoring behavior regimen.

The traditional definition of a peer tutor involved instruction of one child by another who has thus been trained to act as teacher for some component of the *educational* program. Poorman's (1980) peer tutoring program included teaching principles of reinforcement and contingent extinction. Such programs also have included training nonhandicapped children to collect data monitoring the handicapped child's performance during the tutoring sessions (e.g., Kohl et al., 1984).

Gaylord-Ross and Pitts-Conway (1984) have proposed a continuum of possible social interactions between children which they consider to vary in the degree of structure. They viewed peer tutoring as a high structure, first step which guarantees success for the nonhandicapped child because it clearly delineates expected behaviors and the teacher provides direct assistance. They maintained that lower structure interactions could follow and be facilitated by an initial peer tutoring program; these lower structure interactions include leisure and transient exchanges (both intermediate structure) and friendships with no staff input (low structure).

Perhaps the distinction which should be made is between a high structure horizontal interaction and a high structure vertical interaction. In both cases, the children would receive specific and careful training for their interactions. The difference would lie in the nature of the activities in which they engage. Hence, several programs which have been referred to as peer tutoring might best be thought of as high structure horizontal interactions. In the peer tutoring program, the emphasis is upon one child teaching another child self-help, toileting, or academic skills (e.g., Poorman, 1980), and the interaction is clearly a replication of teacher-child instructional events (i.e., vertical interaction), which one would not expect to find in normalized peer interactions. The term *buddy system*, on the other hand, seems to accurately characterize high structure horizontal interactions where the nonhandicapped child is trained to assist a handicapped peer. This assistance is to facilitate the participation of the handicapped child in the various leisure and transient social exchanges which occur in natural environments and which do reflect the usual kinds of interactions seen among peers. Buddies may be trained to accompany the handicapped student at lunch, recess, extracurricular events, and to and from the school bus. These are activities in which all children normally engage and activities with which a severely handicapped child could benefit from models and help provided by peers rather than by paid and professional staff. Similarly, the cooperative goal structure research describes a high structure horizontal context for handicapped and nonhandicapped students to engage in normalized leisure time activities (Rynders et al., 1980). By providing the peer dyad with structure and supervision, the nonhandicapped child has access to the appropriate helper and model for normalized social exchanges in various school and community environments. The Special Friends program developed in Hawaii is another example of a high structure horizontal interaction program which focuses upon heterogeneous friendship patterns (Voeltz,

Hemphill et al. 1983). The Donder and Nietupski (1981) program, where nonhandicapped students taught playground activities to their severely handicapped peers, added a novel component; nonhandicapped children were asked to make suggestions for age appropriate games they would teach their handicapped peers.

In most peer interaction programs, the emphasis is upon friendship and social/leisure activity interactions. This model is based upon the assumption that handicapped and nonhandicapped children can develop meaningful social relationships (e.g., friendships) which will endure over time and extend outside of and beyond the school careers of these children. It is essential to this model that children be matched in ways which parallel other friendship patterns, e.g., similar ages, perhaps same sex (depending upon the children's age vis-a-vis "normalized" same vs. cross-sex friendships), physical accessibility to one another, shared interests and enjoyment of similar activities, and, of course, whether or not the children like one another. Programs of this nature generally involve less emphasis on information about handicapping conditions and view attitude changes as outcomes of the social contact between the children. The focus of information is on personal knowledge regarding the individual handicapped peer and how to interact with one another. Hence, the model assumes that both the nonhandicapped and the handicapped child must acquire social, play, and communication skills essential to that interaction. The nonhandicapped child generally would not be taught tutoring or management skills, though s/he may be taught the forms of the behavioral responses to be used by a handicapped peer, such as sign language. These programs can vary from high structure (Voeltz, Hemphill et al., 1983) to low structure (Gaylord-Ross & Pitts-Conway, 1984).

Theoretically, the special friends and the cooperative group instructional structures are the normalized patterns of interactions which occur in the mainstream between children. The buddy system variation as discussed earlier is also quite common to many environments and activities. However, such buddy systems would not typically be a substitute for more normalized social and friendship interactions, but would be a complement designed to facilitate task performance. Furthermore, patterns of who-helps-whom will vary as a function of the activity or the environment. The peer tutoring program in which the nonhandicapped child is always the helper and the handicapped child is receiving instruction from someone other than a teacher or parent is clearly not a parallel to normalized social peer relationships even though peer tutoring does occur in regular education settings for various reasons. The peer tutoring approach may serve other functions and produce other outcomes; as discussed earlier, the approach may provide a realistic context for initial interactions between children whose abilities and skill levels are quite discrepant. Such programs, however, do not appear to be a substitute for friendships in the long term.

Summary Discussion on Outcome Data

We have little, if any, data on the relative outcomes of various approaches to peer interactions. Simpson (1983) reported that information plus systematic social interaction contact between handicapped and nonhandicapped children resulted in significantly greater acceptance and more positive interaction behaviors than information alone. Voeltz's (1980a; 1982) work supported the superiority of systematic social (special friends) contact over physical proximity alone, which was nevertheless also superior to no exposure at all on a measure of children's attitudes toward their handicapped peers. Only Gaylord-Ross and Peck (1985) have reported the preliminary results of a direct comparison between a special friend vs. a peer tutoring program. Their data favored the special friends program after the first year of data collection. This condition was associated with higher levels of generalized social interactions with handicapped peers outside the program context by the nonhandicapped teenagers in their study.

Clearly, given the ready willingness of professionals to argue emphatically in support of one or more of these models, data are needed to refine such programs as well as to justify further efforts with one approach rather than another. It may well be, of course, that different outcomes are associated with different approaches, and each may be valued for different reasons. The available research does suggest that both the attitudinal and behavioral outcomes of interactions are positive. There is much work to be done to qualify what this means with respect to our ultimate goal of longitudinal and normalized interactions between nonhandicapped persons and persons with severe handicaps.*

REFERENCES

Asher, S. R., & Taylor, A. R. The social outcomes of mainstreaming: Sociometric assessment and beyond. *Exceptional Education Quarterly*, 1981, *1*, 13–30.

Brinker, R. P. *The rate and quality of social behavior of severely handicapped students in integrated*

*An earlier version of portions of this chapter appeared in Voeltz, L. M., Johnson, R. E., and McQuarter, R. J. (1983). *The integration of school-aged children and youth with severe disabilities: A comprehensive bibliography and a selective review of research and program development needs to address discrepancies in state-of-the-art.* Minneapolis: University of Minnesota Consortium Institute.

Preparation of this chapter was supported in part by Contract No. 300-82-0363 awarded to the University of Minnesota from the Division of Innovation and Development, Special Education Programs, U.S. Department of Education. The opinions expressed herein do not necessarily reflect the position or policy of the U.S. Department of Education, and no official endorsement should be inferred.

and non-integrated settings. Princeton: Educational Testing Service, 1982.

Brown, F., & Holvoet, J. Effect of systematic peer interaction on the incidental learning of two severely handicapped students. *Journal of the Association for the Severely Handicapped,* 1982, 7, 19–28.

Brown, L., Branston, M. D., Baumgart, D., Vincent, L., Falvey, M., & Schroder, J. Using the characteristics of current and subsequent least restrictive environments in the development of curricular context for severely handicapped students. *AAESPH Review,* 1979, 4, 407–424.

Brown, L., Nietupski, J., & Hamre-Nieuptski, S. The criterion of ultimate functioning and public school services for the severely handicapped student. In M. A. Thomas (Ed.), *Hey, don't forget about me.* Reston, VA: Council for Exceptional Children, 1976.

Brown, L., Nisbet, J., Ford, A., Sweet, M., Shiraga, B., York, J., & Loomis, R. The critical need for nonschool instruction in educational programs for severely handicapped students. *Journal of the Association for the Severely Handicapped,* 1983, 8, 71–77.

Bruininks, R., & Lakin, K. C. (Eds.). *Living and learning in the least restrictive environment.* Baltimore: Paul H. Brookes, in press.

Burton, T. A., & Hirshoren, A. Some further thoughts and clarifications on the education of severely and profoundly retarded children. *Exceptional Children,* 1979, 45, 618–625.

Cronbach, L. J., Ambron, S. R., Dornbusch, S. M., Hess, R. D., Hornik, R. C., Phillips, D. C., Walker, D. F., & Weiner, S. S. *Toward reform of program evaluation: Aims, methods, and institutional arrangements.* San Francisco: Jossey-Bass, 1980.

Donaldson, J. Changing attitudes toward handicapping persons: A review and analysis of research. *Exceptional Children,* 1980, 46, 504–514.

Donder, D., & Nietupski, J. Nonhandicapped adolescents teaching playground skills to their mentally retarded peers: Toward a less restrictive middle school environment. *Education and Training of the Mentally Retarded,* 1981, 16, 270–276.

Falvey, M., Brown, L., Lyon, S., Baumgart, D., & Schroder, J. Strategies for using cues and correction procedures. In W. Sailor, B. Wilcox, & L. Brown (Eds.), *Methods of instruction for severely handicapped students.* Baltimore: Paul H. Brookes, 1980.

Fenrick, N., & McDonnell, J. Junior high school students as teachers of the severely retarded: Training and generalization. *Education and Training of the Mentally Retarded,* 1980, 15, 187–194.

Ford, A., Brown, L., Pumpian, I., Baumgart, D., Nisbet, J., Schroder, J., & Loomis, R. Strategies for developing individualized recreation and leisure programs for severely handicapped students. In N. Certo, N. Haring, & R. York (Eds.), *Public school integration of severely handicapped students: Rational issues and progressive alternatives.* Baltimore: Paul H. Brookes, 1984.

Freagon, S., Wheeler, J., Brankin, G., McDannel, K., Stern, L., Usilton, R., & Keiser, N. Increasing severely handicapped students' personal competence in the community. In S. Freagon, J. Wheeler, G. Brankin, K. McDannel, D. Costello, & W. M. Peters (Eds.), *Curricular processes for the school and community integration of severely handicapped students ages 6–21.* DeKalb, IL: Northern Illinois University and DeKalb County Special Education Association, 1983.

Gable, R. A., Hendrickson, J. M., & Strain, P. S. Assessment, modification, and generalization of social interaction among severely retarded, multihandicapped children. *Education and Training of the Mentally Retarded,* 1978, 13, 279–286.

Gaylord-Ross, R. J., & Peck, C. A. Integration efforts for students with severe mental handicaps. In D. Bricker, & J. Filler (Eds.), *Serving the severely retarded: From research to practice.* Reston, VA: Council for Exceptional Children, 1985.

Gaylord-Ross, R. J., & Pitts-Conway, V. Social behavior development in integrated secondary autistic programs. In N. Certo, N. Haring, & R. York (Eds.), *Public school integration of severely handicapped students: Rational issues and progressive alternatives.* Baltimore: Paul H. Brookes, 1984.

Gottlieb, J. Observing social adaptation in schools. In G. P. Sackett (Ed.), *Observing behavior. Vol. I: Theory and applications in mental retardation.* Baltimore: University Park Press, 1978.

Gottlieb, J. Improving attitudes toward retarded children by using group discussion. *Exceptional Children*, 1980, *47*, 106–111.

Gottlieb, J. Mainstreaming: Fulfilling the promise? *American Journal of Mental Deficiency*, 1981, *86*, 115–126.

Guess, P., & Helmstetter, E. Skill cluster instruction and the individualized curriculum sequencing model. In R. H. Horner, L. Meyer, & H. D. Fredericks (Eds.), *Education of learners with severe handicaps: Exemplary service strategies.* Baltimore: Paul H. Brookes, in press.

Johnson, R., Johnson, D. W., DeWeerdt, N., Lyons, V., & Zaidman, B. Integrating severely adaptively handicapped seventh-grade students into constructive relationships with nonhandicapped peers in science class. *American Journal of Mental Deficiency*, 1983, *87*, 611–619.

Johnson, D. W., Johnson, R. T., & Maruyama, G. Interdependence and interpersonal attraction among heterogeneous and homogeneous individuals: A theoretical formulation and a meta-analysis of the research. *Review of Educational Research*, 1983, *53*, 5–54.

Johnson, R., Rynders, J., Johnson, D. W., Schmidt, B., & Haider, S. Interaction between handicapped and nonhandicapped teenagers as a function of situational goal structuring: Implications for mainstreaming. *American Educational Research Journal*, 1979, *16*, 161–167.

Kohl, F. L., Moses, L. G., & Stettner-Eaton, B. A. A systematic training program for teaching nonhandicapped students to be instructional trainers of severely handicapped schoolmates. In N. Certo, N. Haring, & R. York (Eds.), *Public school integration of severely handicapped students: Rational issues and progressive alternatives.* Baltimore: Paul H. Brookes, 1984.

McHale, S., & Simeonsson, R. J. Effects of interaction on nonhandicapped children's attitudes about autistic children. *American Journal of Mental Deficiency*, 1980, *85*, 18–24.

Meyer, L. H., Fox, A., Schermer, A., Ketelsen, D., Montan, N., Maley, K., & Cole, D. The effects of teacher intrusion on social play interactions between autistic and nonhandicapped peers. Submitted for publication, 1984.

Meyer, L. H., & Kishi, G. S. School integration strategies. In R. J. Brunininks & K. D. Lakin (Eds.), *Strategies for achieving community integration of developmentally disabled children.* Baltimore: Paul H. Brookes, 1984.

Meyer, L. H., McQuarter, R. J., & Kishi, G. S. Assessing and teaching social interaction skills. In W. Stainback & S. Stainback (Eds.), *Integration of severely handicapped students with their nonhandicapped peers: A handbook for teachers.* Reston, VA: Council for Exceptional Children, in press.

Neel, R. S., Billingsley, F. F., McCarty, F., Symonds, D., Lambert, C., Lewis-Smith, N., & Hanashiro, R. *Teaching autistic children: A functional curriculum approach.* Seattle: University of Washington, College of Education, 1983.

Noonan, M. J., Hemphill, N. J., & Levy, G. K. L. *Social skills curricular strategy for students with severe disabilities.* Honolulu: University of Hawaii, Department of Special Education, 1983.

Poorman, C. Mainstreaming in reverse with a special friend. *Teaching Exceptional Children*, 1980, *12*, 136–144.

Putnam, J. W. *Social integration of moderately handicapped students through cooperative structuring:*

Influence of teacher instruction on cooperation. Unpublished doctoral dissertation, University of Minnesota, 1983.

Russo, D. C., & Koegel, R. L. A method for integrating an autistic child into a normal public school classroom. *Journal of Applied Behavior Analysis,* 1977, *10,* 579–590.

Rynders, J. E., Johnson, R. T., Johnson, D. W., & Schmidt, B. Producing positive interaction among Down Syndrome and nonhandicapped teenagers through cooperative goal structuring. *American Journal of Mental Deficiency,* 1980, *85,* 268–283.

Simpson, R. J. *Severely handicapped learning project: Joint dissemination review panel report.* Lawrence, KS: University of Kansas Department of Special Education, 1983.

Siperstein, G., Bak, J., & Gottlieb, J. Effects of group discussion on children's attitudes toward handicapped peers. *Journal of Educational Research,* 1977, *70,* 131–134.

Stokes, T. F., Baer, D. M., & Jackson, R. L. Programming the generalization of a greeting response in four retarded children. *Journal of Applied Behavior Analysis,* 1974, *7,* 599–610.

Voeltz, L. M. Children's attitudes toward handicapped peers. *American Journal of Mental Deficiency,* 1980, *84,* 455–464. (a)

Voeltz, L. M. Special friends in Hawaii. *Education Unlimited,* 1980, *2,* 10–11. (b)

Voeltz, L. M. Effects of structured interactions with severely handicapped peers on children's attitudes. *American Journal of Mental Deficiency,* 1982, *86,* 380–390.

Voeltz, L. M. Programs and curriculum innovations to prepare children for integration. In N. Certo, N. Haring, & R. York (Eds.), *Public school integration for severely handicapped students: Rational issues and progressive alternatives.* Baltimore: Paul H. Brookes, 1984.

Voeltz, L. M., & Brennan, J. Analysis of interactions between nonhandicapped and severely handicapped peers using multiple measures. In J. M. Berg (Ed.), *Perspectives and progress in mental retardation, Vol. I: Social, psychological, and educational aspects.* Baltimore: University Park Press, 1984.

Voeltz, L. M., Hemphill, N. J., Brown, S., Kishi, G., Klein, R., Fruehling, R., Collie, J., Levy, G., & Kube, C. *The special friends program: A trainer's manual for integrated school settings* (rev. ed.). Honolulu: University of Hawaii, Department of Special Education, 1983.

Voeltz, L. M., Johnson, R. E., & McQuarter, R. J. *The integration of school aged children and youth with severe disabilities: A comprehensive bibliography and a selective review of research and program development needs to address discrepancies in the state-of-the-art.* Minneapolis, MN: Minnesota Consortium Institute, University of Minnesota, 1983.

Wilcox, B., & Bellamy, G. T. *Design of high school programs for severely handicapped students.* Baltimore: Paul H. Brookes, 1982.

Wilcox, B., & Sailor, W. Service delivery issues: Integrated educational systems. In B. Wilcox & R. York (Eds.), *Quality education for the severely handicapped: The federal investment.* Washington, DC: U.S. Department of Education, 1980.

Young, C., & Kerr, M. The effects of a retarded child's social initiations on the behavior of severely retarded school-age peers. *Education and Training of the Mentally Retarded,* 1979, *14,* 185–190.

Ziegler, S., & Hambleton, D. Integration of young TMR children in a regular elementary school. *Exceptional Children,* 1976, *42,* 459–461.

CHAPTER 6

VOCATIONAL TRAINING OF MODERATELY AND SEVERELY HANDICAPPED PERSONS: SUCCESS, FAILURE, AND THE FUTURE

PHIL GUNTER AND SID LEVY

For many years, it was thought that most moderately and severely handicapped individuals did not have the capability to participate in society. They were perceived as a burden on society without the ability to care for their own needs. During the past two decades, the accuracy of these perceptions have been questioned. As a result of the development of training technology, many moderately and severely handicapped people have been taught skills that allow them to care for themselves, to work, and to be contributing members of their community. Yet, even with the verification of their ability to learn those skills, presently, the vast majority of severely handicapped people are not integrated members of society and the work force. It is proposed that their exclusion is the result of societal restrictions and not their inability to contribute in meaningful ways. Further, it is suggested that the negative attitudes held by both the public and professionals contribute to their exclusion. Finally, the present governmental regulations and employment structure inhibit integration into society's work force. Unless the bureaucratic restraints are removed and societal attitudes changed, severely handicapped individuals will remain as noncontributing members of society. The following chapter reviews the research literature which has contributed to this conceptualization of moderately and severely handicapped people and attempts to predict the direction for the future of this population in the nation's work force.

Phil Gunter is currently the Coordinator of Exceptional Student Services, Lee County Schools, Fort Myers, Florida. He received his Ph.D. from George Peabody College of Vanderbilt University. He has been a classroom instructor of behavior disordered and severely and moderately handicapped children and adolescents, coordinator of a vocational training grant for mildly and moderately handicapped students, and a school administrator. His current research involves control of stereotypic behaviors of persons with severe handicaps and methodological issues of social validation research.

Sidney M. Levy received his Ph.D. from the University of Illinois. He is currently an Assistant Professor of Special Education at George Peabody College of Vanderbilt University. Dr. Levy has made substantial contributions to the vocational training technology used with severely handicapped persons. He continues to be involved with observational studies of handicapped and nonhandicapped workers.

Training Progress

Advances in training and behavioral technology have allowed many severely and moderately handicapped people to demonstrate their competence on numerous skills (Bellamy, Peterson, & Close, 1975; Levy, Pomerantz, & Gold, 1977). Some of the strategies include: task analysis, systematic training, and behavior modification. Each of these procedures has been demonstrated to be highly effective in training situations (Levy, 1983).

With this technology, the initial goals of instruction for moderately and severely retarded people were attempts to teach self-help and survival skills. It was believed that possessing these skills would allow handicapped people to achieve some degree of independence. The skills taught included: toothbrushing (Lattal, 1969), toileting (Foxx & Azrin, 1973), grooming skills (Lewis, Ferneti, & Keilitz, 1975), travel skills (Neef, Iwata, & Page, 1978), telephone dialing (Leff, 1974, 1975), coin equivalence (Trace, Cuvo, & Criswell, 1977), shopping skills (Matson, 1981), basic eating skills (Stainback, Healy, Stainback, & Healy, 1976), restaurant eating skills (van den Pol, Iwata, Ivancic, Page, Neef, & Whitley, 1981), and dressing skills (Nutter & Reid, 1978).

As a result of achieving success in teaching survival skills to this population, the focus was then directed to teaching job skills. Gold (1972) successfully taught moderately and severely retarded people to assemble bicycle brakes through the use of task analysis and systematic training procedures. From this beginning, research on teaching other difficult industrial tasks were conducted including cam switch assembly (Bellamy et al., 1975) and electric circuit boards (Levy et al., 1977). These were intended to be job skills that could be performed either in a work activity center, sheltered workshop, or community job placement. Cuvo, Leaf, and Borakove (1978) broadened this community work view by training handicapped people to work in the service area. In their study, six moderately retarded adolescents were taught restroom cleaning skills. The students were found to generalize the skills to other restroom settings with little training.

Once it was demonstrated that severely handicapped people could acquire job task skills, the relevant issue became whether they could produce at acceptable industrial rates and quality. Bellamy (1976) discussed the importance of production: "The practical utility of these skills (vocational skills) will depend to a large extent upon the rates at which they are ultimately performed . . . " (p. 54). Production rate (Bellamy, 1976) is the basis for supervisors' "global performance ratings" (p. 54) of employees in industrial settings. Brown and Pearce (1970) demonstrated that by using nonhandicapped peer models the production rate of handicapped people on an envelope stuffing task could be increased. Sharpton (1981) used competition to increase production rates in a sheltered employment setting. Martin, Pallotta-Cornick, Johnstone, and Goyos (1980) increased productivity rates in a sheltered setting by using a multiple component strategy of reduction of distractions, initial instructions, picture prompts, reinforcement through pay, and social approval for on-task behavior. Brown, Van Deventer, Perlmutter, Jones, and Sontag (1972) used only monetary payments to increase production, while Cotter (1971) used contingent music for the same purpose. Research has clearly demonstrated that under the appropriate conditions, handicapped workers could improve their productivity.

The next logical step was to place severely handicapped persons into community job settings. In order to successfully accomplish competitive work integration, appropriate behaviors, other than direct work task behaviors, needed to be developed. Appropriate use of social skills with coworkers and supervisors became increasingly important. The teaching of these skills is presently at the forefront, and the many successes include teaching severely handicapped people to increase smiling at others (Hopkins, 1968), to ask questions of adults and peers (Twardosz & Baer, 1973), conversing with friends, table manners, and social etiquette skills (Perry & Cerreto, 1977), reduction of stereotypic behaviors in a socially acceptable manner (Gunter, Brady, Shores, Fox, Owen, & Goldzweig, 1984), generalization of social initiation bids (Fox, Gunter, Brady, Bambara, Spiegel-McGill, & Shores, 1984), and to interact appropriately with members of the opposite sex (Hamre-Nietupski & Williams, 1977). For severely and moderately handicapped persons to be integrated into communities as "well rounded" individuals, development of skills in use of leisure time were targeted. Schleien, Ash, Kiernan, and Wehman (1981) taught cooking skills to a profoundly retarded woman. Restaurant skills, including ordering and paying (van den Pol, Iwata, Ivancic, Page, Neff, & Whitley, 1981); running and jogging (Gunter, 1981); an age-appropriate dart game (Schleien, Wehman, & Kiernan, 1981); a pinball machine game with appropriate social behavior while using this activity (Hill, Wehman, & Horst, 1982); physical fitness skills and table games (Wehman, Renzaglia, Berry, Schutz, & Karan, 1978); and swimming (Sherrill, 1981) are additional leisure activities which have been taught. With the knowledge that many moderately and severely handicapped persons can be trained to perform the skills necessary for community employment and living, the focus of attention will now shift to the employment sites of the handicapped.

Workshops and Community Employment

There are two primary types of work options available to handicapped people. One option is sheltered work facilities and the other is competitive community employment. As Levy (1983) recognized, the sheltered facilities were primarily for the moderately, severely, or profoundly handicapped; community job placement strategies were traditionally strategies geared toward the mildly handicapped. As a result of the demonstration of their ability to acquire work skills and the passage of legislation mandating equal opportunity for all handicapped people (1973 Vocational Rehabilitation Act and P. L. 94-142), there seems to be a current trend to involve lower functioning populations in community job settings (Flexer & Martin, 1978).

Sheltered work programs are of basically two types: the sheltered workshop and the work activity center (Levy, 1983). Sheltered workshops typically serve a higher functioning handicapped population than do work activity centers even though the two may be housed in the same facility. Although both populations are of concern, due to limited literature on work activity centers, this chapter will focus on sheltered workshops.

It is the goal of the sheltered workshop to aid handicapped individuals to achieve and maintain their maximum work potential. "The traditional workshop attempts to place the handicapped into competitive employment after a period of evaluation, work adjustment, and/or vocational training" (Flexer & Martin, 1978, p. 416). This is in contrast to the extended employment workshops which Flexer and Martin (1978) describe as providing "remunerative or profitable work to the more severely handicapped person who is considered unable to compete in the open labor market" (p. 416).

Gold (1973) maintained that whether the workshop is of the traditional or the extended employment type, work should be utilized "as the primary medium for client development" (p. 5); but he also asserted that in most cases the type of work found in workshops does not achieve this goal. Most of the work currently found in sheltered workshops is highly repetitious and simplistic. Such types of tasks provide little opportunity for training of useable work skills. In addition, insufficient quantities of work do not allow for sustained production, resulting in considerable worker down time. Worker inactivity often leads to inappropriate behavior (Levy & Glascoe, 1983). A final criticism of sheltered workshops is the fact that they are usually not run as effective businesses; "workshops do not have the business acumen and industrial know how to bid and produce competitively" (Flexer & Martin, 1978, p. 418).

Several suggestions have been made as to how workshops might improve in the accomplishment of their goals. First, Pomerantz and Marholin (1977) suggested that workshops should specialize in the production of one type of item. This would allow for specialization in contracts received and greater efficiency in production. A second suggestion might be for several workshops to form a cooperative in order to facilitate contract procurement (Flexer & Martin, 1978). However, the availability of work alone will not resolve the problems of the workshop situation.

Another source of problems are organizational and bureaucratic constraints. A contributor to these constraints are governmental regulations and guidelines for services delivered to handicapped persons. Pomerantz and Marholin (1977) suggested four factors which prevent sheltered workshops from achieving their maximum potential. These are: (a) inadequate accountability, (b) funding for quantity rather than quality, (c) consequences of community client placement, and (d) consequences of increased earnings of clients. Inadequate accountability refers to the fact that essentially all workshops are entitled to the same funding through the Fair Labor Standards Act and the Developmental Disabilities Act; therefore, little difference is established between funding of superior programs and programs of poorer quality (Pomerantz & Marholin, 1977). Grossman and Rowitz (1973) elaborated on the fact that funds are allocated by these agencies based on the number of clients served in the workshop rather than "qualitative changes in the clients."

A major stated objective of sheltered workshops is the placement of clients in community employment settings, yet far too often this has not happened. A reason for this not being accomplished is that the clients ready for community employment tend to function at higher rates of productivity, and community placement would decrease the workshop's ability to quickly complete contracts (Pomerantz & Marholin, 1977). Thus the emphasis is on producing work in order to secure more contracts, in contrast to training individuals which is a stated goal of many workshops. Also contributing to this problem is the previously mentioned fact that workshops are funded according to the number of clients served rather than the client's improvement.

Another reason for the limited success of job placement of the severely handicapped is the fact that many workshops are extremely understaffed and have little time for investigation of potential community placements. This factor is exaggerated in depressed economic periods which results in high rates of unemployment. Finally, the environmental limits of the sheltered workshop are not conducive to generalization into industrial or community based employment settings. This is especially true of production rates and wages.

It is suggested that instead of encouraging high productivity rates, workshops in fact reinforce low productivity. Increased earnings of clients through higher productivity has been a problem in that support from several service agencies is contingent on low productivity (if the client's earnings exceed a certain point, funding from these agencies is stopped for that individual). Included in these agencies are Social Security, medical assistance, welfare insurance, and mental health monies (Pomerantz & Marholin, 1977). Reinforcement of low productivity is also a factor brought about by insufficient work; this phenomenon was discussed earlier in this chapter. The design of the workshop itself is usually not conducive to high productivity, and often there are few role models to encourage increased productivity in the workshop. Workers often observe less capable peers receiving the same compensation for less work. This cause for failure to encourage maximum work potential will be discussed at a later point in this chapter.

Levy (1980) pointed out that staff trained in industrial methodology are also missing from this setting, and this factor "contributes to the situation" (p. 135). Gold (1973) explained that industry has for some time been studying and developing information in the areas of productivity, job design, methods of time measurement, and training. His suggestion was for the adaptation of this information to improve the operation and management of sheltered workshops.

Competitive Community Jobs

The second work option for the handicapped, community job sites, has produced two models which have experienced some initial success: the enclave and the trainer advocate models. Both models were developed for moderate and severely handicapped populations.

Greenleigh Associates, Inc. (1975) has reported success with the enclave model for community based employment of handicapped individuals. The enclave concept involves a station or department of handicapped individuals working in a community work site under the supervision of trainers and supervisors. The advantages of this model are resources for high production and quality based accountability (Pomerantz & Marholin, 1977) as well as opportunities to interact with nonhandicapped peers. Production rate is not based on the contracts or subcontracts a workshop can procure. If the client cannot perform at the expected job rate, his/her salary is adjusted accordingly. Therefore, production rate has a meaningful and natural contingency.

The trainer-advocate (T-A) model (Levy, 1983) incorporates a systematic and gradual entry of the handicapped individual into the community job setting. This is done by identifying and analyzing jobs in the community; training handicapped individuals for the jobs; supervising the clients one-to-one on the job, and gradually fading the supervisor's involvement. This model has been very successful in achieving placement of the handicapped individual in community employment.

Even though supporters of each of these models have reported a great deal of success, the severity of the population served by these models should be closely scrutinized due to the wide range of abilities found in those clients labeled severely retarded. For example, a severely handicapped person with good motor ability, physical stamina, and a pleasant disposition might stand a better chance of success in community based employment than an individual with similar mental ability but less motor ability, strength, and an unpleasant personality. The point being made here is that IQ alone should not be the critical factor in the prediction of success or failure of handicapped persons. Rather, identification of critical skill factors required by employers would be a better indicator of success. This information could provide replication of the models with a greater probability of success. A second concern is the risk involved in elevating clients' salaries above the point at which supplementary services that are being received can be abruptly ended. This point will be discussed in more detail. These seem to be some of the concerns regarding community work for the severely retarded. Finally, community employment is subject to fluctuating economic conditions; and in depressed periods, the handicapped are usually among the first to become unemployed.

Wage and Employment Factors Limiting Successful Integration

Projections in 1972 were that only 21% of handicapped students leaving school would be fully employed (Martin, 1972), another 40% would be underemployed, and 26% would be unemployed. Recent reports have not disputed those figures (D'Alonzo, 1978). Prior to the enactment of the 1973 Vocational Rehabilitation Act, vocational training for the most severely handicapped people occurred in sheltered workshops or work activity centers only (Pomerantz & Marholin, 1977), and wages earned by handicapped workers in activity centers and sheltered workshops have been insufficient for their support. In 1975, an average hourly wage paid at work activity centers was $.33; sheltered workshop clients earned an average of $.75 per hour (Greenleigh Associates, Inc., 1975). It is clear that such low income does not allow handicapped people the opportunity to be self-supportive and to gain independence.

An Attempt at Correction

The probable reasons for handicapped peoples' low productivity and subsequent low income were discussed previously. Through organizational systems change, much of the problem could be lessened. Governmental support is essential for remedying the situation. One positive change that has occurred is the 1980 Social Security Disability Amendments (P.L. 96-265) which provides changes in Social Security and SSI Disability Protection. This change allows more flexibility and incentive for the disabled person to enter and/or re-enter the job world. These changes were included in the *1980 Disability Amendments, A Training Aid for Vocational Rehabilitation Counselors,* and are as follows:

1. Providing automatic re-entitlement of Social Security disability insurance benefits and SSI disability payments if an attempt to go to or return to work fails any time within the 15 months following the initial trial work period.
2. Continuing medical protection for up to three years after cash benefits stop.
3. Treating sheltered workshop income as earned income.
4. No longer deeming parental income and resources to SSI students.
5. Allowing impairment related work expenses to be deducted from an individual's earnings in order to determine earned income for monthly payments.
6. Eliminating the need for the 24-month medicare period to be "consecutive" months.
7. Extending continuance in vocational rehabilitation programs if it increases the likelihood of permanent work. (p. 5)

However, it appears that advantage is not being taken of these benefits. A possible explanation might be the bureaucratic red tape involved in processing the paperwork. Another explanation could be a lack of awareness of the law on the part of the workshop administrators. These changes, if utilized, should facilitate the movement of severely handicapped people into competitive employment which would improve the likelihood of their success in society.

Also remaining unanswered are the questions of why the retarded are still failing in attempts at successful community job integration. Nihira and Nihira (1975) determined that safety risks were the chief factors inhibiting community placement of handicapped individuals. D'Alonzo (1977) reported that lack of physical stamina, limited self-help, and lack of appropriate social emotional maturity were the major reasons why retarded people fail to keep jobs. Bellamy, Horner, and Inman (1979) also commented on "work behavior" of the severely retarded. Work behaviors are those behaviors which are associated with work but not specifically required for task completion. Bellamy et al. (1979) stressed that inappropriate work behavior is the leading cause of failure to succeed at employment by this population.

The earlier review of training literature in this chapter has revealed the success experienced in teaching work skills. A question posed is: Where is the breakdown? If we can teach these skills, why is not possessing the skills suggested as the leading cause for job failure for many moderately and severely handicapped persons?

A Cause of Failure

Gold (1973) reported an extreme concern about the failure of those providing services directly to the severely retarded to acquire recent knowledge from the literature. Experimentally, we have trained many vocationally related skills to the handicapped; but all too often these experimental results remain on shelves, unread, and unusued. "The need is to facilitate meaningful, perpetual, and direct communication between researchers and practitioners" (Gold, 1973, p. 21).

Gold (1973) suggested that most educational research is written for scientific publications and is not easily understood by practitioners. He proposed that attempts be made to disseminate this research to the practitioner in applicable form. Prehm (1976) reiterated this point: "A major impediment to the application and extension of educational research with the handicapped is lack of efficient, speedy, comprehensive systems for the dissemination of its results" (p. 18). Hopefully, if the information is available, it will be utilized. However, Gunter and Brady (1984) point out that this is not guaranteed.

If the services are to be improved and the opportunities increased for the moderately and severely handicapped, then changes must occur. Not only must we concern ourselves with effective communication among service agencies, practitioners, and researchers, but there needs to be a new view taken of job markets and labor managements systems. This view is shared by both Levy (1983) and Gold (1973) who suggested that learning from the fields of industrial management and engineering could open new avenues for viewing and providing success for future vocational programs for the handicapped. But more effective strategies must be developed to deliver this information, as well as previous information, to the practitioner quickly and in a more digestable manner (Gunter & Brady, 1984). These, then, seem the appropriate areas in which to direct our energies for the immediate future.

Conclusion

In spite of clear and convincing evidence that these individuals have demonstrated their self-worth, their ability to work, and their desire and ability to become self-sufficient, the vast majority still remain unemployed or underemployed (DuRand & DuRand, 1978). Is it too late to refocus our thinking about the possibilities of employment for a large number of the severely handicapped? In the opinion of the authors, the answer is "no."

Considering the huge investment that has been made in educating handicapped people in recent years, one might expect greater changes in vocational skill levels and greater opportunities to apply those skills. The reality of the situation is that handicapped workers are performing the same tasks they were 50 years ago and earning approximately the same level of income. To remedy the situation, it is suggested that a complete re-evaluation of vocational services be conducted and realistic changes in the system be made. A careful analysis of the predicted changes in industrial technology and the consequential changes in labor needs must be made in order to effectively redirect programming for handicapped individuals. It is fruitless to continue funding programs that are preparing people for jobs that are no longer available. Both the professional and lay populations' literature abounds with discussions about industrial technology and future manpower changes (Alexander, 1983; Halberstam, 1983; Office of Technology Assessment, 1982); yet, if the rest of the world is concerned with the eminent changes, rehabilitation and habilitation personnel do not appear to be. The interpretation of this might be either a lack of awareness or possibly a lack of interest. Regardless of the suggested reason or reasons, if effectiveness is to be achieved, then change must start immediately.

The first step is analysis of job forecasting information to determine what positions will be avaialble in the future. Once the types of jobs are determined, the task becomes how to best prepare the handicapped to be competitive. If we are not able to prepare them for competitive jobs, then acceptable alternatives must be found.

If it appears that most unskilled or semi-skilled jobs will be in the service areas (e.g., fast food restaurants or janitorial work), then training should be structured toward providing those skills. If it can be determined that the use of robots will replace most of the unskilled labor force as we traditionally know it, then what will happen to those workers? Where will they go? It might be that production and use of robots will create new jobs that handicapped workers could competently fill. Unless habilitation personnel can anticipate those jobs, handicapped workers will not be prepared to fill them. The results will be what has been the case throughout the history of vocational services for the handicapped: we will be there too late, with too little.

The second possibility is not as positive, but might be more realistic. The readjustment of the labor force may result in a severe reduction or the elimination of unskilled jobs. Another likelihood might be the filtering down of a displaced semi-skilled work force to the unskilled ranks. In any event, there might not be available competitive jobs for handicapped persons.

If we believe that handicapped people have a right to participate in the labor market, then new noncompetitive alternatives may need to be developed.

A potential alternative is the establishment of government supported work facilities. These would be factory type work sites where handicapped people would be guaranteed a job and the opportunity to earn a wage. These facilities would not be conceived as profit-making businesses, but could function as self-sustaining enterprises. The work would be supplied through government contracts and would be designed to require hand labor although it might be more profitably produced through automation. This form of program would be more economical to operate than existing human service programs because it would result in usable production, wages being earned, and the handicapped person possibly paying taxes. Unlike the present sheltered workshop system, the objective would not be habilitation, but an opportunity to work. The quantity of available work should be sufficient to allow workers to produce at rates commensurate to their individual capacities. It is suggested that if competitive employment opportunities are not available, federally supported work facilities might be the best alternative for the handicapped.

It is clear that to date vocational services for moderately and severely handicapped individuals have not accomplished their objectives. Most handicapped people have not profited maximally from society's investment in their education. To continue in the same vein does not make sense. If meaningful change in the lives of handicapped people is to occur, then it is imperative that other pathways be explored.

REFERENCES

Alexander, C. P. The new economy. *Time,* May 30, 1983, pp. 62–70.

Bellamy, G. T. Habilitation of the severely and profoundly handicapped: A review of research on work productivity. In G. T. Bellamy (Ed.), *Habilitation of the severely and profoundly handicapped: Reports from the specialized training program.* Eugene, OR: Center on Human Development, 1976.

Bellamy, G. T., Horner, R. H., & Inman, D. P. *Vocational habilitation of severely retarded adults: A direct service technology.* Baltimore, MD: University Park Press, 1979.

Bellamy, G. T., Peterson, L., & Close, D. Habilitation of the severely and profoundly retarded: Illustrations of competence. *Education and Training of the Mentally Retarded.* 1975. *10.* 174–186.

Brown, S., & Pearce, E. Increasing the production rates of trainable retarded students in a public school simulated workshop. *Education and Training of the Mentally Retarded.* 1970. *5.* 15–22.

Brown, L., Van Deventer, P., Perlmutter, L., Jones, S., & Sontag, E. Effects of consequences on production rates of trainable retarded and severely emotionally disturbed students in a public school workshop. *Education and Training of the Mentally Retarded,* 1972, *7,* 74–81.

Cotter, V. W. Effects of music on performance of manual tasks with retarded adolescent females. *American Journal of Mental Deficiency,* 1971, 76(2), 242–248.

Cuvo, A. J., Leaf, R. B., & Borakove, T. S. Teaching janitorial skills to the mentally retarded: Acquisition, generalization, and maintenance. *Journal of Applied Behavior Analysis,* 1978, *11,* 345–355.

D'Alonzo, B. J. Trends and issues in career education for the mentally retarded. *Education and Training of the Mentally Retarded,* 1977, *12,* 156–158.

D'Alonzo, B. J. Career education for handicapped youth and adults in '70s. *Career Development for Exceptional Individuals,* 1978, *1*(1), 4–12.

DuRand, L., & DuRand, J. *The affirmative industry.* St. Paul, MN: Diversified Industries, 1978.

Flexer, R. W., & Martin, A. S. Sheltered workshops and vocational training settings. In M. E. Snell (Ed.), *Systematic instruction of the moderately and severely handicapped.* Columbus, OH: Merrill Publishing Co., 1978.

Fox, J. J., Gunter, P., Brady, M. P., Bambara, L., Spiegel-McGill, P., & Shores, R. E. Using multiple peer exemplars to develop generalized social responding of an autistic girl. In R. B. Rutherford & C. M. Nelson (Eds.), *Monograph on severe behavioral disorders of children and youth,* Vol. 7. Reston, VA: Council for Exceptional Children, 1984.

Foxx, R. M., & Azrin, M. H. *Toilet training the retarded.* Champaign, IL: Research Press, 1973.

Gold, M. W. Stimulus factors in skill training of retarded adolescents on a complex assembly task: Acquisition, transfer, and retention. *American Journal of Mental Deficiency,* 1972, 76(5), 517–526.

Gold, M. W. Research on the vocational habilitation of the retarded: The present, the future. In N. R. Ellis (Ed.), *International review of research in mental retardation.* New York: Academic Press, 1973.

Greenleigh Associates, Inc. *The role of the sheltered workshop in the rehabilitation of severely handicapped.* Washington, DC: Department of Health, Education and Welfare, Rehabilitation Services Administration, 1975.

Grossman, H., & Rowitz, L. A community approach to services for the retarded. In G. Tarjan, R. Eymand, & C. Myers (Eds.), *Social behavior studies in mental retardation.* Monograph of the American Association of Mental Deficiency, 1973.

Gunter, P. L. *Development of a positive self-concept for TMR adolescents through distance running.* Unpublished Ed.S. paper, Library of West Georgia College, Carrolton, GA, 1981.

Gunter, P. L., & Brady, M. P. Increasing the practitioner's utilization of research: A dilemma in regular and special education. *Education,* 1984, *105*(1), 92–98.

Gunter, P. L., Brady, M. P., Shores, R. E., Fox, J. J., Owen, S., & Goldzweig, S. The reduction of aberrant vocalizations with auditory feedback and resulting collateral behavior change of two autistic boys. *Behavioral Disorders,* 1984, *9,* 254–263

Halberstam, D. The quiet revolution: Robots enter our lives. *Parade Magazine,* April 10, 1983, pp. 17, 19–20.

Hamre-Nietupski, S., & Williams, W. Implementation of selected sex education and social skills to severely handicapped students. *Education and Training of the Mentally Retarded,* 1977, *12*(4), 364–372.

Hill, J. W., Wehman, P., & Horst, G. Toward generalization of appropriate leisure and social behavior in severely handicapped youth: Pinball machine use. *Journal of the Association for the Severely Handicapped,* 1982, *6,* 38–44.

Hopkins, B. L. Effects of candy and social reinforcement, instruction, and reinforcement schedule learning on the modification and maintenance of smiling. *Journal of Applied Behavior Analysis,* 1968, *1,* 121–129.

Lattal, K. A. Contingency management of tooth brushing behavior in a summer camp for children. *Journal of Applied Behavior Analysis,* 1969, *2,* 195–198.

Leff, R. B. Teaching the TMR to dial the telephone. *Mental Retardation,* 1974, *12*(2), 12–13.

Leff, R. B. Teaching TMR children and adults to dial a telephone. *Mental Retardation,* 1975, *13,* 9–12.

Levy, S. M. The debilitating effects of the habilitation process. In C. Hansen, & N. Haring (Eds.), *Expanding opportunities: Vocational education for the handicapped.* Seattle: University of Washington, 1980.

Levy, S. M. School doesn't last forever: Then what? Some vocational alternatives. In E. Schopler, & G. B. Mesibov (Eds.), *Autism in adolescents and adults.* Chapel Hill, NC: Plenum Press, 1983.

Levy, S. M., & Glascoe, F. P. *Do we know what to teach? An evaluation of work-related social skills.* Manuscript submitted for publication, 1983.

Levy, S. M., Pomerantz, D. J., & Gold, M. W. Work skill development. In N. G. Haring, & L. J. Brown (Eds.), *Teaching the severely handicapped* (Vol. 2). New York: Grune & Stratton, 1977.

Lewis, P. J., Ferneti, C. L., & Keilitz, I. *Project MORE: Hair washing.* Bellevue, WA: Edmark, 1975.

Martin, E. W. Individualism and behaviorism as future trends in educating handicapped children. *Exceptional Children,* 1972, *38,* 517–525.

Martin, G., Pallotta-Cornick, A., Johnstone, G., & Goyos, A. C. A supervisory strategy to improve work performance for low functioning retarded clients in a sheltered workshop. *Journal of Applied Behavior Analysis,* 1980, *13,* 183–190.

Matson, J. S. Use of independence training to teach shopping skills to mildly mentally retarded adults. *American Journal of Mental Deficiency,* 1981, *86,* 178–183.

Neef, N., Iwata, B., & Page, T. Public transportation training versus classroom instruction. *Journal of Applied Behavior Analysis,* 1978, *11,* 331–334.

Nihira, L., & Nihira, K. Jeopardy in community placement. *American Journal of Mental Deficiency,* 1975, *79,* 538–544.

Nutter, D., & Reid, D. Teaching retarded women a clothing selection skill using community norms. *Journal of Applied Behavior Analysis,* 1978, *11,* 475–487.

Office of Technology Assessment. *Social impacts of robotics* (OTA Publication No. OTA–BP–-CIT-11). Washington, DC: U.S. Government Printing Office, 1982.

Perry, M. A., & Cerreto, M. C. Structured learning training of social skills. *Mental Retardation,* 1977, *15,* 31–34.

Prehm, H. J. Special education research: Retrospect and prospect. *Exceptional Children,* 1976, *43,* 10–19.

Pomerantz, D. J., & Marholin, D. Vocational habilitation: A time for change in existing service delivery systems. In E. Sontag, N. Certo, & J. Smith (Eds.), *Educational programming for the severely handicapped.* Reston, VA: Council for Exceptional Children, 1977.

Schleien, S. J., Ash, T., Kiernan, J., & Wehman, P. Developing independent cooking skills in a profoundly retarded woman. *Journal of the Association for the Severely Handicapped,* 1981, *6,* 23–29.

Schleien, S. J., Wehman, P., & Kiernan, J. Teaching leisure skills to severely handicapped adults: An age-appropriate darts game. *Journal of Applied Behavior Analysis,* 1981, *14*(4), 513–519.

Sharpton, W. R. The effects of three feedback procedures on the productivity of severely retarded workers (Doctoral dissertation, Georgia State University, 1981). *Dissertation Abstracts International,* 1981, *42,* 2618-A.

Sherrill, C. *Adapted physical education and recreation: A multidisciplinary approach.* Dubuque, IA: Brown, 1981.

Stainback, S., Healy, H., Stainback, W., & Healy, J. Teaching basic eating skills. *AAESPH Review,* 1976, *1*(7), 26–35.

Trace. M.. Cuvo. A.. & Criswell. J. Teaching coin equvalence to the mentally retarded. *Journal of Applied Behavior Analysis.* 1977. *10.* 85–97.

Twardosz. S.. & Baer. D. M. Training two severely retarded adolescents to ask questions. *Journal of Applied Behavior Analysis.* 1973. *6.* 655–661.

van den Pol. R. A.. Iwata. B. A.. Ivancic. M. T.. Page. T. J.. Neff. N. A.. & Whitely. F. P. Teaching the handicapped to eat in public places: Acquisition. generalization. and maintenance of restaurant skills. *Journal of Applied Behavior Analysis.* 1981. *14.* 61–69.

Wehman. P.. Renzaglia. A.. Berry. G.. Schutz. R.. & Karan. O. C. Developing a leisure skill repertoire in severely and profoundly handicapped adolescents and adults. *AAESPH Review.* 1978. *3.* 162–172.

Section III
STRATEGIES FOR PLANNING
INDIVIDUALIZED PROGRAMS

CHAPTER 7*

SYNTHESIZING CURRICULUM AND INSTRUCTION: A MODEL FOR TEACHERS IN COMMUNITY BASED SETTINGS

MICHAEL P. BRADY

Recent developments in basic and applied research, instructional technology, teaching strategies, and curriculum design have provided classroom teachers with a wealth of valuable information concerning the education of severely handicapped children and youth. Local and state responses to court ordered and federally mandated changes in education systems have drastically increased demands on these teachers, often leading to job dissatisfaction and a feeling of being overwhelmed (Weatherley & Lipsky, 1977). Educators integrating severely handicapped students into community based schools find this task both difficult and challenging (Brady & Dennis, 1984; Brady & Gunter, in press). While both information and service demands have increased, little has been done to help the classroom teacher synthesize these developments into usable instructional models (Gunter & Brady, 1984; Prehm, 1976). The gap between the development and use of technologies led some educators (Gold, 1973; Gunter & Brady, 1984) to call for increased efforts toward dissemination of information to direct service providers. This chapter reviews a number of curriculum and instruction principles and technologies presently available to teachers of severely handicapped students. This information is integrated into a model that sequentially leads teachers and other service providers through goal selection, techniques of instruction, and program modification.

*Michael P. Brady is a Special Education Research Fellow and a Ph.D. candidate at George Peabody College of Vanderbilt University. His current interests and publications include legal issues related to integration, community based education models, handicapped children's social development, applications of instructional technology and applied behavior analysis in special education, and cross-cultural aspects of disability and habilitation. He has worked in school, district, and state education agencies in the U.S. and abroad, and is a member of the Association of Retarded Citizens and the Association for Persons with Severe Handicaps.

119

Curriculum and Instruction Components

Numerous authors have emphasized the need for curricular components such as long term planning (Brown, Nietupski, & Hamre-Nietupski, 1976), determination of instructional needs (Belmore & Brown, 1978), curricular mapping (Larsen & Poplin, 1980), and age appropriateness (Brown, Branston, Hamre-Nietupski, Pumpian, Certo, & Gruenewald, 1979). Others have focused on instructional procedures which include task analysis (William & Gotts, 1977), specific instructional strategies (Gold, 1980b), task presentation and correction procedures (Falvey, Brown, Lyon, Baumgart, & Schroeder, 1980), generalization strategies (Stokes & Baer, 1977), and progress measurement (Burney & Shores, 1979; White & Haring, 1976).

Brown (1973) and Williams, Brown, and Certo (1974) outlined a number of necessary curricular components for moderately and severely handicapped students which generally include: (a) the skill the student must perform; (b) a rationale for the necessary skill; (c) a description of how it will be taught; (d) a measurement system for evaluating progress; (e) types of materials necessary; (f) an approach to ascertain generalization across persons, places, materials, and cues; and (g) strategies for promoting independent use of the skill.

Current trends in curriculum development are either content (what to teach) or process (how to teach) oriented. Popham and Baker (1970) designated the use of commercial curricula and activity guides as a content orientation. Teachers who place their planning focus on instructional strategies and methods are considered process oriented. A review of curriculum guides by Billingsley and Neafsey (1978) identified several content and process curricula. Examination of the literature reveals that there are also a number of guides which combine content and process variables.

While there is a substantial amount of instruction related information available, the gap between theory and practice in instructional programming is a major barrier to the development of effective programs for handicapped learners (Gold, 1973; Gunter & Brady, 1984). Bridging this gap requires intermediary or transition steps prior to implementing instruction (Carmichael & Vogel, 1978). Dick and Carey (1978) advocated a systems approach to instructional design as a means of integrating a variety of theoretical and research concepts into a coherent instructional program.

A Synthesis Model

The model presented in this chapter divides curriculum and instruction into three global areas: (a) goal selection variables, (b) instructional variables, and (c) curriculum modification. The model is presented in Table 1. The literature on curriculum and instruction is reviewed in terms of each of these three components. Little or no attempt is made to introduce new instructional variables; rather, this model presents one way to synthesize a vast amount of information into an efficient and effective tool for developing individual educational programs (IEPs) for severely handicapped learners in integrated, community based settings.

TABLE 7-1
CURRICULUM AND INSTRUCTION SYNTHESIS MODEL

Goal Selection Variables	*Instructional Variables*		*Curriculum Variables*
Trainer variables	*Instructional content*	*Instructional processes*	Direct measurement
Task knowledge	Organizing goals	Formats:	Task analysis revisions
Training control	Short-term objectives	Discrimination	Eco-behavioral models
Learner variables	Methods	Oddity	Extended evaluation
Normalization	Task analysis:	Match-to-sample	Discrepancy measures
Less restrictive environments	Content	Chaining	Restrictiveness
Age appropriateness	Process	Total task	continuum
Ultimate functioning:		Generalization	Microtechnology
Current/future		Feedback:	systems
environments		Natural cues	
Community referenced		Cue redundancy	
Partial participation		Level of assistance	
		Modeling	
		Shaping/Fading	
		Other behavioral strategies:	
		Restrictiveness	
		continuum	

Goal Selection Variables

The instructional component of an IEP requires that specific goals and objectives be determined yearly. Numerous forces influence the choice of goals. Parents often have priorities that they want built into the student's program; aggressive or self-injurious behaviors, for instance, may demand immediate intervention. Other goals may seek to promote freer access to community based vocational or social environments. Official school policy may require a "balanced" curriculum by prescribing content domains. Few sets of guidelines have been developed to assist with goal selection for severely handicapped persons. Numerous authors, however, have suggested variables which teachers need to consider; these have been divided into trainer and learner related variables.

Trainer Variables

Task knowledge. Obviously a teacher should be competent in performing a task that he/she is teaching; unfortunately, this logic is not always applied. Teachers are often called upon to teach academic, social, leisure, self-help, or vocational tasks with which they themselves have had little experience. Yet, the more difficulty the student experiences in learning a task, the more knowledge the trainer should have of that task; fewer skill prerequisites may then be required of the learner (Gold, 1976). Gold suggested that a trainer best gains information about a task by performing it. The emphasis of Gold's position is that the most productive information about efficient performance can be gained only by doing the task oneself.

Control over training. Numerous authors (Fowler, Johnson, Whitman, & Zukotynski, 1978; Lovaas, 1981; Stokes & Baer, 1977; Whitman, Hurley, Johnson, & Christian, 1978) have cited the need to program instruction across environments and persons. By using this approach, teachers and parents complement each other's efforts by selecting goals that promote skill development in school, home, and community environments. A team approach to goal selection implies parental involvement in instruction. The expansion of instructional input (time, trainers, settings) is generally an efficient means of promoting skill development and use.

Learner Variables

Normalization. Wolfensberger (1972) stressed both environmental and behavioral considerations when explaining his conceptualization of normalization. Behaviors considered normal differ across environments and cultures; normal methods used to teach these behaviors also vary. Certainly, child behaviors and training methodologies that are considered normal in many remote, rural, or multicultural settings differ dramatically from those in urban or suburban environments (Brady & Anderson, 1983). Unfortunately, an examination of numerous IEPs might suggest that normalization principles are largely ignored when selecting goals for severely handicapped learners. Every potential goal should satisfy two criteria for inclusion in a program:

1. The goal should promote student behaviors that are considered normal in his/her community.
2. The goal should be taught by methods considered normal in that community.

Least restrictive environments. Closely related to normalization is the need to teach persons in less restrictive settings. Instructional programs therefore should promote a student's access to less restrictive living and learning environments. Goal selection should reflect the student's need to increase the personal competencies required for successful integration into less restrictive settings, and should include planned interactions with nonhandicapped learners (Bellamy & Wilcox, 1980; Voeltz, 1980).

Age appropriateness. Brown, Branston, Hamre-Nietupski, Pumpian, Certo, and Gruenewald (1979) stressed the need to develop chronological age appropriate goals and strategies for handicapped learners. There is little chance of a severely handicapped person becoming less dependent in normal community environments unless goals and teaching strategies reflect his/her chronological age; society will not afford citizens' rights, responsibilities, expectations, and dignity to an "external child" (Wolfensberger, 1975). Social expectations differ for 6, 10, and 14 year olds; therefore, a teacher should consider age appropriateness, both in goal and method selection.

Ultimate functioning in current and future environments. IEP team members must examine and inventory skills that will ultimately be necessary for a student to function more independently in current and future environments. Brown, Branston-McClean, Baumgart, Vincent, Falvey, and Schroeder (1979) described a three part strategy for curriculum development that focuses on both these environments:

1. The teacher identifies current and future least restrictive environments in which the student lives or will live.
2. The teacher identifies the skills required in each setting.
3. The teacher systematically teaches the student to perform or participate in as many of those skills as possible.

Goal selection thus depends on the skills necessary for a student to ultimately function in those environments (Brown, Nietupski, & Hamre-Nietupski, 1976).

Brown, Branston-McClean, Baumgart, Vincent, Falvey, and Schroeder (1979) and Falvey, Brown, Lyon, Baumgart, and Schroeder (1980) reviewed both ecological and student behavior inventory procedures for identifying skills required in a variety of settings. Unfortunately, such powerful assessment and planning information is not included in most diagnostic reports. If IEP teams are to become particularly effective, ecological and student behavior inventories may need to become essential skills of both teachers and diagnosticians. (The Mattison and Rosenberg chapter in this text provides a number of practical guidelines for ecological inventory development.)

Community referenced skills. To increase students' competence in their natural environments, goals should be community referenced. Bellamy and Wilcox (1980) specified the difference between community referenced curricula and programs that follow traditional academic or child development sequences. Community referenced curricula are future oriented; they prepare students for demands made by local work settings, recreational opportunities, and community and residential environments. In locally referenced curriculum development, goal selection need not follow a hierarchy of traditional skill sequences. Skills necessary or useful for integration into community environments (e.g., using public buses, shaving, purchasing a movie ticket) are often resistant to developmental sequencing models. Such models offer little insight into goal selection decisions. (For a more thorough discussion, the reader is referred to the chapter by Freagon et al. in this text.)

Partial participation. It is unlikely that severely handicapped students will be taught all the skills needed to function independently in work, leisure, home, and community settings. However, situations to promote students' partial participation in previously restricted settings can be designed and adapted. Brown, Branston-McClean, Baumgart, Vincent, Falvey, and Schroeder (1979), for instance, have described three types of adaptations designed to foster student participation to the maximum extent possible: (a) providing personal assistance to the learner; (b) adapting materials, rules, or procedures; rearranging activity sequences, or providing adaptive devices; and (c) adapting physical and/or social environments.

Summary

When deciding which goals to select for a severely handicapped student's IEP, teachers, parents, and other members of an IEP team are faced with an enormous responsibility. In contrast to decisions based solely on available commercial resources or other chance factors, a systematic goal selection strategy has been presented. The strategy can be used alone or with more formal social validation procedures (cf. Voeltz, Wuerch, & Brockhaut, 1982; Wuerch & Voeltz, 1982).

Instructional Variables

After educational goals are selected, a teacher must choose between a number of instructional strategies. Williams, Brown, and Certo (1974) differentiated between content and process instructional variables. In this model, content refers to student-focused behaviors. Content includes goals, objectives, methods, and task analysis. Process variables refer to procedural strategies including instructional formats, feedback, and additional behavioral strategies.

Instructional Content

Organizing Goals

Larsen and Poplin (1980) used a process called curricular mapping as an organizational tool for instructional development. Maps can be refined to include specific longitudinal goals (Brown, Falvey, Vincent, Kaye, Johnson, Ferrara-Parrish, & Gruenewald, 1979) to promote skill use in a variety of situations. Longitudinal goals may be translated into IEP annual goals which should be specific enough to avoid ambiguity both in daily programming and longitudinal planning.

Objectives

Writers in a variety of disciplines (e.g., educational psychology, industry, management) have prescribed methods of writing behavioral objectives. Apparently, there are as many methods for developing goals and objectives as there are instructional texts and departments of education guidelines. Generally, objectives should be short term, focus on specific learner behaviors, and be capable of easy measurement (Mager, 1975; Popovich, 1981).

Method

The terms method, technique, and strategy are often used interchangeably. To avoid confusion, in this model "method" is used to refer to the way a task is performed. In one training film (Roberts, 1975), Gold described two different methods of putting on a coat:

1. Hold the open coat in front of your body, zipper facing away from your body. Reach across the top and put your arms in the holes. Flip the coat over your head. Adjust the coat on your body.
2. Hold the open coat behind you, zipper facing your back. Reach behind and place your arms in the sleeves. Adjust the coat on your body. Note that this conceptualization of "method" differs from the "strategies" in subsequent sections of this chapter.

Task Analysis

Williams and Gotts (1977) have listed a number of steps involved in performing a task analysis:

1. Delineate the behavioral objective.
2. Review instructionally relevant resources.

3. Derive and sequence the component skills of the objectives.
4. Eliminate unnecessary or redundant component skills.
5. Determine prerequisite skills.
6. Monitor student performance and revise the sequences accordingly (p. 22).

Gold (1980b) differentiated between a content and a process task analysis; the former refers to the teachable steps into which a task can be divided; the latter "means everything the trainer does to teach the content to the learner" (Gold, 1980b, p. 13). The distinction is an important one. While many commercial curricula consist of content task analyses, teachers often improve instruction by sequential changes in the teaching process. (A useful skill analysis strategy is presented in the Salzberg and Lignugaris/Kraft chapter of this text.)

Instructional Processes

Instructional processes refer to the strategies used to teach IEP content. Gold (1980b) differentiated between instructional formats and feedback. The utility of specific behavioral strategies has been demonstrated in the literature by numerous writers.

Formats

Discrimination training. Spellman, DeBriere, Jarboe, Campbell, and Harris (1978) described a discrimination format using pictures of objects to teach daily living skills. Blake (1976) noted six classes of discrimination learning related to the presentation of materials and the method of presentation: (a) distinctive features of a stimulus, (b) irrelevant features, (c) redundancy, (d) sequence, (e) dimensions of stimuli, and (f) contiguity or proximity of stimuli.

Oddity. Research involving discrimination training led to the use of oddity as a training format. Gold (1980a) described oddity as a useful format for identifying an inappropriate object in a category, a common requirement in numerous vocational tasks. Use of an oddity format requires a student to discriminate at least one of the six classes described by Blake (1976).

Match to sample. Match to sample strategies have been used successfully to teach sight-word reading (Sidman & Cresson, 1973), math skills (Williams, Coyne, DeSpain, Johnson, Scheuerman, Stengert, Swetlik, & York, 1978), and complex assembly skills (Levy, 1975; Levy, Pomerantz, & Gold, 1977). This is among the most useful whole task strategies for students with significant learning problems.

Forward and backward chaining. Once a skill has been task analyzed, a decision must be made regarding the order of the steps. A number of self-help (e.g., dressing) and leisure (e.g., volleyball) skills are taught more easily by presenting the last step first (Wehman, 1979). This process of teaching steps in reverse order is called backward chaining. Academic skills are often taught in a forward chain; the first step is presented first. Popovich (1981) described forward and backward chaining in more detail and is recommended as a resource.

Total task. In contrast to learning a skill in a step-by-step process, total task presentation requires a student to perform the entire skill each time it is presented (Gold, 1980b). Instrumental to the success of this technique is the use of graduated guidance, which is particularly useful for students who do not respond to simple verbal or gestural prompts. Popovich (1981) identified the three components of graduated guidance as: (a) full guidance, (b) partial guidance, and (c) shadowing.

Generalization. Severely handicapped persons do not readily generalize newly acquired skills to different settings, cues, people, and situations. In reviewing programming for generalization, Stokes and Baer (1977) concluded that an active generalization technology is still in its infancy. Nevertheless, training for generalization is an integral part of instruction and should be implemented either during instruction itself or after a student has reached performance criteria (Sulzer-Azaroff & Mayer, 1977). Lovaas (1981) suggested that teachers consider both stimulus generalization and response generalization. Procedures to ensure stimulus generalization include:

1. Working in several environments.
2. The use of several "teachers."
3. The use of common stimuli in different environments, followed by systematic alteration of stimuli.
4. The use of common reinforcement schedules in different environments.

Procedures to promote generalization of a single skill to a larger set of skills (response generalization) include:

1. Building communicative responses.
2. Building practical self-help skills.
3. Teaching appropriate play.
4. Building compliance.
5. Teaching observational learning.
6. Building new social rewards.
7. Building intrinsic rewards (Lovaas, 1981, pp. 110–111).

Three current lines of research hold promise for generalization programming. First, the use of multiple peers appears to be a very effective means of promoting the generalization of social interaction skills within a relatively short period of time (Fox, Gunter, Brady, Bambara, Spiegel-McGill, & Shores, 1984). Second, choosing multiple "best examples" of objects (a number of materials that most closely resemble an object's category) is a more effective way of promoting acquisition and generalization of cognitive skills than simply choosing multiple examples or presenting good and poor examples (Hupp & Mervis, 1981). Finally, the use of milieu techniques and naturalistic teaching and measurement strategies has become an effective means of facilitating language generalization (Hart, in press; Warren, in press). While the problems of developing effective and efficient generalization strategies and generalization measurement systems remain, the implications of current research is very promising. (For an excellent discussion of generalization strategies, the reader is referred to several chapters in Warren and Rogers-Warren, in press).

Feedback

Feedback is the information exchanged between teacher and student which promotes task completion. Feedback is commonly conceptualized as the consequence of an instructional sequence. In this model, however, both cues and consequences are included under the category of feedback.

Natural cues and consequences. Falvey et al. (1980) differentiated between instructional and natural cues and consequences. Instructional cues and consequences are used when a learner does not respond appropriately to information available in the natural environment. In developing cues and consequences that promote skill usage, teachers may alter the duration, intensity, or frequency of the instructional information. It is useful to conceptualize "natural" and "instructional" as two ends of a continuum. Teachers should use naturally occurring cues and consequences as much as possible. Where the duration, intensity, or frequency of information giving must be altered to increase teaching effectiveness, a teacher should move away from the naturally occurring situation to the least degree necessary.

Two exciting steps in the development of naturalistic teaching procedures have been milieu strategies (Hart, in press; Hart & Rogers-Warren, 1978) and distributed trial training (Mulligan, Guess, Holvoet, & Brown, 1980). Milieu strategies consist of a number of techniques including mand model, delayed cue, and incidental teaching. Such strategies emphasize students' functional responding and arranging teaching environments to more closely reflect natural, nontraining environments. Distributing trials across different settings, teachers, materials, and times of the day may result in a better use of instructional time, reduce cognitive and motor fatigue, and aid in planning instruction of skills that cross curriculum areas. The characteristic common to all of these procedures is the arrangement of naturally occurring cues and consequences in students' natural environments.

Cue redundancy. A common characteristic of severely handicapped people is their inattentiveness to stimuli. Gold (1972, 1974) successfully used color, shape, and size coding and sequential arrangement of stimulus materials to facilitate acquisition of complex tasks. Strategies which shape, then fade cues (stimuli) rather than student responses generally are known as errorless learning strategies. Cue manipulations can yield high rates of responding in a short period of time. However, during transfer from such instructional cues to more natural ones (generally unconditioned stimuli), students may increase their rates of errors (Touchette, 1971). At this point teachers need to use caution in using correction procedures not available in natural environment.

Levels of assistance. A basic teaching strategy used in a number of curricula (Fredericks et al., 1976; Lent, 1974) involves four levels of assistance to strengthen cues and consequences. These levels resemble graduated guidance; the information (assistance), however, is usually built into a task analysis and systematically presented. Levels vary in terms of the degree of help given which ranges from (a) total physical assistance, (b) partial physical assistance (prompting or priming), (c) modeling, (d) verbal cues, to (e) no help. A number of problems are inherent in using levels of assistance: priming and total assistance are seldom available in natural environments; over use of assistance can lead to student dependency; teachers may not fade assistance appropriately as a student learns a skill. If a teacher decides that powerful information such as physical assistance is needed, escape or fading mechanisms need to be preplanned.

Modeling. Modeling or imitation strategies have been powerful tools for teaching social skills (Levy, 1983), vocational skills (Bellamy, Peterson, & Close, 1975), and language (Lovaas, 1981). Modeling can be used as both a cue and as a correction procedure. A teacher can combine a modeling strategy with forward or backward chaining and successive approximations to shape information and student responses to more natural occurrences of behavior. Modeling is a cue with a high occurrence, and is available across a variety of environments, skills, and people (cf. Striefel, 1974).

Shaping and fading. Shaping and fading procedures can be used at three points of an instructional sequence. Gold (1972) focused on shaping and fading of instructional cues; others (Lovaas, 1981; Sulzer-Azaroff, & Mayer, 1977) concentrated on shaping student responses. Finally, there is a growing body of literature which emphasizes shaping and fading of reinforcement and other consequences (Falvey et al., 1980; Sulzer-Azaroff, & Mayer, 1977). Of utmost importance for instructional programming, external information eventually must be removed from a teaching situation so that the learner is performing in response to natural demands. In contrast to traditional shaping and fading procedures, Snell and Gast (1981) have reported that a time delay procedure may be a more effective way of promoting independent skill usage.

Additional Strategies for Reducing Interferring Behavior

Numerous behavioral techniques have been shown to be effective means of reducing stereotypic, aggressive, and/or self-injurious behaviors. Most of these techniques are either contrived (e.g., overcorrection, timeout from positive reinforcement), risk side effects (punishment), or are physically difficult for teachers to implement. The decision to implement specific techniques often may put a teacher at odds with the principles of normalization, least restrictiveness, and age appropriateness. Keith (1979) has suggested that the relationship between behavioral strategies and normalization be viewed as a continuum rather than as a dichotomy. Much abnormal behavior serves to dehumanize and restrict access for severely handicapped people; these behaviors may need to be changed to promote social participation (Gunter. 1984). If such behavior does not respond to ordinary techniques, it may be useful to isolate motivating or etiological influences (Gunter, 1984). Consequently, a teacher can select a more powerful tool that is the least restrictive, yet most effective one available. A teacher should then fade the extraordinary technique while pairing it with more "normal" means of influencing behavior. This process prescribes the use of such powerful means of behavior change: (a) when less powerful means are not effective. (b) as the extraordinary means are being faded out, and (c) when the target behavior must be changed to promote student competence, safety, and community access. Such guidelines may be necessary to avoid questions of potential teacher liability (Brady & Dennis, 1984).

Popovich (1981) assigned behavior change procedures to a three component model based on their aversive qualities. Level 1 contains no aversive properties, Level 2 has some aversive qualities, while Level 3 is completely aversive. The use of a restrictiveness continuum holds promise for conceptualizing the relationship between behavioral strategies and normalization. Brady (1984) presented a model which includes strategies for reducing and increasing behaviors in terms of this continuum.

Curriculum Modification

Instruction of a selected objective does not last indefinately; any of the variables related to students, teachers, settings, and instructional procedures may yield an unsuccessful outcome and adaptation may be necessary.

Burney and Shores (1979) and White and Haring (1976) have developed decision rules useful for analyzing student performance rate data. Teachers who collect frequency, duration or latency data, however, do not have validated guidelines for changing instructional programs (Haring, Liberty, & White, 1980). Gold (1976, 1980a, 1980b) suggested another approach to instructional adaptation. An unsuccessful training interaction can be adapted in a three step revision sequence:

1. Revise the process task analysis.
   1.1 Feedback revisions
   1.2 Format revisions
2. Revise the content task analysis. Branching may be necessary for difficult steps.
3. Revise the methods. Select a different way of performing the task.

In an attempt to expand the adaptation process to include noninstructional variables, Gaylord-Ross (1980) outlined a decision model for aberrant behavior. He suggested a five component model which first assesses the necessity for a behavior change program. If such a program is warranted, reinforcement procedures are suggested. If the behavior is not brought under control, then a teacher would systematically proceed through ecological, curriculum, and finally punishment procedures, until a successful reduction of the behavior has taken place. Karan, Bernstein, Harvey, Bates, Renzaglia, and Rosenthal (1979) employed an extended evaluation system. Their approach to adapting unsuccessful interventions included problem analysis, direct observation (which may include several assessment procedures), identification of the problem and its parameters, treatment strategies, and treatment evaluation.

A decision to change a student's instructional program need not be a debate over the merits of the adaptation systems described above. A more useful approach would include several of these recommendations and an analysis of the variables outlined in this chapter. An appropriate strategy is to evaluate the discrepancy between a student's ideal and present behavior (Mager & Pipe, 1970). First, a teacher might progress through the goal selection variables to ascertain the appropriateness of a target behavior. Next, the teacher might employ strategies suggested by Gaylord-Ross (1980) and Karan et al. (1979) to isolate and remediate other ecological factors. Analysis and adaptation of instruction should follow a least restrictiveness paradigm, shaping instructional materials, cues, and consequences to those found in natural environments. Managing the adaptation process should be as streamlined and efficient as possible. The increasing use of microcomputer technology for the collection, analysis, presentation, and storage of student performance and program data holds tremendous promise and has already become a useful tool for many special education teachers (Brady & Langford. in press).

Conclusion

As a result of a decade of work with severely handicapped learners. teachers have been overwhelmed with strategies. suggestions. ideas. and techniques. The gap between research and practice. however. limits state of the art educational programming in integrated. community based settings. This chapter did not examine other models that assist teachers in delivering quality services. Models such as IEP managers (Brady, 1983), education synthesizers (Bricker, 1976), research synthesizers (Gunter & Brady, 1984), transdisciplinary teams (Hart, 1977), consulting teachers/clinical researchers (Nevin, Paolucci-Whitcomb, Duncan, & Thibodeau, 1982), and teacher training program evaluation based on student performance (Shores, 1979) also add valuable resources to teachers and staff on the "front line." The model presented does provide a structure for the synthesis of the many curriculum and instruction variables referred to in the current literature. With it. perhaps teachers and other service providers will approach planning and instruction in a more systematic and effective manner.*

REFERENCES

Bellamy, G. T., Peterson, L., & Close, D. Habilitation of the severely and profoundly retarded: Illustrations of competence. *Education and Training of the Mentally Retarded*, 1975. *10*. 174–186.

Bellamy, G. T., & Wilcox, B. Secondary education for severely handicapped students: Guidelines for quality services. In B. Wilcox & A. Thompson (Eds.). *Critical issues in educating autistic children and youth*. Washington. DC: U.S. Department of Education. 1980.

Belmore, K., & Brown, L. A job skill inventory for use in a public school vocational training program for severely handicapped potential workers. In N. G. Haring & D. Bricker (Eds.). *Teaching the severely handicapped* (vol. 3). Seattle: American Association for the Education of the Severely and Profoundly Handicapped, 1978.

Billingsley, F. F., & Neafsey, S. S. Curriculum/training guides: A survey of content and evaluation procedures. *AAESPH Review*, 1978, *3*(1), 42–57.

---

*The author wishes to acknowledge and thank the many people who provided valuable input into this chapter: Sam Ashcroft. Phil Gunter. Marilyn Rousseau, and Steve Warren. Also. appreciation is extended to Sylvia Scruggs and Vaoi'iva Brown for their unending assistance with the preparation of the manuscript. Preparation of this chapter was supported in part by a grant from the U.S. Department of Education. Special Education Programs, Grant No. G008301035.

Portions of this chapter were published earlier in *The Exceptional Child*. 1984. *31*(10), 19–32. Permission to reprint is gratefully acknowledged.

Blake. K. A. *The mentally retarded: An educational psychology.* Englewood Cliffs, NJ: Prentice-Hall. 1976.

Brady. M. P. A curriculum and instruction synthesis model for teachers of the severely handicapped. *The Exceptional Child,* 1984, *31*(1), 19–32.

Brady. M. P. Rural special education teacher training: Issues in the Pacific Basin territories. *Teacher Education and Special Education,* 1983. *6*(1), 71–76.

Brady, M. P.. & Anderson. D. D. Some issues in the implementation of P. L. 94-142 in the Pacific Basin territories. *Education,* 1983, *103*(3), 259–269.

Brady. M. P.. & Dennis. H. F. Integrating severely handicapped learners: Potential teacher liability in community based programs. *Remedial and Special Education,* 1984, *5*(5), 29–36.

Brady. M. P.. & Gunter. P. Educating severely handicapped students: Legal issues in integrated. community based educational programs. *Executive Educator, 6,* in press.

Brady. M. P.. & Langford. C. A. Microcomputer technology in special education: Teacher uses and concerns. *Contemporary Education,* in press.

Bricker. D. D. Educational synthesizer. In M. A. Thomas (Ed.), *Hey, don't forget about me!* Reston. VA: Council for Exceptional Children, 1976.

Brown. L. Instructional programs for trainable-level retarded students. In L. Mann & D. A. Sabatino (Eds.). *The first review of special education* (vol. 2). Philadelphia: JSE Press, 1973.

Brown. L.. Branston, M. B.. Hamre-Nietupski, S., Pumpian, I., Certo, N., & Gruenewald. L. A strategy for developing chronological age appropriate and functional curricular content for severely handicapped adolescents and young adults. *Journal of Special Education,* 1979, *13*(1), 81–90.

Brown. L.. Branston-McClean. M. B.. Baumgart. D., Vincent, L., Falvey. M., & Schroeder, J. Using the characteristics of current and subsequent least restrictive environments for severely handicapped students. *AAESPH Review,* 1979, *4*(4), 407–424.

Brown. L.. Falvey. M.. Vincent. L., Kaye. N., Johnson. F., Ferrara-Parrish, P., & Gruenewald, L. Strategies for generating comprehensive, longitudinal and chronological age appropriate individual educational plans for adolescent and young adult severely handicapped students. In L. Brown. M. Falvey. D. Baumgart, I. Pumpian, J. Schroeder, & L. Gruenewald (Eds.). *Strategies for teaching chronological age appropriate functional skills to adolescent and young adult severely handicapped students* (vol. IX. Part 1). Madison, WI: Madison Metropolitan School District. 1979.

Brown. L.. Nietupski. J.. & Hamre-Nietupski. S. The criterion of ultimate functioning and public school services for the severely handicapped student. In M. A. Thomas (Ed.), *Hey, don't forget about me: Education's investment in the severely, profoundly, and multiply handicapped.* Reston. VA: Council for Exceptional Children, 1976, 2–15.

Burney. J. D.. & Shores. R. E. A study of relationships between instructional planning and pupil behavior. *Journal of Special Education Technology,* 1979, *2*(3), 16–25.

Carmichael. L.. & Vogel. P. Research into practice. *Journal of Physical Education and Recreation,* 1978. *49,* 29–30.

Dick. W., & Carey. L. *The systematic design of instruction.* Glenview, IL: Scott, Foresman, 1978.

Falvey. M.. Brown, L.. Lyon. S.. Baumgart. D., & Schroeder. J. Strategies for using cues and correction procedures. In W. Sailor, B. Wilcox, & L. Brown (Eds.), *Methods of instruction for severely handicapped students.* Baltimore: Paul H. Brookes, 1980.

Fowler. S. A., Johnson. M. R., Whitman. T. L., & Zukotynski, G. Teaching a parent in the home to train self-help skills and increase compliance in her profoundly retarded daughter. *AAESPH Review,* 1978, *3*(3), 151–161.

Fox. J. J., Gunter, P., Brady. M. P., Bambara, L., Spiegel-McGill, P., & Shores. R. E. Using multiple peer exemplars to develop generalized social responding of an autistic girl. In

R. B. Rutherford & C. M. Nelson (Eds.). *Monograph on severe behavioral disorders of children and youth*. Vol. 7. Reston. VA: Council for Exceptional Children. 1984.

Fredericks, H. D., Riggs, C., Furey, T., Grove, D., Moore, W., McDonnell, J., Jordon, E., Hanson, W., Baldwin, V., & Wadlow, M. *The teaching research curriculum for moderately and severely handicapped*. Springfield. IL: Charles C Thomas. 1976.

Gaylord-Ross, R. A decision model for the treatment of aberrant behavior in applied settings. In W. Sailor, B., Wilcox, & L. Brown (Eds.), *Methods of instruction for severely handicapped students*. Baltimore: Paul H. Brookes. 1980.

Gold, M. W. Stimulus factors in skill training of the retarded on a complex assembly task: Acquisition. transfer, and retention. *American Journal of Mental Deficiency*. 1972, 76(5), 517-526.

Gold, M. W. Research on the vocational habilitation of the retarded: The present, the future. In N. R. Ellis (Eds.), *International review of research in mental retardation*. New York: Academic Press, 1973.

Gold, M. W. Redundant cue removal in skill training for the mildly and moderately retarded. *Education and Training of the Mentally Retarded*. 1974, 9(1), 5-8.

Gold, M. W. Task analysis of a complex assembly task by the retarded blind. *Exceptional Children*, 1976, 43(2), 78-84.

Gold, M. W. *"Did I say that?" Articles and commentary on the Try Another Way system*. Champaign, IL: Research Press Co., 1980. (a)

Gold, M. W. *Try another way training manual*. Champaign, IL: Research Press, 1980. (b)

Gunter, P., & Brady, M. P. Increasing the practitioner's utilization of research: A dilemma in regular and special education. *Education*, 1984, 105(1), 92-98.

Gunter, P. L., Self-injurious behavior: Characteristics, etiology and treatment. *The Exceptional Child*, 1984, 31(2), 91-98.

Haring, N. G., Liberty, K. A., & White, O. R. Rules for data based strategy decisions in instructional programs: Current research and instructional implications. In W. Sailor, B. Wilcox, & L. Brown (Eds.), *Methods of instruction for severely handicapped students*. Baltimore: Paul H. Brookes, 1980.

Hart, B. Environmental techniques that may facilitate language generalization and acquisition. In S. F. Warren & A. Rogers-Warren (Eds.), *Teaching functional language*. Baltimore: University Park Press, in press.

Hart, B., & Rogers-Warren, A. A milieu approach to teaching language. In R. Schiefelbush (Ed.), *Language intervention strategies*. Baltimore: University Park Press, 1978.

Hart, V. The use of many disciplines with the severely and profoundly handicapped. In E. Sontag, J. Smith, & N. Certo (Eds.), *Educational programming for the severely and profoundly handicapped*. Reston, VA: Council for Exceptional Children, 1977.

Hupp, S. C., & Mervis, C. B. Development of generalized concepts by severely handicapped students. *Journal of the Association for the Severely Handicapped*, 1981, 6(1), 14-21.

Karan, O. C., Bernstein, G. S., Harvey, J., Bates, P., Renzaglia, A., & Rosenthal, D. An extended evaluation model for severely handicapped persons. *AAESPH Review*, 1979, 4(4), 374-398.

Keith, K. D. Behavior analysis and the principle of normalization. *AAESPH Review*, 1979, 4(2), 148-151.

Larsen, S. C., & Poplin, M. S. *Methods for educating the handicapped: An individualized education program approach*. Boston: Allyn and Bacon, 1980.

Lent, J. R. *Project MORE: Daily living skills program*. Bellevue, WA: Edmark Associates, 1974.

Levy, S. M. The development of work skill training procedures for the assembly of printed circuit boards by the severely handicapped. *AAESPH Review*, 1975, 1(1), 1-10.

Levy, S. M. School doesn't last forever, then what? Some vocational alternatives. In E. Schopler & G. Meisbov (Eds.), *Autism in adolescents and adults.* Chapel Hill, NC: Plenum Press, 1983.

Levy, S. M., Pomerantz, D. J., & Gold, M. W. Work skill development. In N. G. Haring & L. J. Brown (Eds.), *Teaching the severely handicapped: A yearly publication of the American Association on Education of the Severely Profoundly Handicapped* (vol. II). New York: Grune & Stratton, 1977.

Lovaas, O. I. *Teaching developmentally disabled children: The ME book.* Baltimore: University Park Press, 1981.

Mager, R. F. *Preparing instructional objectives.* Palo Alto, CA: Pitman Learning, 1975.

Mager, R. F., & Pipe, P. *Analyzing performance problems or "you really oughta wanna".* Belmont, CA: Fearon Pitman, 1970.

Mulligan, M., Guess, D., Holvoet, J., & Brown, F. The individualized curriculum sequencing model (1): Implications from research on massed, distributed or spaced trial training. *Journal of the Association for the Severely Handicapped,* 1980, *5*(4), 325–336.

Nevin, A., Paolucci-Whitcomb, P., Duncan, D., & Thibodeau, L. A. The consulting teacher as a clinical researcher. *Teacher Education and Special Education,* 1982, *5*(4), 19–29.

Popham, W. J., & Baker, E. L. *Systematic instruction.* Englewood Cliffs, NJ: Prentice-Hall, 1970.

Popovich, D. *Effective educational and behavioral programming for severely and profoundly handicapped students: A manual for teachers and aides.* Baltimore: Paul H. Brookes, 1981.

Prehm, H. J. Special education research: Retrospect and prospect. *Exceptional Children,* 1976, *43,* 10–19.

Roberts, G. (Producer). *Task analysis: An introduction to a technology of instruction.* Indianapolis: Film Productions of Indianapolis, 1975. (Film)

Shores, R. E. Evaluation and research. *Teacher Education and Special Education,* 1979, *2*(3), 68–71.

Sidman, M., & Cresson, O. Reading and cross model transfer of stimulus equivalences in severe retardation. *American Journal of Mental Deficiency,* 1973, *77,* 515–523.

Snell, M. E., & Gast, D. L. Applying time delay procedure to the instruction of the severely handicapped. *Journal of the Association for the Severely Handicapped,* 1981, *6*(3), 3–14.

Spellman, C., DeBriere, T., Jarboe, D., Campbell, S., & Harris, C. Pictoral instruction: Training daily living skills. In M. Snell (Ed.), *Systematic instruction of the moderately and severely handicapped.* Columbus: Charles E. Merrill, 1978.

Stokes, T. F., & Baer, D. M. An implicit technology of generalization. *Journal of Applied Behavior Analysis,* 1977, *10,* 349–367.

Striefel, S. *Managing behavior, part 7: Teaching a child to imitate.* Lawrence, KS: H & H Enterprises, 1974.

Sulzer-Azaroff, B., & Mayer, G. R. *Applying behavior analysis procedures with children and youth.* New York: Holt, Rinehart & Winston, 1977.

Touchette, P. E. Transfer of stimulus control: Measuring the moment of transfer. *Journal of Experimental Analysis of Behavior,* 1971, *15,* 347–354.

Voeltz, L. M. Children's attitudes toward handicapped peers. *American Journal of Mental Deficiency,* 1980, *84*(5), 455–464.

Voeltz, L. M., Wuerch, B. B., & Brockhaut, C. H. Social validation of leisure time activities training with severely handicapped youth. *Journal of the Association for the Severely Handicapped,* 1982, *7*(2), 3–13.

Warren, S. F. Clinical strategies for the measurement of language generalization. In. S. F. Warren & A. Rogers-Warren (Eds.), *Teaching functional language.* Baltimore: University Park Press, in press.

Warren, S. F., & Rogers-Warren, A. (Eds.), *Teaching functional language*. Baltimore: University Park Press, in press.

Warren, S. F., & Rogers-Warren, A. (Eds.), *Teaching functional language*. Baltimore: University Park Press, in press.

Weatherley, R., & Lipsky, M. Street-level bureaucrats and institutional innovation: Implementing special education reform. *Harvard Educational Review*, 1977, *47*(2), 171–197.

Wehman, D. Instructional strategies for improving toy play skills of severely handicapped children, *AAESPH Review*, 1979, *4*(2), 125–135.

White, O. R., & Haring, N. G. *Exceptional teaching*. Columbus, OH: Charles E. Merrill, 1976.

Whitman, T. L., Hurley, J. D., Johnson, M. R., & Christian, J. C. Direct and generalized reduction of inappropriate behavior in a severely retarded child through a parent-administered behavior modification program. *AAESPH Review*, 1978, *3*(2), 68–77.

Williams, W., Brown, L., & Certo, N. Basic components of instructional programs. *Theory Into Practice*, 1974, *14*(2), 123–136.

Williams, W., Coyne, P., DeSpain, C., Johnson, F., Scheuerman, N., Stengert, J., Swetlik, B., & York, R. Teaching math skills using longitudinal sequences. In M. E. Snell (Ed.), *Systematic instruction of the moderately and severely handicapped*. Columbus, OH: Charles E. Merrill, 1978.

Williams, W., & Gotts, E. A. Selected considerations on developing curriculum for severely handicapped students. In E. Sontag, J. Smith, & N. Certo (Eds.), *Educational programming for the severely and profoundly handicapped*. Reston, VA: Council for Exceptional Children, 1977.

Wolfensberger, W. *The principle of normalization in human services*. Toronto: National Institute of Mental Retardation, York University Campus, 1972.

Wolfensberger, W. *The origin and nature of our institutional models*. Syracuse: Human Policy Press, 1975.

Wuerch, B. B., & Voeltz, L. M. *Longitudinal leisure skills for severely handicapped learners: The Ho'onanea curriculum component*. Baltimore: Paul H. Brookes, 1982.

CHAPTER 8

THE USE OF AN ECOLOGICAL INVENTORY TO SELECT INDIVIDUAL EDUCATION PROGRAM OBJECTIVES

MARTY E. MATTISON, II AND REBECCA ROSENBERG

Over the past decade there has been a gradual shift in the curriculum emphasis for moderately and severely handicapped persons. This shift has been from a developmental, data-based instructional model to a model which focuses on practical life skill experiences in a student's present and future environment (Wilcox & Bellamy, 1982). Specifically, much of the curriculum and instruction literature has repeatedly recommended that valid curricula must emphasize age appropriate functional skills demonstrated in natural community settings (Brown, Branston-McClean, Baumgart, Vincent, Falvey, & Schroeder. 1979; Brown, Nietupski, & Hamre-Nietupski, 1976; Freagon, Pajon, Brankin, Galloway, Rich, Karel, Wilson, Costello, Peters, & Hurd, 1981; Neel, Billingsley, McCarthy, Symonds, Lambert, Lewis-Smith, & Hanashiro, 1983). Such a functional curriculum requires teachers to re-examine their methods of assessment and IEP goal selection for moderately and severely handicapped students.

The Ecological Inventory as an Assessment Tool

There are very few guidelines available for selecting IEP goals and objectives. Until recently, diagnosticians and teachers have assessed students using developmental checklists and sequences such as Uniform Performance Assessment Systems (UPAS) by White, Haring, Edgar, and Bendersky

*Marty E. Mattison, II received an M.Ed. in Educational Psychology (Special Education) from the University of Hawaii in 1979. During this time, Marty received a grant to work at the University of Washington, University of Kansas, and Teaching Research in Monmouth, OR. He has been working on a Ph.D. at the University of Oregon. Marty is currently a special education district resource teacher with the Windard Oahu District in Hawaii. He is a member of The Association for Persons with Severe Handicaps (TASH) and is active as an inservice trainer for teachers of severely handicapped students in the State of Hawaii.

Rebecca Rosenberg received an M.Ed. in Special Education in 1978 from the University of Hawaii. While a masters student, she received a grant to visit three model special education programs for severely handicapped students in Miami, Wisconsin, and Vermont. She has been a teacher of severely multiply handicapped students and presently is a special education resource teacher at the Leeward, Oahu District serving elementary and intermediate-age students of all handicapping conditions.

(1978), The Behavioral Characteristics Progression (1973), the Bayley Scales (1969), or the Brigance Diagnostic Inventory of Early Development (1978). Based on the developmental assessment used in conjunction with commercial curriculum task analyses or activity guides, IEP goals and objectives were derived that addressed the next developmental milestone that the student lacked. Unfortunately, inappropriate and/or insufficient assessment data has resulted in some IEP goals and objectives which were inappropriate to the chronological age and immediate functional needs of many severely handicapped students (e.g., teaching a 15-year-old to stack blocks). In addition, the curriculum was neither locally referenced nor did it provide for individual options (e.g., high technology vocational options in Seattle versus pineapple picking and packing in Hawaii).

The logic of traditional developmental sequences leading to acquisition of functional life skills no longer holds. Many other factors, however, have been suggested for consideration in goal selection: normalization, least restrictive environments, age appropriateness, ultimate functioning in current and future environments, community referenced skills, and finally, the principle of partial participation (Brady, 1984). Low learning rates and the problems of generalization, retention and regression point toward a need for age appropriate functional skills and applying what Brown et al. (1976) termed the "criterion of ultimate functioning." That is, we must consider the skills that each student must possess in order to function as independently and productively as possible in various environments. In order to select and define such objectives, the criterion of ultimate functioning has been applied to assessment and goal selection.

These authors have found that an ecological inventory is the most functional and useful decision making assessment tool for approaching the problem of "what to teach" moderately and severely handicapped students. Ecological inventories are individualized processes and instruments which provide educators with (a) a list of current and potential future environments and specific subenvironments in which a student functions or may function, and (b) a list of activities and specific skills that are required to perform those activities that occur within each subenvironment (Sailor & Guess, 1983). An inventory assessment strategy is geared to a curriculum that stresses functionality, age appropriateness, and training in natural environments. Rather than remediation of developmental lags, the inventory is oriented toward student needs in the "here and now" and in the future.

The ecological inventory process provides teachers with information on skills necessary for functioning in five major domains: vocational, recreation/leisure, domestic, school and community—as they occur in home, school, and community settings. The inventory also allows the teacher to assess the student's present level of functioning in the various domains across environments. For example, completion of an inventory might indicate that a student can partially participate in the domestic skill of cooking rice, fully participate in the leisure skill of playing video games, but can not use community buses. Based on information gained from the inventory, the teacher, in conjunction with parents and others concerned with the student's educational program, can begin to select IEP goals and objectives.

Selection of IEP goals and objectives is also dependent on the student's age. An older student's IEP might emphasize goals and objectives in the vocational domain whereas the emphasis in a younger student's IEP might be in the school domain. For example, the IEP for a student in the elementary grades might include such objectives as beginning feeding and dressing or toileting skills in their respective natural environments. IEP objectives for an 18-year-old student would include more vocationally oriented objectives such as using communication cards to make purchases at a fast food counter (Christoph, Nietupski, & Pumpian, 1979), or crossing streets (Page, Iwata, & Neef, 1976).

Current teaching techniques are not changed by the use of an ecological inventory. Techniques such as task anlaysis, match-to-sample, forward and backward chaining, generalization tactics, levels of assistance, natural cues and consequences, modeling, data collection and decision making follow the inventory process as they would follow other assessment strategies.

Developing An Ecological Inventory

The initial step in conducting an ecological inventory is to list opportunities to participate in home, school, and local community activities. To discover these opportunities, Wilcox and Bellamy (1982) identified three strategies: (a) observation of activities engaged in by nonhandicapped peers and adults, (b) interviews with knowledgeable individuals in the community, and (c) "logical analysis"—determining present and future activities necessary or helpful for moderately and severely handicapped individuals to participate to the maximum extent possible. Activities selected should reflect critical functions. Critical functions are defined in terms of the purpose that a behavior serves rather than the specific motor act of the behavior (White 1980a, 1980b). Sailor and Guess (1983) identified eight functions crucial to successful participation in home, school, and community environments:

1. Eating
2. Toileting
3. Mobility
4. Expressive communication

   5. Receptive communication
   6. Hygiene/appearance
   7. Recreation/leisure
   8. Horizontal social interactions

An inventory should reflect various location-specific training activities, since individual communities vary in lifestyles and population size. There appear to be certain critical survival competencies, however, that are important to general survival across communities and settings. These require further empirical research but are presented in the inventory as a general guide.

The authors used these strategies as well as brainstorming with other educators to develop a locally referenced inventory that has been transformed to a parent and teacher questionnaire presented in Table 1. (Only the school domain is presented here for illustrative purposes. However, the entire inventory may be obtained from the authors.) The questionnaire is sent home to be completed by parents and an identical questionnaire is completed by the teacher.

For those teachers who find the task of designing an entire ecological inventory overwhelming, there are a few ecological inventories available, in addition to the version presented here, that may serve as a starting point. These examples include inventories developed by Neel et al. (1983) for Project IMPACT; Freagon et al. (1981) for their community based program; and Wilcox and Bellamy (1982) for secondary programming suggestions. Information previously published by Project MAZE, Volume IX (Madison Metropolitan School District, 1979) by Brown et al. at the University of Wisconsin also provides information on how to develop an ecological inventory. Teachers must again be cautioned, however, that the inventory should survey local environments and opportunities if it is to be directly relevant to student goal selection.

Conducting the Inventory

Many teacher hours are currently spent assessing, planning instruction, and writing each student's IEP. Initially an ecological inventory may require more teacher planning hours but, eventually, the extra time will pay off in three areas. First, careful ecological analysis will provide a teacher with a wealth of useful IEP planning data. Second, skill acquisition is facilitated if those skills are functional and taught in natural settings (Freagon & Rotatori, 1982). Finally, if new skills are immediately useful, they are more likely to be maintained. Indeed, instruction may be more efficient because the need for additional training for generalization and maintenance may be minimized (Brown et al., 1976).

The ecological inventory procedure could be facilitated for teachers by having diagnostic evaluation teams participate in the information gathering

TABLE 8-1
ECOLOGICAL INVENTORY

Domain: School *Activity Area:*	*Independent*	*Model Verbal Gestural*	*Physical Assistance*	*Does Youngster Participate?*
Leisure				
Grasps, holds objects				
Puts puzzle together				# of pieces: ____
Pages through book				
Puts on headphones				
Plays tape recorder				
Turns on and watches T.V.				
Plays video games				
Plays outdoor games				Types of games:
Plays indoor games				

Note preferred activities:

Instruction				
Sits in chair				
Turns head both sides; lifts head				
Attends to task				How long? ____
Holds pencil, crayon				
Cleans up after task completed				
Points				
Responds to verbal, gestural, or physical cues				
Changes activity at appropriate time				
Other:				

Bathroom				
Indicates need to use bathroom				
Uses right/left limbs				
Eliminates/urinates in toilet				
Flushes toilet				
Uses toilet paper				
Pulls paper towel from dispenser				
Opens/closes doors				
Washes and dries hands				
Brushes teeth				

TABLE 8-1 (Continued)
ECOLOGICAL INVENTORY

Domain: School Activity Area:	Independent	Model Verbal Gestural	Physical Assistance	Does Youngster Participate?
Undresses				
Puts on clothes				
Applies deodorant				
Brushes hair in mirror				
General Skills				
Communicates to others				
Goes to correct classroom				
Finds classroom door				
Opens door to classroom				
Drinks from fountain				
Puts personal items in cubby area				
Other:				
Kitchen Area				
Prepares simple snacks				
Serves others				
Reaches out to preferred object/food				
Cleans up after snack				
Takes items to sink				
Other:				
Room Cleaning				
Washes windows				
Arranged chairs				
Sweeps/mops floor				
Vacuums carpet				
Opens/Closes windows				
Takes out trash				
Rest Area/Simulated Bedroom				
Makes bed				
Changes bedding				
Hangs up clothes				
Puts away clothes				
Other:				

TABLE 8-1 (Continued)
ECOLOGICAL INVENTORY

Domain: School Activity Area:	Independent	Model Verbal Gestural	Physical Assistance	Does Youngster Participate?
Utility Room				
Puts dirty clothes in hamper				
Sorts clothes				
Brings clothes to washer				
Puts detergent in washer				
Washes clothes				
Puts in dryer/set times				
Folds clothes				
Hangs clothes				
Picks up. delivers clothing				
Irons clothes				
Other:				
Playground/Recess				
Rides assorted playground equipment				Does student play without adult supervision? Yes ___ No ___
List equipment:				
Interacts with peers (initiates. responds)				
Shares materials				
Indicates needs assistance on playground				
Other:				
Cafeteria				
Waits in line				
Pays for meal				
Selects utensil for meal				
Carries lunch tray				
Drinks with straw or from cup				
Eats finger foods				
Pierces food with fork				
Cuts food with fork/spoon/knife				

TABLE 8-1 (Continued)
ECOLOGICAL INVENTORY

Domain: School Activity Area:	Independent	Model Verbal Gestural	Physical Assistance	Does Youngster Participate?
Remains in proper eating position				
Finishes meal				
Other:				
Mobility Between Settings				
Propels self between settings				
Walks between settings				
Finds new setting				
Finds areas within setting				
Other:				
SCHOOL WORK FUNCTIONS				
Cafeteria				
Says "thank you"				
Serves food				
Passes out milk				
Sweeps floors				
Wipes tables				
Scrapes plates				
Wipes pots and pans				
Other:				
Office				
Staples				
Folds				
Collates				
Stuffs envelopes				
Delivers messages				
Says "excuse me"				
Other:				
Library				
Checks out book				
Stamps books with date				
Puts books in cart				
Other:				

TABLE 8-1 (Continued)
ECOLOGICAL INVENTORY

Domain: School Activity Area:	Independent	Model Verbal Gestural	Physical Assistance	Does Youngster Participate?
Grounds Maintenance				
Waters plants				
Cuts grass				
Plants				
Pulls weeds				
Rakes leaves				
Picks up trash				
Deposits trash in receptacle				
Other:				

process. In Hawaii, diagnostic team members include a diagnostic prescriptive teacher, social worker, speech therapist, psychological examiner, and may include an occupational and/or physical therapist. Presently, these team members evaluate severely handicapped students with standardized developmental assessment instruments. While some developmental data may be useful to teachers, information such as "cognitive functioning is at the 18-22 month level" does not assist the teacher in planning an age appropriate, functional curriculum.

The authors would like to see the inventory process begin with diagnostic personnel. For example, a social worker might gather information on the activities in which the student participates, the skills the student presently demonstrates at home, and specific parent/caregiver expectations and desires for the future. The survey located in the Appendix might be used as an introductory instrument. Rather than administer developmental checklists, diagnostic prescriptive teachers could assess the student's level of attainment of critical functions across the various environmental domains. Speech therapists could assess communicative forms (e.g., sign language, gestures) and functions (to request needs, to protest, etc.) that the student presently exhibits.

Selecting Goals

Once the survey is completed, goals and objectives for each student based on information derived from the inventory are developed. When prioritizing student needs, parents and teachers should consider those skills, activities, and behaviors that lead to student skill improvement in multiple environments, are longitudinal, and are relevant and valued by those who interact with the student. Sailor and Guess (1983) offer some very practical suggestions on functional goal/objective selection:

1. Is the goal/objective appropriate?
2. Is it taught in the least restrictive community setting?
3. Can it be seen as a specific, useful normalized skill?
4. Can the goal/objective be met by a student within a year if carefully planned, monitored, and intensively trained?
5. Can the larger skill be broken down into subskills that can be taught as short-term instructional objectives?
6. Is the skill useful and functional? Will it increase a student's independence in normal environments?
7. Does the goal/objective fit into the student's overall education program?
8. Was the goal/objective selected only after careful analysis of the student's immediate critical function needs within multiple, normalized environments, taking into consideration modifying characteristics that might be needed (e.g., environment modifications or prosthetic equipment)?

Mobility and travel skills about the school campus might be a potential goal selected from an ecological inventory. Rather than teach such travel skills by assisting (or "herding") students in a large group, a teacher might choose the more natural, relevant and age appropriate objective of having the student walk independently to lunch. Guess, Horner, Utley, Holvoet, Maxon, Tucker, and Warren (1978) presented a curriculum sequencing model for severely handicapped students which emphasizes functional and age appropriate skills while also considering the topographical similarity of skills. Holvoet, Guess, Mulligan, and Brown (1980) further detailed their Individualized Curriculum Sequencing Model (ICS) and related the model to assessment and functional goal/objective selection. This deals more with classroom programming and curriculum in general and is beyond the scope of this chapter. The emphasis, however, is that the results of an ecological inventory yield a rich supply of curriculum and instruction data that teachers can readily use for IEP planning and daily instruction.

Even with these guidelines, however, questions remain as to the validity of the goal/objective selection process. Voeltz and Evans (1983) have noted the following concerns:

1. Selecting goals because they appear to be functional now does not guarantee they will be functional in the future;
2. Selecting goals because they are functional in California does not guarantee they will be functional in Illinois;
3. We do not know if it would help to teach the functional goals in any particular order;

4. Teachers, parents, employers, etc. may not even agree which skills are functional; and
5. Education for severely handicapped learners could be restricted to teaching minimum levels of competence and deviance reduction (i.e., teaching easiest forms and leaving it at that; teaching students how to use a toilet or eat at McDonald's, but not how to work, play, and make friends; teaching what the environment wants with little regard for what the person wants (p. 10).

Obviously, even with a more functional process for selecting goals and objectives questions remain. However, teachers cannot afford the luxury of waiting for yet another decade before instituting assessment procedures and instruments that yield useful data. To date, the ecological inventory has proven to be the best available classroom assessment tool for teachers of moderately and severely handicapped students.

Conclusion

A shift in curriculum emphasis to community based, practical life skills programs has required a change in assessment and goal selection procedures currently used with moderately and severely handicapped individuals. Current literature and practice suggests the use of a localized ecological inventory to fulfill that need. Understandably, some teachers may find that task overwhelming. However, the authors have presented a model to assist with the selection of goals and objectives and to help teachers develop their own inventories. Ecological inventories will help teachers and parents consider functional, age appropriate IEP goals and objectives that will allow a student to participate as fully as possible in current and future living styles and settings.*

REFERENCES

Bayley, N. *Bayley scales of infant development.* Atlanta: The Psychological Corporation, 1969.
Behavioral characteristics progression. Palo Alto, CA: Vort Corp., 1973.
Brady, M. P. A curriculum and instruction synthesis model for teachers of the severely handicapped. *The Exceptional Child,* 1984, *31*(1), 19–32.
Brigance, A. *Brigance diagnostic inventory of early development.* North Billerica, MA: Curriculum Associates, 1978.

*The writers wish to acknowledge Dr. Mary Jo Noonan (Department of Special Education, University of Hawaii at Manoa), Mr. William C. Mertes (Ruby Van Meter School, Des Moines, Iowa), and our colleagues and loved ones for their input and support throughout this project. Also, our warmest mahalo to the people throughout the country who have challenged and guided us toward better serving handicapped students in our schools.

Brown, L., Branston-McClean, M., Baumgart, D., Vincent, L., Falvey, M., & Schroeder, J. Using the characteristics of current and subsequent least restrictive environments in the development of content for severely handicapped students. *AAESPH Review.* 1979, *4,* 407–424.

Brown, L., Nietupski, J., & Hamre-Nietupski, S. The criterion of ultimate functioning and public school services for severely handicapped children. In M. A. Thomas (Ed.). *Hey, don't forget about me!* Reston, VA: Council for Exceptional Children, 1976, 2–15.

Christoph, D., Nietupski, J., & Pumpian, I. Teaching severely handicapped adolescents and young adults to use communication cards to make purchases at a fast food counter. In L. Brown, M. Falvey, D. Baumgart, I. Pumpian, J. Schroeder, & L. Gruenewald (Eds.), *Strategies for teaching chronological age appropriate functional skills to adolescent and young adult severely handicapped students.* Vol. IX, Part I. Madison, WI: Madison Metropolitan School District, 1979.

Freagon, S., & Rotatori, A. F. Comparing natural and artificial environments in training self-care skills to group home residents. *Journal of the Association of the Severely Handicapped.* 1982, *7,* 73–86.

Freagon, S., Pajon, M. Brankin, G., Galloway, A., Rich, D., Karel, P., Wilson, M., Costello, D., Peters, W. M., & Hurd, D. *Teaching severely handicapped children in the community: Processes and procedures.* DeKalb, IL: Northern Illinois University, 1981.

Guess, D. Horner, R. D., Utley, B., Holvoet, J., Maxon, D., Tucker, D., & Warren, S. A functional curriculum sequencing model for teaching the severely handicapped. *AAESPH Review.* 1978, *3,* 202–215.

Holvoet, J., Guess, D., Mulligan, M., & Brown, F. The individualized curriculum sequencing model (II): A teaching strategy for severely handicapped students. *Journal of the Association for the Severely Handicapped.* 1980. *5*(4), 337–351.

Neel, R., Billingsley, F., McCarthy, F., Symonds, D., Lambert, C., Lewis-Smith, N., & Hanashiro. R. *Teaching autistic children: A functional curriculum approach.* Project IMPACT. Seattle: University of Washington College of Education, 1983.

Page, T., Iwata, B., & Neef, N. Teaching pedestrian skills to retarded persons: Generalization from the classroom to the natural environment. *Journal of Applied Behavior Analysis.* 1976. *9,* 433–444.

Sailor, W., & Guess, D. *Severely handicapped students: An instructional design.* Boston: Houghton Mifflin, 1983.

Voeltz, L. M., & Evans, I. M. Educational validity: Procedures to evaluate outcomes in programs for severely handicapped learners. *Journal of the Association for the Severely Handicapped.* 1983, *8,* 3–15.

White, O. R. Adaptive performance objectives: Form versus function. In W. Sailor, B. Wilcox, & L. Brown (Eds.), *Methods of instruction for severely handicapped students.* Baltimore: Paul H. Brookes, 1980. (a)

White, O. R. Child assessment. In B. Wilcox & R. York (Eds.), *Quality education for the severely handicapped.* Washington, DC: U.S. Department of Education. Office of Special Education. 1980. (b)

White, O. R., Haring, N. G., Edgar, E., & Bendersky, J. *Uniform performance assessment systems (UPAS).* Seattle: College of Education, Experimental Education Unit, Child Development and Mental Retardation Center, University of Washington, 1978.

Wilcox, B., & Bellamy, G. T. *Design of high school programs for severely handicapped students.* Baltimore: Paul H. Brookes, 1982.

CHAPTER 9*

A CURRICULUM BASED APPROACH TO DECISION MAKING AND DATA COLLECTION FOR COMMUNITY BASED PROGRAMS

CHARLES L. SALZBERG AND BENJAMIN LIGNUGARIS/KRAFT
UTAH STATE UNIVERSITY

Don't collect data! There seems to be a proliferation of data collection these days. Every time you turn around, someone is recording some bit of information; what you wear, what car you drive, how much schooling you've had, what you think about this topic or that. Professional program developers have made great strides in systematizing processes for habilitating mentally retarded people in vocational areas (Bellamy, Horner, & Inman, 1979; Connis, Sowers, & Thompson, 1981; Wehman, 1981; Wehman, Renzaglia, & Schutz, 1977), residential areas (Schalock, Harper, & Carver, 1981; Skarnulis, 1976), and in community programming (Wuerch & Voeltz, 1982). We have all been urged to keep more and more information about what we do and about the people with whom we do it. Laws, regulations, and funding agencies require a myriad of overlapping data for accountability. At times we are literally awash in required paperwork. The total effect can be an aversion to data, data collection, to the people who advocate it, and to the laws that require it.

Is all this data collection really necessary? Is it helpful? Are there ways to simplify the process and reduce the burden? Perhaps! But first, let's consider some of the reasons why collecting data is so often an irritant. For one thing, we often find ourselves recording information that has no obvious

Charles L. Salzberg is an Associate Professor of Special Education at Utah State University. He received his doctorate from the University of Kansas in 1972. Since then, his focus has been on education and community integration of handicapped children and adults and on teacher training. His research has encompassed basic learning skills of severely and profoundly handicapped individuals, parent-mediated training programs, the use of peers and siblings as teachers, and the development of social-competence in behavior disordered youth. His current activities include research on vocational training and placement and the development of personnel preparation programs for vocational special educators.

Benjamin Lignugaris/Kraft is a doctoral candidate in Special Education at Utah State University. He has been a teacher of handicapped youth, has designed community based career education programs, and has published research and curricula on community based habilitation for mentally retarded people. He is currently conducting research in the areas of vocational and social-vocational training of mentally retarded people and personnel preparation of special education teachers.

purpose. It may satisfy a need that some other person or agency has but, if so, we have no idea what it is used for. In many cases, it simply clutters files. Also, we seem to collect overlapping sets of data for different agencies because the procedures, reporting forms, and time intervals are unrelated to one another. The effect is that similar information ends up being taken in three different ways, at three different times, and at three times the effort and cost. If things were coordinated, one set of data would suffice. Perhaps the most frustrating aspect of data collection is that sometimes the tail seems to be wagging the dog. That is, data requirements may begin to dictate programming strategies rather than programming decisions determining data requirements. For example, rehabilitation facilities in one state required client data in a particular format that forced programs to divide skills into smaller units than usual. Those units often impaired the teaching process because they were inappropriately small for the clients who were undergoing training. That problem can occur in schools, in residential programs, and in vocational programs.

Comprehensive data-based decision strategies and curriculum design for use in schools with moderately and severely handicapped students have been described elsewhere (Fredericks, Baldwin, Moore, Templeman, Grove, Moore, Gage, Blair, Alrick, Wadlow, Fruin, Bunse, Makohon, Samples, Moses, Rogers, & Toews, 1975; Haring, Liberty, & White, 1980; Wehman, 1979). The purpose of this chapter is to address decision making and data collection for community based programs such as residential living programs, vocational habilitation and training programs, leisure and recreation programs, and community survival programs.

Principles for Data Collection

Numerous factors that make data collection irritating have led us to suggest several principles that might be useful in designing data collection systems for community agencies.

Data Are for Decision Making

Collect data that you can use! Sometimes data provide a basis for a decision about program *placement* for an individual. Sometimes it is needed to identify the *skills* that are important to teach. Continuous data may be used to assess the effects of a teaching process. Data collection is also necessary to evaluate the general quality or scope of a service agency or program. In any case, data are for decision making. The question of what data to collect begins with identification of the decisions that will have to be made and, subsequently, the kinds of information that would be most useful in making those decisions.

Simpler Is Better

In all cases, the most direct means of recording information is preferred. This is not to imply that one should shy away from complex problems. However, complexity is no virtue in the process of decision making. In the context of measurement, increased complexity implies increased expenditures of time and resources.

One MultiPurpose Data System Is Better Than Many Single Purpose Data Sets

To the maximum extent possible, each data system should be designed to meet as many of an agency's or a teacher's information requirements as possible. Even in cases in which different reporting formats are required, it may be possible for one data system to provide all of the needed information; the information can then be easily converted to the required formats.

Data Collection Systems Should Be Fitted To, Not Determinants Of, Programming Strategies

Data systems should not dictate programming strategies. Programming strategies should be designed to meet client needs in light of individual abilities, staffing patterns, and available facilities.

Each residential living program, vocational habilitation and training program, and leisure and recreation program is different in size and structure. Moreover, each type of program has its own mission, operating procedures, staffing patterns, and decision making requirements. There are large differences even within one type of vocational or residential program. Therefore, no one system will be optimal for the entire gamut of available programs.

This chapter will present an approach to decision making for community based programs that is broadly applicable. For purposes of clarity, the approach will be illustrated with two examples: one drawn from the area of residential living; the other from community affairs. Space limitations preclude presentation of comprehensive examples for each type of program. Even if that were possible, it is unlikely that any community agency could directly copy a data system and expect that system to perfectly fit its needs. In fact, it is our belief that every program needs a data system tailored to its own specific decision making requirements. For that reason, the two examples of habilitation programs presented in this chapter are accompanied by a detailed narrative recounting the logic that guided their development. An understanding of that logic will allow readers to replicate the approach and tailor it to their own needs.

From Mission To Decision To Data

One should not set out initially to collect data. In fact. designing data collection procedures comes last. The beginning point is defining the mission that guides the actions of an agency or the development of a treatment plan for an individual (see Anderson's chapter in this text). Next comes the process of determining the goals that relate to each mission. Goals subsequently are reduced to subgoals and those to objectives. Activities to accomplish goals provide the impetus for making decisions. Decisions can be only as astute as the information upon which they are based. Hence the need for data.

In the examples in Tables 1 and 2, questions about data collection focus on data useful for making decisions about client training goals. Training goals are derived logically and, to some extent, empirically from the primary mission for agencies and individual clients. Data collection is, then, the last step in a purposeful approach to human service delivery.

TABLE 9-1
AN EXAMPLE OF AN AGENCY DECISION

The general mission of the Kraft Habilitation Center (pseudonym) is to provide broad ranging habilitation programs for mentally retarded adults between the ages of 21 and 65. One agency goal derived from that mission is to develop a continuum of community residential programs that lead toward independent living. That goal, in turn, raises the need to make a variety of decisions about the number. configuration. and credentials for staff in each of the programs. Another decision to be made is the number of clients that each program should be designed to accommodate. A third set of decisions relates to staff training. career advancement. and morale. Useful data for making these decisions might include: the number of clients currently in the agency's programs; the skill levels of clients: the size of the waiting lists for each program: the movement of clients across the continuum of residential programs: and employee satisfaction and turnover.

A Curriculum Based Decision Making System

The figures in this chapter reflect decisions about individual client programs rather than administrative problems. Each figure relates individual client program decisions to a comprehensive habilitation curriculum. A curriculum based data system can accommodate a variety of functions. First, it enables the development of individually tailored habilitation plans. Second, it provides data for program decisions at all levels, i.e., it can meet Individual Habilitation Plan (IHP) demands as well as provide information for the variety of reports that are required of habilitation service agencies. Third.

TABLE 9-2
AN EXAMPLE OF AN HABILITATION PROGRAM DECISION

The primary mission of the habilitation program for Ms. Susan Post (a mentally retarded adult in a habilitation facility), is to increase her ability to function independently in the community. One goal derived from that mission is competitive employment. A subgoal for Ms. Post is to learn the necessary skills for travel to and from work. There are numerous decisions to be made in regard to this subgoal. What specific skills are most important to teach to Ms. Post? How should each skill be taught? What staff, materials, and time will be needed to teach these skills? How long will it take? Different kinds of data are applicable to these questions: the types of transportation available to Ms. Post; the skills that are needed to use community transportation; the skills that Ms. Post already possesses. Once training is under way, data about Ms. Post's rate of learning will be needed to predict her future program needs and to adjust training to make it maximally effective.

this system provides straightforward information in a simple manner to facilitate client and guardian involvement in program planning and review. Finally, it should ease the paperwork burden by providing a relatively efficient means of collecting data and by collecting only data that are needed.

Building Blocks for Program Decisions

Figure 1 illustrates the structure of a curriculum based decision making process for a community habilitation program. In this illustration, program planning begins at the top with the general habilitation mission of helping the client function more independently. It becomes progressively more specific as it proceeds downward through each successive block of the decision making hierarchy. In planning and executing a training program, one may reach down to whatever level of specificity is required by a particular client. Similarly, data may be collected on any combination of hierarchical levels that will best meet staff, client, and agency needs.

Block 1: Choice of domains. The mission of many community service agencies is to help their clients become more independent in the community. This begins by determining how adequately the client presently functions in each major area of community life. These areas, referred to as domains, are illustrated in Table 3. The clients' habilitation goals require progressively greater self-sufficiency at home, at work, and in the community. In addition, there are skills, referred to in Table 3 as generically applicable skills, that are fundamental to the development of independence in all three domains. The first set of decisions in developing a client's program is whether a priority should be given to one or two domains or whether the client's program should attend equally to all of them. The factors most likely to affect this decision are imminent placements that require a specific set of skills or the existence of skill deficits that are viewed as especially debilitat-

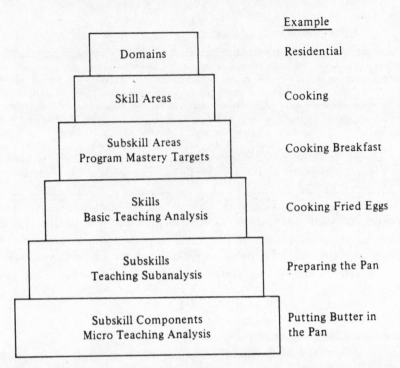

Figure 9-1. The structural components for a curriculum based data system for a community habilitation program.

ing by staff in the client's residential and vocational programs. For example, the staff might consider the inability to follow simple instructions as a serious impediment to placement in any community training program.

Block 2: Selecting skill areas. The next level of decision making is selecting high priority skill areas within each domain. Sample skill areas within each domain are illustrated in Table 3 and, in more detail, in Table 4. For example, in the community affairs domain, skill areas include grocery shopping, eating out, banking skills, and community entertainment. This list of skill areas must be developed by each service agency and tailored to its own needs and to available community resources. The skill areas that are targeted for training should be directed toward a criteria of increased client self-sufficiency or toward meeting an immediate client need.

Block 3: Subskill area. The skill area level is the base for developing individual program plans. Further delineation of skill areas into subskill areas is usually necessary to provide manageable, realistic goals from which to design programming. For example, banking may be a targeted client skill area (see Table 4). Its potential subskill areas include: (a) depositing money, (b) withdrawing money, and (c) writing checks. Each subskill is a complete repertoire. It can stand by itself. For that reason, mastery at the level of

TABLE 9-3
LIST OF DOMAINS AND SKILL AREAS
(Partial List Intended as an Illustration)

Residential Living	Vocational	Community Affairs
Household care	Getting along with	Grocery shopping
Care of clothes	supervisor	RESTAURANT USE
Yard care	Getting along with	Banking
Food shopping	Co-workers	Attending spectator
COOKING	Carrying out work	sports events
Leisure at home	instructions	Community recreation
Bill paying	Reliable attendance	(e.g., bowling,
Responding to emergencies	Steady on-task behavior	swimming, YMCA)
	Punctuality	Community entertainment
	Groups of vocational	(e.g., movies, theater,
	tasks (e.g., hand	night clubs)
	tools, assembly,	Clothes shopping
	custodial, etc.)	

Generically Applicable Skills

Money handling
Instruction following
Basic expressive and receptive language
Basic self-care (e.g., eating, bathing, toileting)
Conversation skills
Community mobility
Survival reading

subskill areas is often a good unit to use as a primary measure of client progress.

Block 4: Skills. Subskill areas are generally complex, multiple-component repertoires. To teach a subskill area (e.g., withdrawing money from a bank), it must often be analyzed into smaller units (e.g., completing the withdrawal form, teller interaction skills, and completing the transaction). In many cases, teaching units at this level will be small enough for many individuals to progress at a satisfactory pace. Data at the skill level of analysis are helpful for making decisions about a client's specific training needs and for making decisions concerning client progress. If data collected at the skill level indicate that a client is not progressing satisfactorily skills have to be further divided into subskills.

Block 5: Subskills. In the subskill analysis, the trainer identifies the behaviors that make up a skill. For example, completing a bank withdrawal form includes writing the correct date, entering the amount of money desired, and signing the withdrawal form. Data at the subskill level focuses on the precise components that must be performed to master skills. Thus, data at this level are useful when making teaching decisions about skills that the client is having difficulty mastering. For example, gains in client

TABLE 9-4
GROUP MASTERY CHECKLIST

	John	George	Susan
COMMUNITY AFFAIRS			
Restaurant			
Fast food	_____	_____	_____
Cafeteria	_____	_____	_____
Sit down	_____	_____	_____
Grocery Shopping			
Dairy products	_____	_____	_____
Fruits and vegetables	_____	_____	_____
Meat, fish and poultry	_____	_____	_____
Banking			
Depositing money	_____	_____	_____
Withdrawing money	_____	_____	_____
Writing checks	_____	_____	_____
Community Entertainment			
Active recreation	_____	_____	_____
Spectator sports	_____	_____	_____
Theatre—Night clubs	_____	_____	_____
RESIDENTIAL SKILLS			
Cooking			
Breakfast	_____	_____	_____
Lunch	_____	_____	_____
Dinner	_____	_____	_____
Household Care			
Kitchen Care	_____	_____	_____
Living room/Den care	_____	_____	_____
Bedroom care	_____	_____	_____
Yard Care			
Care of lawn	_____	_____	_____
Trees and shrubs	_____	_____	_____
Care of sidewalks	_____	_____	_____
Bill Paying			
Rent	_____	_____	_____
Utilities	_____	_____	_____
Other periodic	_____	_____	_____

Checks skills that have been targeted. When a skill has been mastered, write the date.

progress are more likely to be seen in data on entering the correct date on a bank withdrawal form than on mastering the whole skill of withdrawing money. Measurement units at the skill level (e.g., withdrawing money) might be too large to be a sensitive indicator of progress for some clients. In most cases, the subskill level of analysis will be sufficiently specific to serve as teaching units to monitor client progress. However, programming with more severely handicapped clients often requires a microteaching analysis in which subskills have to be even further subdivided. That process is the same as that described for dividing skills into subskills. As a general guideline, each level of measurement should not be divided into more than about six constituent parts. Beyond that, it is usually more efficient to shift to a more specific level of analysis and thus, a more sensitive measure of client behavior. For example, the subskill area of banking should not be divided into more than six skills. If those teaching units are too large for a particular client as indicated by a lack of measurable progress in weekly data analysis, training, and progress monitoring should shift to the next level of specificity, in this case, the subskill level (see Haring et al., 1980 for a detailed presentation of decision rules). Using this approach, teaching and data collection units are constantly adjusted to remain optimally sized for each client.

A Case Study

In order to illustrate specifically how an IHP and an associated data system are developed, a case study is presented below. The name and places have been changed to protect the confidentiality of the individuals involved.

John Young is a 22-year-old man who is moderately mentally retarded, living in a small group home in Salt Lake City. He gets along well with his five roommates and is well liked by the group home staff. John is usually eager to please others and with systematic instruction, he acquires skills readily. John works at a local sheltered workshop assembling exercise equipment. His production rate at the workshop has been increasing steadily. As a result, the workshop personnel have become eager to place John in competitive employment. The group home staff are faced with a number of decisions in updating John's habilitation plan. They begin the decision making process by considering which *domains* most urgently need to be considered. John's upcoming placement into competitive employment is the most striking change in his living circumstances. The staff certainly want John to have every chance at success in his new job placement since working successfully in competitive employment would be a major step forward in his life. In light of that, the group home staff took the time to visit John's future work site. They met some of John's future coworkers and followed them through the day. They came to several realizations. First, John would be out on his own more often. He would have substantially more spending money to use at his own discretion. Most important, the staff found that most of John's co-workers eat lunch at neighborhood restaurants in the downtown area near where they work. John would need to join his co-workers at lunch, and therefore he must learn how to eat at a restaurant (*skill area*). Next, the staff considered the various kinds of restaurants. There are fast food restaurants, cafeterias, and restaurants with table service in the downtown area. It turned out that there were many fast food restaurants near John's intended job site and that was where John's co-workers usually ate. For that reason, they decided to concentrate their efforts with John on eating at fast food restaurants (*subskill area*). Third, the staff had to analyze the skill of eating in a fast food restaurant. The process of analyzing skills into their constituent parts, referred to as task analysis, has been explained in a variety of texts (Bellamy et al., 1979; Gold, 1976; Thiagarajan, Semmel, & Semmel, 1974) and will not be discussed here. However, it should be noted that there are, inevitably, many ways to divide tasks into their constituent parts and that no particular analysis is best for all purposes. In this case, the group home staff divided eating at a fast food restaurant into five *skills:* (a) entering the restaurant, (b) ordering the food, (c) eating the food, (d) asking necessary questions of restaurant employees, and (e) handling money. Armed with this analysis, the group home staff took John to several fast food restaurants where they led him through the process of getting food so that they could find out which of the five skills John already knew and which he did not. They used a simple recording form, illustrated in Table 5 on which they noted John's performance. The group home staff merely recorded a "y" (yes) and the date in the appropriate assessment block when John performed a skill correctly. If John performed a skill incorrectly, the group home staff helped him through it and recorded an "n" (no) and the date in the assessment block. Thus, in Table 5, one can see that John has difficulty ordering food, asking for water from the waitress, and paying for the meal. The group home staff realized that each of the skills that John needed to learn was itself composed of several parts. The problem they faced was how to most rapidly prepare John to eat with his co-workers without calling unflattering attention to himself. John immediately needed a minimally functional way to get through the meal, not a complete or polished set of dining subskills. For example, money handling covers a broad range of skills. Some money handling skills are highly complex and difficult to learn even for non-handicapped people. However, John did not need complex money handling skills to be self-sufficient in a fast food restaurant. He only needed to be taught how to present a five dollar bill and wait for change. If that would get John by for the moment, he could later be taught how to count dollar bills and change. The point is that the group home staff had to divide skills into *subskills* with an eye toward the most efficient way to prepare John to function credibly in a new, more advanced situation. Further, it is important to note that the primary teaching analysis for John was at the subskill level. The data system, therefore, also tracked John's progress at the subskill level (see Table 6). When John had learned all the subskills for money handling in the fast food restaurant, money handling was checked off as mastered. When John had learned all the skills necessary to conduct himself appropriately in fast food restaurants, then mastery of eating out at a fast food restaurant was checked off on the Group Mastery Checklist (see Table 4).

TABLE 9-5

INDIVIDUAL TARGET SKILL SPECIFICATION AND RECORD SHEET

Client: __John Young__   Domain: Community Affairs

Staff: __Sarah Rule__   Skill Area: Restaurant

                                            Subskill Area: Fast Food

Skill Specification	Assessments							
	Date	*Y/N*	*Date*	*Y/N*	*Date*	*Y/N*	*Date*	*Y/N*
1. Entering								
2. *Ordering								
3. Table Skills								
4. *Make Inquiries								
5. *Money Handling								

Instructions:

Record the data that the skills are reviewed next to each item. Enter a Y (yes) if a skill is performed correctly and a N (no) if the skill is performed incorrectly, in the box next to the date.

When a skill has been performed correctly on three consecutive occasions, check it off on the Individual Mastery Checklist for Restaurant Skills and the Group Mastery Checklist for Community Affairs.

In their redesign of John's habilitation program, the group home staff also considered his situation in the group home (*residential domain*). They could see that John was steadily developing skills that would allow him to become more self-sufficient. If they planned carefully, it seemed possible that John could move from a group home to a semi-sheltered apartment. Moreover, they realized that when John moved to his new job, his schedule would no longer be aligned with other group home residents who were still in the sheltered workshop. John would have to get up and get going earlier in the morning than the other residents. John likes to eat a big breakfast which, thus far, had always been prepared by one of the group home staff. However, that would not be possible when he started his new job. For those reasons, learning to cook (*skill area*) and, especially, learning to cook breakfast (*subskill area*) became an important part of John's new habilitation program. After developing the Individual Master Checklist for Cooking Skills (see Table 7), the group home staff realized that many different foods could go into a breakfast. It would take a long time for John to learn to prepare all items. For the moment, they decided to teach John to cook a breakfast composed of the foods that he liked the most and that would provide good nutrition. Thus, the staff decided to teach John to prepare

TABLE 9-6

SEQUENTIAL TASK ANALYSIS AND TRAINING DATA SHEET

Client: _____

Staff: _____

Domain: Community Affairs
Area: Restaurant Use
Subskill Area: Fast Foods
Skill: Money Handling

Money Handling for Fast Food Restaurants

	Probes						
	Date	Y/N	Date	Y/N	Date	Y/N	Date	Y/N

1. When cashier requests payment, take a $5 bill from wallet or purse and hand it to cashier.

2. Wait until cashier hands back change.

3. Receive change and:
   (a) if cashier says nothing, say "thank you," or
   (b) if cashier says "thank you," say "you're welcome."

4. Put change away and wait for food.

Enter a Y or N in the box next to each item when the client does that step correctly without help. Record the date of each training session on the top of the column. When the client has correctly handled money in a fast food restaurant three times in a row, discontinue recording data on this level.

juice, coffee, toast, fried eggs (over well because that's the way John liked them), and bacon. In order to find out what John already knew, they watched while John tried to prepare each of these goods. They found that John knew how to make coffee, juice, and toast. The staff hoped that John could readily learn to cook fried eggs and bacon but they realized that, if learning to cook fried eggs and bacon proved to be too difficult, easier foods such as cold or hot cereal could be substituted. The group home staff initially set out to teach John to cook fried eggs in one step. They ran John through the entire process of cooking fried eggs several times. Data collected at the target skill level suggested that John was not making very much progress. Therefore, the group home staff decided to divide the skill of preparing fried eggs into small (*subskill*) units. That task analysis is presented in Table 8. An analysis revealed that John's problems were breaking eggs in the skillet and transferring the eggs from the skillet to the plate after they were cooked. Intensive practice on these two subskills brought John rapidly to the point where he could successfully cook his own fried eggs every morning. After that, John's data reflected mastery of all subskills on the task analysis, success in cooking fried eggs and cooking bacon (see Table 7) and a check mark on the Group Checklist (Table 4) for cooking breakfast. Subsequently, the group home staff continued to periodically monitor John's ability to cook breakfast to make sure that he retained that skill.

TABLE 9-7
INDIVIDUAL MASTER CHECKLIST FOR COOKING SKILLS
(Partial list intended as an illustration)

Breakfast		Lunch		Dinner	
•Toast	8/ 3/83	Cold meat sandwich	_____	Tossed salad	_____
•Juice	8/ 2/83	Soups from can	_____	Fruit salad	_____
Cold cereal	_____	Soups from dry pkg.	_____	Fresh vegetable	_____
Hot cereal	_____	Canned meat	_____	Canned vegetable	_____
•Fried eggs	8/22/83	Fresh fruit	_____	Broiled chops	_____
Scrambled eggs	_____	Yogurt	_____	Broiled fish	_____
Boiled eggs	_____	Cottage cheese	_____	Hamburger	_____
•Bacon	8/22/83	Tuna fish sandwich	_____	Roast chicken	_____
Sausage	_____	Cheese sandwich	_____	Baked ham	_____
•Coffee	8/ 2/83	Grilled cheese sandwich	_____	Baked chicken	_____
Tea	_____	Bacon, lettuce & tomato sandwich	_____	Baked potatoes	_____
Pancakes	_____	Iced Tea	_____	Baked potatoes	_____
French Toast	_____			Pan fry steak	_____

TABLE 9-8
TASK ANALYSIS FOR COOKING FRIED EGGS

1. Prepare to cook (get eggs, prepare skillet, burner on)

2. Put eggs in skillet (crack eggs into skillet, discard shells)

3. Cook eggs (unstick eggs with spatula, adjust burner)

4. Transfer eggs to plate (unstick eggs and slide them onto plate), turn off the burner

5. Clean up (clear table, wash, dry, put dishes away)

Now that John had learned to eat at a fast food restaurant and had learned to cook his own breakfast, the group home staff needed to repeat the process of redesigning John's habilitation program. The same procedures for decision making, skill analysis, and data collection would be reapplied to direct John toward self-sufficiency in yet another way.

Instruction and Data Collection

The curriculum based approach to data collection for community programs is based on the operating principles presented earlier. This section will expand the discussion of those principles and point out some of their more important implications for collecting data. It should be noted that data collection is related to the instruction process. One collects data on client mastery of the skills that one is trying to teach. Thus, the measures directly reflect the effectiveness and scope of the instructional processes. The measurement units, like the teaching units, can range from broad skill areas to very specific subskills. The advantage in this approach is that testing and teaching are mutually supportive. Moreover, if the selection of teaching targets is directed by an habilitation curriculum, then the data will reflect meaningful progress toward independent functioning in community life.

Data Should Reflect Independent Performance in the Natural Environment

Although data collection is linked closely to teaching procedures, it need not be identical with it. For example, in teaching a client such as John to cook fried eggs, the group home staff will often assist him in performing the necessary steps. Thus, the group home staff might remind the client, "Now it's time to break the egg" or they might even take his hand and help him crack the egg into the frying pan. It is important for the data collection process that assisted performance not be mistaken for independent performance. The purpose of the data is to indicate when the client has mastered a particular skill or subskill. A "yes" will be meaningful only if it consistently reflects independent performance. Thus, on the data collection sheet, in those instances in which staff helped the client. an "n" should be recorded. A "y" should be reserved for occasions in which the client does it correctly without reminders or other kinds of help. Similarly, the data system should reflect client performance of a skill in the situation where that skill is ultimately needed rather than in a teaching situation, if the two are different. For example, to teach a client to eat at a fast food restaurant, it might be helpful to simulate some of the restaurant procedures in the group home first. Thus, a copy of a menu could be put on the wall in the group home and the client could be taught how to place a food order before actually being taken to the fast food restaurant. However, client performance in this simulated condition should not be equated with performance in the fast food restaurant. It may turn out that the client, after simulation training, can order food at the restaurant without further training. However, it is likely that some additional training will be necessary. In any case, a "yes" on the fast food data sheet should be recorded only when the client performs the behavior in the natural environment.

Time Savers

There are potential time saving techniques in data collection processes that result from manipulating the relationship between teaching and data collection. First, not all teaching sessions have to result in data collection. In fact, teaching may occur far more frequently and more intensively than the level of data needed. Thus, when John was learning to cook breakfast, teaching sessions may have occurred every day. Moreover, at one point, teaching was conducted at relatively microscopic levels to help John learn how to crack an egg. *It was not necessary for the staff to collect data in all those teaching sessions or to collect data at that microscopic level.* In fact, the staff recorded information on John's breakfast cooking skills only twice each week. That was sufficient to assess John's progress. This sampling procedure reduced time and effort while retaining enough information to make the decisions that were required.

Second, the teaching process should use the largest teaching units to which a client can successfully respond. Thus, John learned to make toast by being shown the entire process at one time (*skill level*). There was no need to divide that skill into subskills. Consequently, the staff did not. On the other hand, learning to fry eggs was considerably more difficult for John. In that case, they had to divide frying eggs into its constituent subskills and, in the case of cracking the egg, they even had to divide a subskill into its constituents. Often this fine grained analysis may become necessary. However, resisting the temptation to analyze skills into smaller units than is necessary can save time and prevent boredom.

Third, the process of recording information in this data based approach is very easy. It requires only a check mark or a "yes" or "no" in a prescribed place on a list of skills or subskills. Because it is so simple, many clients can learn to do the recording with a little supervision from the staff. To the extent that clients can record their own progress, staff are relieved of that burden. Moreover, the process has educational benefits in that it increases clients' awareness of their skill growth and of the purpose of the staff's teaching efforts. As they become accustomed to this process, clients become progressively more involved in planning their own programs and monitoring their own habilitation gains. The process of client self-recording also provides a natural, frequent opportunity for informal counseling by the staff.

Last, this data based approach is inherently compatible with computer technology. The entire habilitation curriculum can be stored on a micro-computer. Subsequently, the procedures for developing client program plans and monitoring client progress can be computer based. A more detailed discussion of the use of microcomputers in special education and teachers' attitudes toward them is available in Brady and Langford (in press), Hofmeister (1983), and Stowitschek and Stowitschek (1984). To the extent that this system is mated with microcomputer technology, the efficiency of the planning process, the data collection process, and the analysis and summary process will be significantly enhanced.

Summary and Conclusions

In this chapter, a curriculum based approach to data systems for habilitation programs has been presented. A central theme has been that data should not be burdensome. Rather, the data should help staff be more effective decision makers. Data collection procedures should not dictate the kinds of questions asked. The data should provide the information needed to answer questions that are posed by client training needs and agency concerns.

One key to escaping the "data burden" is to begin program analyses at a general level and move toward progressively smaller units. In the system presented, analysis begins with broadly defined domains and moves toward highly specific subskills. In this way, training targets become focused and skills mastered at lower levels cumulate toward functional habilitation goals and community independence. If program planning started at a microscopic level or was based exclusively on a general assessment instrument such as the Adaptive Behavior Scale (Nihra, Foster, Shellhas, & Leland, 1974), skill targets would not necessarily sum to functional skills (see Mattison & Rosenberg's chapter in this text).

Community agencies need not start from scratch in developing habilitation curricula upon which to build teaching and data collection units. Most curriculum analysis work has already been accomplished (e.g., Wehman, 1979). There are comprehensive training programs for a variety of skill areas such as cooking (Taylor, Carlson, Close, & Larrabee, 1981), banking and budgeting (Carlson, Taylor, Lignugaris/Kraft, Close, & Larrabee, 1981), community social skills (Lignugaris/Kraft & Close, 1981), and household management (Close, Taylor, Carlson, & Larrabee, 1981). The challenge is to use the available material to develop a data system that provides the information needed for decision making.

Another advantage of a curriculum based data system is that it may strengthen the habilitation focus of an agency's staff. IHPs may become more functional when targeted skills are expressed in pragmatic, clear terms (e.g., cooking breakfast). Staff may also gain encouragement to focus on pro-social repertoires rather than being exclusively occupied with decreasing maladaptive behaviors.

Data systems that are simple and direct are more likely to be used by administrators, staff, and parents. In the system presented, data collection merely requires skill checks once or twice a week. These may be accomplished by skilled trainers or relatively untrained parents or group home staff. If checklists are posted on a wall, supervisors and administrators can stay abreast of client progress by looking at the data board as they pass by on their way to their offices.

A simple data system may also be useful in building client self-direction. A self-monitoring program can begin with the Group Mastery Checklist. As clients' skills develop, they may learn to track their own progress in greater detail and to take an increasing role in selecting their own training targets.

This chapter has provided a model for integrating curriculum and data collection. It has assumed knowledge of essential teaching skills. A data system can help staff see the effects of their teaching efforts, but it will not necessarily direct them to the most effective teaching practices. A lack of client progress may reflect poorly chosen objectives or inadequate curriculum units. Lack of client progress is often symptomatic of inappropriate teaching procedures. Consequently, people with instructional expertise must be available to service agency staff to get the maximum benefit from a curriculum based program planning and data collection system (see Brady's chapter in this text).

This chapter began with the admonition, *"Don't collect data!"* That admonition has since been qualified. *Only collect data that will be used to make decisions.* Collect data in units small enough to reflect client progress but no smaller than necessary to make decisions about the instructional process. Whenever possible, teach clients to monitor their own progress and use that process to help them learn how to take a more active part in determining their own future. Finally, don't let data collection become the master of the habilitation process. Rather, let client mastery data be the servant of effective programming toward independent community functioning.

REFERENCES

Bellamy, G. T., Horner, R. H., & Inman, D. P. *Vocational habilitation of severely retarded adults: A direct service technology.* Baltimore: University Park Press, 1979.

Brady, M. P., & Langford, C. Microcomputer technology in special education: Teacher uses and concerns. *Contemporary Education,* in press.

Carlson, C., Taylor, V., Lignugaris/Kraft, B., Close, D., & Larrabee, D. *Budgeting and bill paying.* Eugene, OR: Rehabilitation Research and Training Center, 1981.

Close, D., Taylor, V., Carlson, C., & Larrabee, D. *Household management and home safety.* Eugene, OR: Rehabilitation Research and Training Center, 1981.

Connis, R. T., Sowers, J., & Thompson, L. E. *Training the mentally handicapped for employment: A comprehensive manual.* New York: Human Sciences Press, 1981.

Fredericks, H. P., Baldwin, V. L., Moore, W., Templeman, V. P., Grove, D., Moore, M., Gage,

M. A., Blair, L., Alrick, G., Wadlow, M., Fruin, C., Bunse, C., Makohon, L., Samples, B., Moses, C., Rogers, G., & Toews, J. *A data based classroom for the moderately and severely handicapped.* Monmouth, OR: Instructional Development Corporation, 1975.

Gold, M. W. Task analysis of a complex assembly task by the retarded blind. *Exceptional Children,* 1976, *43,* 78–84.

Haring, N. G., Liberty, K. A., & White, O. R. Rules for data based strategy decisions in instructional programs: Current research and instructional implications. In W. Sailor, B. Wilcox, & L. Brown (Eds.), *Methods of instruction for severely handicapped students.* Baltimore: Paul H. Brookes, 1980.

Hofmeister, A. *Microcomputer applications in the classroom.* New York: Holt, Rinehart, and Winston, 1983.

Lignugaris/Kraft, B., & Close, D. *Technical assistance package: Social skills.* Eugene, OR: Rehabilitation Research and Training Center, 1981.

Nihra, K., Foster, R., Shellhas, M., & Leland, H. *AAMD adaptive behavior scale.* Washington, D.C.: American Association on Mental Deficiency, 1974.

Schalock, R. L., Harper, R. S., & Carver, G. Independent living placement: Five years later. *American Journal of Mental Deficiency,* 1981, *86,* 170–177.

Skarnulis, E. Less restrictive alternatives in residential programming. *AAESPH Review,* 1976, *1,* 42–46.

Stowitschek, J. J., & Stowitschek, C. E. Once more with feeling: The absence of research on teacher use of microcomputers. *Exceptional Education Quarterly,* 1984, *4*(4), 23–29.

Taylor, V., Carlson, C., Close, D., & Larrabee, D. *Simply cooking.* Eugene, OR: Rehabilitation Research and Training Center, 1981.

Thiagarajan, S., Semmel, D. S., & Semmel, M. I. *Instructional development for training teachers of exceptional children: A sourcebook.* Minneapolis: Council for Exceptional Children, 1974.

Wehman, P. *Curriculum design for the severely and profoundly handicapped.* New York: Human Services Press, 1979.

Wehman, P. *Competitive employment: New horizons for severely disabled individuals.* Baltimore: Paul H. Brookes, 1981.

Wehman, P., Renzaglia, A., & Schutz, R. Behavioral training in sheltered workshops for the severely disabled. *AAESPH Review,* 1977, *2,* 24–36.

Wuerch, B. B., & Voeltz, L. M. *Longitudinal leisure skills for severely handicapped learners.* Baltimore: Paul H. Brookes, 1982.

Section IV
STRATEGIES FOR IMPLEMENTING INDIVIDUALIZED PROGRAMS

CHAPTER 10

BEHAVIOR ANALYTIC STRATEGIES IN COMMUNITY SETTINGS: PROBLEMS AND SOLUTIONS

WILLIAM SHARPTON AND PAUL A. ALBERTO

The philosophical principle of normalization (Wolfensberger, 1972) has come to define the desired goal for the lives of moderately and severely handicapped individuals. Normalization suggests that optimal development and functioning occur when individuals are allowed access to integrated settings for educational, residential, and vocational opportunities. These settings have been operationalized variously with continua depicting degrees of independence versus restriction. Specifically, these continua include educational settings ranging from self-contained placement to integrated regular education placement (Deno, 1970); vocational settings ranging from activity centers to competitive employment (Rusch & Mithaug, 1980); and residential settings ranging from full-time residential institutions to independent apartment living (Braddock, 1977).

To be successful in least restrictive adult settings, a handicapped individual must have patterns of behavior in his/her repertoire which are as normal as possible. Maximizing behavior patterns which allow for success in adult settings is the role of the educator. To succeed in this role, educators must apply the principle of normalization to the settings and strategies of instruction.

Normalizing the setting of instruction necessitates moving from the classroom to the community. This movement will enable students to experience first hand the naturally occurring antecedents of behaviors being taught as well as the naturally occurring consequences of their behaviors. In community based instructional settings, students will learn to use environmental context cues which cannot be duplicated in the classroom. Students will

---

*William Sharpton completed his doctorate at Georgia State University. Presently, he is an Assistant Professor of Special Education at the University of New Orleans. His current interests include community based training of such skills as transportation, shopping, and recreation activities.

Paul A. Alberto is an Associate Professor of Special Education at Georgia State University and Director of the training program in moderate and severe handicaps. Dr. Alberto has published articles and books related to applied behavior analysis in education and instructional programming for severely handicapped persons. He is actively involved with the Georgia State Department of Education's inservice training efforts as well as all levels of personnel preparation at Georgia State University.

experience the natural reinforcement associated with the successful completion of tasks such as using a shopping list to fill a grocery cart. doing the laundry in a public laundromat. or crossing a street safely. Instruction in the natural setting in which the skill is used also allows the student to learn to recognize the undesirable consequences of crossing against the light. getting off the bus at the wrong stop. or forgetting to buy ice cream.

The normalization of instructional strategies requires that functional adaptations dictated by community settings be made to the strategies of applied behavior analysis. Over the years. it has been shown that the learning principles which serve as the foundation for applied behavior analysis, and the systems of monitoring and affirming student performance. are extremely effective with handicapped individuals (Sailor & Guess. 1983). The transfer of instruction from the classroom to the community will present the teacher with new instructional management problems. These problems relate to a loss of instructional control. In the classroom. the teacher can artificially and conveniently arrange the environment to assure desired outcomes. Teachers can assure errorless learning by utilizing clear. distinct. and consistent antecedent stimuli (S^Ds), as well as immediate and artificially obvious consequences or feedback. Such is not the case in the community setting where the teacher cannot hope to completely control or manipulate the multitude of stimuli associated with a particular environment. Community based instruction assures that teachers select functional activity sequences because students are confronted with the real demands of a situation rather than hypothetical demands arranged in a classroom setting based on a packaged curriculum.

Often the teacher views community based instruction as a frustrating challenge. This chapter will present the design of strategies for five of the instructional problems that arise when instruction is moved outside the classroom. These instructional problems include: (a) structuring content. (b) selecting antecedent stimuli. (c) transfer of learning. (d) student initiation of tasks and activities, and (e) monitoring behavior.

Structuring Content

As soon as instruction is moved from the classroom to the wider community. the teacher's perspective must simultaneously widen from the narrow focus of individual task instruction to the more complex sequencing of tasks which naturally occur in the everyday world outside the classroom. The teacher must take the view that tasks are part of larger activities; activities are part of larger sequences. It is by performing these larger sequences that nonhandicapped persons negotiate the completion of the events in their day. Instruction of isolated, and therefore seemingly unrelated tasks does not present the student with an understanding of the interrelatedness of events nor the flow and rhythm of the day which is so much a part of a normalized life style (Wolfensberger, 1972). For example, the task of operating a washing machine is part of the larger activity of doing laundry. Laundry may only be a part of the larger sequence of events that one may engage in during a day (e.g.. cashing bills for change, riding a bus to get to the laundromat. doing the laundry, and buying milk on the way home).

Once a task has been selected for instruction based on the demands of an activity. a more precise delineation of responses involved in the performance of the task should be identified. Assuming that it may be required in a group home that each resident do one's own laundry, a traditional task analysis may be performed to enumerate the sequence of discrete responses which result in task completion. Most teachers were trained to do exhaustive task analyses which list every step in the chain. However, these task analyses often exceed those behaviors which are functionally necessary for actual task completion. Thus, this approach can consume precious instructional time (and the student's patience). For example, Cuvo, Jacobi, and Sipko (1981) initially identified 37 steps in a task analysis for using a washing machine, but subsequently determined that only nine were actually essential for task completion.

When preparing a task analysis, it is also important to remember that a task can be performed in a variety of ways. Just as there are at least two ways to tie a shoe and at least three ways to put on a coat, there is probably more than one way to stack a dishwasher or sort dirty clothes. In determining which analysis is best suited to a particular student in a given situation, two considerations are important. Assuming that all analyses yield equal effectiveness. the efficiency of each sequence should be determined. The more efficient procedure would be one that requires the student to perform the least number of individual steps, takes the student the least number of minutes to complete. and provides the least margin of potential error on the part of the student. Also, the task should conform to any rules which may be in effect in a given environment. For example, when teaching the relevant tasks for operating a dishwasher, it can be noted that the dish racks can be filled in a variety of ways. A particular restaurant, however, may require that a preferred system be used such as placing all cups in one rack, all saucers in another, and all plates in another. Similarly, the transit system in one city may provide for drivers to give change to customers boarding the bus; another city, however, may require that passengers have the exact change prior to boarding.

A critical variable in the decision for selecting or not selecting a task for instruction must center on its functional utility. For a task to be useful, the student must independently perform the task in the natural setting as soon as possible. The concern of instruction becomes twofold: (a) to teach tasks that can be immediately applied independently, and (b) to increase the sophistication of existing responses. Often, the student can perform the task only when the environment is adapted in terms of additional cues or adaptive materials, or can only partially participate in an activity (Baumgart et al., 1982). Such environmental adaptation may be applied initially to ensure that the student can perform the task in the natural setting as independently as possible, and to make the student aware of his/her ability to act upon and effect change in the environment. Over time, it should be the teacher's goal to increase the sophistication of the student's response by decreasing the degree of adaptation. This approach also should ensure that a student is not withheld from community based instruction on the premise that she/he is "not ready" for a given activity due to presumed deficits in skills. Rather, instruction is designed to accommodate a range of competency levels in the natural environment as soon as possible (Wilcox & Bellamy, 1982).

It is rare that the target of instruction is ever the performance of an isolated task. Rather, some combination of tasks are performed toward an end that alters the environment in some desirable and beneficial manner. Such a combination or sequence of tasks when looked at as a whole is called an activity (Horner, Sprague, & Wilcox, 1982). Discrete tasks such as "point to green" are rarely called for in community settings. Generally, the identification of green would merely be a part of the activity of crossing the street. Similarly, discriminating la-els is a discrete task which is part of the activity of shopping; utensil use is a discreta task which is part of the activity of eating in a restaurant. When tasks are viewed and taught as activities, the student is provided a context for engaging in the task(s), as well as an experience with the naturally occurring antecedents and reinforcers associated with their performance. The implication for designing instruction is to move from the massing of discrete behaviors to the integration of these behaviors into teaching sequences (Sailor & Guess, 1983). Under this principle, "milk" would not simply be taught as ten trials of sight word identification. Instead, the student would recognize the word (or label) in the context of reading a shopping list and filling a shopping cart.

To increase the likelihood that a student will recognize the functional worth of an activity, instruction should evolve to the combination of activities in community based activity sequences. An activity sequence is a behavioral chain which involves two or more activities. The activity sequences may occur totally in one setting. For example, in a bowling alley, an activity sequence might include entering the alley, requesting a lane, bowling, eating at the snack bar, then calling home for a ride. Yet, some activity sequences require individuals to function in more than one setting. A trip to the grocery store might involve crossing a street (community), riding a bus (community/bus), cashing a check (bank), shopping (store), and returning home (community/bus).

In designing activity sequences to be taught, the teacher should approximate the order in which the activities will actually be applied in the natural course of a daily routine. This order of events should approximate the pattern used by nonhandicapped persons. For example, the individual preparing for a trip to the grocery store must first make sure that she/he has money, and then travel to the bank if she/he needs cash prior to arriving at the store. Before going to the grocery store, the student has probably identified needs based on a review of the food shelves in the kitchen. The same temporal pattern should be utilized in planning community based experiences in order to maximize opportunities to rehearse coherent activity sequences.

Activity sequences can be adjusted to allow for the repeated practice of previously acquired activities as well as the introduction of new ones. For example, the activities in Figure 1 have been mastered at different levels of sophistication by a given student. Every attempt should be made to introduce only one activity at the level of acquisition in a sequence. The other activities should be performed at a higher level of mastery such as fluency, maintenance, or generalization.

Mrs. Williams has designed the following activity chain for Robert. Note that the instructional goal for each activity is at a different level of instruction.

Activity	*Goal*
CROSS 2-LANE STREET	Fluency: Increase speed of crossing.
CASH CHECK AT BANK	Maintenance: Experience to provide planned practice of acquired skill.
GROCERY SHOPPING	Generalization: Instruction takes place in a different store to program performance across settings.
PREPARE MEAL	Acquisition: Robert is engaged in his first experience preparing a meal using pictoral recipe cards.

Figure 10-1. Activity sequence chain with activities at different levels of instruction.

Selecting Antecedent Stimuli

Inherent in a behavioral approach to instruction is the determination of relationships between antecedent stimuli and the responses which follow. When preparing to teach a task or activity in a community setting, the teacher cannot select and arrange antecedents as she/he can in the classroom.

Rather, the teacher must make successful use of the antecedents that occur naturally in the community setting. When preparing to teach a task or activity in a community setting three factors should be considered. First, an appropriate, naturally occurring antecedent stimulus (S^D) must be identified. Second, the possible variations that may occur in the stimulus as it appears in various settings must be noted. Third, strategies must be designed for use if, after repeated training, the student still does not respond to the naturally occurring antecedent.

To the maximum extent possible, students should be instructed to respond to the same S^Ds available to nonhandicapped persons. Therefore, as often as possible, behavior of handicapped individuals should be cued by S^Ds that occur naturally in the environment. Acknowledging teacher vocal-cue control for a task antecedent is an inappropriate final goal of instruction. When planning instruction the teacher should analyze the available cues and setting to train the student to respond to just one S^D, thereby avoiding confusion by focusing a student's attention. In a situation where a student is being taught to cross a two lane intersection, there are a variety of S^Ds used by nonhandicapped persons. These may include use of a traffic light, a "walk"/"don't walk" sign, a reduced flow of traffic, or the crossing of other pedestrians. When teaching this task, the teacher should select only one of the available, naturally occurring S^Ds; thus the student will know exactly what to focus on and will not have to evaluate the relative weights of cues (e.g., the number of cars passing, or the presence of a yellow light). The basis for selection may depend upon which S^D is easier to discriminate, faster to teach, and results in quicker student independence. In street crossing training, a red/green light discrimination is faster and more certain of correct responding by the student than is training to a "walk"/"don't walk" sign. The appropriateness of teaching the light color discrimination is heightened if more intersections are controlled by traffic lights than "walk" signs in the training community.

Equally important, the student should not be trained to respond to an S^D that, upon reflection, should in fact be an S-delta (inappropriate antecedent) for the handicapped student even though it may be employed by a nonhandicapped student. For example, even though the number of other pedestrians crossing at an intersection may be used by nonhandicapped persons as an S^D for crossing, the relative surety and safety factors to be considered and the inability to quantify a critical number during training should cause the teacher to deal with this stimulus as an S-delta.

A problem in the variations of the appearance of antecedent stimuli (stimulus generalization) is exemplified by the fact that price tags do not appear the same in all settings. For example, in various locations (e.g., grocery store, clothing store) price labels appear on the shelf, on the package, or on the items themselves. The numbers appear in varying sizes and styles of print. The teacher should provide as many exemplars as possible drawn from the actual shops which the student will encounter in the neighborhood (see Stokes & Baer, 1977). The teacher first should present and instruct those examples which occur most frequently across locations and then probe the necessity for training the succeeding examples.

If after repeated training trials, the naturally occurring antecedent is still not being responded to appropriately by the student, the teacher will have to use supplementary antecedents. Supplementary antecedents, or prompts, are added by the teacher to the naturally occurring antecedents to assist the initiation of student performance on the original response or to refine performance of the response.

The example in Figure 2 illustrates a variation in the operation of a vending machine which makes use of an additional prompt. Note that the antecedent in both cases is the same, with the exception of the counting card. This card represents the addition of an artificial S^D to the environment. Assuming that several cards representing the various values most often found on machines in the community were supplied, the student would be competent in using a large variety of machines.

Normal Operation	*Alternative Strategy*
Identify & approach machine	Identify & approach machine
Determine amount needed	Determine amount needed
Select coins	Match adaptive counting card to amount on machine
Place coins in machine	Remove coins from card and place in machine
Activate appropriate choice	Activate appropriate choice
Retrieve item	Retrieve item

Figure 10-2. Vending machine operation with and without prompts.

Artificial S^Ds should not be considered universally undesirable. In Figure 2, the addition of the counting card allowed the individual to perform the task independently. Over time, every effort should be made to reduce the reliance of the learner on artificial S^Ds by focusing on the relevant dimensions of naturally occurring antecedents. This process is known as the prompting of natural S^Ds. Alberto and Troutman (1982) discussed four factors which should influence the use of prompts.

Prompts should not distract from the natural S^D, but should focus the student's attention on it. An example of this can be seen in the design of the counting card itself. If the card is made from two layers of cardboard with appropriately sized holes cut for the coins, then the student only focuses on size as the relevant cue. If commercially available coin stamps are used to provide a visual cue for each coin within the hole, then the student also focuses on the design of the coin. Because the fronts of all coins have a face on it, the back of coins provide a grosser discrimination; therefore the use of "tails" side coin stamps will maximize the likelihood of success.

Prompts should be as weak as possible. The best prompt is the weakest one which will result in the emission of the desired behavior. Every attempt should be made to use the least intrusive prompt first. This point may be illustrated using the task of street crossing. A student and teacher are waiting at the curb to cross the street. The light turns green and the student hesitates; the teacher touches the student's arm and says "the light is green." A more appropriate prompt would have been a simple verbal cue "look at the light."

Prompts should be faded as rapidly as possible. The natural S^D may not acquire control over the response if prompts are extended longer than necessary. In using the vending machines, the student is successful when provided with counting cards. At some point the student may learn to identify the coins on the basis of their attributes if he/she is not allowed to use the cards during certain trials (i.e., by fading out use of the prompt). However, it must be remembered that successful functioning independent of third parties in as many community-essential skills as possible is the goal of instruction for young adults. If the student's independent functioning is jeopardized or limited without the use of a prompt, the prompt should remain as an appropriate alternative performance strategy (Wilcox & Bellamy, 1982).

Unplanned prompts should be avoided. For example, while waiting to cross the street, the student may remain stationary when the light turns green. Realizing that the light only remains green a short period of time, the teacher leans forward out of nervousness or anticipation; the student crosses the street and the teacher scores the response as an independently initiated correct response. However, the teacher's unplanned action actually served as the S^D for the student crossing the street.

Transfer of Learning

Too often community based experiences are merely a series of field trips resulting in exposure to community settings rather than the systematic assurance of competence in normative community behaviors. In designing the secondary curriculum, an increasing percentage of instructional time should take place in the setting in which the activity will take place rather than in the classroom (Wilcox & Bellamy, 1982). This is not to imply that all instruction will take place in shopping centers, on buses, and in neighborhood fast food restaurants. Administrative constraints on public school life often limit the number of opportunities in the community. Therefore, the teacher must be sure that the time spent in the community is quality educational time, and that there is a logical transition from in-class instruction to community based instruction. Classroom instruction may best be used to (a) instruct prerequisite skills needed to insure that a fluent chain of behavior is produced in the community setting, and (b) provide practice for tasks in the behavioral chain which the student is having particular difficulty in performing.

As with any analysis of a behavior chain, step one of the chain assumes a certain level of skill competence on the part of the student, prerequisite to performance of the chain. These entry level or prerequisite skills may be taught in the classroom, at least to initial acquisition, with generalization occurring in the community setting. For example, a prerequisite to the activity of street crossing is the ability to discriminate the colors red and green; a prerequisite to the activity of bus riding may be number recognition (for correct bus identification); a prerequisite to the activity of grocery shopping may be the identification of certain sight words or labels. Without competence in these prerequisite skills, valuable community time is consumed, thereby taking away from practice of the functional application of the community based task or activity. Additionally, the student is distracted from the sequence of the actual activity at hand by the need for teacher interruption to deal with the remediation or guidance of the prerequisite skills.

Classroom time may be used to remediate the deficit of a particular skill needed to complete a behavior chain. Often in the performance of a chain there are steps within the chain that the student cannot perform. The first thing the teacher should do is simply guide the student through that one step and allow the student to perform the next step(s) independently (Bellamy, Horner, & Inman, 1979). If following repeated trials, the student fails to perform the task independently, the teacher may decide to use classroom time to remediate. First, the teacher must decide if the student's inability to perform the step is due to a motor-practice problem or a continuing problem in recognizing the naturally occurring antecedent stimulus. If the problem relates to motor performance, the teacher may choose to provide the student with massed practice in the classroom. For example, if the difficulty in the travel chain is stepping onto the bus, the teacher may arrange massed practice of this skill in the classroom with a step of equal height as that on a city bus. Similarly, the student may experience a power problem such as the inability to push a door open at the Social Security Office. The student may have a strength problem exemplified by an inability to lift a full rack of dishes during the job training experience.

If the continuing problem with a particular step is in recognition of the natural antecedent stimulus, classroom instruction can focus attention on the S^D to maximize the probability that the student will attend to the appropriate cue when in the community and perform the desired response. Assume that the teacher has repeatedly prompted the student to look at the traffic signal; however, the student is distracted by other stimuli inherent to the setting (e.g., other signs). The teacher may decide to maximize the probability that the student will concentrate on the relevant cue by using a set of closeup slides depicting various traffic signals (i.e., red, green, and yellow) (Sharpton, 1981). Classroom time is used to show the slides to the student one at a time while providing the verbal cue "Can you cross?" After the student responds correctly to an established criterion, slides are used which systematically introduce into the picture more and more distracting variables that occur in the natural setting. Such massed practice in the classroom will facilitate community success.

The same idea can be used in bus training. It is necessary for the student to recognize the approach of certain landmarks as the S^D for signaling the bus to stop. If the student continually misses the landmark, a set of slides similar to the ones used for street crossing may be prepared. These slides would depict the relevant landmark, first in isolation and then with increasing distractors, that appear along the bus route. Distractor slides of similar landmarks should be included to ensure that the student can correctly identify the appropriate landmark. Following performance of this skill to an established criterion, a videotape of the bus route may be shown to verify that the student can recognize the landmark when the scenery is in motion. The time length of each trial can be gradually increased to approximate the length of the bus ride. In this case, a simulated setting affords more learning trials than are available in the natural setting. Simulated performance trials also may be recommended when safety or expense are of concern (Horner, McDonnell, Vogelsburg, & Williams, 1983).

A third possibility is the use of classroom time to perfect an instructional adaptation that has been selected due to continuing difficulty with a particular step. For example, if the student can perform all steps in the bus chain but either cannot select the appropriate coins for bus fare or lacks the appropriate fluency for competent coin selection, the teacher may decide for now (or forever) to teach the student to use an adaptation. With the adaptation the student is independent in the performance of the chain. The teacher may attach to the student's coin holder a card with a pictoral sample of the appropriate coins needed to get on the bus. Before leaving home or work, the student matches the coins to the sample, thereby guaranteeing the correct coins for riding the bus. The use of such a strategy overcomes a continuing inability to recognize coins.

Student Initiation of Tasks and Activities

When designing instruction in the classroom, the teacher makes out a schedule of instructional activities. The teacher thereby decides when a given task will be undertaken and initiates the student's performance of each task. In most instructional circumstances verbal cues are used to prompt the student to initiate, continue, or correct task performance. However, a critical factor in training handicapped students for independence is the ability to self-initiate behavior. As one analyzes the cues nonhandicapped persons use as prompting strategies for initiating behavior, they appear to group into three types of functional antecedents.

The first group of functional antecedents are those that depend on recognition of the need to replenish materials based upon an existing depletion. Nonhandicapped persons initiate many of what may be considered community based skills based on notice of depletion. For example, we go to the grocery when we need goods; we do laundry because there are no clean clothes in the drawer; and go to the bank because our wallet is empty. Prompts may be taught as the functional antecedent for self-initiation of these and similar behaviors. The teacher may need to exaggerate this rather abstract S^D by employing a more concrete stimulus. For example, a teacher can arrange for the student to buy all white underwear with the exception of one blue pair. As a component of the laundry activity, the student is taught to always place his underwear in his drawer with the blue pair on the bottom of the stack. When he gets to the blue pair in his drawer, his supply is depleted, indicating it is time to do the laundry.

A second functional antecedent for self-initiation is the self-administration of a specific stimulus which signals that the behavior should begin. This system is practiced on an everyday basis by most people when they awaken to an alarm clock. For some handicapped individuals, an adaptation of this procedure may be needed. For example, an individual can be taught to activate an alarm clock and be provided with two preset clocks. When the first alarm rings, it signals initiation of a sequence which includes rising, washing, dressing, and eating. When the second alarm rings, the individual initiates a sequence which includes picking up the bus money on the dresser, picking up lunch, and leaving the house. The alarm should be set in such a manner to allow enough time to walk to the bus stop.

The third functional antecedent is responding to a noted schedule of events or "listing". This is particularly appropriate when a prompt is needed at various points in a chain of events, not just at the initiation of an activity sequence. An example of this self-initiation (or self-continuation) technique is seen when pictures illustrating tasks to be performed are placed in the desired sequence in a book or on a ring. If house cleaning is scheduled, the student is trained to use picture prompts to initiate each activity in the sequence (e.g., dusting, cleaning the bathtub, vacuuming). In this case, photographs depicting each task could be used. The student performs each task and turns each page in sequence until the book, and thus the chores, are completed.

In the previous example, all of the activities were performed in the same setting. This same procedure could be used to initiate behavior across several settings. For example, the student could be provided with pictures corresponding to the sequence of community based activities (e.g., banking, riding the bus, eating lunch, grocery shopping, returning home). In this manner, the teacher could increase the likelihood that a complex activity sequence will be carried out. (For detailed descriptions and examples of picture prompts, see the chapter by Freagon et al. in this text.)

The design of an appropriate self-initiation strategy is a crucial component of community based instruction. In selecting such a strategy, the teacher should ensure that the system is effective, generalizable to a number of settings, and as unobtrusive as possible. Effectiveness can only be verified when the student is allowed to rely on the strategy to initiate behavior. That is, if the teacher continues to supply verbal or physical cues at this stage of instruction, self-initiation will not be realized.

The purpose of these procedures is merely to initiate behavior, not direct the form of specific responses. Therefore, the same procedure can be modified for use with a variety of tasks, activities, and activity sequences. These strategies will be useful in future settings only if they are communicated to service providers and family members associated with settings outside the school.

Monitoring Behavior

Well documented instructional strategies include the use of varying levels of assistance to bring about independent performance (Billingsley & Romer, 1983). When planning instruction of community activities, an important consideration should be what the student will do following an error in either a supervised or a nonsupervised setting. Initially, the teacher arranges the environment in such a manner that errorless learning is maximized. Following documentation that the student can perform the given task or activity to a predetermined level of proficiency, the teacher is ready to consider the next level of performance. Since errors can occur at any level of performance, the teacher should include instruction which will provide the student with a procedure for independently coping with an error whether in a supervised or nonsupervised community setting.

The first step in designing an independent error correction procedure is to examine the functional consequences of an error after it is committed. Certainly an error can be made in the performance of any community activity; however, the results of various errors can differ in terms of their effect on the student's well being or the functional completion of the task. Consider the case of shopping with one-dollar bills. If the student has successfully mastered paying to the next highest dollar value, at worst an error can result in losing 99 cents in most situations. When the amount shown on the register is $4.30, the student hands the cashier five one-dollar bills and waits for change. Four errors are possible in this exchange. The student may hand the cashier six dollars instead of five dollars. At worst, the cashier will not return the extra dollar. The student may hand the cashier only four dollars, in which case the cashier will ask for more money, and the student will either hand another dollar bill or reduce the number of items purchased. The student may forget to wait for change; if so, the cashier will call the student back to give the change, or at worst, the student will lose 70 cents. Finally, the student could be given an incorrect amount of change, in which case he/she will either lose less than 70 cents or benefit by the cashier's error.

In any of these possible outcomes of error, the functional purpose of the task has been fulfilled, and in no instance has the student's well being been affected. Is it, therefore, worth utilizing valuable instructional time to train an error correction procedure to cover these cases?

Now consider the task of riding a municipal bus. If the student misidentifies a bus stop, he/she will exit the bus in an unfamiliar setting. The consequences of this behavior may be serious and warrant the instruction of a correction procedure. Prior planning will have considered, given the nature of the task and the functioning of the student, whether the appropriate error correction will call for (a) terminating the task, or (b) compensating for the results of the error.

If terminating the task is required, the following type of error correction may be taught during instruction since it can be generalized to a variety of settings throughout the city.

The student:

1. Identifies and locates a payphone with a printed telephone number on the dial or under the pushbuttons.
2. Identifies and retrieves appropriate coin(s) to operate the phone.
3. Uses emergency telephone number card in his wallet to locate appropriate telephone number (e.g., that of the teacher, parent, employer, house parent).

4. Dials phone.
5. Says. "My name is _____. I am lost. The number of this phone is
_____."
6. Waits for person at telephone location.

Upon receiving the call, the teacher. house parent. etc. calls the operator. explains the emergency, and gives the telephone number of the payphone at which the student is located. With this information. the operator can cross reference the number and give the exact location of the payphone at which the student is waiting.

A higher functioning student who you want and expect to get to the functional conclusion of the activity may have been taught a different error correction procedure. Assume that the student did not see the S^D landmark for exiting the bus until the bus had already passed the stop. The student is taught to exit at the next stop. He/She then walks back to the stop or landmark (asking directions if necessary) and continues the steps of the chain in the journey to the destination. Thus, instead of terminating the activity, the student is taught a procedure which will compensate for the error.

Effective instruction of an error correction procedure must occur in a sequential manner, in the natural setting. following errorless instruction for initial acquisition of the target activity. Error correction training is an active process. As such, it must be planned in coordination with the development of the targeted community activity sequence. Instruction in the correction procedure should occur at the time that an error is made. Thus. the teacher must be prepared for the student's error before it occurs. For error correction procedures to be competently performed and rationally understood by the student, the student must be able to perform the correction independently at the appropriate point in time. That is, the *error* should prompt the student to initiate the correction procedure rather than a verbal prompt from the teacher. An added step of training may involve the arrangement of the environment so that an error will occur when the student does not see the teacher physically present for reassurance and assistance. For example. a student may be placed on an unfamiliar bus route. with only shadow supervision, to ensure that the "lost" procedure is competently performed.

Summary

Each of the instructional concerns discussed in this chapter must be minimized to successfully transfer an educational program from the classroom to the community. Within each, the goal remains to fade out teacher assistance as quickly as possible, yet to design the instructional program in such a way that the likelihood of successful, independent performance by the student is maximized.

Content should be selected from immediate and potential community environments and structured to present the opportunity for the student to engage in functional and coherent patterns of activities. Instructional strategies should be structured to accommodate a range of student competence as well as different levels of mastery of particular tasks. By the time students are adolescents and young adults, the term "not ready for" should no longer enter our goal selection process. Natural antecedents must be attended to and artificial ones substituted only when their presence enhances the immediate capability of the student to perform an activity. With student independence as the goal, it is important to train students to take responsibility for their functioning including initiating daily activities and compensating for inappropriate performance.

Each of these points should be considered in order to design an instructional program which builds independence in the performance of normalized or adapted normalized patterns of living. The skills needed by students for such patterns of living must be taught systematically and verified if the concept of normalization is to be applied to educational programs serving moderately and severely handicapped people.

REFERENCES

Alberto, P. A., & Troutman, A. C. *Applied behavior analysis for teachers: Influencing student performance.* Columbus, OH: Charles Merrill, 1982.

Baumgart, D., Brown, L., Pumpian, I., Nisbet, J., Ford, A., Sweet, M., Messina, R., & Schroeder. J. Principle of partial participation and individualized adaptations in educational programs for severely handicapped students. *Journal of the Association for the Severely Handicapped.* 1982, *7*, 17–27.

Bellamy, G. T., Horner, R., & Inman, D. *Vocational habilitation of severely retarded adults.* Baltimore: University Park Press, 1979.

Billingsley, F., & Romer, L. Response prompting and the transfer of stimulus control: Methods, research, and a conceptual framework. *Journal of the Association for the Severely Handicapped.* 1983, *8,* 3–12.

Braddock, D. *Opening closed doors: The deinstitutionalization of disabled individuals.* Reston, VA: Council for Exceptional Children, 1977.

Cuvo, A., Jacobi, L., & Sipko, R. Teaching laundry skills to mentally retarded students. *Education and Training of the Mentally Retarded,* 1981, *16,* 54–64.

Deno, E. Special education as developmental capital. *Exceptional Children,* 1970, *37,* 229–237.

Horner, R. H., McDonnel, J., Vogelsburg, R. T., & Williams, J. *Simulation training: Strategies for conducting in-class training that results in adaptive performance in the community.* Presentation at National Conference of the Association for the Severely Handicapped, November 1983, San Francisco.

Horner, R. H., Sprague, J., & Wilcox, B. General case programming for community activities.

In B. Wilcox & G. T. Bellamy (Eds.), *Design of high school programs for severely handicapped students*. Baltimore: Paul H. Brookes, 1982.

Rusch, F. R., & Mithaug, D. E. *Vocational training for mentally retarded adults: A behavior analytic approach*. Champaign, IL: Research Press, 1980.

Sailor, W., & Guess, D. *Severely handicapped students: An instructional design*. Boston: Houghton Mifflin, 1983.

Sharpton, W. Adapting media and materials for community skills instruction. *Journal of Special Education Technology*, 1981, *4*, 20–24.

Stokes, T., & Baer, D. An implicit technology of generalization. *Journal of Applied Behavior Analysis*, 1977, *10*, 349–367.

Wilcox, B., & Bellamy, G. T. *Design of high school programs for severely handicapped students*. Baltimore: Paul H. Brookes, 1982.

Wolfensberger, W. (Ed.). *The principle of normalization in human services*. Toronto: Toronto Institute on Mental Retardation, 1972.

CHAPTER 11

UTILIZATION OF INTEGRATED SETTINGS AND ACTIVITIES TO DEVELOP AND EXPAND COMMUNICATION SKILLS

KATHLEEN STREMEL-CAMPBELL, ROBERT CAMPBELL AND NANCY JOHNSON-DORN

A defining characteristic of persons with moderate and severe handicaps (Grossman, 1977) is the inability to engage in interpersonal communication. These individuals often are deficient in verbal communication skills and are placed at an added disadvantage since few augmentative language programs provide for language intervention through social interactions (Schutz, Williams, Iverson, & Duncan, 1984; Siebert & Oller, 1981). Consequently, the lack of specific motor, vocational, social skills, and the absence of a language system are sometimes given to exclude these individuals from integrated environments and activities. Schutz et al. (1984) further pointed out that if these individuals are to be excluded from integrated activities and experiences until they demonstrate acceptable levels of social skills, they may never have an opportunity to participate in community integration. Additionally, if individuals with moderate/severe handicaps do not receive an opportunity to participate in integrated activities, there are few reasons for them to learn more effective social and communication skills.

In the past 10 years, alternative or augmentative language systems for individuals with handicaps have been widely used and accepted (Harris & Vanderheiden, 1977; Musselwhite & St. Louis, 1982; Stremel-Campbell,

---

*Kathleen Stremel-Campbell conducts research, curricula development, and teacher training on language acquisition and generalization strategies for persons with moderate and severe handicaps. She is known nationally for her work in both verbal and nonverbal communication. She previously worked with Project MESH (Model Education for the Severely Handicapped) in Parsons, KS and with Teaching Research in Monmouth, OR.

Robert Campbell formerly worked with the Bureau of Child Research at the University of Kansas and Teaching Research in Monmouth, OR. Presently he is conducting research involving the generalization of social-communication skills. Other interests and publications include telecommunications and microtechnology. Dr. Campbell is currently Director of Rainbow Center, a preschool organization for handicapped children in Wichita, KS.

Nancy Johnson-Dorn has worked in activity centers, group homes, and classroom settings with moderately and severely handicapped persons. Currently, she is a teacher trainer on an integration project at Teaching Research and a student at Western Oregon State College.

Cantrell, & Halle, 1977). The need for a vocal language system (i.e., speech) has therefore been minimized, and the use of alternative systems (i.e., manual signs and communication boards) have been advocated. For a number of individuals with more severe developmental disabilities, the development of a formal language system that includes abstract symbols and rules for ordering these symbols may not be a reality. While we as interventionists strive to meet each individual's ultimate level of language functioning, we cannot emphasize the development of a *language* system to the exclusion of developing, using, and expanding the person's *communication* system. Communication is a social interaction between a speaker and listener in which information is exchanged (Sailor, Guess, Goetz, Schuler, Utley, & Baldwin, 1980). The medium by which a message is shared may be through prelanguage (e.g., extending objects, pointing, gesturing) or language (e.g., speech, manual signs, Bliss symbols, written words). Years are often spent training a few language vocabulary items (e.g., eat, bathroom) without first assessing if the individual is communicating intentionally by nonlanguage means. There is a high probability that teaching a language response will not be functional if the individual is not demonstrating a communication response. Individuals will not learn a language response and suddenly begin to use it to communicate. However, they may use a newly acquired language behavior to more effectively communicate a "message" that they could communicate previously by a nonlanguage behavior, especially if the language behavior is reinforced by the environment.

Rather than pinpoint the specific language skills that are necessary for successful integration into public school and community settings, the present chapter will discuss the importance of utilizing integrated settings and activities to develop and expand each individual's communication system. Four major areas are critical for developing more efficient and effective communication within integrated environments:

1. Developing communication within social context;
2. Selecting and developing effective communication systems and content;
3. Utilizing systematic training to increase interpersonal communication; and
4. Programming for generalization.

Developing Communication Within a Social Context

Mahoney (1975) stated that language should be viewed as a continuously evolving system with the structure serving as a means for achieving the goal of efficient communication within an extended environment. He stressed that models of language intervention should view language as developing from more primative communication systems that include the social interaction and nonverbal communication systems that exist between language learning children and their primary language models. Additionally, the relationship between social, cognitive, and linguistic skills must be considered in developing prelanguage or language communication programs for each individual (McLean & Snyder-McLean, 1978). The recent research on the development of normal child language (Bates, Benigni, Bretherton, Camaloni, & Volterra, 1979; Bruner, 1975; Halliday, 1975) focuses on three major aspects that have implications for developing communication programs for individuals with handicaps. First, nonverbal (i.e., prelanguage) communication systems serve the basis for emergent language. Second, communicative acts (i.e., prelanguage and language) can serve an array of social functions. Third, communication must be trained in a social context in which the sender and receiver share a communication system.

Prelanguage Communication Systems

Often alternative language systems are selected for individuals as though the system is a final "product." The development of a communication system must be considered as an evolving "process" in which the student's current level of communication across different social environments is analyzed continuously. This continuous assessment of communication within natural interpersonal interactions provides information for determining the next level of the individual's communication system. One of the first sets of questions that interventionists should attempt to answer includes: (a) Is the specific environment providing opportunities for communication?, (b) Is the individual communicating purposefully in *any* form?, (c) Are various forms of communication used for generalized functioning?, and (d) Is the individual's communication system effective and efficient with others?

Individuals who do not display language responses (e.g., speech, signs, pointing to pictures) or who demonstrate very limited language vocabulary often are not provided opportunities for making choices or requesting objects/activities. A majority of the interactions between the individual and professionals consists of directives in which the individual is not given opportunities to control his/her environment (Certo & Kohl, 1984; Voeltz, 1984). These individuals begin to rely on adult figures to provide cues and prompts to direct their actions. In these cases, initial IEP communication objectives may necessarily include increasing the opportunities across integrated environments for any form of communication to occur. In order to use a language response in a functional manner, an individual must have the concept that the word, sign, or symbol represents a specific object, event, or activity. Many individuals demonstrate the ability to use a limited number of signs or pictures, but they may nondiscriminatingly use the words in their repertoire, not demonstrating a one-to-one correspondence between the sign and the object that is being requested. It can be difficult to determine the individual's communicative intent if they consistently use only trained signs to refer to new referents.

Prelanguage or prelinguistic communication can be defined as nonsymbolic behaviors that an individual intentionally uses to communicate a specific message to another person. Adults use prelanguage behaviors concurrent with speech to communicate their message more effectively. Individuals who have limited receptive language skills may respond primarily to prelanguage responses as well. While individuals with cognitive and/or sensory impairments may display slightly different levels of acquiring the prelanguage behaviors as compared to young children (Bates et al., 1979), ongoing training data (Stremel-Campbell, Clark-Guida, & Johnson-Dorn, 1984) indicate that a tentative easy-to-difficult hierarchy can be proposed. The hierarchy of prelanguage behaviors is presented in Table 1. Students with severe physical impairments may require the use of adaptive devices and switches that can be trained prior to the development of more formal communication boards or books. The student's acquisition rate for different types of prelanguage behaviors may be used as a selection criteria in determining an appropriate augmentative system at a later point. For example, young developmentally delayed children may demonstrate that their speech development is quite delayed in relation to their cognitive/social development in object use, imitation, and receptive communication. A number of these children demonstrate that they acquire gestures more rapidly than they can identify pictures or use pictures to request. Other children point to objects and pictures more readily than they can use gestures to communicate. The student's acquisition data can be used to develop an augmentative language system so that the child is learning a language system concurrently with training or speech development if this is an appropriate objective. Therefore, the student's language development does not have to become even more delayed while speech is being trained.

The analysis of prelanguage communication behavior is important for additional reasons as well. These include:

1. Individuals demonstrating profound cognitive and sensory handicaps may not acquire a language system;
2. Other individuals may need to communicate by more concrete forms of behavior prior to learning a more abstract form of language;
3. Individuals with limited language skills need to be able to use prelanguage means to communicate when a vocabulary item is unknown (sign) or not available (communication board); and

TABLE 11-1
HIERARCHY OF PRELANGUAGE BEHAVIORS

Uses body movement
Averts head/pushes away
Touches object/person
Manipulates person physically
Extends objects
Reaches for out-of-reach objects
Extends hand
Points to request
Points to show
Uses object-person-object-person gaze
Extends objects to show
Vocalizes
Uses simple gestures
Uses Yes/No gestures
Points to pictures

4. Individuals at the one-word stage of language development may use combined language and prelanguage forms to communicate about different things at the same time.

Interventionists must learn to observe the more subtle forms of prelanguage behavior to develop more functional communication programs. For example, if we can determine what objects, events, and activities the student is referring to by eye gaze, object extension, or pointing, we can expand the student's language on a functional basis by utilizing the student's communicative intent to select new language vocabulary items. Additionally, we can select more appropriate two-word relations if the student's communication system is used as a basis for our selection. Our ultimate goal should be to continuously move the student from lower levels of prelanguage behaviors, if the student is not utilizing these behaviors, to higher prelanguage forms while expanding the content (i.e., what the student is communicating about). Next, the student may be using prelanguage behaviors to initiate communication while being trained to use signs or communication boards as responses. Once the student is able to use a one-word language system both to initiate and respond, combinations of prelanguage behaviors and language behaviors can be targeted prior to training different semantic relations at the two-word stage (e.g., cracker please, Mom help, my coat, no paper, paper-trash).

It is critical to develop a student's program both vertically (to higher forms) and horizontally (to expanded context). Two major errors in programming communication frequently are made. The first is to move the student only in a vertical direction so that the student learns to sign: (a) "juice," (b) "want juice," (c) "want juice please," and (d) "I want juice please." This strategy provides the student with a limited number of four-word utterances.

While the student's progress may look good on paper, the educational significance of this progress is questionable since the student is using only longer combinations to request the same limited set of objects/activities. The second frequent error is to expand the student's acquisition and generalization at one level so that the student can request a large number of objects and activities (by pushing the adult's hands toward the object or by pointing) with the same form. In this case, the student's behavior is strongly reinforced, and the student is not encouraged to use higher forms of communication or language. Unfortunately, there are not specific criteria for moving a student to a higher level and expanding a student's current level prior to training a new form. Perhaps a criterion of limited generalization could be used once the student generalizes a learned form to request untrained but relevant objects in a horizontal fashion; a higher language form is then targeted. An example might be moving a student from touching an object or person to gesturing to request objects/actions during breakfast. In this way, new content is taught through trained forms (e.g., "Touch eggs" or "Touch milk"), and new forms are taught initially by using trained content (e.g., "Point to eggs" or "Point to milk") (Bloom & Lahey, 1978). Later, new content can be taught concurrently with new forms to determine if the student can generalize trained content to new forms without direction training. Once a student has learned to generalize different prelanguage forms across content, the student may demonstrate the use of different forms concurrently so that he/she extends his/her cup for "more milk," extends his/her hand to request a spoon, and points or vocalizes to receive a napkin.

Social Functions Served by Communicative Behaviors

The previous examples have emphasized the use of prelanguage behaviors for two primary social functions to request objects or assistance and to protest or request removal of objects or assistance. These two functions are probably the first functions to develop for individuals with more severe handicaps. It is critical that the student learns other social functions (e.g., greeting, calling, commenting). As students get older, they are trained to be more independent, to obtain objects, and to not request assistance. If these students have been taught that the major function of communication is to request, it is likely that their overall use of communicative behaviors will decrease as they become more independent.

It is necessary to analyze the integrated environments to determine which social functions are a natural part of interpersonal interactions that typically occur or could occur within those settings and to arrange those environments (e.g., community, work, home) so that students continue to have a reason to initiate communication as well as to respond to the communication from others (Seibert & Kimbrough-Oller, 1981). While integrated settings have the potential to increase the opportunities for communication, direct training within those environments is often necessary, especially for students with more severe handicaps. Opportunities for communication also set the occasion for different social functions to be trained. While the overall function of communication is to exchange information (Sailor et al., 1980), the types of information that can be shared between a sender and a receiver (i.e., speaker and listener) are numerous. Various terminology typically is used in the literature (see McLean & Snyder-McLean, 1978 for a review).

The following types of social functions (based on Dore, 1975) can be expressed by different communicative acts:

1. Protecting/rejecting;
2. Requesting continuation of an object/activity;
3. Requesting object/action;
4. Repeating;
5. Social (greeting, thank you);
6. Calling;
7. Requesting attention to self;
8. Requesting attention to a referent (object, activity, event);
9. Offering;
10. Answering (yes/no, wh question);
11. Requesting permission;
12. Commenting;
13. Requesting answer; and
14. Giving unknown information.

A number of functions may be achieved more effectively with language. In fact, Halliday (1975) pointed out that learning vocabulary (a) allows new meaning for functions that the child currently is using; (b) allows for functions to be combined; and (c) later allows the child to communicate an experience to someone who has not shared that experience. He found that young children's vocabulary and early language structures are specific to one function or another, but they initially do not use an utterance for multifunctions. For example, a child may use "more meat" (I want:) as a request, and "my shoe" (here is:) as a comment. Only later is the child able to use an utterance for different functions. These normal developmental data have implications for developing communication sequences. Often, individuals with severe handicaps use their language responses only as request functions and not to comment on changes or observations that occur. The deficiency may be more directly related to training procedures than the student's lack of potential communication skills. Students may learn only request and protest functions if communication training is restricted to teacher-student interactions in a one-to-one training format.

Communication targeted within integrated social contexts. The concept of integration as an ongoing process of interactions (Hoben. 1980; Stainback & Stainback, 1981) has lead to the challenge of classifying. defining, training. and measuring social skills for individuals with severe handicaps. In the past. social skills curricula consisted primarily of increasing self-help. decreasing aberrant behaviors. and/or targeting isolated social interaction skills. Even though the conceptualization of social skills remains to be strengthened, a number of authors have pointed out that communicative and noncommunicative social skills are a critical part of our daily living skills (Schutz, Williams, Iverson, & Duncan, 1984).

The ability to communicate effectively in initiating and in maintaining interactions appears to facilitate peer acceptance in children with mild handicaps (Gottman, Gonso, & Rasmussen. 1975; LaGreca & Mesibov. 1979). Changes in the communicative behavior of preschool children with moderate and severe handicaps have the potential to affect social integration (Guralnick. 1981), particularly if communication skills are trained in conjunction with other social behaviors. Additionally. communication serves as a more appropriate means to engage in many types of social interactions. The variation of the social content across integrated settings provides natural opportunities for communicative interaction and for different social functions to be expressed. Social skills are an essential component of school and community activities. A number of authors advocate programming social skills in natural contexts due to the nonsegmented nature of interactions, and the need to generalize appropriate social behavior (Certo & Kohl, 1984; Schutz et al., 1984; Voeltz. 1984). Subsequently integrated settings provide the natural social contexts that may be necessary to teach effective communication.

However, special considerations need to be made since many handicapped students demonstrate such limited communication skills or limited abilities to generalize acquired communication skills. Since many of these individuals use prelanguage or alternative methods to communicate. additional considerations become critical. First, other forms of alternative communication systems may need to be trained so that persons unfamiliar with the student can communicate with him/her. Second, persons within integrated settings may require specialized training in order to maximize the opportunities for appropriate interactions.

Selecting and Developing Effective Communication Systems and Content

For students involved in integrated settings, three major questions need to be asked:

1. Is the communication system that the student currently uses with his/her primary language models (parents, teachers, professionals) effective and efficient with those persons?
2. Is the same communication system also effective and efficient with unfamiliar persons who may become significant persons in interactions with integrated settings?
3. Does the manner in which the student uses his/her communication system present more of a disadvantage to promote positive attitudes and positive interactions rather than an advantage?

It is important that the student's current communication system be evaluated across different integrated activities based on: (a) effectiveness, (b) efficiency, and (c) appropriateness. While many students with moderate handicaps are able to use manual signs effectively and efficiently in their primary environments (e.g., home and classroom), these students may not be able to communicate effectively with school peers who are nonhandicapped or with other persons in the community. Concurrent augmentative systems, such as pointing to a picture book or card, may need to be trained for the student to communicate and participate in integrated settings. This does not mean that manual sign communication can not be expanded in those settings by training other persons to discriminate and use manual signs. In many cases, manual signs may be the student's most efficient system when communicating with familiar persons. The time that it takes to transmit a message is also very critical. Often students with physical handicaps who are quite skilled with a communication board system use vocalizations concurrent with prelanguage behaviors (e.g., facial expressions, body movements, eye gaze) instead of using their communication system. The communication board may be more effective if the vocabulary items are present; however, in certain contexts the use of prelanguage behaviors may be more efficient. Therefore, it is important to train the most effective and efficient communication responses across different integrated settings. For example, a student who can use two-word sign combinations may need to learn the following discrimination to demonstrate the most effective and efficient communication:

1. Use signs at home and in the classroom;
2. Use signs with classmates and peers who sign;
3. Use prelanguage forms to peers who do not know signs (e.g., wave, point, gestures);

4. Use picture books to order meals. shop. and participate in community recreational activities; and

5. Use prelanguage responses that are natural to all environments when they are most efficient (such as nodding head yes/no) instead of pointing to pictures or written words.

Therefore, the student must learn *how, when,* and with *whom* to communicate. Once a student engages in basic communication interactions. other aspects that contribute to the effectiveness and appropriateness of the communication exchange must be considered. Each society has cultural and social rules specific to interpersonal interactions. The distance that we stand from a listener, eye contact. forms of address, and touching a listener are important variables in communication programming within integrated settings.

Students who use speech to communicate are frequently at a disadvantage when priorities are made. Since they usually can communicate effectively with familiar persons who understand their speech approximations in routine contexts, their communication abilities within integrated settings may not be adequately assessed or targeted for intervention. In addition, while other individuals have intelligible speech and display fairly appropriate language structures, they often demonstrate related social behaviors that label them as "handicapped." These social behaviors that are critical to the appropriateness of language within interpersonal interactions are illustrated in the conversation checklist shown in Table 2. The checklist format can be used across various integrated contexts in order that specific training procedures can be implemented.

The interpersonal communication skills of individuals with moderate and severe handicaps can be extremely varied. Many of these individuals may never achieve "conversation skills" in which they engage in dialogue and adhere to all of the subtle social rules specific to our culture. Consequently. no one set of intervention strategies and procedures will be applicable across the variations of communication skills and needs. An integral relationship must exist between the validity of the responses selected for training. and the training procedures that are implemented (McFall, 1982).

Utilizing Systematic Training to Increase Interpersonal Communication

Wilcox and Sailor (1980) stressed that the major integration issues to be addressed by administrators, educators, and parents no longer should focus on "does integration work?" Instead, efforts should be directed to "how to make integration work?" The purpose of integrating is not simply the physical placement of a student with special needs in the public schools and community; rather integration activities should result in regular and sus-

TABLE 11-2
CONVERSATIONAL CHECKLIST

Name:	*Consistently Displays = X*
Date:	*Inconsistently Displays = X0*
Setting:	*Never Displays = 0*

Behaviors	Dates		
1. Initiates conversation with a number of persons.			
2. Looks at listener during conversation.			
3. Touches listener only appropriately.			
4. Stands at appropriate distance during conversation.			
5. Addresses listener.			
6. Gives enough information.			
7. Gives truthful information.			
8. Gives only nonredundant information.			
9. Gives relevant information.			
10. Uses polite forms.			
11. Listens to speaker without frequent interruptions.			
12. Responds appropriately to speaker's questions.			
13. Inquires about others.			
14. Maintains topic of other.			
15. Says several things about one topic.			
16. Requests only needed information.			
17. Uses statements or declarative sentences.			
18. Asks questions.			
19. Requests action of another (Imperatives).			
20. Uses appropriate tone for negative statements or requests.			
21. Initiations (tally frequency).			
22. Responses (tally frequency).			

tained interactions between nonhandicapped students and students with special needs (Taylor, 1982). There is a growing agreement among educators that positive interactions between nonhandicapped and handicapped students are important to the overall development and socialization of both groups even when the handicaps are so severe that integration into regular classrooms may be difficult (Rynders, Johnson, Johnson, & Schmidt, 1980). A number of studies (McHale & Simeonsson, 1980; Voeltz, 1980, 1982) showed that increased contact of nonhandicapped and severely handicapped students can influence the accepting attitudes of nonhandicapped students toward their handicapped peers. However, positive attitudes do not necessarily assure that increases in social interactions will occur. The work of a number of educators (Bricker, 1978; Fredericks et al., 1978; Guralnick, 1980; Hamre-Nietupski & Nietupski, 1981; Stainback & Stainback, 1981) indicated that specialized arrangements of the environment and programming may be necessary if positive interactions are to occur.

Communication should not be targeted in isolation but rather within other social interactions, such as leisure skills, daily living skills, and community activities (Gaylord-Ross, Stremel-Campbell, & Storey, 1984). Therefore, the strategies to be discussed are applicable to the communication skills discussed earlier as well as other social skills. The selection of the strategies that are effective to increase interpersonal social skills will depend upon the amount of support the handicapped individual and the peers need to initiate and sustain interactions between one another. The extent of environmental and trainer support necessary will depend upon the social, communicative, and cognitive skills of the peers with handicaps. Individuals with higher levels of skills will require less trainer support during the interactions. Subsequently, individuals with limited social, communication, and cognitive skills will require greater environmental manipulation and trainer support.

The instructional strategies discussed within this section are applicable to preschool children through secondary students. Both the age and the functioning level of each individual are major factors that need to be considered in selecting intervention procedures. The major point to be made is that communication training will be discussed as an ongoing component of social interaction training. Both nonhandicapped peers and other handicapped peers will be described as "peer partners," since interactions necessarily include the behavior of two or more persons. It is equally important to increase the communication between other handicapped peers and between handicapped and nonhandicapped peers if we are to increase the communication effectiveness of ultimate functioning within integrated environments.

Stainback, Stainback, Raschke, and Anderson (1981) discussed three methods to facilitate interactions between handicapped and nonhandicapped peers. These are (a) classroom organization, structure, and materials; (b) training severely handicapped students in interactional skills, and (c) training nonhandicapped peers to interact with severely handicapped students. The strategies presented in this chapter for increasing social and communication interactions are variations of these and include:

1. Systematic design and arrangement of the environment;
2. Peer mediated strategies; and
3. Trainer mediated strategies.

Systematic Design and Arrangement of the Environment

Environmentally mediated interventions are strategies in which the interaction routine is arranged to facilitate positive social and communicative interactions between the handicapped individual and other persons. This intervention strategy may be used in isolation for individuals who exhibit social skills in some settings, but who do not generalize these skills to other relevant settings and persons. For individuals with limited or low baseline rates of social and communication skills, the environmentally mediated interventions are used in conjunction with other strategies. Four major procedures are included within environmental mediations: (a) selection of peers, (b) selection of activities and materials, (c) arrangement of the physical environment, and (d) selection of the type of programming.

Selection of peers. Research relevant to peer selection variables with elementary and secondary students is limited. The majority of information available is from studies that have been conducted with preschool children with mild or moderate handicaps. There is evidence that cross-age interactions are different than same-age interactions when children are placed in social contact situations (Loagee, Gruenich, & Hartup, 1977). These authors found that three year olds were more active socially when interacting with a five year old than when interacting with another three year old; five year olds were more active socially when interacting with another five year old than with three year olds. Other studies (Goldman, 1976) also showed that specific social learning opportunities may be unique to mixed-age interactions. Sex differences also seem to influence positive social interactions. Fagot and Patterson (1969) found that three year old boys rewarded one another about five times as frequently as they rewarded girls, and girls rewarded each other approximately seven times as frequently as they rewarded boys. The friendship status between two children also determines the incentive value of peer rewards. Hartup (1964) found that rewards are more effective when given by a low friendship status peer than when given by a friend. These peer variables should be taken into account when programming the use of other peers as reinforcing agents in the training and socialization of handicapped children.

However, the data specific to preschool children cannot be generalized to older students. Table 3 outlines a list of considerations teachers have used to select peers for older students. One of the major factors is selecting an age appropriate peer. A number of teachers involved in the Teaching Research Integration Project have indicated that peers with special needs (although not characterized as handicapped by the school) have made excellent peer partners and also have benefited from the interactions. Other teachers have recruited groups of school leaders (e.g., the football team) to serve as peer advocates to model positive social interactions to the school body. The social "rules" of each peer group (i.e., preschool, elementary, middle school, and secondary) vary widely and must be considered in selecting peers and determining appropriate activities.

Selection of activities and materials. One of the most important steps in arranging the environment for social-communication interactions is to include the handicapped student in integrated activities in which communication naturally occurs. To increase the student's communication effectiveness. it may be necessary to assess his/her communication skills with different persons across different settings. The student's communicative competence with a parent or teacher may not represent his/her competencies with peers in integrated settings To increase the student's communication with class-mates and other peers, it is critical that assessment procedures and IEP objectives reflect peer interaction and communication. Hopefully. a wide range of communication skills will be trained incidentally within social interactions. However, development of specific IEP objectives will assist the teacher in targeting and evaluating the major communicative behaviors. Initially, the integrated activities need to be analyzed to determine the communication that is mandatory to complete the task, and the communica-tion that is optional to the task-related interaction (Certo & Kohl. 1984). Next, the teacher must observe the student within the relevant interactions to assess skills and needs. Once age appropriate and functional communica-tion needs have been identified within the diverse integrated settings. the specific instructional techniques must be determined.

TABLE 11-3
SELECTION OF PEERS AND ACTIVITIES

Selection of Peers	Selection of Activities
Select a peer who is within two years of age of the student with handicaps.	Select activities that the student with severe handicaps has most of the skills to perform.
Select a peer for whom the student with handicaps indicated a preference.	Select activities that provide natural opportunities for interaction.
Select a peer who will continue attending the same schools as the student with handicaps.	Select activities that require the peer to take a peer role rather than a supervisor role.
Select a peer who is familiar to the student with handicaps.	Select activities that provide opportunities for *varied* interactions.
Conduct an integrated activity with a small group of students. Select a peer who is most comfortable and interested in becoming a peer partner with a student who is handicapped.	
Ask the student with handicaps who he/she would like for a peer partner.	

While the student hopefully is included in a wide variety of integrated activities, certain integrated activities are more conducive to communication. Frequent reciprocal interactions, cooperation (Rynders et al., 1980) and interactions that are mutually reinforcing serve as the major activities in which peer communication can be trained. For example, breakfast and dinner may be appropriate activities to increase communication skills with siblings or housemates for older students. Task-related communication skills may be trained during "eating in a restaurant" activity. However, lunch within a public school may not afford as many appropriate opportunities for the student to communicate at his/her level. This does not mean that opportunities for interactions with peers should not be encouraged. Rather, independent eating skills may be a priority IEP objective in which the student is *not* to request that others get his/her napkin, open his/her milk, or return the tray.

The scheduling of specific activities must also be considered in arranging the environment. Less rigorous activities can be rotated with more rigorous activities; more reinforcing activities can follow less reinforcing activities. The establishment of routines also is important so that the environment itself can set the occasion for specific responses. Infrequent changes within the routine have the potential to evoke verbal initiations and questioning behavior.

Four of the important aspects of selecting appropriate activities for increasing communication in integrated settings include: (a) activities for a small group of participants, (b) activities that are natural and age appropriate to all persons, (c) activities that are mutually reinforcing to both the handicapped and nonhandicapped students, and (d) activities that will continue to be functional in post-school environments. Table 3 presents additional considerations to be made in selecting activities. Table 4 outlines specific activities across age groupings that have been effective in targeting both prelanguage and language interactions for individuals with moderate and severe handicaps.

The selection of materials also is an important consideration in arranging the integrated environment. A review of the preschool literature shows that more conflicts are likely to occur between preschool children when play space is restricted or when a limited number of objects or pieces of equipment are available. Also, the presence of specific materials such as climbing equipment, blocks, trucks, tricycles, and clay cause fewer conflicts than sand or water play (Quilitch & Risley, 1973).

Quilitch and Risley (1973) demonstrated that some toys are primarily "isolate" (i.e., played with by one child at a time), and other toys are "social" (i.e., played with by two to four children at a time). They suggested that through the selection of appropriate play materials, educators can create environments to maximize children's opportunities to practice social interaction. Therefore, the social interaction trainer should use materials that generally are used by more than one person at a time. Sometimes the peer partners will prefer "isolate" materials to the "social" materials selected by the trainer. In these situations, the trainer can use a strategy, "cooperative goal structuring" (Rynders et al., 1980), in which isolate materials or activi-

TABLE 11-4
SUGGESTED ACTIVITIES SOCIAL INTERACTION TRAINING

Younger Student	Older Student
Playing with blocks	Taking turns shooting baskets
Playing with cars and trucks	Playing darts on a Velcro Dart Board
Taking turns jumping on a small trampoline	Playing Frisbee golf
Taking turns rocking on rocking horse	Going to the store
Swinging on swing	Going to the snack bar
Rolling ball back and forth	Making a scrapbook
Playing make believe kitchen	Cooking
Singing	Painting
Playing outside on equipment	Making a collage
Dancing	Playing Table Games (e.g.. Sorry. Dominoes)
Playing tape recorder/record player	Playing Video games
Putting on lotion	Playing records/albums
Snack time activity	Playing radio
Making simple snacks	Going to restaurant
Blowing bubbles	Bowling
Taking turns activating toy	Playing cards
Riding/pulling wagon	Playing Simon
Playing musical instruments	Looking at books or magazines
Playing with dolls	Playing Juke Box
Playing "dress-up"	Dancing (appropriate context)
Playing with clay	Playing tape recorder
Playing at sand table	Playing pinball
Playing with Lite Bright	Riding bikes
Playing with Sno Cone machine	Going out for coffee
Playing with puppets	Going for a beer

ties can be used to increase social interaction between the peer partners.

It is also important that duplicates of materials be available for the students so that opportunities for modeling and imitation are available. Providing two students with materials that must be used together is also a strategy to promote peer interactions. Finally, rotation of materials and changes in the environment can set the occasion for children to increase initiations directed toward both adults and peers.

Arrangement of the physical environment. The trainer should arrange the physical environment of the social interaction setting so it is conducive to positive interaction between the peers. Peers that cannot see each other. are cold, or are distracted will have a difficult time interacting with each other. Some suggestions for arranging the physical environment are:

1. Position the peers so they can see or orient themselves toward each other. Young children attempting to interact with a peer in a wheelchair may need something to stand on so they can see over the wheelchair tray.
2. Make sure the peers are not too hot or too cold. If it is a cold, windy

day, have them wear their coats outside or stay inside. If it is hot outside, have them interact with each other in the shade.

3. Be sensitive to the noise level in the interaction setting. It should be quiet enough for the peers to hear each other.
4. Arrange for the peers to interact with each other in settings that are comfortable to them. The setting should not be too large or too small.

A number of students with moderate handicaps demonstrate interpersonal communication directed toward an adult but demonstrate few communication interactions toward their peers. If individuals do exhibit the social and communicative skills but do not generalize these skills, a simple strategy may be to remove the adult from the activity.

Selection of the type of programming. Rydners et al. (1980) found that cooperative goal structuring (i.e., teaming students in groups to complete a task) was more effective in producing positive interactions between students with handicaps and their peers than other structures traditionally used by teachers. Other structures included competitive goal structure (i.e., the students compete with each other) and individualistic goal structure (i.e., the student's attainment of the goal is unrelated to the other students). Cooperative goal structuring can be used during social interaction training by having peer partners complete projects or use objects together. This strategy also allows the trainer to use isolate toys (Quilitch & Risley, 1973) because the peers can use them at the same time (e.g., peers playing with a puzzle together, peers making one object out of Play-Doh). There are numerous possibilities for increasing positive interaction between peer partners by using this strategy.

Peer Mediated Strategies

Peer mediated strategies include any peer training that occurs outside of the ongoing interaction. Peers involved in integrated activities may need a general level of training that is specific to the individual with a handicap. For example, when students have limited communication and imitation skills or nonvocal language systems, training may be necessary for the peer partner. The individuals within the communicative interaction must have a "shared system of communication" in which the partner can use and receive additional prelanguage behaviors, manual signs, or the functions of a communication board. Peer partners who are trained to use the students' language system may require additional training to serve as models and to learn to be more tolerant of the time it may take to transmit a message via augmentative systems. Also, the student is more likely to utilize the augmentative system and not revert back to gestures, unintelligible speech or vocalizations if the peer shares the communication system.

Knowing the manner in which the student communicates sets the occasion for communication to occur, but does not assure that these interactions will occur. Often, additional training and arrangements of the environment will be necessary. A number of features of the training should include:

1. Training or facilitating a proper position for communication;
2. Training the peer to use specific cues to increase the student's responding and initiating;
3. Providing the peer with specific knowledge concerning what the student can communicate about; and
4. Training the peer to make social bids and to serve as a model and reinforcing agent.

Peers who interact with students with physical or sensory handicaps need to learn the importance of their position when communicating. Often, peers will push the student in a wheelchair and talk to the student without establishing eye contact. The student's efforts to establish or maintain eye contact may force them out of the most appropriate physical position. Interactions with students with auditory and visual impairments may require additional attention to the peers' method of approach and positioning.

Older peers may need to learn to reduce the complexity of their language and to provide different levels of cues to increase the student's initiations and appropriate responses. Guralnick and Paul-Brown (1980) found that nonhandicapped children adapted their communication according to the communication competence of a listener with different developmental levels. However, these data cannot be generalized to older students and adults (Seigal, 1963) without supporting data. The types of cues used by teachers (see Table 5) are also applicable to peers so that more independent communicative behavior occurs between the student and the peer.

Two peer mediated strategies that recently have appeared in the literature include *peer modeling* and *peer social initiations.* Peer modeling involves having the nonhandicapped peers model specific, positive social behaviors to the handicapped student. Peer social initiations is a strategy which the peer is taught to deliver "social bids" or social invitations to the student with handicaps. Both strategies also include reinforcement and role play provided by the social interaction trainer. Strain (1981) concluded that the peer social initiation strategy was more advantageous than the peer modeling strategy based on success with students with severe handicaps. However, available data indicate (Strain, Kerr, & Ragland, 1979) that more information is needed regarding how to use this strategy in a way that will facilitate generalization.

TABLE 11-5

TYPES OF CUES FOR COMMUNICATION

Environmental Cues — to increase initiations

Arrangement of materials

Routines

Indirect Cues — to increase initiations

Focused attention — "Johnny. it's your turn."

"Johnny. look what we have."

Nothing is free — Require student to request what is wanted or needed.

"Playing naive" — Require student to express himself at the level he is capable.

Direct Cues

Demand for communication — "Tell me what you want."

Wh questions — "What do you want?"

Yes/no questions — "Do you want an apple?"

Prompt Cues

Closure — "You need a _____." Student responds "napkin."

Gesture/sign prompts — "You have a napkin." Student signs. *napkin.*

"You have a _____" while signing cracker.

Child/student says "cracker."

Verbal prompt for a sign response.

Model

Prelanguage — Trainer models the gesture. "no" — Student imitates gesture.

Sign — Trainer models the sign *cheese.* Student imitates the sign.

Verbal — Trainer models. "juice." Student imitates "juice."

Physical Assist (use fading procedures so less assistance is gradually provided)

Prelanguage responses

Sign

Trainer Mediated Interventions

Trainer mediated interventions are strategies in which both nonhandi-capped peers and the students with handicaps are directly taught to interact with each other by an adult. While peer intervention strategies without direct teacher facilitation (Strain, 1981) may be successful with students who exhibit certain levels of initiation and communication skills, additional techniques (e.g., adult prompting and reinforcement) may be necessary initially to increase positive communicative interactions (Apolloni, Cooke, & Cooke, 1977; Cooke, Cooke, & Apolloni, 1978; Peck, Cooke, & Apolloni, 1981). Unfortunately, adult facilitation also may interfere with ongoing interactions (Certo & Kohl, 1984). Additional research with older students is necessary to determine when adult mediated techniques facilitate interactions, and when they decrease ongoing levels on interactions. One thing is certain —

social interactions have to occur before they can be decreased.

Perhaps a more critical aspect of the use of trainer mediated techniques would include "when and how" they are used rather than if they should be used. Preliminary data (Stremel-Campbell, Clark-Guiida, Johnson-Dorn, 1984) show that even though peers were trained to use manual signs and speech and used signs in a cooking integration activity, 80% of the students did not use speech or natural volume in conjunction with signs without adult prompts and reinforcement. A focus on appropriate uses of trainer mediated strategies includes: (a) cues and reinforcement, (b), demonstration, (c) role play, and (d) partial participation.

Cues and reinforcement. Cues are used by the trainer to tell the peers what to do. The cue training should include a minimal assist strategy so that a final objective of training would be reciprocal communication initiations and responses by both the peer and the student *without* direct trainer mediation. These levels of cues for communication were Presented in Table 5. In addition, cues given to the peer may range from subtle "hints" or suggestions (e.g., "John really likes bubbles.") to more direct instructions (i.e., "Use the bubbles to get him to look.").

Initially cues should be used in conjunction with reinforcement. A number of considerations are critical if the interactions are to become more naturally reinforcing without direct trainer mediation. These considerations include:

1. Change the activity or try another type of interaction if the peers do not use a suggestion or if they do not want to join in the activity.
2. Use language that the peers understand. For example, say "Get him to look at you" rather than "Be sure to get eye contact."
3. Feel free to cue *both* peers.
4. Do not over cue. This will encourage the peers to rely on the trainer for information on how to interact with each other. Use a delay technique of waiting for the peers to initiate interaction.
5. Fade cues as quickly as possible.
6. Be subtle when reinforcing the peer.
7. Do not interrupt or inhibit interaction between the peers by reinforcing them. Try to make reinforcement as unobtrusive as possible.
8. Only use social reinforcement unless it has been determined that the peers need additional reinforcers to motivate them to interact with each other. Some preschool teachers use reinforcement charts, stickers, or a special activity at the end of the session to motivate specific students.

Demonstration. Demonstrations can be used by the trainer to show the peers how to interact with each other. They particularly are desirable when teaching the nonhandicapped peer how to communicate or to greet, take turns, or share with the handicapped student. The following are suggestions for the social interaction trainer using demonstration as a strategy for increasing positive social interactions between the peer partners.

1. Keep the directions and actions simple in the demonstration.
2. Demonstrate the interaction as a peer model rather than a teacher model. This will encourage the peers to interact with each other in a peer-peer interaction model rather than a teacher-peer model.
3. Accept approximation of the action demonstrated.

Role play. Role play is used to "act out" the interactions before they actually occur between the peer partners. Using role play can help prepare the peers for what will happen during the interaction. This strategy can be very successful if it is used in the correct manner. Usually, role play is used only with the nonhandicapped peer. Some suggestions for the trainer using role play are:

1. Make the peer as comfortable as possible when using this strategy.
2. Portray the student with handicaps in a realistic but positive manner.
3. Reverse roles and have the nonhandicapped peer portray the partner. This can be helpful when teaching the peer how his/her partner uses his/her communication system. For example, the trainer asks the peer how he/she would ask for more juice if he/she could not talk. The peer might extend the glass to the juice can or point to the glass to request. Then the behavior possibly could be encouraged when he/she interacts with his/her peer partner.

Principle of partial participation. The trainer also can use, as a supplement to other training strategies, the principle of partial participation (Baumgart, Brown, Pumpian, Nisbet, Ford, Sweet, Messina, & Schroeder, 1982). The principle of partial participation is the orientation that persons with severe handicaps should not be excluded from activities they only can partially perform; rather the activity, skill, environment, or their performance should be altered in some way so they can participate as fully as possible.

There are four different ways the principle of partial participation typically is used with handicapped students. First, activities can be adapted so the student with handicaps can participate. For example, a preschool student with no verbal language skills was unable to join a small group of her peers in a singing activity. The trainer adapted the activity by having the student provide music for the singing. In this way, the student was able to participate with her peers. Second, materials can be adapted so the student with handicaps can participate in activities with age appropriate peers. Some examples of adapted materials are: (a) color coded dominoes, (b) velcro covered mitt and ball, (c) switch-operated tape recorder, and

(d) switch-operated toys. A variety of adapted switches (e.g., joy stick, push panel, grasp switch) can be made by the trainer to help students participate in activities they otherwise would miss (Burkhart, 1982). Third, adaptation may include changing the rules of the game or activity. For example, a middle school student with limited physical ability attempted to play "pick-up-sticks" with his peer partner. Unfortunately, he was unable to pick up a stick without touching other sticks (a rule of the game). The rules were adapted so he had to pick up only one stick but was allowed to touch the other sticks. The original rules remained the same for his partner. In this way, the peer partners were able to play a game they both enjoyed. Fourth, adaptations that can be helpful when working with young children is to add rules to the activity. This can help structure the activity so increased interactions can occur between the peer partners. A rule that commonly is added to activities is turn taking. The trainer can structure an activity so the peers take turns activating an object or working on a joint project.

As a trainer mediated intervention, partial participation takes the form of assistance provided to the student with handicaps so the student can participate at least partially in the activity. The assistance provided refers to verbal, gestural, physical, or supervisory assistance provided by the social interaction trainer. The following are important points to consider when providing assistance:

1. Adapt the materials, skills, or rules whenever possible. This is the most preferred type of partial participation the trainer can use.
2. Only provide assistance that the handicapped student needs to participate in the activity.
3. Provide the assistance in an unobtrusive manner.
4. Begin fading the assistance immediately.

Programming for Generalization

The acquisition of communication and language skills requires a continual process of discrimination and generalization. The student must learn to discriminate the relevant and irrelevant environmental cues, persons, and settings in which selected communication behaviors *should* and *should not* occur. Additionally, the student must learn to generalize appropriate communicative skills to relevant stimuli (e.g., including language cues, objects, events, persons, and settings). The generalization of social skills and communication skills possibly presents one of the greatest challenges because the environmental cues are often subtle and infinite. The student must learn:

1. When to communicate in different situations;
2. What to communicate about and with whom;

3. In what form to communicate;
4. How to sustain communication interactions; and
5. When to terminate communication.

The generalization of social skills also differs somewhat from the generalization of familiar persons in designated settings (Gaylord-Ross et al., 1984). Other social behaviors may be specific to the context of task related behaviors (e.g., shopping, eating in a restaurant) (Certo & Kohl, 1984). The literature points out that generalization of communication and social skills is not a natural outcome of training for individuals with moderate and severe handicaps (Strain, 1981; Stremel-Campbell & Campbell, 1984; Stokes & Baer, 1977; Wehman & Hill, 1982).

Utilizing Integration Training to Promote Generalization

The diversity and range of the activities, events, materials, and persons within integrated settings serve as facilitators to form the relevant discriminations and generalizations that are necessary for effective communication and language use. A number of the active generalization techniques categorized by Stokes and Baer (1977) can be more easily achieved if training occurs across integrated environments rather than being confined to structured 1:1 training in only a classroom setting. However, simply providing the student with access to integrated activities will not assure that generalization will occur. Generalization must still be a planned outcome of well developed intervention programs (Warren, 1977).

Integrated settings provide us with a range of multiple exemplars across materials, persons, and settings. Since training occurs within specific natural environments, concurrent training, natural consequences, and indiscriminable contingencies of reinforcement can readily be programmed during intervention. However, the trainer must take advantage of these integrated environmental features that have the potential to facilitate the generalization of communication. Initially, the most critical communication skills that are necessary to function effectively across different settings must be prioritized (Gaylord-Ross et al., 1984). An environmental inventory across settings and activities will enable the trainer to determine: (a) the communication skills that are critical to specific activities, and (b) the natural opportunities for communication across different activities (Brown et al., 1979; Stremel-Campbell & Campbell, 1984). As pointed out earlier, not all integrated activities provide maximum opportunities for communication and language to occur. Since the student cannot be trained in every activity or setting, care must be taken to select multiple activities and settings for training in which maximum opportunities for communication interactions do exist. Subsequently, the trainer also must select a range of social settings and activities (Horner, McDonnell, & Bellamy, 1984) that will provide for relevant discriminations to be made.

Persons within the integrated settings provide relationship cues (Voeltz, 1984) that are critical if generalization is to be achieved. Nonhandicapped peers have the potential to serve as age appropriate models for both the students and the trainer. Additionally, the criterion levels of communication skills (e.g., greeting, calling, initiating interactions, etc.) can best be determined by utilizing these peers to determine natural rates of behavior so that these behaviors are socially valid (Warren, 1977). Other adults who are significant to domestic and leisure activities provide a range of appropriate nonverbal and verbal cues (e.g., "Are you ready to order," "Do you want to order now," or "Have you decided what you wanted?") and to vary responses to similar cues (e.g. "Help me please," "I need Kleenex," "Where's the magazine?").

The activities within integrated environments provide natural cues that should ultimately control the student's communication interactions. For example, a waitress may simply approach the table, smile, and position her pencil to take the student's order for dinner. The trainers gradually must fade their prompts, "Order now," or "Tell her what you want," so that the student's communication exchange is not dependent on the verbal or nonverbal cues of the trainer. Therefore, it is critical to analyze the integrated environments to determine the range of stimuli that may control a similar response, the common stimuli that may control a similar response, and the common stimuli that may call for diverse responses. Integrated settings also provide communication trainers with more examples of natural cues. Persons who are socially skilled often use polite requests (e.g., "Are you ready to order," "Would you get that for me?") to get someone to give information or perform an action. Yet, many programs emphasize giving the student a direct command (e.g., "Work now," "Give me the _____."). It is important that the student learn to respond to polite requests and indirect cues as well as direct cues if they are to function appropriately within integrated activities.

Measuring Generalization

While specific integrated activities may be selected for direct communication training, other integrated settings and activities serve as generalization settings. That is, generalization can be measured in those settings in which training did not directly occur. However, care must be taken to determine that opportunities for the student to generalize trained communication skills are present. Opportunities to request, protest, greet, call, or comment may be more significant in some activities than in others. Additionally, the opportunities to use more specific language structures (e.g., "I want _____, please.") will be further limited to specific activities. Therefore, we must determine what aspects of communication and language to measure and in which settings to conduct our measurements. The ultimate criterion for determining the success of a student's communication program should include the effectiveness of a communicative interaction across different persons. The student must transmit a specific message that can be understood across various listeners. The student must also understand the messages directed to them and respond appropriately. In this way, the communication skills that are targeted within training become extremely important. If we target only vocabulary or specific utterances, we cannot expect the student ultimately to use "language" to communicate. Rather, we must focus on communication interactions and gradually present more specific and effective ways (through language) for the student to interact.

The effectiveness of techniques to increase communicative interactions with adults, siblings, classmates, or peers without handicaps can best be determined by the ongoing collection of data. Since communication is reciprocal, dyadic observational systems (Strain & Shores, 1977) which include the behavior of both partners will provide us with more information to make program modifications, rather than one in which only the student is observed. Observation procedures may include a variety of recording techniques (Sackett, 1978) in which the choice of a recording technique will depend on the IEP objectives, and the activities and settings where training occurs and/or generalization is expected.

Summary

This chapter outlined the important aspects of communicative behavior, and the training and generalization strategies used within integrated environments. This chapter stressed the importance of using these integrated settings to increase social and communicative interactions, rather than specifying communication and language systems as prerequisites, which typically exclude students with moderate and severe handicaps.

This chapter outlines four major points. First, language and communication skills cannot be trained in a restricted, isolated manner if these skills are to be used by the student across a variety of situations, persons, and settings. Rather, language and communication skills should be trained in a number of social interactions that are common to the student's living, school, work, and community environments. Second, the student's communication system should be evaluated across different integrated activities based on: (a) effectiveness, (b) efficiency, (c) and appropriateness. Third, instructional strategies for increasing communication effectiveness across integrated settings must be utilized. Fourth, the primary evaluation of programming must include the student's generalization of language and communication skills within various integrated environments to different persons since we cannot train in every possible environment.

Hopefully, these interactions will benefit both the students with handicaps as well as persons without apparent handicaps.*

REFERENCES

Apolloni, T. A., Cooke, S. R., & Cooke, T. P. Establishing a normal peer as a behavioral model for developmentally delayed children. *Perceptual and Motor Skills.* 1977, *44,* 231–241.

Bates, E., Benigni, L., Bretherton, I., Camaioni, L., & Volterra, V. *The emergence of symbols.* New York: Academic Press, 1979.

Baumgart, D., Brown, L., Pumpian, I., Nisbet, J., Ford, A., Sweet, M., Messina, R., & Schroeder, J. Principle of partial participation and individualized adaptations in educational programs for severely handicapped students. *The Journal of the Association for the Severely Handicapped,* 1982, *7*(6), 17–27.

Bloom, L., & Lahey, M. *Language development and language disorders.* New York: John Wiley & Sons, 1978.

Bricker, D. D. A rationale for the integration of handicapped and nonhandicapped school children. In M. Guralnick (Ed.), *Early intervention and integration of handicapped and nonhandicapped children.* Baltimore: University Park Press, 1978.

Brown, L., Branston, M., Hamre-Nieuptski, S., Pumpian, I., Certo, N., & Gruenewald, L. A strategy for developing chronological age appropriate and functional curriculum content for severely handicapped adolescents and young adults. *Journal of Special Education.* 1979, *13,* 81–90.

Bruner, J. From communication to language: A psychological perspective. *Cognition.* 1975, *3,* 255–289.

Burkhart, L. J. *More homemade battery devices for severely handicapped children with suggested activities.* College Park, MD: Author, 1982.

Certo, N., & Kohl, F. L. A strategy for developing interpersonal interaction instructional content for severely handicapped students. In N. Certo, N. Haring, & R. York (Eds.), *Public school integration of severely handicapped students.* Baltimore: Paul H. Brookes, 1984.

Cooke, T. P., Cooke, S. R., & Apolloni, T. Developing nonretarded toddlers as verbal models for retarded classmates. *Child Study Journal,* 1978, *8,* 1–8.

Dore, J. Holophrases, speech acts, and language universals. *Journal of Child Language,* 1975, *2,* 21–40.

Fagot, B. I., & Patterson, G. R. An in vivo analysis of reinforcing contingencies for sex-role behaviors in the preschool child. *Developmental Psychology.* 1969, *1,* 563–568.

Fredericks, H. D., Baldwin, V., Groves, D., Moore, W., Riggs, C., & Lyons, B. Integrating the moderately and severely handicapped preschool child into a normal day care setting. In M. Guralnick (Ed.), *Early intervention and the integration of handicapped and nonhandicapped children.* Baltimore: University Park Press, 1978.

*This chapter was produced under Contract Number 300-81-0411 from the Office of Special Education. U. S. Department of Education. The information and opinions expressed herein do not necessary reflect the position or policy of the Office of Special Education, and no official endorsement should be inferred.

Gaylord-Ross, R., Stremel-Campbell, K. & Storey, K. Social skills training in natural contexts. In R. H. Horner, L. M. Voeltz, & H. D. Fredericks (Eds.), *Education of learners with severe handicaps: Exemplary service strategies.* Baltimore: Paul H. Brookes, 1984.

Goldman, J. A. *The social participation of preschool children in same-age versus mixed-age groupings.* Unpublished doctoral dissertation, University of Wisconsin, 1976.

Gottman, J., Gonso, J., & Rasmussen, B. Friendships in children. *Child Development,* 1975, *46,* 709–718.

Grossman, H. J. *Manual on terminology and classification in mental retardation.* Washington, DC: American Association on Mental Deficiency, 1977.

Guralnick, M. Social interactions among preschool children. *Exceptional Children,* 1980, *16,* 248–253.

Guralnick, M. J., & Paul-Brown, D. Functional and discourse analyses of nonhandicapped preschool children's speech to handicapped children. *American Journal of Mental Deficiency,* 1980, *84*(5), 444–454.

Guralnick, M. J. Programmatic factors affecting child-child social interactions in mainstreamed preschool programs. *Exceptional Education Quarterly,* 1981, *1*(4), 71–91.

Halliday, M. Learning how to mean. In E. Lenneberg, & E. Lenneberg (Eds.), *Foundations of language development: A multi-disciplinary approach,* (Vol. 1), New York: Academic Press, 1975.

Hamre-Nietupski, S., & Nietupski, J. Integral involvement of severely handicapped students within regular public schools. *Journal of the Association for the Severely Handicapped,* 1981, *6,* 30–39.

Harris, D., & Vanderheiden, G. Enhancing the development of communicative interactions. In R. Schiefelbush (Ed.), *Nonspeech language and communication: Analysis and intervention.* Baltimore: University Park Press, 1980.

Hartup, W. W. Friendship status and the effectiveness of peers as reinforcing agents. *Journal of Experimental Child Psychology,* 1964, *1,* 154–162.

Hoben, M. Toward integration in the mainstream. *Exceptional Children,* 1980, *47*(2), 100–105.

Horner, R. H., McDonnell, J. J., & Bellamy, T. Efficient instruction of generalized behaviors: General case programming in simulation and natural settings. In R. H. Horner, L. M., Voeltz, & H. D. Fredericks (Eds.), *Education of learners with severe handicaps: Exemplary service strategies.* Baltimore: Paul H. Brookes, 1984.

LaGrecca, A. M., & Mesibou, G. B. Social skills intervention with learning disabled children: Selecting skills and implementing training. *Journal of Clinical Child Psychology,* 1979, *8,* 234–241.

Loager, M. D., Grueneich, R., & Hartup, W. W. Social interaction in same and mixed-age dyads of preschool children. *Child Development,* 1977, *48,* 1353–1365.

Mahoney, G. Etiological approach to delayed language acquisition. *American Journal of Mental Deficiency,* 1975, *80*(2), 139–148.

McFall, R. M. A review and reformulation of the concept of social skills. *Behavioral Assessment,* 1982, *4,* 1–33.

McHale, S., & Simeonsson, R. Effects of interaction on nonhandicapped children's attitudes toward autistic children. *American Journal of Mental Deficiency,* 1980, *85,* 18–24.

McLean, J. E., & Snyder-McLean, L. K. *A transactional approach to early language training.* Columbus, OH: Merrill, 1978.

Musselwhite, C. R., & St. Louis, K. W. *Communication programming for the severely handicapped: Vocal and nonvocal strategies.* Houston: College Hill Press, 1982.

Peck, C. A., Cooke, T. P., & Apolloni, T. Utilization of peer imitation in therapeutic and instructional contexts. In P. S. Strain (Ed.), *Peers as classroom change agents.* New York: Plenum, 1981.

Quilitch, H. R., & Risley, T. R. The effects of play materials on social play. *Journal of Applied Behavior Analysis*, 1973, *6*, 573–578.

Rynders, J., Johnson, R., Johnson, D., & Schmidt, B. Producing positive interaction among Downs Syndrome and nonhandicapped teenagers through cooperative goal structuring. *American Journal of Mental Deficiency*, 1980, *85*, 268–273.

Sackett, G. P. (Ed.). *Observing behavior (Vol. 2): Data collection and analysis methods*. Baltimore: University Park Press, 1978.

Sailor, W., Guess, D., Goetz, L., Schuler, A., Utley, B., & Baldwin, M. Language and severely handicapped persons: Deciding what to teach to whom. In W. Sailor, B. Wilcox, & L. Brown (Eds.), *Methods of instruction for severely handicapped students*. Baltimore: Paul H. Brookes, 1980.

Schutz, R. P., Williams, W., Iverson, G. S., & Duncan, D. Social integration of severely handicapped students. In N. Certo, N. Haring, & R. York (Eds.), *Public school integration of severely handicapped students*, 1984, 15–42.

Seibert, J. M., & Kimbrough-Oller, D. Linguistic pragmatics and language intervention strategies. *Journal of Autism and Developmental Disorders*, 1981, *11*(1), 75–86.

Siegel, G. M. Adult verbal behavior with retarded children labeled as "high" or "low" in verbal ability. *American Journal of Mental Deficiency*. 1963, *3*, 417–424.

Stokes, T. F., & Baer, D. M. An implicit technology of generalization. *Journal of Applied Behavior Analysis*, 1977, *10*, 349–367.

Stainback, W., & Stainback, S. A review of research on interactions between severely handicapped and nonhandicapped students. *The Journal of the Association for the Severely Handicapped*, 1981, *6*, 75–81.

Stainback, W., Stainback, S., Raschke, D., & Anderson, R. Three methods for encouraging interactions between severely handicapped and nonhandicapped students. *Education and Training of the Mentally Retarded*, 1981, *16*, 188–192.

Strain, P. S. Peer-mediated treatment of exceptional children's social withdrawal. *Exceptional Education Quarterly*, 1981, *4*, 93–105.

Strain, P. K., Kerr, M. M., & Ragland, E. U. Effects of peer-mediated social initiations and prompting/reinforcement procedures on the social behavior of autistic children. *Journal of Autism and Developmental Disorders*, 1979, *9*(1), 41–53.

Strain, P. S., & Shores, R. E. Social reciprocity: Review of research and educational implications. *Exceptional Children*, 1977, *43*, 526–531.

Stremel-Campbell, K., & Campbell, R. Training techniques that may facilitate generalization. In S. Warren & A. Rogers-Warren (Eds.), *Teaching functional language*. Baltimore: University Park Press, 1984.

Stremel-Campbell, K., Cantrell, D., & Halle, J. Manual signing as a language system and as a speech initiator for the nonverbal severely handicapped student. In E. Sontag, J. Smith, & N. Certo (Eds.), *Educational programming for the severely and profoundly handicapped*. Reston, VA: CEC Division on Mental Retardation, 1977.

Stremel-Campbell, K., Clark-Guiida, J., & Johnson-Dorn, N. *Prelanguage and language communication for children/youth with severe handicaps*. Monmouth, OR: Teaching Research, 1984.

Taylor, S. From segregation to integration: Strategies for integrating severely handicapped students in normal school and community settings. *Journal of the Association for the Severely Handicapped*, 1982, *8*, 42–49.

Voeltz, L. M. Children's attitudes toward handicapped peers. *American Journal of Mental Deficiency*, 1980, *84*, 455–464.

Voeltz, L. M. Effects of structured interactions with severely handicapped peers on children's attitudes. *American Journal of Mental Deficiency*, 1982, *86*, 380–390.

Voeltz, L. M. Program and curriculum innovations to prepare children for integration. In N. Certo, N. Haring, & R. York (Eds.), *Public school integration of severely handicapped students.* Baltimore: Paul H. Brookes, 1984.

Warren, S. Useful ecobehavioral perspective for applied behavior analysis. In A. Rogers-Warren & S. Warren (Eds.), *Ecological perspectives in behavior analysis.* Baltimore: University Park Press, 1977.

Warren, S., & Rogers-Warren, A. (Eds.), *Teaching functional language.* Baltimore: University Park Press, 1984.

Wehman, P., & Hill, J. Preparing severely handicapped youth for less restrictive environments. *Journal of the Association for the Severely Handicapped,* 1982, 7, 33–39.

Wilcox, R., & Sailor, W. Service delivery issues: Integrated education systems. In B. Wilcox, & R. York (Eds.), *Quality education for the severely handicapped: The federal investment.* Washington, DC: U.S. Department of Education, 1980.

CHAPTER 12*

DESIGNING AND IMPLEMENTING LEISURE PROGRAMS FOR INDIVIDUALS WITH SEVERE HANDICAPS

PAUL WEHMAN AND M. SHERRILL MOON

Leisure instruction for severely handicapped persons has begun to receive serious attention by researchers and teachers alike (Wehman, 1979a; Wehman & Schleien, 1981; Wuerch & Voeltz, 1982). Several years ago there were virtually no data-based studies available which investigated the leisure activity of severely handicapped persons. Within the past 6 to 8 years, however, there has been a substantial increase in the number of papers published in this important area (Voeltz, Wuerch, & Wilcox, 1982). It has become apparent to educators working with schoolaged severely handicapped children (Hopper & Wambold, 1978; Wehman & Marchant, 1977, 1978), as well as adult service providers (Corcoran & French, 1977), that the free time of moderately and severely handicapped people is a crucial aspect of community integration and community acceptance.

Before going further, it will be helpful to review the terminology used in this chapter and specifically to highlight the major elements of an appropriate leisure program. The terms leisure, recreation, and play will be used interchangeably throughout our discussion. We will leave the definitional nuances of play and leisure to other authors (Ellis, 1973; McCall, 1974; Nunnally & Lemond, 1973). Rather, we will focus on four elements that should characterize leisure programs: (a) *fun or enjoyment,* (b) *constructive or purposeful behavior,* (c) *participation,* and (d) *self-initiated behavior and choice.*

Voeltz, Wuerch, and Wilcox (1982) noted that *fun and enjoyment* are critical in the design of a leisure program. This element is perhaps the most differentiating characteristic between leisure and other major skill domains

---

Paul Wehman is an Associate Professor of Special Education and Director of Virginia Commonwealth University's Rehabilitation Research and Training Center. He has been a national leader in creating competitive employment opportunities for mentally retarded persons for a number of years. He has also published extensively in the areas of community based leisure, recreation, and educational programming.

Sherrill Moon is an Instructor of Special Education and is Director of Training at Virginia Commonwealth University's Rehabilitation Research and Training Center. Her research interests and publications have included physical fitness for mentally retarded persons, leisure-recreation programming and vocational transition issues.

such as work, domestic/home living, and community functioning. Certainly in implementing a leisure program the teacher must be sensitive to providing an enjoyable and fun atmosphere for the student with activities which, ideally, are naturally reinforcing. Teaching students to tie shoe laces, sort circuit breakers, or label pictures, on the other hand, are not activities which will usually be considered "fun."

The second aspect of leisure which must be considered is the *purposefulness* and/or *constructive nature* of the activity. Admittedly, this can be a highly subjective concept, but it must be evaluated. Consider the likelihood of an institutionalized profoundly retarded woman who body rocks constantly in the day room, smiling and laughing all the time. Of course, this is not the type of leisure which is normalizing and which service providers want to encourage. Hence, some attempt to assess appropriate object function as well as duration of time with activity must be made.

The third component which must be considered is *participation*, even if it is only partial participation (Baumgart et al., 1982). Leisure is one curriculum area in which total proficiency and competence is not essential. If one can enjoy an activity by limited involvement, the same recreational goals will be met. More discussion will follow in this chapter on how to improve participation through adaptations.

A fourth element of leisure programs involves client choice or preference, and specifically, the ability to *self-initiate* activities which are desirable. It is significant that virtually all of the leisure studies which have been performed with severely handicapped persons (and other mentally retarded individuals as well) do not demonstrate self-initiated responses. Instead, behaviors typically have been shaped, generalized, and maintained, but self-initiation has not been specifically addressed. Yet leisure is perhaps more of a choice activity than any other life skill domain. We must be sensitive to this component.

In sum, the ultimate result of an appropriate leisure program should allow for the client to be able to self-initiate constructive leisure activities that are enjoyable and satisfying. There should be a repertoire of activities that have been taught, and subsequently for which materials are made available. Rote and mechanical use of one object for months and months is not the ultimate objective of a well-designed leisure program.

The Importance of Leisure Programs

Leisure programs need to be formalized and structured for moderately and severely handicapped individuals. As we have noted repeatedly in earlier writings (Wehman, 1977; 1979a) leisure skills cannot be assumed to develop normally but will require systematic instruction. Since leisure objectives need to be formalized, what logically follows is that most students' Individual Education Plans (IEPs) or adults' Individual Habilitation Plans (IHPs) should reflect leisure objectives for acquisition and/or generalization. There are numerous reasons for emphasizing leisure programs for severely handicapped individuals. Some of these reasons follow.

Enhancing Quality of Life

Many severely handicapped people frequently have a large amount of free time available. Since the likelihood of full employment is not good in the near future, the necessity of appropriate use of leisure is evident. Schleien, Wehman, and Kiernan (1981) recognized this fact in their study of low quality, high quality, and inappropriate leisure activity of moderately retarded adults in a community based group home. The amount of low quality or inappropriate leisure was markedly high before specific leisure instruction was provided. Improved leisure capabilities of severely handicapped persons can have a markedly positive affect on their quality of life. With severely multiply handicapped and nonambulatory profoundly retarded individuals, the amount of free time is extensive. It is necessary that we study ways in which to expand the leisure opportunities for these individuals.

Prevention of Institutionalization

Developing appropriate leisure programs can facilitate community retention of severely handicapped individuals. Respite care programs and community recreation programs are two vehicles for helping maintain severely handicapped persons in the community. In developing a training program for volunteers to work in a respite care program, we have found that recreation and leisure instruction is an essential aspect of reducing the probability of institutionalization (Inge, Moon, & Hill, 1983). It is increasingly apparent that persons and other caretakers will be more willing to maintain a child at home who can play independently and not exhibit destructive behaviors.

Community and Vocational Adjustment

There is little doubt that severely handicapped individuals who have a repertoire of appropriate leisure and other social interaction skills have a superior opportunity to maintain a job and to retain a community living placement. Greenspan and Shultz (1981) found in an extended review of retarded employees in Nebraska that job loss was directly related to inadequacy of social skills. Our own employment research (Wehman, 1981) confirms this deficit as one major problem severely handicapped workers face in job retention. Similarly, Novak and Heal (1981) also noted that competence in social, leisure, and other critical community skills is crucial in helping moderately and severely handicapped individuals adjust in the community and become fully integrated.

Behavior Management

One common characteristic of many severely handicapped individuals is behavioral excesses which can lead to serious management problems. These problems often include property destruction, self-abuse, pica, and assault. Numerous investigators (Favell, 1973) have found that leisure skill training is an excellent means of reducing these behaviors. Constructive leisure responses are often incompatible with inappropriate social behaviors.

These reasons only briefly touch on the value of leisure instruction. Hopefully, the reader can see the multi-faceted benefits of a well-planned recreation program.

Leisure in the Home and Community

In a recent summary of previously published literature in the leisure area (Wehman, Renzaglia, & Bates, in press), it was observed that in approximately 30 studies, few of the leisure activities described actually took place in either the client's home or community. Most leisure programs occurred in school classrooms or institutional environments. This review underscored the fact that much more attention must be paid to providing community based leisure instruction (Wehman & Hill, 1982).

It is somewhat ironic that leisure, a skill area which is consistently practiced and should occur most frequently either at home (Burch, date unknown) or in a community setting (Hill, Wehman, & Horst, 1982), has attracted so little literature addressing this concern. Many more home training programs and efforts at generalization of leisure skills must be initiated. In addition, there needs to be an awareness on the part of practitioners that leisure programs, regardless of how well the design, are of very limited value if they are not practiced in the natural environments in which they are supposed to occur. This issue relates directly to the identification and selection of leisure skills for instruction.

Identifying and Selecting Leisure Skills for Instruction

Wehman and Schleien (1981) and Wuerch and Voeltz (1982) have more than adequately described the importance of selecting leisure skills carefully. Wuerch and Voeltz (1982) have especially gone to great lengths on this topic and have successfully expanded and improved our earlier work.

There are several important factors which need to be considered. The first is chronological age appropriateness (would the skill selected also be of interest to and be performed by a nonhandicapped peer of similar age?). Selection of age appropriate activities is necessary to communicate to others the competence and dignity of severely handicapped persons. A second factor relates to the attitudes of parents and other family members and the availability of leisure materials in the home environment. Without sensitivity to this issue, the carry over of leisure programs into the home will be greatly limited. The types of community resources in a given locality is also essential to deciding what skills should be prioritized for instruction. Urban areas will suggest and provide for certain leisure outlets while sparsely populated rural locations will probably have dissimilar types of leisure opportunities. Finally, the attitude, aptitude, and skills of the client or child are crucial. If an activity is to be fully enjoyed, the client should have input in deciding which activities will be emphasized for training.

In Table 1, a leisure skill selection chart is reprinted from the Wuerch and Voeltz text. They have broken skill selection into major categories of normalization philosophy, individualization, and environment. Thirteen items are arranged across these categories.

One final word is in order about leisure skill selection. This is potentially the most important part of the leisure program design process. Identifying the appropriate activities for instruction will set the tone, positively or negatively, of the entire program. This area of program development may, in fact, be where most activity therapists and teachers show limitations. Skills are selected capriciously and on the basis of administrative convenience, grouping arrangements, Special Olympics acceptance, or supply of funds. There needs to be as much effort placed into the skill selection process as there is in the actual instruction provided.

Types of Leisure

Leisure and recreational activities have been categorized in a variety of ways to include: physical, cultural, social and mental activities; outdoor and indoor activities; spectator and participant activities; passive and active activities; independent, cooperative, and competitive activities; community based activities; and sports, games, hobbies, and toy play (Bates & Renzaglia, 1979; Moon & Renzaglia, 1982; Sherrill, 1981; Wehman & Schleien, 1981). We have chosen for purposes of this chapter to classify leisure programs for handicapped individuals into sports, games, hobbies, and toy play because these four categories encompass all types of functional, community based activities. Included within each category are both indoor and outdoor and

TABLE 12-1
LEISURE ACTIVITY SELECTION CHECKLIST

Normalization: A concern for selecting activities that have social validity and that will facilitate normalized play and leisure behaviors, as well as provide opportunities for movement toward increasingly complex interactions.

1. Age Appropriateness — Is this activity something a nonhandicapped peer would enjoy during free time?
2. Attraction — Is this activity likely to promote interest of others who frequently are found in the youth's leisure time settings?
3. Environmental Flexibility — Can this activity be used in a variety of potential leisure time situations on an individual and group basis?
4. Degree of Supervision — Can the activity be used under varying degrees of caregiver supervision without major modifications?
5. Longitudinal Application — Is use of the activity appropriate for both an adolescent and an adult?

Individualization: Concerns related to meeting the unique and ever-changing needs and skills of handicapped youth.

1. Skill Level Flexibility — Can the activity be adapted for low to high entry skill levels without major modifications?
2. Prosthetic Capabilities — Can the activity be adapted to varying handicapping conditions (sensory, motor, behavior)?
3. Reinforcement Power — Is the activity sufficiently novel or stimulating to maintain interest?

Environmental: Concerns related to logistical and physical demands of leisure activities on current and future environments and free time situations.

1. Availability — Is the activity available (or can it easily be made so) across the youth's leisure environments?
2. Durability — Is the activity likely to last without need for major repair or replacement of parts for at least a year?
3. Safety — is the activity safe, i.e., would not pose a serious threat to or harm the handicapped youth, others, or the environment if abused or used inappropriately?
4. Noxiousness — Is the activity not likely to be overly noxious (noisy, space consuming, distracting) to others in the youth's leisure environments?
5. Expense — Is the cost of the activity reasonable? That is, is it likely to be used for multiple purposes?

Reprinted with permission from Wuerch & Voeltz (1982)

independent and cooperative activities. Table 2 provides examples of activities from each category that have been successfully instructed to severely handicapped persons.

Definitions to Types of Leisure

Object manipulation. Appropriate manipulation of leisure materials is the basis of toy play and a precursor to optimally participating in sports, games, and hobbies. Although learning to manipulate leisure materials is the simplest form of leisure participation (Wehman & Schleien, 1981), is appropriate for instruction to adolescents and adults when they cannot interact functionally with certain materials such as balls, music materials, and vending machines.

Object manipulation skills can be taught simultaneously as separate leisure objectives (e.g., catching a ball) and within the context of more complex

TABLE 12-2

SAMPLE SPORTS/FITNESS ACTIVITIES, HOBBIES, GAMES, AND TOY PLAY SKILLS APPROPRIATE FOR SEVERELY HANDICAPPED CITIZENS

SPORTS/FITNESS ACTIVITIES

Independent or Individual Activities

Yoga	Biking	Jumping rope
Walking	Putt-Putt	Horseshoes
Swimming	Aerobic exercise	Dancing
Tumbling	Weight training	Archery
Skating	Horseback riding	Jogging
Hiking	Using playground equipment	Climbing
Skiing	Baton twirling	*Fishing

Dual or Cooperative Activities

**Boating	Horseshoes	Golf
Bowling	Martial arts	**Darts
Boxing	Gymnastics	Handball
**Croquet	**Shuffleboard	Tetherball
**Dancing	Racquet sports	Frisbee

Team Sports

Hockey	Basketball	Dodgeball
Softball	Touch football	Soccer
Lacross	Volleyball	Baseball
Kickball	Water polo	**Stickball

Note: Many of these activities can be included in more than one category.

**May be considered game or hobby.

HOBBIES

Plant care	Woodworking/Furniture refinishing
Pet care	Weaving
Needlework/Sewing	Sports spectating
Painting/Coloring	Books and magazines
Photography	Collecting
Music	Fan Clubs
Cooking, Dining out	Movies/Cultural activities
Ceramics/Pottery	Organized clubs (4-H, Scouts, YMCA)

GAMES

*Cootie	Concentration	Video games
*Mr. Potato Head	UNO	Shuffleboard
Perfection	Twister	Yard games
Trouble	*Candyland	War Slap/Jack
Checkers	Simon	Marbles
Old Maid	Pinball	Ping Pong
Pool	Tick-Tac-Toe	Jacks
*Hop Scotch	Foosball	Pick Up Sticks
Picture Lotto	Charades	

leisure activities (e.g., playing a modified softball game). The younger child and the very unskilled student will have a greater emphasis on specific

TABLE 12-2 (Continued)
SAMPLE SPORTS FITNESS ACTIVITIES, HOBBIES, GAMES, AND TOY PLAY SKILLS APPROPRIATE FOR SEVERELY HANDICAPPED CITIZENS

TOY PLAY/OBJECT MANIPULATION		
Balls	•Lincoln Logs	Marbles
•Blocks	•Tricycle/Bicycle with training	Yo-Yo
•Bucket and shovel	wheels	View Finder
Camera	Needle/Sewing material	Matchbox cars
Crayons	Musical Toys/Instruments	•Big Wheel
•Dolls	Puppets	Record player
Dice	•Rocking toys	Scissors
Etch-a-Sketch	Silly Putty	Telephone
Frisbee	•Slinky	Paints
•Hammer toys	Pinball/Video machine	Plants
Hula Hoop	Trucks/Trains	Vending machine
•Jack-in-the-Box	Magazines/Books	Pick Up Sticks

•Appropriate only for younger students.

Partially adapted from Moon & Renzaglia (1982)

object manipulation skills in his/her leisure skills curriculum. However, even the most profoundly handicapped persons should be given access to age appropriate materials within the framework of a normalized activity. Examples of functional leisure materials that can be included in object manipulation programs are shown in Table 2.

Sports. Sports are organized activities involving some type of rules, complex gross and fine motor movements, and the exertion of physical energy. Some sports involve a single participant while others involve two or more. Sports are an important part of our culture because of their relationship with health and fitness and because much of our leisure time is spent as sports spectators. Some of the sports skills that have been successfully taught to severely handicapped persons include individual exercises (Allen & Iwata, 1980; Stainback, Stainback, Wehman, & Spangiers, 1983; Wehman, Renzaglia, Berry, Schutz, & Karan, 1978); darts (Schleien, Wehman, & Kiernan, 1981); bicycle riding (Peterson & McIntosh, 1973; Wehman & Marchant, 1977); use of playground equipment (Keernan, Grove, & Zachofsky, 1969; Wehman & Marchant, 1977); swimming (Bundschuh, Williams, Hollingsworth, Gooch, & Shirer, 1972; Sherrill, 1981); bowling (Seaman, 1973); weight training (Moon, 1983); and jogging (Gunter, 1984).

Although sports typically involve a number of very complex motor patterns and intricate rules, most severely handicapped persons can at least be taught to partially participate in some community based sport. In many cases, some kind of adaptation will have to be made. The instructor must analyze the sport in terms of the motor patterns involved, the separate skill sequences comprising the activity, and the adaptations possible. Bunker and Moon (1983) suggested that because some sports are so difficult to learn. those which involve the least complicated motor patterns and rules but are still age appropriate should be instructed first. For example, volleyball is a simpler team sport than softball or basketball because it entails only striking. jumping, sliding, and running and has fewer rules. Aerobic weight lifting may be preferable over rope jumping for improving fitness since lifting weights is much simpler motorically than jumping rope. Other examples of sports that may be taught to severely handicapped persons are shown in Table 2.

Games. Like sports, games usually involve some sort of rules. However. games are typically played purely for enjoyment which makes them a true leisure activity (Wehman & Schleien, 1981). Games can be physical, involving complex gross motor patterns (e.g., Simon Says) or more passive, less motorically complicated (e.g., board, table, and card games). They can be open ended like a game of tag or structured like checkers and certain card games. Nearly all games involve some type of competition.

Teaching games to severely handicapped persons can be made relatively simple because of the variety of material, rule, and skill sequence adaptations possible. Two of the major considerations in teaching games are making sure the activities and materials chosen are chronologically age appropriate, and that they provide opportunities for the students to interact and share with each other. Examples of games that can be taught are shown in Table 2.

Hobbies. Hobbies may be the ultimate leisure activity since the only goal of hobby participation is enjoyment. A hobby is any recreational activity in which one can participate on a continuous, sometimes lifelong basis. It may be an activity in which one physically participates or an event which involves spectating (e.g., attending theatrical, music, or sports programs). Hobbies do not have to entail particular goals or rules.

Very often, severely handicapped persons do not have hobbies because they have never been taught to participate in certain activities purely for enjoyment over an extended period of time. For a person to really have a hobby, he or she initially should be taught a variety of activities and then be allowed to choose the ones that are most enjoyable.

Hobbies can involve sports, games, cooking, or more "cognitive" activities such as creating, reading, painting, observing, and listening. Examples of hobbies are delineated in Table 2.

Leisure Skills and Socialization

Our previous discussion should familiarize the reader with the various types of leisure content for which programs may be designed. However, it is essential to remember that leisure programs will take place in a variety of social contexts. For example, a student may play a game such a picture lotto (Marchant & Wehman, 1979) with a peer. This may be considered in either a cooperative or possibly even a competitive context. On the other hand, a similar game may be played alone by the student. This would be considered as an independent or isolate leisure situation. Independent, cooperative, and competitive social contexts can exist for many of the four types of leisure described in the earlier section. What will be presented next is a brief overview of each of these social situations, their relative importance, and selected program development information relevant to each. Also included in this section are discussions of Special Olympics and the impact of sexual expression on the socialization and leisure of moderately and severely handicapped individuals.

Independent Leisure

Independent or isolative leisure usually refers to an individual interacting with an object or engaging in an activity alone. This situation suggests that the person is able to exhibit appropriate leisure for a sustained period with minimal adult supervision. Independent or isolative leisure has received much attention in the literature (Hill, Wehman, & Horst, 1982; Hopper & Wambold, 1978; Schleien, Wehman, & Kiernan, 1981) since many severely and profoundly retarded individuals have no leisure skills. Hence the first stage in the development of independent leisure activities is learning to complete one or more simple leisure activities independently.

Value of independent leisure. When one reviews the classic Parten (1932) scales of play skill development, as well as literature applying these scales to evaluation of the play of mentally retarded (Wehman, 1977), it is apparent that cooperative and associative play levels are more advanced and hence give the appearance of being of greater value. To the extent that these levels of socialization reflect more sophisticated behavior this may be true. Yet when one considers the critical nature of independent play by a severely handicapped child at home, and concomittantly the necessity for constant adult supervision, a different light is shed on the value of independent play. The ability to interact with objects *constructively* and for a *sustained period of time* eases tension on the part of the family members, eases the search for babysitters, and usually enhances the acceptance of the child in the home and community. In addition, it should also be noted that many students will have no peers to play with after school. Hence independent leisure will be the only social context available.

There are other reasons for promoting independent play. These relate to the student feeling better about him/herself because of competence in initiating different leisure skills, the likelihood of reduced behavior management

problems (Lockwood et al. 1982), and the facility with which other important collateral skills such as communication and motor skills may be trained
(Cavallaro & Bambara, 1982). A comprehensive leisure education program
is complete only if it contains instruction for the development of independent leisure skills.

Basic program principles involved in developing independent leisure. There
are numerous techniques available for improving independent play and
most of these are related to applied behavior analysis strategies. Specifically,
if an individual refuses to interact with objects, the instructor can consider
simply placing the materials physically closer to the participant. We demonstrated the effectiveness of the physical proximity approach in an earlier
study with severely handicapped youth (Wehman, 1978a,b).

The use of verbal instructions and/or modeling of appropriate actions
are two other techniques which have frequently been used in the literature
to teach use of an instamatic camera (Wehman & Schleien, 1981) and use of
tricycles and other playground equipment (Wehman & Marchant, 1978).
Modeling, in particular, has been an essential component of most play and
leisure skill training programs for severely and profoundly mentally retarded
persons (Hopper & Wambold, 1978; Schleien, Wehman, & Kiernan, 1981).

Physical prompting and chaining also have been heavily relied upon,
especially in the initial stages of training individuals who are either under
very poor verbal control or who have had no previous instruction in leisure
skills. The principle danger with physical guidance is that when this form of
help is extended over time, it may become difficult to withdraw teacher
assistance and allow for more independent behaviors. When modeling,
verbal instructions, and physical prompting are employed in a cue hierarchy arrangement, the use of a task analysis for leisure instruction is greatly
enhanced.

Cooperative Leisure

The ability to participate jointly in an activity with a peer or in a group is
a developmentally more advanced level of socialization. Many activities
within the four types of leisure demand cooperative behavior. As noted
earlier, social play skills have received substantial attention by investigators
(Gable, Hendrickson, & Strain, 1978; Morris & Dolker, 1974; Peterson &
Haralock, 1977; Strain, 1977).

Value of cooperative leisure. Interacting appropriately with peers has several positive aspects associated with it. First, cooperative leisure facilitates
friendships. When handicapped youths are paired with nonhandicapped
peers the severely handicapped student may be perceived in a more normal
light. This is especially true of value given the negative perceptions which

nonhandicapped children often have of severely handicapped peers (Stainback & Stainback, 1982; Voeltz, 1980). Second, cooperative leisure usually requires taking turns, sharing, and waiting for others. These are each general skills which are essential for acceptance in work and community living. Finally, cooperative leisure activities also promote higher order communication and functional academic skills. The likelihood of communication is heightened when social reciprocity emerges between peers.

Basic program principles involved in developing cooperative leisure. There are several ways of improving cooperative leisure skills in severely handicapped individuals. We have detailed many of these strategies in our earlier work (Wehman, 1979b), but some of these techniques have been repeated here. Social interaction techniques can be viewed as a hierarchy of least intrusive interventions to most intrusive interventions. Here are six strategies which may be employed. First, with higher functioning students, sociodramatic techniques of roleplaying cooperative activities can be utilized. Strain (1977) successfully used this technique in small group play with young retarded children. A second strategy involves providing each student with an interdependent activity, that is, one which requires both individuals to participate. Games like checkers and tetherball are illustrations of interdependent activities (Mithaug, 1976). Hendrickson, Tremblay, Strain, and Shores (1981) also listed a series of toys and leisure materials which may be of interest.

Pairing a nonhandicapped peer with a severely handicapped child is a third means of promoting social interactions. By "coaching" or prompting the nonhandicapped peer, the probability of appropriate interactions is greatly enhanced. A fourth technique involves using a more capable retarded person to facilitate interactions. If none of these less intrusive techniques work, the teacher may have to manually guide both students through structured interactions (Wehman & Marchant, 1978). Finally, if both individuals will not cooperate, the instructor will then have to be the other participant and provide instruction in this format. These strategies, although not inclusive, begin to lay a foundation for designing cooperative interactions. *It is not our belief that isolative leisure is a prerequisite skill to cooperative actions.* These behaviors can be taught concurrently and each have their own respective value.

Competition

Although competition has been a principle aspect of American life, little attention has been directed to competition in the context of leisure for moderately and severely handicapped individuals. With some severely handicapped individuals who are so substantially handicapped intellectually (i.e., profoundly retarded persons) this is understandable. However, with many trainable retarded, some severely retarded and autistic, and some multi-handicapped individuals the social context of competition probably requires greater attention both by teachers and service providers as well as researchers.

Value of competition. Competition teaches students how to win and how to lose and provides a context for developing appropriate social behaviors which should occur with either of these events. Many moderately and severely handicapped individuals are not at a competence level which allows them to be aware of competition factors which surround certain activities. However, for those individuals who are capable, it will be of value to periodically structure activities in such a way as to enhance competition. Knapczyk and Yoppi (1975) observed that competitive play skills were necessary for adjustment of mildly retarded, behavior disordered students into the pressures of normal school programs and society. It would appear that competition has a limited role in leisure education programs for most moderately and severely handicapped individuals. However, with the influence of Special Olympics (to be discussed later) and other organized programs, we must be sensitive to this aspect of recreation.

Basic program principles involved in developing competitive skills. Any type of competition involves matching one's skill level against some standard. This standard can be *direct* in which there is competition between or among contestants to see who can perform the "best," or it can be *indirect* in which each competitor sets his or her own individual goal (Bunker, 1980). Most recreational activities can be adapted to include either or both forms of competition.

Indirect competition in which each person tries to improve upon some internal standard or criteria is probably the best way initially to train competitive skills to severely handicapped persons. By setting different "winning" criteria according to each student's current level of performance, everyone is given the opportunity to be successful. Once the student has had ample opportunities to experience success and failure in meeting some internal winning criteria and can deal with not always matching this standard, then direct competition can be introduced.

At the point that direct competition is introduced, both forms of competition can be used simultaneously. This allows for students to be reinforced for bettering individual performance levels even when they lose the direct competition. For example, four severely handicapped adolescents in a fitness-training program may compete against each other to see who can ride the stationary bicycle continuously for the longest period at a certain difficult tension level. At the same time, each of the four students can try to ride longer than they did the day before. Different reinforcers can be established so that all students may earn something for outdoing his or her previous performance and so that the overall winner receives a reward for the "best performance of the day."

The Role of Special Olympics

A major form of socialization in leisure for mentally retarded children has been Special Olympics. As a nationally recognized recreation program for mentally retarded persons, Special Olympics has enjoyed widespread participation (Orelove, Wehman, & Wood, 1982; Polloway & Smith, 1978). Thousands of mentally retarded children have competed in a variety of athletic activities since its inception in 1968. Special Olympics is the only recreation opportunity for many mentally retarded children and it involves cooperative and competitive leisure activity throughout. As significant an impact as Special Olympics has had, it has not been without controversy. Advocates feel that this program allows for leisure participation by retarded children and also their parents, socialization experiences, and opportunities for school training. Critics of Special Olympics believe that the principle of normalization is not being followed (cf., Wolfensberger, 1972) and that there has been too much emphasis on competition and nonfunctional physical education activities. There probably is some merit to each argument. Hence we have chosen to take a constructive posture and provide selected suggestions for improving Special Olympics.

Include Nonhandicapped Individuals

If enough school and community interest is demonstrated for retaining an olympic type activity for retarded persons, then one might alter the format to permit nonhandicapped individuals to participate. As with all effective integrated programs, the addition of nonhandicapped peers would be done gradually and systematically.

The first stage of integration might include the nonhandicapped children as volunteers within the actual olympic events, as is already done in several areas of the country. Several functions the children could perform include timekeeper, scorekeeper, messenger, refreshment server, musician, and coach. On the other hand, the role of "huggers" may be stigmatizing and probably should be reconsidered as a position with Special Olympics.

The second level would involve nonhandicapped children as teachers during regular physical education classes at school. Retarded children could be taught by their peers to throw, run, jump, etc., thereby allowing individualized attention to specific motor skills whenever necessary.

The net result of this integration would be the minimization of separate and unequal policy of motor skills training practices in many schools, especially with more severely retarded children. In addition. handicapped children would still be able to experience the same benefit Special Olympics offer, and nonhandicapped children would gain greater exposure to and, it is hoped, understanding of all of their classmates.

Develop a Well-Balanced Recreation Program

In many schools, as stated earlier, Special Olympics is the major or even sole focus of the physical education program for retarded students. It must be kept in mind that Special Olympics was conceived at a time when special education service delivery systems segregated most mildly handicapped children in self-contained schools and rejected almost all severely handicapped children from public schools altogether.

As we continue to service handicapped children in less restrictive placements (i.e., with planned and programmed interactions with nonhandicapped children), we face the need to provide them with a recreation and fitness program that will make them healthier. It is questionable whether Special Olympics provides a vehicle for promoting independence and socialization. Its narrowness is especially apparent in children who have several physical and social interaction deficits. Is "throwing a softball" a meaningful activity to a girl with severe spastic quadriplegia? Does running the 50-yard dash permit a 16-year-old retarded boy as much independence and ability to interact with others as learning the latest dance?

In short, the specific activities of the Special Olympics must be measured against the overall goals of the individual student. Where they overlap, they should be incorporated. In few cases, however, can the Special Olympics supplant a balanced physical education program of fitness, fun, and social independence (Bunker & Moon, 1983). The lack of stringent experimental studies evaluating the different facets of Special Olympics is a highly fertile area for further research.

Include handicapped students in community based recreation. Close scrutiny of the previous two suggestions reveals the need for retarded students to have access to a full range of physical and recreational activities with nonhandicapped peers. The obvious (although not necessarily simple) solution is to provide handicapped children and youth with the opportunity to participate in community recreation programs. Such programs include church and community center dances, little league events, 4-H groups, and community swimming classes. A community or school system may even want to use the familiarity and popularity of the Special Olympics to begin its own olympic events. The activities would be open to all citizens or students regardless of their race, sex, national origin, religion, political affiliation, or impairment. The recent dramatic increase in the number of marathons and other running events reveals a clear enthusiasm for such community activities.

Sexual Expression

Another form of socialization in leisure which has received limited attention is sexual expression and interaction of moderately and severely handicapped individuals. What work there has been has focused on basic sex education (Bender & Valletutti, 1976; Fischer & Krajicek, 1974; Hamre-Nietupski & Williams, 1977) as opposed to promoting sexual expression or appropriate social behaviors such as private vs. public masturbation, social interaction, dating, and physical expression of sexual behaviors such as holding hands, kissing, or sexual intercourse. Clearly this is a sensitive topic not only with handicapped individuals but also nonhandicapped youth. The sensitivity of the topic probably relates to the service delivery arrangement where students reside. Adams, Tallon, and Alcorn (1982) found that community based staff were generally more tolerant of physical expression of sexual behavior than institution staff. Hall and Morris (1976) found that institutionalized retarded persons were less knowledgeable about sex than those retarded persons living in the community.

Heshusius (1982) has written an excellent paper which reviews what mentally retarded persons think about sexual intimacy and also what we, as service providers think. He concluded that far too many publications for retarded individuals deal with the image of genital sex which he, as well as Edgerton (1973), noted as an absurdly narrow definition. Heshusius went on to say, "In conclusion, the problem of 'sex and the retarded' does not seem to lie in the particular brand of sexuality we have claimed for the less competent, but rather with our ideologies and with the stereotypes we hold about the 'retarded'." (p. 167)

In short, sexual expression is an area which should be included in leisure instructional programs in the future. As Ward (1983) observed, this is a normal type of leisure, not a leisure activity invented only for nonhandicapped persons.

Adapting Leisure Programs

We now move from socialization and leisure into methods of *adaptation*, that is, how to modify leisure programs for severely handicapped individuals to participate. An adaptation is a specific manipulation or change in any component of an activity (Wehman & Schleien, 1981). Very often adaptations must be made in leisure skills programs to allow severely handicapped individuals to fully or partially participate. Appropriate adaptations not only enhance the skill level and participation of the handicapped person but also improve the attitudes of nonhandicapped citizens in community based programs.

There are a number of considerations in formulating leisure skills adaptations. First, no adaptation should be considered until it is determined through systematic assessment, particularly task analysis of the skill, that the client absolutely cannot learn to participate in the activity with standard rules and materials. Second, adaptations should be considered temporary. As the client becomes more proficient at the adapted activity, the instructor should try to fade or change the adaptation to a less intrusive type. If a client needs a permanent adaptation, care must be taken to choose the most normalizing alteration so that he or she can participate with nonhandicapped persons. Finally, adaptations that will be most accessible across environments should be tried initially. Elaborate and/or expensive devices which are not portable usually limit the utility of an adaptation. However, such adaptations are sometimes necessary for the severely physically impaired individual (Campbell, 1983).

The Principle of Partial Participation

Even with adaptations some severely handicapped persons will not be able to participate independently in community based leisure programs. The principle of partial participation (Baumgart et al., 1982) asserts that even limited participation in an age appropriate, functional activity is more desirable *than independent performance in an age appropriate, segregated activity.* This principle has particular applicability to leisure skills programs in which the primary objective should be enjoyment rather than total independence. Utilizing this principle in designing and adapting leisure programs should prevent the following instructional pitfalls: (a) training activities because the student is at a particular developmental level; (b) teaching isolated splinter or prerequisite skills to independence instead of teaching all skills within the context of a functional activity; and (c) teaching within segregated or unnatural environments simply because the student cannot perform independently.

Baumgart et al. (1982) suggested that every skill be closely analyzed in terms of the skill components which the student can and cannot *ever* be expected to perform independently. This requires systematic assessment and instruction in some instances before applying an adaptation. This type of skill analysis permits for a single activity adaptation on some components and the opportunity for independent performance on others.

Types of Individual Adaptations

Once it has been determined that an activity needs to be adapted to allow for full or partial participation, the instructor must decide what kind of adaptation is most practical and normalizing. A number of types of adaptations have been suggested for use in leisure programs (Brown et al., 1979; Wehman & Schleien, 1981; Williams, Briggs, & Williams, 1979).

Materials and devices. It may be necessary to alter recreational materials and equipment or to create additional devices that allow the severely handicapped student to more efficiently handle materials. Material adaptations can be as simple as color coding certain dials to the addition of electromechanical switches. Material adaptations are particularly beneficial to the severely physically involved clients, and most recently, the use of inexpensive electromechanical switches for operating toys and record/cassette players has proved very successful. Burkhart (1980; 1982) has outlined specific directions for building and using these battery operated switches, some of which make leisure participation possible for clients who do not even exhibit full head and trunk control. Although the list is by no means complete, several other references for adapting materials are shown in Table 3. Some specific examples of material adaptations related to the four types of leisure programs are provided in Table 4.

TABLE 12-3

REFERENCES ON MATERIAL ADAPTATIONS FOR LEISURE SKILLS PROGRAMS

Source	Material	Type of Material Adaptation
•Adams, Daniel, & Pullman (1975)	sports/games	material modifications
Burkhart, L. (1980; 1982)	toy play, use of record/cassette player	electro-mechanical switches
American Alliance for Health, Physical Education Recreation, and Dance (1977)	sports	19 pieces of equipment and adaptive devices
Ford & Duckworth (1976)	sports, games, hobbies	material modifications adaptive devices
Wehman & Schleien (1981)	sports, games, hobbies, toy play	material modifications adaptive devices
•Cowart, J. (1979)	sports-archery, badminton, baseball, softball, bowling, golf, table tennis	material and equipment modifications, adaptive devices
•Aharoui, H. (1982)	sports-basketball, frisbee, soccer, aquatics	material and equipment modifications; adaptive devices
•Bauer, D. (1981)	sports-physical fitness activities, biking, roller skating, running	material and equipment modifications; adaptive devices

NOTE: These references also contain many ideas for rule/procedural, skill sequence, and environmental adaptations.

TABLE 12-4

EXAMPLES OF ADAPTATIONS APPLIED TO THE FOUR CATEGORIES OF LEISURE SKILLS

Activity	Type of Adaptation
	Sports/Fitness Activities
Badminton	Material
	• Short-handed racket
	• Enlarged foam rubber racket handle
	• Indoor play (eliminate wind factor)
	• Lowered net
	• Lightweight ball (or yarn or heavier weighted birdie)
Basketball	Procedural/Rule
	• More than 5 players (increase court coverage and eliminate need for long passes)
	• Use of half a court
	• Allow two-handed dribbling
	• Allow two or more steps per dribble
Bowling	Skill Sequence
	• Trainer picks up ball and gives to bowler to perform a "two handed" bowl
Baseball	Lead Up Activity
	• Kickball to learn concepts of scoring runs, running bases, fielding
	• Punchball to develop gross motor coordination
	• Tee ball to practice batting swing and hitting any size ball
	• Suspend ball from ceiling for continuous batting practice
	• Whiffle ball: slower, safer version of baseball
	Hobbies
Photography	Material
	• Extend button with attachment
	• Color designated buttons
	• Polaroid camera
Plant care	• Use 1 cup measure to prevent overwatering
Cooking	• Color code dials and temperatures on stove
	• Picture recipes
Needlework	Lead Up Activity
	• Lacing board with plastic needle attached to nylon cord
	• Sewing cards to learn basic movements necessary for sewing
Collecting/Fan Club	• Cutting pictures from magazines (to be categorized by someone else)
	Games
Ping Pong	Material
	• Nerf balls and paddles
	• Large paddle head
Pool	Procedural/Rule
	• Rather than designate striped or solid balls, shoot at any ball and record number of balls hit into pockets

Rule/procedural adaptations. Complicated rules and procedures can be extreme barriers to the participation of mentally and physically disabled

TABLE 12-4 (Continued)

EXAMPLES OF ADAPTATIONS APPLIED TO THE FOUR CATEGORIES OF LEISURE SKILLS

Activity	*Type of Adaptation*
Playing Cards	Skill Sequence • Pick up cards only after all have been dealt to all players • Allow some players to have "silent partner"
Darts	Lead Up Activities • Cricket requiring player to count number of darts thrown on board instead of adding numbers • Using numbers 1 through 6 as designated scoring numbers rather than 15 through 20 as usually done in Cricket, allowing for easier number identification
	Objective Manipulation
Telephone	Material • Use shoulder supporter to hold phone • Push buttons
Balls	• Start with large, light balls and progress to smaller, heavier ones
Viewfinder	Skill Sequence • Have second person push button to change picture
Vending Machine	• Having picture cards denoting items and corresponding correct coins

persons in community based leisure programs, especially games and sports. Rules and procedures can be altered for some individuals and remain unchanged for others so that handicapped individuals can participate with their nonhandicapped peers. The following sources have outlined a number of specific rule and procedural adaptations for severely handicapped children and adults: Adams, Daniel, & Pullman (1975); Grosse (1971); Information and Research Utilization Center (1976); Wehman and Schleien (1981). Specific examples of rule and procedural adaptations are also shown in Table 4.

Environmental adaptations. Many handicapped citizens are denied participation in community based leisure programs due to the inaccessibility of recreational facilities. Narrow doors, lack of ramps, and poorly designed toilet facilities are common problems. Another type of environmental adaptation that most recreational facilities do not have is special equipment to aid in positioning, handling, and mobility of the physically involved individual. There is federal and state legislation (e.g., 1973 Vocational Rehabilitation Act, Section 504) which mandates the construction of public facilities to include access for the handicapped. There are also various guidelines available for making environmental adaptations (Virginia Commission, 1976) and commercially available mobility and positioning equipment.

Skill sequence adaptations. The use of a task analysis is the best way to teach a leisure activity to a severely handicapped person. However, the typical sequence of steps in a task analysis may have to be adapted for some individuals. For example, some steps may have to be done for the client or eliminated and others may need to be done in reverse order (see Sharpton and Alberto's chapter in this text).

Lead up activities. Wehman and Schleien (1981) described lead up activities as a simplified form of an activity that allows for participation in some component part. Lead up activities can be taught separately or simultaneously and then linked together and modified and instructed with the context of the more complicated activity.

One of the best ways to train lead up activities is to analyze an activity into its individual skills and train one or more of the simpler component skills. Other lead up activities can be based around the use of modified rules or equipment. Some other examples of lead up activities are also provided in Table 5.

Conclusion

This chapter has provided an overview of leisure skill programming guidelines for individuals with severe handicaps. In this chapter, we have discussed several types of leisure programs which can be used for facilitating recreational skills in severely handicapped youth. A number of exemplar instructional programs were provided as well. The issues of Special Olympics, social skill development, and sexual expression were also addressed as critical elements to consider in leisure skill development. Finally, adaptation and modification of leisure materials was described as a means of improving participation.*

REFERENCES

Adams, R., Daniel, A., & Pullman, L. *Games, sports, and exercise for the physically handicapped.* Philadelphia: Lea and Febiger, 1975.

Adams, G., Tallon, R., & Alcorn, D. Attitudes toward the sexuality of mentally retarded and nonretarded persons. *Education and Training of the Mentally Retarded.* 1982, *17*(4), 307–312.

Aharoui, H. Games and activities for severely handicapped students utilizing small space and minimal equipment. *Practical Pointers,* 1982, *5*(11), 1–27.

Allen, L. D., & Iwata, B. A. Reinforcing exercise maintenance using existing high rate activities. *Behavior Modification,* 1980, *4,* 337–354.

American Alliance for Health, Physical Education and Recreation. Making physical education and recreation facilities accessible to all ... planning ... designing ... adapting. Washington, DC: Author, May, 1977.

Bates, P., & Renzaglia, A. Community based recreation programs. In P. Wehman (Ed.). *Recreation programming for developmentally disabled persons.* Baltimore: University Park Press, 1979.

---

*The development of this chapter was partially supported by grant number G008301124 from the U.S. Department of Education.

Portions of several tables appeared previously in *Systematic Instruction of the Moderately and Severely Handicapped, Journal of Special Education,* and *Longitudinal Leisure Skills for Severely Handicapped Learners.* Reprinted with permission.

Bauer. D. Aerobic fitness for the moderately retarded. *Practical Pointers.* 1981. 5(5). 1–32.

Baumgart. D.. Brown. L.. Pumpian. I.. Nisbet. J.. Ford. A.. Sweet. M.. Messina. R.. & Schroeder. J. Principle of partial participation and individualized adaptations in educational programs for severely handicapped students. *Journal of the Association for the Severely Handicapped.* 1982. 7. 16–27.

Bender. M.. & Valletutti. P. *Teaching the moderately and severely handicapped.* Baltimore: University Park Press. 1976.

Brown. L.. Branston-McLean. M.. Baumgart. D.. Vincent. B.. Falvey. M.. & Schroeder. J. *Using the characteristics of current and subsequent least restrictive* environments in the development of curricular content for severely handicapped students. *AAESPH Review.* 1979. 4(4). 407–424.

Bundschuh. E. L.. Williams. W. C.. Hollingsworth. J. D.. Gooch. S., & Shirer. C. Teaching the retarded to swim. *Mental Retardation.* 1972. 10(5). 32–35.

Bunker. L. K. Nature-nurture and the future of co-ed sports. *The proceedings of the National Association for Physical Education in Higher Education.* (Vol. II). Champaign. IL: Human Kinetics Press. 1980.

Bunker. L.. & Moon. S. Motor skills. In M. E. Snell (Ed.). *Systematic instruction of the moderately and severely handicapped.* Columbus. OH: Charles Merrill. 1983.

Burch. M. *Generalization of leisure skills in retarded adult women.* Unpublished doctoral dissertation. Florida State University. Tallahassee. FL.. date unknown.

Burkhart. L. J. *Home made battery powered toys and educational devices for severely handicapped children.* College Park. MD: Author. 1980.

Burkhart. L. J. *More home made battery devices for severely handicapped children with suggested activities.* College Park. MD: Author. 1982.

Campbell. P. Students with movement difficulties. In M. E. Snell (Ed.) *Systematic instruction of the moderately and severely handicapped.* Columbus. OH: Charles E. Merrill. 1983.

Cavallaro. C.. & Bambara. L. Two strategies for teaching language during free play. *The Journal of the Association for the Severely Handicapped.* 1982. 7(2). 80–92.

Corcoran. E. L.. & French. R. W. Leisure activity for the retarded adult in the community. *Mental Retardation.* 1977. 15(2). 21–23.

Cowart. J. Sports adaptations of unilateral and bilateral upper-limb amputees. *Practical Pointers.* 1979. 7(10). 1–13.

Edgerton. R. Some socio-cultural research considerations. In F. de la Cruz. & G. Laveck (Eds.), *Human sexuality and the mentally retarded.* New York: Brunner/Mazel. 1973.

Ellis. M. *Why people play.* Englewood Cliffs. NJ: Prentice-Hall. 1973.

Favell. J. Reduction of stereotypies by reinforcement of toy play. *Mental Retardation.* 1973. 11. 24–27.

Fischer. H.. & Krajicek. M. *Sex education for the developmentally disabled: A guide for parents, teachers, and professionals.* Baltimore: University Park Press. 1974.

Ford. J.. & Duckworth. B. *Physical management for the quadriplegic patient.* Philadelphis: Davis. 1976.

Gable. R.. Hendrickson. J. M.. & Strain. P. S. Assessment, modification, and generalization of social interaction among severely retarded multihandicapped children. *Education and Training of the Mentally Retarded.* 1978. 13(3). 279–286.

Groose. S. Indoor target gold. *Journal of Health, Physical Education, and Recreation.* 1971. 42(1).

Greenspan. S., & Schultz. B. Why mentally retarded workers lose their jobs: Social competence as a factor in work adjustment. *Applied Research in Mental Retardation,* 1981. 2(2). 23–38.

Gunter. P. An age appropriate, community leisure skill for the moderately and severely handicapped. Manuscript submitted for publication. 1984.

Hamre-Nietupski. S.. & Williams. W. Implementation of selected sex education and social skills to severely handicapped students. *Education and Training of the Mentally Retarded,* 1977. 12. 364–372.

Hendrickson. J. M.. Tremblay. A.. Strain. P. S.. & Shores. R. E. Relationship between toy and material use and the occurrence of social interactive behaviors by normally developing preschool children. *Psychology in the Schools*, 1981. *18*(4), 500–504.

Heshusius, L. Sexuality, intimacy, and persons we label mentally retarded: What they think—what we think. *Mental Retardation*, 1982, *20*(4), 164–168.

Hill, J., Wehman, P., & Horst, G. Toward generalization of appropriate leisure and social behavior in severely handicapped youth: Pinball machine use. *The Journal of the Association for the Severely Handicapped*, 1982, *6*, 38–44.

Hopper, C., & Wambold, C. Improving the independent play of severely mentally retarded children. *Education and Training of the Mentally Retarded*, 1978, *13*, 42–46.

Information and Research Utilization Center in Physical Education and Recreation for the Handicapped. *Physical activities for impaired, disabled, and handicapped individuals*. Washington. DC: Author, 1976.

Inge, K., Moon, S., & Hill, J. *Developing a respite care training program for adult volunteers*. Unpublished manuscript. Virginia Commonwealth University Severely Handicapped Community Training Project, Richmond, VA., 1983.

Keernan, C., Grove, F., & Zachofsky, T. Assessing the playground skills of the severely retarded. *Mental Retardation*, 1969, *7*, 29–32.

Knapczyk, P., & Yoppi, J. Development of cooperative and competitive play responses in developmentally disabled children. *American Journal of Mental Deficiency*, 1975. *80*. 245–255.

Marchant, J., & Wehman, P. Teaching table games to severely retarded children. *Mental Retardation*, 1979. *17*. 150–151.

McCall, R. *Exploratory manipulation and play in the human infant*. Monograph of the Society for Research in Human Development. Chicago: University of Chicago Press, 1974.

Mithaug, D. Employing task arrangements and verbal contingencies to promote verbalizations between retarded children. *Journal of Applied Behavior Analysis*, 1976, *9*, 301–314.

Moon, S. *The effects of nonhandicapped peer participation and different reinforcement procedures on the maintenance of fitness activities in severely handicapped adolescents*. Unpublished doctoral dissertation. University of Virginia, Charlottesville, VA, 1983.

Moon, S.. & Renzaglia, A. Physical fitness and the mentally retarded: A critical review of the literature. *The Journal of Special Education*, 1982. *16*, 269–287.

Morris, R., & Dolker, M. Developing cooperative play in socially withdrawn children. *Mental Retardation*, 1974, *12*, 24–27.

Novak, A., & Heal, L. (Eds.), *Community integration*. Baltimore: Paul H. Brookes, 1981.

Nunnally, J. C., & Lemond, L. Exploratory behavior and human development. In H. W. Reese (Ed.), *Advances in child development and behavior* (Vol. 8). Chicago: Academic Press, 1973.

Orelove, F., Wehman, P., & Wood, J. An evaluative review of Special Olympics: Implications for community integration. *Education and Training of the Mentally Retarded*, 1982. *17*, 519–524.

Parten, M. Social play among preschool children. *Journal of Abnormal Psychology*, 1932. *28*, 136–147.

Peterson, N., & Haralock, J. Integration of handicapped and nonhandicapped preschoolers: An analysis of play behavior and social interactions. *Education and Training of the Mentally Retarded*, 1977, *12*(3), 235–246.

Polloway, E., & Smith, J. Special Olympics: A second look. *Education and Training of the Mentally Retarded*, 1978, *13*, 432–433.

Schleien, S., Wehman, P., & Kiernan, J. Teaching leisure skills to severely handicapped adults: An age appropriate darts game. *Journal of Applied Behavior Analysis*, 1981, *14*(4), 513–519.

Seaman, J. A. Right up their alley. *Teaching Exceptional Children*, 1973, *5*, 196–198.

Sherrill, C. *Adapted physical education and recreation: A multidisciplinary approach*. Dubuque. IA: Brown, 1981.

Stainback, S., & Stainback, W. The need for research on training nonhandicapped students to interact with severely handicapped students. *Education and Training of the Mentally Retarded,* 1982, *17,* 12–16.

Stainback, S., Stainback, W., Wehman, P., & Spangiers, L. Acquisition and generalization of physical fitness skills in three profoundly retarded adults. *Journal of the Association for the Severely Handicapped,* 1983, *8*(2), 47–55.

Strain, P. Effects of peer interactions on withdrawn preschool children. *Journal of Abnormal Child Psychology,* 1977, *5,* 445–455.

Virginia Commission of Outdoor Recreation — Recreation Services Section. *Architectural accessibility for the disabled in park and recreation facilities.* Richmond, VA: Virginia Commission of Outdoor Recreation, 1976.

Voeltz, L. Children's attitudes toward handicapped peers. *American Journal of Mental Deficiency,* 1980, *84,* 455–464.

Voeltz, L., Wuerch, B., & Wilcox, B. Leisure and recreation: Preparation for independence, integration, and self-fulfillment. In B. Wilcox, & G. T. Bellamy (Eds.), *Designing high school programs for severely handicapped students.* Baltimore: Paul H. Brookes, 1982.

Ward, M. From my perspective. No more checkers . . . Let's rap. *Teaching Exceptional Children,* 1983, *15*(4), 234–241.

Wehman, P. *Helping the mentally retarded acquire play skills: A behavioral approach.* Springfield, IL: Charles C Thomas, 1977.

Wehman, P. Teaching recreational skills to severely and profoundly handicapped persons. In E. Edgar, & R. York (Eds.), *Teaching severely handicapped persons,* Vol. IV. Seattle: AAESPH, 1978. (a)

Wehman, P. (Ed.). *Recreation programming for developmentally disabled persons.* Baltimore: University Park Press, 1978. (b)

Wehman, P. Instructional strategies for improving play skills of severely and profoundly handicapped children. *AAESPH Review,* 1979, *4*(2), 125–135. (a)

Wehman, P. *Curricula design for the severely handicapped.* New York: Human Sciences Press, 1979. (b)

Wehman, P. *Competitive employment: New horizons for severely disabled persons.* Baltimore: Paul H. Brookes, 1981.

Wehman, P., & Hill, J. *Leisure skill instructional guide for severely handicapped youth.* Richmond: Virginia Commonwealth University, 1982.

Wehman, P., & Marchant, J. A. Developing gross motor recreational skills in children with severe behavioral handicaps. *Therapeutic Recreation Journal,* 1977, *11*(2), 48–54.

Wehman, P., & Marchant, J. Improving free play skills of severely retarded children. *The American Journal of Occupational Therapy,* 1978, *32,* 100–104.

Wehman, P., Renzaglia, A., & Bates, P. *Functional living skills for moderately and severely handicapped persons.* Baltimore: University Park Press, in press.

Wehman, P., Renzaglia, A., Berry, Schutz, R., & Karan, O. Developing a leisure skill repertoire in severely and profoundly handicapped persons. *AAESPH Review,* 1978, *3,* 162–172.

Wehman, P., & Schleien, S. *Leisure programs for handicapped persons.* Baltimore: University Park Press, 1981.

Williams, B., Briggs, N., & Williams, R. Selecting, adapting, and understanding toys and recreation materials. In P. Wehman (Ed.), *Recreation programming for developmentally disabled persons.* Baltimore: University Park Press, 1979.

Wolfensberger, W. *Principles of normalization.* Toronto: National Institute of Mental Retardation, 1972.

Wuerch, B., & Voeltz, L. *Longitudinal leisure skills for severely handicapped learners.* Baltimore: Paul H. Brookes, 1982.

CHAPTER 13*

INCREASING PERSONAL COMPETENCE
IN THE COMMUNITY†

SHARON FREAGON, JILL WHEELER, GAYLE P. BRANKIN, KIM MCDANNEL,
LISA STERN, RUTH USILTON, NANCY KEISER

With the advent of Public Law 94-142, Section 504 of the Rehabilitation Act of 1973 and deinstitutionalization suits in a large number of states, persons with severe handicaps are increasingly participating in public school and natural, domestic, vocational, recreation-leisure, and community-at-large environments. These persons' right to participate in normalized or natural environments has necessitated the development of technology and strategies to facilitate greater participation and/or increased independent functioning.

Prior to the recognition of these rights, persons with severe handicaps were viewed as perennial children with mental ages and/or developmental ages of infants or very young children. As a consequence, they were not expected to order independently in a restaurant, make choices regarding food preferences, communicate in a competitive work situation, communicate bowling shoe size in a bowling alley or clothing size in a department

*The development of this chapter was partially supported by Federal Contract No. 300-80.0646. "Implementation of Quality Educational Service Systems for Severely Handicapped Children and Youth: Rural," with the Special Needs Section, Special Education Programs, U.S. Office of Education.

†*Sharon Freagon* is an Associate Professor in the Department of Learning, Development, and Special Education at Northern Illinois University in DeKalb. While at Northern Illinois, Dr. Freagon has been involved with the school, vocational, recreation-leisure, domestic, and community-at-large integration of students with severe handicaps and the development of small community based residential alternatives to institutionalization. Currently, she is the Director of two federally funded projects—one involving the school and community integration of students with severe handicaps on a state-wide basis in Illinois and the other involving the transition to adulthood of secondary-aged students in DeKalb County.

Jill Wheeler is a doctoral student at Northern Illinois University. She is currently Project Coordinator of a federally funded project awarded to Northern Illinois University involving the school and community integration of Illinois' school-age children and youth who have severe handicaps. Jill also supervises two community based residential alternatives for youths who have been deinstitutionalized.

Gayle Brankin is currently Implementation Coordinator of a federally funded project awarded to Northern Illinois University involving the school and community integration of Illinois' school-age children and youth who have severe handicaps. In this capacity, Gayle coordinates and directs the technical assistance to individual school districts and cooperatives selected as implementation sites for the project. Gayle was a classroom, vocational, and transition teacher for students with severe handicaps prior to her present position.

store and so on. Guess, Horner, Utley, Holvoet, Maxon, Tucker, and Warren (1978) distinguished between developmental logic and remedial logic in instructional programs for persons with severe handicaps. The developmental logic assumes that children, adolescents, and adults with severe handicaps learn and grow in the same general sequences that have been normed for persons not identified as handicapped. Remedial logic, on the other hand, does not make the assumption that persons with severe handicaps learn and grow in a pattern similar to persons not identified as handicapped. Rather, remedial logic assumes that actual environmental skill expectations can be assessed and severely handicapped persons can be instructed to perform the skill requirements of a given environment independent of how persons not identified as handicapped acquire the same skills.

Largely due to the early work of Dr. Lou Brown of the University of Wisconsin and his colleagues in the Madison Metropolitan School District, many programs for persons with severe handicaps throughout the nation have incorporated the remedial logic. Programs employing the remedial logic are generally said to be chronologically age appropriate, functional, and preparatory for future environments. Wilcox and Bellamy (1982) described the criteria to measure the effectiveness of programs for severely handicapped individuals. These are *independence, productivity,* and *participation.* The criteria of independence, productivity, and participation require progress measurement in those natural environments where persons with severe handicaps are expected to exhibit the required skills. One only has to inventory those environments (i.e., grocery stores, restaurants, competitive work sites, department stores, public schools) to see that they require a wide variety of reading, writing, math, and communication skills. Since it is unreasonable to assume that most severely handicapped individuals will ever perform all of the reading, writing, math, and communication require-

Kim McDannel is currently Field-Based Practicum Supervisor for masters students preparing to be teachers of students with severe handicaps and/or autism at Northern Illinois University. In the past, Kim was a Research Associate on a federally funded project awarded Northern Illinois University evaluating the outcome of the school and community integration of DeKalb County's students with severe handicaps.

Lisa Stern is currently a secondary teacher of students with severe handicaps at DeKalb High School. She drew the many illustrations that are contained in the present chapter. As a teacher in an age appropriate high school, Lisa is involved with her students' daily training in nonschool natural community environments and their interactions with nonhandicapped students.

Ruth Usilton is currently a teacher of students with severe handicaps at Littlejohn Elementary School in DeKalb. In her current position, she developed many of the compensatory strategies illustrated in the present chapter. Ruth's past experience as a teacher of secondary-age students contributed to the design of transition strategies for elementary-age students to next school and community environments.

Nancy Keiser is currently a teacher of students with severe handicaps at Littlejohn Elementary School in DeKalb. Prior to this position, Nancy served as an Alternative Communication Specialist. Her experience contributes to the design and adaptation of communication systems for heterogeneous groups of students with severe handicaps in natural community environments.

ments of multiple natural environments, it is imperative that alternative or compensatory strategies be developed to ensure their maximum independence, productivity, and participation. This chapter, then, is concerned with the development of alternative or compensatory strategies that can be used when severely handicapped persons cannot perform the reading, writing, math, and communication requirements of natural environments. The chapter includes: (a) a rationale for compensatory strategies, (b) the ecological inventory process for determining severely handicapped persons' needs for alternative or compensatory strategies, (c) the reading, writing, math, and communication requirements of community environments, and (d) compensatory strategies.

Rationale for Compensatory Strategies

Arguments regarding instructional programs for severely handicapped persons persons are prevalent in the literature. While they generally are concerned with school-age youth, they also have relevance to the postschool adult population. Most likely the concern with children, youth, and young adults has been facilitated with the implementation of P.L. 94-142. Programs for adults with severe handicaps are not as clearly mandated as are programs for school-age persons. Therefore, to make the rationale for compensatory strategies, the present authors had to rely on the literature relating to school-age populations. The authors believe, however, that the information provided also has direct relevance to programs serving adults.

Current Arguments Regarding Instructional Programs

Arguments regarding instructional programs for persons with severe handicaps center around issues of educability, expectation, instructional content, and methodology. *First,* considering the issue of educability, Baer (1981a) wrote that no matter how severely handicapped a person is, a well designed instructional program will find some behavior to reinforce independent of the instructor's criteria for progress. Ellis (1981) suggested that presently no means exists to ensure that a given behavior is unteachable in a given person and that the "set of procedures to be tried is too large and not yet totally invented" (p. 96).

Second, regarding educational expectations, Brown, Branston, Hamre-Nieuptski, Johnson, Wilcox, and Gruenewald (1978) argued that because severely handicapped students manifest significant skill deficits, they frequently receive instruction on curriculum objectives characteristically offered to infants or very young children. This results in the delivery of instruction which is nonfunctional, artificial, and inappropriate for severely handi-

capped students' chronological ages. This type of curriculum runs the
danger of a prophecy fulfilled (Brown, Wilcox, Sontag, Vincent, Dodd, &
Gruenewald, 1977). Since severely handicapped children will never meet all
the developmental milestones that nonhandicapped children meet, they
receive years and years of training with this curricular perspective. This
tends to keep them looking, in the eyes of others, as children all their lives,
e.g., at 18 they keep playing their "Sesame Street" records, bringing their
dolls to school, and still cannot meet the instructional objective to count 10
red blocks. Freagon (1982) argued that use of the medical model communicates a curriculum in the public schools dealing with disability as opposed
to ability and it therefore would be better utilized in a hospital than in the
public schools. Services provided by medically associated personnel are
needed in the schools, but how they are delivered needs rethinking. Gliedman
and Roth (1980) believed that the medical model's use in the public schools
characterizes handicapped children as sick and always patients. As a consequence, they are never considered human beings with all the wants, desires,
and needs that nonhandicapped persons have.

Finally, regarding instructional content and methodology, Donnellan (1980)
and Brown (1981) noted that instructional content should be judged by its
functional nature. For example, if the person does not perform the particular skill in question, will someone else have to do it for him or her? Brown,
Nietupski, and Hamre-Nieuptski (1976) advised that the "criterion of ultimate functioning" be employed in selection of instructional content; i.e.,
what do severely handicapped students have to learn in order to function in
heterogeneous, postschool domestic, recreation-leisure, work, and community environments? York and Williams (1977) advocated that the functional
curriculum model held the most promise for severely handicapped students'
participation in least restrictive environments. The functional curriculum
model is based upon skills that students must be able to perform in current
and subsequent least restrictive environments (Williams, Brown, & Certo,
1975).

A number of researchers and authors suggest that severely handicapped
students' generalization of skills (e.g., stimulus and response generalization;
transfer of training; and performance across persons, places, instructional
materials, and language cues) will not occur unless severely handicapped
students are taught in the natural settings where the skills have to be utilized
(Baer, 1981b; Reese & Lipsitt, 1970; Williams, Brown, & Certo, 1975). The
full stimulus properties of least restrictive natural environments in which
severely handicapped students need to function currently and in the
future cannot be replicated within the walls of any school. Therefore,
Brown et al. (1977) advocated that severely handicapped students be educated in:

settings that encourage and support extensive long-term interactions and that only such settings be considered "least restrictive" . . . Settings include at least self-contained classes for severely handicapped students in public school buildings, regular classes, nonclassroom but school-related activities both on and off school grounds, and nonschool settings and activities involving nonhandicapped people of all ages and levels of function. (p. 196)

Advancing Technology

While the arguments over the merits of employing developmental vs. remedial logic will continue, Holvoet, Guess, Mulligan, and Brown (1980) suggested that both logics have merit and that they be combined in programs for severely handicapped persons. The authors pointed out that severely handicapped persons, like those who are not identified as handicapped, do not learn skills in isolation and that an interdependence exists between cognitive, social, and motor development. The development of cognitive, social, and motor skills, however, has typically been associated with developmental logic and in practice has relegated severely handicapped persons to skills characteristic of very young children. Holvoet et al. (1980) explained that when developmental logic is combined with remedial logic, the latter can guard against this tendency. Voeltz and Evans (1983) found the concept of interrelated behaviors promising in that severely handicapped learners do not have the time to learn the wide variety of specific behaviors needed in all environments. A general case programming strategy in community environments has been developed by Horner, Sprague, and Wilcox (1982). According to these authors, general case programming

refers to those behaviors performed by a teacher or trainer that increase the probability that skills learned in one training setting will be successfully performed with different target stimuli, and/or in different settings, from those used during training. (p. 63)

The above researchers, who are also practitioners, would all agree that instruction (a) in chronological age appropriate, functional, and next environment related skills, and (b) in natural domestic, recreation-leisure, vocational, and community-at-large environments is important if severely handicapped persons are going to realize increased participation, productivity, and independence in society. What is not yet clear is the technology of providing services that have these characteristics. One thing is perfectly clear, however, from this advancing technology and practice. Most, if not all, natural domestic, recreation-leisure, vocational, and community-at-large environments have reading, writing, math, and communication skill requirements that many severely handicapped persons will *never* completely acquire unless alternative or compensatory strategies are employed. Most professionals interested in developing services that have the above characteristics would agree with the latter proposition. They may disagree, however, at the age that alternative or compensatory strategies for reading, writing, math, and communication requirements in natural environments should be employed. The present authors contend that alternative or compensatory strategies should be employed whenever persons with severe handicaps, *independent of being very young or very old,* need them to participate more fully, and to be more productive and independent in community environments. The remainder of this chapter delineates systematic procedures to (a) determine natural environments' reading, writing, math, and communication requirements, (b) determine severely handicapped persons' compensatory academic skill needs, and (c) develop compensatory strategies across natural domestic, recreation-leisure, vocational, community-at-large, and public school environments.

The Ecological Inventory Process

The ecological or environmental inventory process developed by Brown, Branston, Hamre-Nietupski, Pumpian, Certo, and Gruenewald (1979) is an especially useful process to determine natural environment requirements for severely handicapped persons' participation and independence. Brown et al. (1979) suggested a six step process to delineate the following: (a) life space domains, (b) the wide variety of current and subsequent natural environments in which severely handicapped persons might function, (c) the subenvironments of the current and subsequent natural environments, (d) the activities that occur in the subenvironments, (e) the skills that are needed to participate in the activities of the subenvironments, and (f) the instructional strategies that will be necessary to insure severely handicapped persons' performance of the skills. The most common life space domains currently being employed are domestic, recreation-leisure, vocational, and community-at-large. Natural environments included in the domestic domain are home, group home, and domestic training environments. Natural home, bowling alleys, movie theatres, roller rinks, etc. comprise the recreation-leisure domain while clerical, janitorial, housekeeping, industrial, and food service competitive employment sites would be included in the vocational domain. Grocery, department, and drug stores; sit down and fast food restaurants; schools; banks and laundromats would be included in the community-at-large domain. Subenvironments of a natural home in the domestic domain would include kitchen, bathroom, bedroom, etc., while a grocery store in the community-at-large domain would include the entry way, carts, departments, purchase counter, etc.

Following is an example of activities and skills delineated for a fast food restaurant. The activities and skills are organized into phases as suggested by Brown et al. If needed, the parts can be further broken down into skill steps.

The inventory in Table 1 was devised by Freagon, Wheeler, McDannel, Brankin, and Costello (1983) for use in a profile system to assess, monitor, and evaluate severely handicapped students' longitudinal progress in a wide variety of natural domestic, recreation-leisure, vocational, and community-at-large environments. It is also used to generate Individual Education Programs (IEPs) and Individual Instructional Programs (IIPs) content and to determine students' alternative or compensatory strategy needs. Every fall students' baselines in environments are determined in the spring IEP/IIP meeting. This process utilizes the previous year's alternative or compensatory strategies. Based on the baseline information and instructional personnels' and parents' recommendations at the spring IEP meeting, the previous year's alternative or compensatory strategies are either maintained or modified. Individual student's performance in natural environments throughout the course of the school year are recorded on the profile in the spring. Used in this manner, the ecological inventory process is an invaluable tool to assess skill requirements in natural environments and the subsequent alternative or compensatory strategy needs. (For further information and a different approach to ecological inventories, the reader is referred to the Mattison and Rosenberg chapter in this text).

Reading, Writing, Math, and
Communication Requirements of Community Environments

From the described ecological inventory process, the reading, writing, math, and communication requirements of natural current and subsequent community environments can be ascertained. These four requirements in community environments are those with which severely handicapped persons often have considerable difficulty. They also represent the content that has traditionally been used in educational programs. As discussed earlier, this content has been taught primarily using developmental logic. Therefore, severely handicapped persons have generally been instructed using strategies to teach very young children. Because severely handicapped persons have not learned and generalized these skills from isolated and segregated environments to natural environments, they have been systematically kept from realizing their full potential in the community.

Following is a series of figures which illustrate the reading, writing, math, and communication requirements of a representative sample of activities in the domestic domain, environments in the recreation-leisure and community-

TABLE 13-1
FAST FOOD RESTAURANT

I. Preparation to Use Fast Food Restaurant

A. Collects all necessary materials (including order cards, money, etc.)

B. Demonstrates rider safety en route

C. Safely maneuvers in parking lot/streets

D. Enters Fast Food restaurant

II. Preparation to Order

A. Chooses/waits in line (open/closed/shortest)

B. Follows movement of line

C. Determines order (including scan menu selection noting time of day/diet)

D. Uses calculator to determine enough/not enough money for purchase

E. Removes wallet from purse/pocket

III. Orders Food

A. Communicates order upon cue from personnel

B. Communicates type of order (here/to go)

IV. Waits for Order

A. Collects necessary utensils (straw/napkins)

B. Requests condiments (salt, pepper, catsup, etc.)

C. Moves aside for line movement as needed

D. Secures order/leaves counter area

V. Pays for Order

A. Removes money from purse/wallet

B. Pays cashier appropriate amount over total: dollar, dollar/cents, cents

C. Waits for change

D. Places change in purse/wallet

VI. Sit Down Service

A. Chooses seating (account for number of group, cleanliness of table, smoking, nonsmoking)

B. Places belongings aside for comfort

VII. Eats Meal

A. Uses napkin

B. Uses silverware appropriately

C. Uses appropriate amount of condiments

D. Displays good table manners

VIII. Disposes of Garbage

A. Collects garbage

B. Empties into garbage can

C. Replaces tray

at-large domains, and job types in the vocational domain. These requirements are also illustrated for elementary, middle, and high schools since
schools are also current and subsequent natural environments for severely
handicapped persons. The requirements illustrated were taken from the
wide variety of environmental inventories comprising the student profile
system devised by Freagon et al. (1983).

Table 2 illustrates some of the reading, writing, math, and communication requirements of personal health and daily living skills, housekeeping,
and meal preparation activities in the domestic domain.

TABLE 13-2
DOMESTIC

Reading/Writing	Math	Communication
Personal Health/Daily Living Skills		
Locates correct bathroom using labels (e.g., men, women, boys, girls)	Demonstrates ability to use emergency phone numbers	Indicates need to use bathroom
Demonstrates ability to use personal identification card	Dials phone numbers accurately	Identifies need for clothing to be laundered, mended, ironed
Recognizes poisonous items/dangers by signs/labels	Weighs self regularly	Identifies various emergency situations (sickness, injury, etc.)
Uses phone book to locate numbers		Reports sickness to adults
		Initiates and responds to phone conversations as appropriate
		Relays phone messages to appropriate persons
Housekeeping		
Follows written or pictoral housekeeping schedule/routine	Measures appropriate amounts of cleaning solution	Identifies items/areas to be cleaned
Locates appropriate cleaning materials using labels	Demonstrates awareness to replenish supplies	Identifies appropriate cleaning materials needed
		Asks for assistance as needed
Meal Preparation		
Classifies various foods into the four basic food groups	Demonstrates ability to use measurement tools	Requests food politely
Plans balanced meals using the food groups	Demonstrates ability to set stove and/or oven temperature	Socializes appropriately during mealtime
Follows a recipe in correct sequence	Demonstrates time-related skills while cooking	
	Serves appropriate quantities of food	

Table 3 indicates some academic requirements of bowling alleys, game
arcades, libraries, and movie theatres in the recreation-leisure domain.

TABLE 13-3
RECREATION/LEISURE

Reading/Writing	Math	Communication
	Bowling	
Includes name on score sheet	Identifies number in group	Requests necessary materials
Write in score/pins down per frame	Obtains correct shoe size	Communicates pins down to scorekeeper
	Scorekeeping	Communicates number of games played to service personnel
	Pay for game(s)	
	Vending	
Scans vending area for desired machine	Deposits proper coins	Asks for assistance as needed
Selects desired items		Responds appropriately to interactions
	Game Arcade	
Follows instructions for using change machine	Obtains proper change/tokens	Requests change/tokens from service personnel
Scans game room, moves to desired area	Dispenses money/tokens into machine	Identifies end of game, winner
Selects game to play		Asks for assistance as needed
Plays game as directed		Responds appropriately to interactions
	Library	
Locates correct drawer for subject/author by alphabet in card catalog	Pays fine on late books	Identifies overdue books
Scans drawer, locates correct card	Locates book "call" number	Identifies amount of money needed to pay fine
Locates specific area/shelf for desired materials		Identifies area to return books
Reads selected materials		Communicates name to check out new materials
		Asks for assistance as needed
	Movie Theater	
Checks paper for what movie is playing	Determines number of tickets to be purchased	Phones theatre for what movies are playing
Selects appropriate movie to attend	Purchases tickets	Communicates number of tickets/movie desired to service personnel
Scans display case of snack bar	Purchases snacks desired	Places snack order to service personnel
Scans lobby for correct movie title/cinema number	Secures seating appropriate for number in group	Asks for assistance as needed
		Responds appropriately to interactions

Table 4 delineates the reading, writing, math, and communication requirements of the bus lines, banks, grocery and department stores, and sit-down and fast-food restaurants in the community-at-large domain.

The academic requirements of clerical, food service, and janitorial-housekeeping job types in the vocational domain are illustrated in Table 5.

Lastly, Table 6 delineates the requirements of elementary, middle, and high schools.

As can be seen from Tables 2 through 6, the reading, writing, math, and communication requirements of natural community environments, including schools, are extensive and it is in these content areas that severely handicapped persons are often said to have the greatest deficits. In addition to those deficits, many, if not most have memory skill deficits (Ellis, 1970; Spitz & Webreck, 1972; Butterfield, Wambold, & Belmont, 1973) that, in the absence of external cuing, contribute to their dependence on others. In addition to the academic skill areas, natural community environments and public schools have many memory skill requirements such as following a daily schedule at school and work. As discussed earlier, Holvoet et al. (1980) pointed out that these skills have an interdependence and, therefore, are not learned in isolation from one another. The remainder of this chapter is concerned with alternative or compensatory strategies that increase severely handicapped individuals' personal competence in community environments including the public schools. The strategies will be illustrated by domain (domestic, recreation-leisure, vocational, community-at-large, and school) and in most instances will attempt to teach multiple skills (e.g., reading in conjunction with number recognition and following a schedule; object and activity identification in conjunction with time telling and reading). As discussed earlier, these strategies should be employed only after instructional personnel have (a) conducted environmental inventories of severely handicapped persons' current and subsequent natural environments, and (b) assessed severely handicapped persons' needs in those environments. Also, the strategies that are developed should be flexible, inexpensive, durable, portable, and nonintrusive. They should allow for inexpensive and easy modification in order to allow greater independent participation as needed. They should be durable to provide for extensive use and they should be portable and nonintrusive to avoid drawing attention to severely handicapped persons in the natural environments. Severely handicapped persons should always receive instruction on the strategies but not necessarily be expected to reach a certain criteria before they are implemented in natural environments.

TABLE 13-4
COMMUNITY

Reading/Writing	Math	Communication
	Bus Line	
Obtains schedule/route guide	Determines bus number appropriate for destination	Identifies destination
Determines correct bus stop for boarding and destination	Determines time bus will depart	Identifies time of bus departure
	Deposits correct change (token) in fare box	Requests transfer
		Verifies destination if uncertain
	Bank	
Chooses correct banking form	Totals check/cash	Identifies banking services needed
Completes deposit/withdrawal slip information	Checks computation on banking form	Indicates banking process to service personnel
Endorses check		Asks for assistance when needed
	Grocery	
Scans shopping list to initiate shopping activity	Determines cost of items	Identifies items to be purchased
Locates departments	Determines enough/not enough money for purchases	Asks for assistance as needed
Uses grocery list	Pays cashier after total is given	Responds appropriately to interactions
Chooses items based on brand. size. weight. and quantity		
	Sit-Down Restaurant	
Identifies wait to be seated/seat yourself	Determines cost of entrees	Communicates number in group to be seated
Scans menu to determine selection	Determines enough/not enough money for selections	Communicates order to waitress
	Identifies check total	Interacts appropriately with peers
	Pays appropriate amount	Requests separate checks
		Asks for service when needed
		Responds appropriately to interactions
	Fast-Food Restaurant	
Scans menu selection board to determine order	Determines price of selections	Communicates order
	Determines enough/not enough money for purchase	Communicates for here or to go
	Pays appropriate amount	Requests condiments
		Asks for assistance as needed
		Responds appropriately to interactions
	Department Store	
Scans shopping list	(clothing) Locates sizes of item	(clothing) Locates store clerk for permission to try on item
Determines departments needed and locates those areas	Checks price tags	Asks for assistance as needed
Chooses items based on size/ quantity/brand	Determines enough/not enough money to buy	Responds appropriately to interactions
	Pays for purchases	

TABLE 13-5
VOCATIONAL

Reading/Writing	Math	Communication
	Clerical	
Follows daily schedule. job routine	Uses time card. records hours worked	Identifies supervisor/location to receive job assignment
Sorts (e.g., mail)	Makes proper number of copies	Places calls as directed
Files	Collates pages in correct order	Takes messages
Uses telephone book	Takes breaks at correct time and for appropriate length of time	Communicates when a particular job is completed
Attaches labels appropriately		
Uses stamper. ink pad appropriately		Responds appropriately to interactions on the job and during breaks
	Food Service	
Follows daily schedule. job routine	Uses time card. reports hours worked	Identifies supervisor/location to receive job assignment
Identifies menu items	Measures soap for dishwasher	Communicates when a particular job is finished
Follows recipe directions	Measures ingredients for menu item(s)	Asks for more work as needed
	Sets oven at proper temperature. time	Asks for assistance as needed
	Takes breaks at correct time and for appropriate length of time	Responds appropriately to interactions on the job and during breaks
	Acting as a Cashier	
	Counts money combinations	
	Totals bill	
	Makes change	
	Operates cash register	
	Vocational	
Follows daily schedule. job routine	Uses time card. records hours worked	Identifies supervisor/location to receive job assignment
	Measures detergent for laundry	Communicates when a particular job is finished
	Operates dryer. including appropriate quantity of clothes and temperature setting	Asks for more work as needed
	Replenish, refill service supplies as needed	Asks for assistance as needed
	Takes breaks at correct time and for appropriate length of time	Responds appropriately to interactions on the job and during breaks

TABLE 13-6
SCHOOL

Reading/Writing	Math	Communication
	Elementary	
Follows daily schedule	Using lockers	Taking/receiving messages
Reads cafeteria menu	Paying for lunch	Interactions with nonhandicapped peers
Leisure reading (books, magazines)	Lunch/milk counts	Interaction with regular education faculty
Check-out library materials	Report attendance	
Grade reports		
	Middle	
Follows daily schedule	Using lockers	Making phone calls
Reads daily announcements	Paying for lunch	Deliver/receive messages
Check/out materials (library and audio visual center)	Attendance count	Making school announcements
Completes assignments	Making school appointments	Interactions with nonhandicapped peers
Leisure reading (books, magazines)	Dialing phone correctly	Interactions with regular education faculty
Secondary		
Follows daily schedule	Using lockers	Making phone calls
Reads daily announcements	Paying for lunch	Deliver/receive messages
Reads snack bar board menu	Attendance count	Making school announcements
Check out materials (library, audio visual center)	Making school appointments	Interactions with nonhandicapped peers
Completes assignments	Dialing phone correctly	Interactions with regular education faculty
Leisure reading (books, magazines)	Use school vending machines	

Domestic Strategies

Freagon, Wheeler, Hill, Brankin, and Costello (1982) described a domestic training environment where up to three severely handicapped students, ages 18 to 21, spent three consecutive overnights for three consecutive weeks a year to practice small group living skills. A certified female teacher and a domestic male trainer assistant worked with the young adults during their stay in the environment. Over the course of approximately 3 years, the majority of the students and/or their parents reported that students could shower or bathe independently. When the domestic trainers sought to verify this, they found that very few of the students cleaned their bodies adequately.

In order to provide these young adults the dignity and respect of privacy, a pictoral cleaning sequence was devised and is illustrated in Figure 1. The sequence is either laminated or covered with plastic and can be hung in a shower or set on the rim of the bathtub. If needed, pictoral checklists can also be devised for materials needed to take a shower or bath. At the same time that appropriate showering or bathing is being performed, student identification of body parts, reading, and number identification skills are reinforced.

Learning to assume responsibility for tasks in natural domestic environments is a skill that is desirable for all persons. Figure 2 illustrates a daily job assignment schedule devised for the domestic training environment. Weekly job schedules can be devised similarily. Both the weekly and daily job schedules are designed to have pictoral representations of the tasks accompanied by a short written description of the task and the student responsible. While these strategies were designed for a domestic training environment, they also have considerable utility in group and natural homes. Their utility is obvious in the group home. In a natural home, instructional personnel at the school could assist families in utilizing these strategies to ensure the handicapped person's participation in family chores for an allowance. At the same time that jobs are being taught, the student's activity, word, and name recognition are reinforced. Other compensatory strategies that can be used in natural domestic environments are (a) pictoral checklists for materials needed for household chores, (b) pictoral sequences for household chores, (c) pictoral recipes, and (d) color coding of temperature gauges on fixtures such as stoves and sinks.

Recreation-Leisure Strategies

As discussed earlier, alternative or compensatory strategies need to be flexible, inexpensive, durable, portable, and nonintrusive. Figure 3 is an illustration of a communication and sequence compensatory strategy for four different natural recreation-leisure environments. The high school student for which this strategy was designed started out with single environment sequences where paying and other requirements were included. As the student learned the sequence, the number of pictoral cues were reduced and more environments included on a single page. The pictoral representations were drawn by instructional personnel and are small so as to slip into a plastic slide protector sheet in a three-ring notebook. The column on the left depicts the four recreation-leisure activities in the community that the student enjoys most. The last picture in the column that allows the student to ask direction to the washroom is placed at the bottom and applies to all four environments. The second column represents the bus line number that

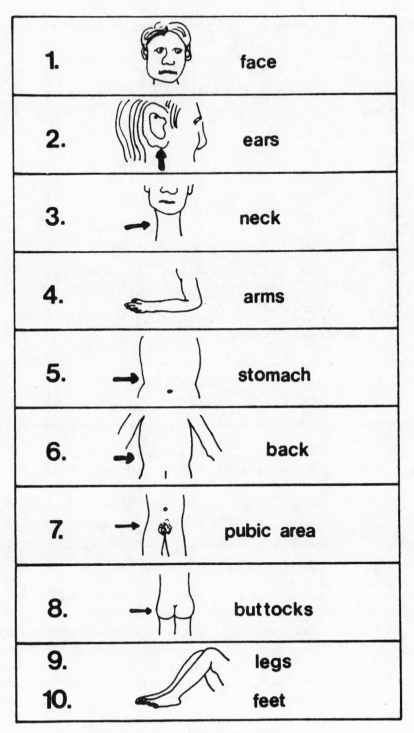

1.		face
2.		ears
3.		neck
4.		arms
5.		stomach
6.		back
7.		pubic area
8.		buttocks
9.		legs
10.		feet

Figure 13-1. Pictoral body cleansing sequence.

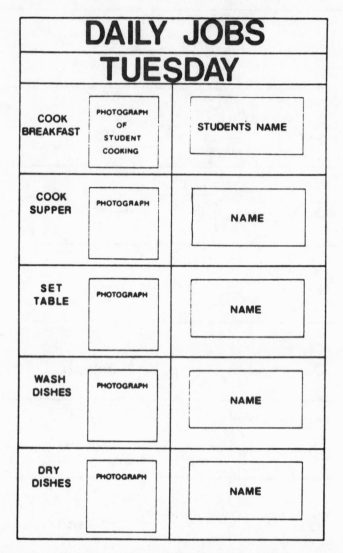

Figure 13-2. Daily jobs for students in the domestic training environment.

the student needs to take from his home to get to the activity. The third and fourth columns contain the messages necessary to engage in this particular activity. All messages are presented in a way that both the student and the service personnel can understand the desired outcome of the interaction. Like the strategies discussed above, this strategy also reinforces word and number recognition while allowing the student increased independent access to community environments.

Figure 13-3. Pictoral communication sequence and compensatory strategy for four natural community recreation-leisure environment.

Community-At-Large Strategies

For the community-at-large domain, a grocery shopping list and payment strategy is illustrated. The pictoral representations utilized in grocery shopping can often be found in women's magazines or in local newspaper advertisements. For many other community-at-large environments, they may have to be drawn.

The strategy that combines item obtainment with paying is illustrated in Figure 4. This strategy has been developed using laminated tag board with plastic slide protector pockets for desired picture items glued onto the tag board. The money is placed in a small ziplock plastic bag which is glued and stapled to the laminated tag board for durability. Once all items are obtained, the card is presented to the cashier in order to pay for the items. This strategy does not require many mathematical or verbal communication skills on the part of the severely handicapped person in order to complete the transaction. The cashier need only to read the printed message, perform the regular transaction and place any change due back in the ziplock bag.

Similar compensatory strategies may be designed for banking, ordering in a restaurant, or various recreation leisure activities. The same compensatory communication strategy may be used for desired interactions in a department store. Communication cards indicating desired items and necessary interactions (e.g., "Where's the dressing room?") are designed in the same manner as those used in the grocery shopping illustration.

Vocational Strategies

If employment for severely handicapped persons in the competitive work force is to be realized, compensatory strategies must be developed that allow for maximum independence on the job. The ability to adequately perform job tasks, while critical, is surely not the sole component involved in securing employment. Memory skills play an important role in relationship to work. The ability to sequence job tasks, identify completion of job components, and determine break and lunch times are all critical job components. Equally important are requirements such as requesting assistance from a coworker, asking for work materials, and responding to supervisors' questions. Because it is unrealistic to expect that severely handicapped persons will consistently be afforded the additional assistance they may often need to fulfill the many job components noted above, compensatory strategies become critical.

Figure 5 represents one method to delineate and sequence a service employment task. The checklist is either laminated or placed in a plastic protector sheet. Job tasks are listed pictorially and are accompanied with words to enhance sight word vocabulary. Pictures are faded when words are mastered. As job tasks are completed, they are checked off with a marker. Upon completion of the job, the checklist is wiped off for reuse the following workday. This particular checklist was designed to be kept in a three ring notebook. Similar checklists can be designed in small 3″ × 5″ notebooks or with flip rings to display only one task at a time.

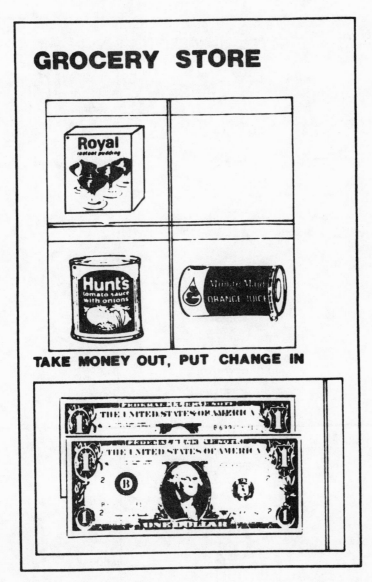

Figure 13-4. Pictoral grocery shopping list and payment strategy made with plastic slide protector pockets and a ziplock bag.

Public School Strategies

As severely handicapped students are integrated into chronologically age appropriate public schools, it is important that they learn to follow schedules similar to students who are not identified as handicapped. Inventories of elementary, middle or junior high, and high schools indicate that by the

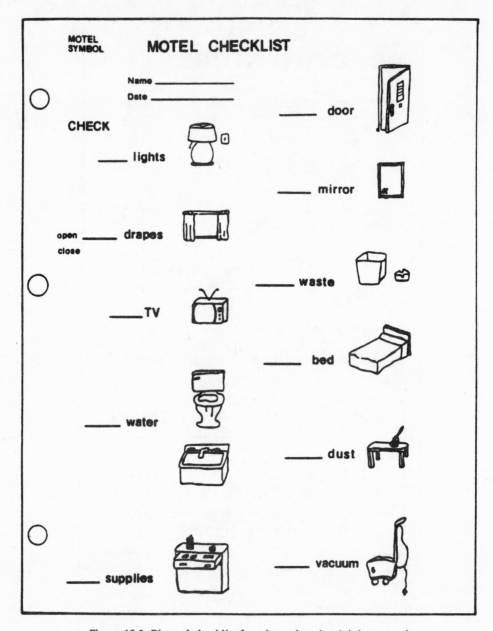

Figure 13-5. Pictoral checklist for a housekeeping job in a motel.

third grade, most nonhandicapped students are expected to be able to independently follow a daily schedule designed by periods.

Figure 6 is a schedule designed for a quadraplegic, severely mentally retarded and blind student. It is a tactile strategy that has actual objects represented for periods or activities in which the student will engage that particular day. The actual objects are attached to laminated tagboard and secured by metal rings to make a book. An actual pencil, city bus token, spoon, and cassette tape are used to represent homeroom, community training, lunch, and recreation-leisure periods respectively. Instructional personnel change the periods daily to correspond with the student's daily activities.

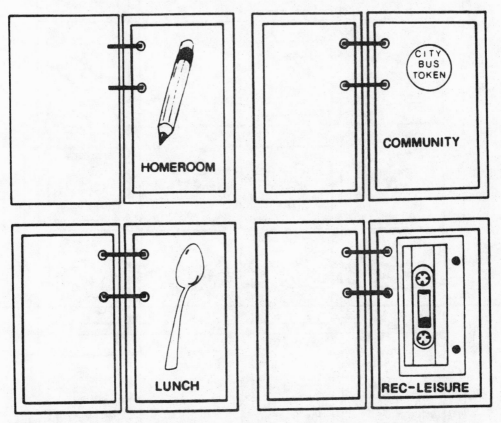

Figure 13-6. Tactile school schedule with actual items secured on 5" × 8" laminated tagboard.

Figure 7 is a more complex schedule of a high school student who does not have visual problems. As with many of the other strategies, a three ring notebook, a slide protector sheet with pockets, and pictoral and sign representations of the student's activities are utilized. Instructional personnel determine the schedule daily and review the individual's schedule during homeroom and at the close of the school day.

Beginning in middle or junior high school, students are issued lockers in which to keep their personal belongings and books. Many severely handicapped students do not have the memory, number, motoric, and visual acuity skills to functionally utilize combination padlocks which are tradi-

Figure 13-7. Pictoral school schedule made with plastic slide protector pockets.

tionally used on school lockers. Two compensatory strategies that can be utilized are (a) a color coded strategy where the student has to learn the number of forward and backward rotations that are associated with each of the three colors, and (b) a simple padlock with a key that can be utilized with more severely handicapped students or by the instructional personnel if students cannot learn to use a key.

Finally, secondary students in most high schools have access to vending machines to purchase soda and other snacks. Many severely handicapped students are incapable of determining the number and types of coins needed to access these machines. A coin matching strategy whereby actual coin imprints are made on a tagboard can be used in these situations. A black ink stamp pad can make the imprint. The tagboard can then be laminated and various combinations put in metal rings or a small ring notebook. Prior to getting in line to purchase the item, the student places his/her available coins on top of the imprints to determine the appropriate combination. This strategy has extended application for purchase of bus tokens and other items in community vending machines.

Conclusion

Increasingly, severely handicapped persons of all ages are being served in natural domestic, recreation-leisure, work, community-at-large, and regular public school environments. The development of the ecological inventory has allowed instructional personnel to assess the skill requirements of these environments and to then develop programs whereby severely handicapped persons may increase their independence, productivity, and participation.

Severely handicapped persons' right to participate in natural environments is now generally accepted. Not as widely accepted, however, is a universal approach to instructing severely handicapped persons in these environments. The present authors have attempted to convey that, independent of age or disability, severely handicapped persons will increase independence, productivity, and participation if compensatory strategies are developed for the reading, writing, math, communication, and memory requirements inherent in natural environments. These requirements are the ones with which severely handicapped persons have the greatest difficulty. Motoric compensatory strategies were not considered as they have been discussed at length elsewhere in the literature. The reading, writing, math, and communication requirements and the illustrations of compensatory strategies in domestic, recreation-leisure, vocational, community-at-large, and regular public schools utilized are by no means all inclusive. We trust that as the technology advances, so will severely handicapped individuals' personal competence in community environments.

REFERENCES

Baer, D. M. A hung jury and a Scottish verdict: "Not proven." *Analysis and Intervention in Developmental Disabilities*, 1981, *1*, 91–97. (a)

Baer, D. M. *Promoting generalization of treatment effects with children: Issues and strategies.* Paper presented at the 15th annual convention of the Association for the Advancement of Behavior Therapy, Toronto, November 1981. (b)

Brown, L. Instructional materials and educational programs for severely handicapped students: Highlights of a presentation by Lou Brown. *Journal of Special Education Technology.* 1981. *4*(2), 1-5.

Brown, L., Branston, M. B., Hamre-Nietupski, A., Johnson, F., Wilcox, B., & Gruenewald. L. A rationale for comprehensive longitudinal interactions between severely handicapped students and nonhandicapped students and other citizens. *AAESPH Review.* 1978. *4*(1). 3-14.

Brown, L., Branston, M., Hamre-Nietupski, S., Pumpian, I., Certo, N., & Gruenewald, L. A strategy for developing chronological age appropriate and functional curricular content for severely handicapped adolescents and young adults. *Journal of Special Education.* 1979. *13*(1), 81-90.

Brown, L., Nietupski, J., & Hamre-Nietupski, S. Criterion of ultimate functioning. In M. A. Thomas (Ed.), *Hey! don't forget about me: Education's investment in the severely, profoundly, and multiply handicapped.* Reston, VA: The Council for Exceptional Children. 1976.

Brown, L., Wilcox, B., Sontag, E., Vincent, L., Dodd, N., & Gruenewald, L. Toward the realization of the least restrictive educational environments for severely handicapped students. *AAESPH Review,* 1977, *2*(4), 195-201.

Butterfield, E. C., Wambold, C., & Belmont, J. M. On the theory and practice of improving short-term memory. *American Journal of Mental Deficiency,* 1973, *77*, 654-669.

Donnellan, A. M. An educational perspective of autism: Implications for curriculum development and personal development. In B. Wilcox & P. Thompson (Eds.), *Critical issues in educating autistic children and youth.* Washington, D.C.: U.S. Department of Education. Office of Special Education, 1980.

Ellis, N. R. Memory processes in retardates and normals. In N. R. Ellis (Ed.), *International review of research in mental retardation* (vol. 4). New York: Academic Press, 1970.

Ellis, N. R. On training the mentally retarded. *Analysis and Intervention in Developmental Disabilities,* 1981, *1*, 99-108.

Freagon, S. A commentary response. In B. Campbell & V. Baldwin (Eds.), *Severely handicapped/hearing impaired students.* Baltimore: Paul H. Brookes, 1982.

Freagon, S., Wheeler, J., Hill, L., Brankin, G., & Costello, D. *A domestic training environment for severely handicapped students.* Paper presented at poster session at the annual convention of the Association for the Severely Handicapped (TASH). Denver, Colorado, November 1982.

Freagon, S., Wheeler, J., McDannel, K., Brankin, G., & Costello, D. *Individual student community life skill profile system for severely handicapped students.* Northern Illinois University-DeKalb and DeKalb County Special Education Association, 1983.

Gliedman, J., & Roth, W. *The unexpected minority: Handicapped children in America.* New York: Harcourt, Brace, Jovanovich, 1980.

Guess, D., Horner, R. D., Utley, B., Holvoet, H., Maxon, D., Tucker, D., & Warren, S. A. A functional curriculum sequencing model for teaching the severely handicapped. *AAESPH Review,* 1978, *3*, 202-215.

Holvoet, H., Guess, D., Mulligan, M., & Brown, F. The individualized curriculum sequencing model (11): A teaching strategy for severely handicapped students. *Journal of the Association for the Severely Handicapped,* 1980, *5*(4), 337-351.

Horner, R. H., Sprague, J., & Wilcox, B. General case programming for community activities. In B. Wilcox & T. Bellamy (Eds.), *Design of high school programs for severely handicapped students.* Baltimore: Paul H. Brookes, 1982.

Reese, H. W., & Lipsitt, L. P. (Eds.), *Experimental child psychology.* New York: Academic Press, 1970.

Spitz. H. H.. & Webreck. C. A. Effects of spontaneous vs. externally-cued learning on the permanent storage of a schema by retardates. *American Journal of Mental Deficiency.* 1972. 77, 163–168.

Voeltz. L. M.. & Evans. I. M. Educational validity: Procedures to evaluate outcomes in programs for severely handicapped learners. *Journal of the Association for the Severely Handicapped.* 1983. 8(1), 3–15.

Wilcox. B.. & Bellamy. T. G. *Design of high school programs for severely handicapped students.* Baltimore: Paul H. Brookes. 1982.

Williams. W.. Brown. L.. & Certo. N. Basic components of instructional programs. *Theory into Practice.* 1975. 14. 123–136.

York. R.. & Williams. W. Curricular and on-going assessment for individualized programming in the classroom. In R. York. P. Thorpe. & R. Minisi (Eds.). *Education of severely and profoundly handicapped people.* New Jersey: Northwestern Regional Resource Center. 1977.

Section V
STRATEGIES FOR THE FUTURE

CHAPTER 14*

RESEARCH NEEDS: EDUCATIONAL, COMMUNITY BASED, SOCIAL, AND POLICY

H. D. "BUD" FREDERICKS

Research seems to have certain characteristics: it is always needed; it is perennially underfunded; and even when accomplished, it is frequently ignored. Without research, we are like people going into the darkness of a strange house, not knowing where the light is or even if there is a light, and groping to turn on that light. We feel, we probe, we stumble, we fall, we get up, we try again, and continue to search for the light. When it goes on, much is revealed to us, at least in the area where the light is shining.

And so it has been with the delivery of services for severely handicapped individuals. How long we were in the dark! How long we were without light! How long severely handicapped people suffered from our ignorance and our lack of knowledge! And then the light seemed to come on, for suddenly we were concerned about delivery of services to severely handicapped people. Everyone credits P. L. 94-142 for seeing that light. But we would hypothesize that the *time* was right. Public Law 94-142 was the catalyst, not the cause. We had come of age. We were ready to serve severely handicapped people. Parents had been advocating for such service for years. Gradually, professionals joined them, and thus P.L. 94-142 was created.

Yet, being ready to serve severely handicapped people and serving them adequately were two different things. In many areas, we were not sure what we should do or what we could do. There were bits of research done on back wards of institutions prior to the advent of P.L. 94-142. However, it was difficult to get an article accepted in publications like *Exceptional Children*

---

*H. D. "Bud" Fredericks turned to a career in special education with the birth of a child with Downs Syndrome in 1966. He received his doctorate from the University of Oregon in 1969 and has been employed at Teaching Research as the Project Director of model demonstration projects for early childhood education, severely handicapped education, and vocational education for students who are deaf and blind and for students with severe handicaps. He has developed curriculum classroom models for children with severe handicaps, group homes for children and adults, adult activity centers, and programs for children with mild handicaps/severe behavioral disorders. In addition, he has studied training techniques and implemented inservice training across all environments from preschool to adult services. Dr. Fredericks has served as the Chair of the Oregon Developmental Disabilities Council, Vice President of a local Association for Retarded Citizens, and is the President for The Association for Persons with Severe Handicaps (TASH).

about severely handicapped people at that time. It was not the "in" subject; consequently, the research that was done focused on institutionalized people and had little applicability to situations in the community.

Yet, P.L. 94-142 mandated the least restrictive environment, and for most, if not all severely handicapped people that meant functioning in the community. The research to show how that should be done was not there. It did not exist in any form, and so what emerged were two trends: a series of conceptualizations by educational philosophers, and major efforts by researchers throughout the country in model building. Certainly, if model building is to be a form of research, it must at least meet certain requirements: (a) it must demonstrate desired effects with severely handicapped individuals; (b) it can be and is replicated; and (c) the same type of effects can be achieved in those replication sites. Model building that meets these requirements has been all too infrequent.

Despite a glaring lack of a data base, we in the field of the education of the severely handicapped have conceptualized much. Like prophets we spoke; perhaps hoping, like prophets, that the faithful followers would adapt our pronouncements as truths—yet, we did not have the data. A few of the standard pronouncements which were presented as truths without support- ive data were such things as:

- Early childhood education is necessary for the maximum development of severely handicapped individuals.
- Parents are essential in the teaching of severely handicapped individuals.
- Integration will achieve good results.
- If some integration is good, more is better.
- Deinstitutionalization is better than institutionalization.
- Around-the-year schooling is necessary at least for some severely handi- capped people.
- Group homes are the way to go.
- Severely handicapped infants should be taught as soon as possible.
- Activity centers are needed in all communities.
- Activity centers have become obsolete, and people should be trained in community settings.
- A functional curriculum is the only type of curriculum that is appropriate for severely handicapped people.

We have been deluged with conceptualizations, beliefs, and prognostica- tions; now we are in desparate need of research to support, refine, revise the pronouncements, and ultimately come closer to truth.

And where are the research needs?

This chapter has as its charge to identify the state-of-the-art in each of these areas and provide suggestions for future research questions. The title of the chapter is, of course, global. It includes just about everything that can happen to a severely handicapped person, and so we have chosen to approach the subject by *not* providing a comprehensive review of the literature. That has already been provided in previous chapters in an effective way. In order to focus on research needs, this chapter will, instead, identify areas in which the research to date has not been adequate or is, in fact, nonexistent. We hope that the chapter will provide a basis for students and professionals to begin to formulate specific research questions and provide valid answers to many of these questions.

At the onset, we think it important to state that truth evolves by the accumulation of evidence. No one research study provides truth. Very frequently in the area of social services, we never can find definitive research that proves beyond a doubt that such-and-such is true for all individuals. Instead, we accumulate evidence that says, "This, perhaps is the best approach for individuals who are severely handicapped." That evidence needs to be accumulated in a variety of ways. It needs to come from the researchers in our country and elsewhere who focus on specific questions, isolate the variables, manipulate the treatments, and arrive at conclusions that are valid. Also, we should be gathering information from practitioners throughout the country. Teachers, group home operators, activity center directors, and vocational trainers all should contribute to this body of knowledge. We have practitioners engaging in excellent programs across our country, finding out information about severely handicapped individuals that is not shared with the rest of the country. Journals seldom accept material for publication that is not "good" research, and so these practitioner reports are only shared in small, regional conferences and are seldom publicized nationally. Often, they are not shared at all. Someone needs to begin to gather best practices and to share them. That is not now occurring to any significant extent.

We have organized this chapter into 13 areas and will try to pinpoint research that is sorely needed. We recognize that we probably will not cover the entire spectrum, but we think that the number of questions we are raising are voluminous enough to demonstrate that we suffer from a dearth of research about essential questions. As indicated earlier, we shall not provide a complete review of the literature for each area, but we shall pinpoint what we consider to be some major critical articles or summaries that are provided by others, so that readers may obtain a bibliography from this chapter that would summarize various research states-of-the-art.

Parents

It is generally agreed by professionals that parents are an integral part of the education and socialization of severely handicapped individuals; yet there is much that we do not know about parents. The entire area of acceptance by parents of their severely handicapped offspring needs to be re-examined. There are some standard conceptions about parents' acceptance and the stages that parents go through when being told that they have a severely handicapped child; yet there is evidence today that these stages may be changing. This subject needs to be examined critically and longitudinally. A good summary of the parents' situation in this research area is contained in Fredericks (in press, a).

There are many different parent training or parent involvement models. These have been developed primarily by projects supported by Special Education Programs (SEP) (formerly Bureau for the Education of the Handicapped) in the Handicapped Children's Early Education Programs. The best ways to involve parents, and how early they should be involved, are still open questions, although each developed model would advocate that it is the best approach. Comparisons between models have been generally nonexistent. The issue of *Exceptional Education Quarterly* edited by Turnbull and Turnbull provides perhaps the best summary of this problem.

The entire relationship of parents with schools is also an area that needs examination. The IEPs alone are a fruitful area for research. Is the process intimidating to parents, as some would suggest, as teachers, specialists, and administrators meet the parents across the table to develop the IEP? Are IEPs effective, and are we in fact devising appropriate and satisfactory programs for our severely handicapped individuals as a result of the IEP process? Are parents satisfied with that process? Is the parents' relationship with the school better because of the IEP process? We have no body of research to answer these questions.

Parents are referred to frequently as partners with the schools in the teaching of severely handicapped individuals. Wolery (1980) provides a nice summary of the types of parent teaching that has occurred, not only for severely handicapped individuals but for mildly handicapped children in the early childhood area. At the time of its publication, the summary indicated a paucity of research in this area. The situation has not improved since then. Few studies systematically investigate the effectiveness of parent involvement. Moreover, the exact role of the parents as teachers is still questionable. There are those who have advocated parents as teachers to teach in conjunction with the school or to teach additional subjects outside the school. Yet we have little research that documents this type of involvement. Thus, the best way to involve parents is open to question.

Finally, what is the most effective way for parents to be advocates for their severely handicapped children? We have instance after instance throughout the country where parents and schools have become polarized, and certainly such polarization does not lead to the development of the best programs for children. Data to demonstrate the best way for parents to achieve success with schools or with any service agency are scarce at best. Even research that has been accomplished is sufficiently ill-defined so that we do not know the impact of socioeconomic status on effectiveness with schools. We do not know the relationship of the severity of the handicap to the effectiveness of the parent as educator, advocate or teacher. Finally, we know little about the effects of single parenthood on handicapped children and relationships to schools.

Early Intervention

It is amazing to realize that SEP has been funding model programs and grants for state implementation of early education for more than 13 years. Yet the amount of information that we have about these programs and their effectiveness is relatively limited. Over the years, approximately 25 new model programs have been funded each year by SEP. These have been very carefully geographically located throughout the United States so that all areas of the country could be exposed to them. Most of the models have persevered over time, and some have demonstrated sizable gains for children while they were in the programs. Yet, 9 years after the implementation of these early childhood programs, when the federal government needed information about the long-range effectiveness of early childhood education, that information was scarce indeed. A handful of studies existed in the country. The most important of these were summarized in the December 1981 issue of the *Journal of the Division for Early Childhood* (cf. Karnes & Cleveland, 1981). Of those, only three or four deal with severely handicapped children. This is an unfortunately small sample because the entire argument for funding of early childhood programs both by federal and state governments has rested on the long-range effects of early childhood education. It would be a sad indictment of any educational system if it was not able to demonstrate that a child in a school program was not gaining more than the child who was not in the school program. The critical question is how those gains are maintained or enhanced over time. There is a critical need for many more long-range studies of specific populations and severities of handicaps.

Moreover, the comparative effects of various types of early intervention are generally unknown. Is it better to provide early intervention through center-based education or through parent involvement? Many of the major models that have lasted over the years advocate their own system without comparing that system to other systems. For instance, the Portage Model, adopted throughout the world, uses parental instruction. The Teaching Research Model, replicated hundreds of times, uses a center-based model combined with parental involvement. Which is more effective? We do not know. There are other questions: Would three days of center involvement plus two days of parental involvement be just as effective as five days of center involvement? How many instructional hours a day achieve optimum effects—does two hours of early childhood intervention produce the same effects as three or four hours?

At what age should early intervention begin? Do we have any data that indicate that early intervention with infants or children below the age of one year is going to produce better results than intervention that may start at age two? And is there a difference by handicapping condition? These are questions for which we do not have answers. These are questions about which we have many biases, but we do not have the data to adequately support those biases. These are basic questions. They are getting at the heart of major programs for which we advocate. Most frequently our advocacy is based on a minimum amount of data and much emotion. (Please do not interpret this comment as being in opposition to early childhood intervention. We are among its greatest supporters, but we recognize that our support is largely based upon intuition and bias).

School

Many of the research questions about school programs for severely handicapped students focus on areas in which there is litigation. This litigation has had two primary foci. The first of these is the length of a school year. There have been a number of cases that examined the need for continued education for severely handicapped individuals during periods when school was not normally in session. In almost all cases, the litigation has been settled in favor of the plaintiff who was seeking an extended school year. Yet in actual fact, the experts knew little about the need for additional school time for severely handicapped individuals. They did not know which individuals or types of students needed that time. Also, they did not know how that additional time could be delivered most effectively. Is it really necessary for all severely handicapped individuals to continue their education during the summer with a standard school day, or is some form of tutorial system possible to prevent regression and long recoupment times? The experts had opinions but few facts based on research. An excellent discussion of problems with year-round special education or the extended school year is contained in Volume 47, Number 4, of *Exceptional Children*. Specifically, the articles by Makuch; Larson, Goodman, and Glean; Stotland and Mancuso; and Leonard are recommended. Finally, a rather provocative article by Edgar, Spence, and Kenowitz (1977), which is still current, points the way to an evaluation design for the effectiveness of extended school year programs. To our knowledge, this evaluation has not been implemented or at least reported in the literature.

The other major litigation area which is currently ongoing is that of integration. A major lawsuit began in August 1983 in Missouri, and we do not anticipate the decision for some time. As the expert witnesses lined up on each side in that particular case, the paucity of evidence was obvious on either side to demonstrate the effectiveness of the integration of the severely handicapped student in public schools with nonhandicapped students. Specific localities throughout the country were pointed to as being areas where successful integration was accomplished, yet each of those localities could not demonstrate that their severely handicapped students were gaining more academically or socially than the students in a segregated setting. Research in this area is critically needed if we are to preserve the concept of least restrictive environment for our severely handicapped students. Conceptualization papers which advocate for integration of severely handicapped students have been prepared by Brown, Wilcox, Sontag, Vincent, Dodd, and Gruenewald (1977); Brown, Branston, Hamre-Nietupski, Johnson, Wilcox, and Gruenewald (1979); and Hamre-Nietupski and Nietupski (1981). Others have focused on the need for research in this area; most notable among those have been Stainback and Stainback (1981, 1982); and Peck and Semmel (1982). These articles provide a nice review of literature but emphasize the total lack of data that is currently extant in this area. Finally, Guralnick (1978) provides a good summary of the effects of integration at the preschool level up to that particular point in time. There is a need to update the effects of integration at the preschool level with current research.

Specifically, these references and others point to the fact that we do not have data that demonstrate the positive effects of integration. However, there are only minor indications throughout the literature that more studies are needed. We do not know how to effectively integrate, although again there are samples from the literature. The effects on children, both the severely handicapped and the nonhandicapped, have not been adequately studied. These effects must be looked at both from an immediate point of view, namely within the school environment, and also as a long-range effect in a community or a region. These studies are massive undertakings but certainly ought to be a focus of future endeavors and federal funding.

Curriculum

One could look into hundreds of research areas regarding curriculum. We cannot cover them all here; however, we have chosen a few which we think are extremely important and for which we do not now have definitive research.

Language

If one reviews the literature in the area of language, one is immediately impressed with the number of studies that have been done by researchers over the years. Yet one major area of research still glares at us in need of solution. When, and for how long, do we teach alternative communication systems to nonverbal children? At what ages should we start? What are the preferred alternative communication systems for children with particular characteristics? How can we be sure that one system is better than another? Bonvillian, Nelson, and Rhyne (1981) provide a review of the findings and issues in teaching sign language to nonspeaking autistic children. They make the point, however, that different sign language teaching methods need to be investigated more fully, including emphasis on training sign language within the children's total environment and with greater staff and parental participation. Fristoe and Lloyd (1979) examined 20 manuals that were designed to teach sign communication to persons with severe communication impairment. They developed a list of what was being taught, not what should have been taught, but it certainly was an indication of our lack of knowledge in this particular area. Goetz, Schuler, and Sailor (1979) reviewed strategies in teaching various types of communication responses to severely handicapped students and provided an excellent discussion of the issues involved. Certainly the utilization of communication boards and the development of electronics to facilitate communications are areas not only of research but of development that need to be tested, tried, and refined.

Socialization

Another curricular area that needs research emphasis is socialization. Much research exists on how to remediate inappropriate social behaviors, but there is little that focuses on social relationships among severely handicapped people and among severely handicapped people and nonhandicapped people.

Studies have been done that have investigated the building of a social response between one, two, or four severely handicapped people. No studies have really examined severely handicapped students in an integrated social milieu and attempted to examine the variables that cause certain severely handicapped students to be more accepted by their nonhandicapped peers. In addition, longitudinal studies are needed to determine the long-range effects of relationships not only between severely handicapped people but also between severely handicapped and nonhandicapped people.

As professionals we have advocated for normalization and integration, and we have done so without a body of data that examines the effects of those policies on severely handicapped people. By placing one or two severely handicapped students in a nonhandicapped school, do we create a favorable social situation for those severely handicapped children, or do we create isolates? If the latter is true, how might we foster more than perfunctory socialization? Where is the data that tell us it is possible to build bona-fide friendships between handicapped and nonhandicapped children? What are the preferences of severely handicapped children? Would they rather be with nonhandicapped children or would they feel more comfortable socializing with other handicapped children?

Finally, the methodology of social behavior research continues to plague researchers. An excellent review of these difficulties is discussed by Fox, Shores, Bambara, McGill, Gunter, and Brady (1983).

Vocational

Vocational curriculum and the adequate training of vocational skills at the secondary level require a rather comprehensive examination and long range testing. There is the need to explore how best to train severely handicapped students in community placements. What students should be trained in those placements, and what students might we better spend our time training to function in a more sedentary sheltered placement?

What should be the emphasis of our vocational training? Should it focus on skill acquisition or are there certain skills which might be more generalizable and thus provide a better benefit to the student in the long run? What is the relationship of emphasis on skill building vis-a-vis the building of appropriate social skills or associated work skills on the job? The experience of Fredericks (in press, b) would indicate that the emphasis should be on associated work skills.

Art and Music

What is the role of art and music in the curriculum for severely handicapped students? Durksen (1981) summarized the current state of the art of music for all exceptional students, but no one has examined its effect on severely handicapped students. We know that many severely handicapped students are interested in and respond to music. We have not adequately taught music as a leisure time skill nor have we adequately used it in therapy or in order to teach other things.

One must extend that question to other art forms. To what extent should severely handicapped students be taught to draw, color, or sketch as an adult leisure time skill? Research is totally lacking in this area.

Functionality

The questions relative to art lead to some concerns about the emphasis on total functionality. Thompson and Rainforth (1979) in their article on a functional fine motor program for severely and profoundly retarded students emphasized the importance of functionality. Functionality has since been espoused as being the prime characteristic that measures the suitability of a curriculum. Yet, we have little data to support the concept that a functional curriculum is better than curricula that are developmentally oriented, nor do we have any data that show how the two should be interrelated. Certainly it is logical to adopt a functional curriculum but in the long run will it provide the best generalization? Will it provide the best array of skills? Is it in fact the most efficient curriculum?

Classroom Size

Curriculum often covers a larger scope than just subject areas. There are many questions about classroom organization and size that remain to be answered. What should be the ratio of severely handicapped students to teachers and aides in an educational environment? What is the best educational format? How many autistic children to a teacher? How many deaf-blind children? How many multiply handicapped children or does etiology not make a difference? Should all autistic children be placed together in the same classroom? Or should we have classrooms that are noncategorical such as are found in Oregon where you have autistic children, deaf-blind children, mentally retarded and multiply handicapped children all being taught by one teacher with an assistant? Class size and organization is a major area of nonresearch. There are many standards voiced by states and by school districts but these are based on "blue sky" bias and teacher union pressure with little data to support their validity.

Support Services

How best do we organize and use support services? Is it better to have the physical therapist actually manipulate arms and legs three times a week for 20 minutes at a time? It is better for the physical therapist to teach others how to do these movements and have them do what the physical therapist does? What kind of data does the physical therapist need to engage in that type of consultive model? Fredericks and the staff of the Teaching Research Infant and Child Center (1982) advocated the consultive model and Bricker (1976) talked about the educational synthesizer. The concept of a consultive model is not new. But these again are theories. We have no data to support the fact that the consultive model does as well for children as does actual personal contact with a therapist. Not only does this apply to physical therapy, but to occupational and language therapy. If one uses a consultive model, how frequently do the programs need to be examined by the consultant? We do not know.

Classroom organization to provide adequate community and vocational training at the secondary level poses monumental questions for administrators, teachers, and parents. Who specifically should be teaching what? Is it appropriate for teachers to teach all cooking skills or should we ask parents to assist? Should parents just be required to aid in the generalization of those skills? What is the relationship between the teacher and the parent relative to shopping skills, budgeting, and all of the other practical living skills that need to be taught before the student can make the transition from student to independent adult.

There is little written about organizational problems. How does one staff a classroom at the secondary level to allow for vocational training, practical living skills, training in the community, and still do classroom work? How does one schedule those events? All of these are questions that have not been adequately researched and for which there are practically no references in the literature. There is a definite lack of various models for secondary education. Wilcox and Bellamy (1982) have developed one. Fredericks and the staff of the Teaching Research Infant and Child Center (1983) have developed another. However, these models have not been tested by others nor compared with other models. They need a wealth of research to prove their worth.

Adult Services

Currently, the severely handicapped population usually is employed by a sheltered workshop or a work activity center. Only recently has Beebe (1982) in Madison, Wisconsin demonstrated the viability of severely handicapped people being trained in vocational skills in competitive employment settings. This has been accomplished in Madison to the extent that there are even vacant slots in the local activity center. Such a situation is phenomenal in this country at this time. In most communities, there is a total lack of availability of slots in work activity centers and sheltered workshops for the severely handicapped. Thus, we need to know more about training in the community. Wehman (1981) and Sowers, Lunderwold, Swonson, and Budd (1980) have perhaps done more than almost anyone in this area. Yet, the vast majority of communities are failing to implement this research and that of Beebe's demonstration project. A chapter in this text by Gunter and Levy describes this dilemma in some detail. The entire community orientation for vocational education is an area that needs to be further researched and explored.

There are many questions involved here. Who can succeed in competitive employment in the community? Who can best be served in an activity center or sheltered workshop? How can we organize to provide training in the community? Can volunteers be used effectively? What should be the emphasis of our training—skill acquisition or associated work skills—or some combination? How do we effect generalization across tasks and working environments?

Residential Facilities

We have advocated long and hard for deinstitutionalization for severely handicapped individuals. The Association for Persons with Severe Handicaps official position states that large institutions are not appropriate, and yet we do not have adequate research to point the way to the optimum size of a group home or the skills which an individual needs to move from a group home setting to a satellite apartment or semi-independent living. In fact, we could probably go so far as to say that we are not too sure exactly what skills are needed to move from one setting to another. Communities, regions, cities, and agencies have developed various guidelines for such movement, but these guidelines are position statements or opinions of professionals, rather than the results of empirical study. Once again, we know very little about alternative residential facilities. We have trouble demonstrating that community residential facilities are better than large institutions. We seem even to have difficulty developing good cost benefit studies or cost comparative studies. We have been so busy providing services that we have not taken the time to determine if the services we provide are really the best for severely handicapped individuals. The few studies that have attempted to analyze some of these areas have been woefully inadequate, incomplete, or parochial. The entire area of foster care or group homes for children or foster care for adults lacks research. Gage, Fredericks, Baldwin, Grove, and Moore (1977) and Templeman, Gage, and Fredericks (1982) described and analyzed costs for one model of a group home found to be effective for children. They did not compare the results with those achieved with children in other models or with costs of other models. Such comparisons are absolutely mandatory if we are going to develop appropriate community resources for severely handicapped people.

Conclusion

As we examine services, education, and policy regarding severely handicapped people, we see a plethora of unanswered questions. In general, research has tended to focus on narrow questions and has avoided the more global "difficult to research" questions. This situation is due to researchers being able to mount mini-studies with little expense and little support. Much of the other funding that has been available in the area of severely handicapped has focused on model building. This has not required comparisons of one model with another, but only a demonstration that a particular model provided some effect. Federal research monies have been slender at best and severely handicapped research has only been able to capture a very small part of those monies.

There is a bright light on the horizon, however. That is the advent of the Severely Handicapped Research Institutes and the potential of a research institute for deaf-blind education to examine communication of deaf-blind children. Four major research institutes have been funded throughout the United States. They are located at the University of Washington, the University of Oregon, the University of Minnesota, and San Francisco State University. Coupled with these are the continuance of research institutes for early childhood education. We can only hope that these institutes will be able to put together a body of programmatic research that will provide the answers to many of the questions we have posed in this chapter.

However, we must be realistic and recognize that these institutes will not be able to provide all of the answers and that we, as practitioners in the field, must continue to add to knowledge in small pieces and bits. This information must eventually by synthesized by those who delight in synthesizing research information and formulating further hypotheses that can then be tested. Moreover, research results must be communicated effectively to practitioners. Gunter and Brady (1984) provide an excellent discussion of the problem of transferring research to practice. At the current time, we see little federal support and practically no state support for research to improve education, the quality, and the provision of services for severely handicapped individuals. It is up to us as practitioners to continue to provide that information and to exhort those at the federal level to provide additional funding so that further research can help answer some of the questions which are critical and for which currently we do not have the answers.

REFERENCES

Beebe, P. Final report to Wisconsin Developmental Disabilities Council. Madison. 1982.

Bonvillian. J. D., Nelson, K. E., & Rhyne. J. M. Sign language and autism. *Journal of Autism and Developmental Disorders*, 1981, *11*(1), 125–137.

Bricker, D. Educational synthesizer. In M. A. Thomas (Ed.), *Hey, don't forget about me*. Reston. VA: Council for Exceptional Children, 1976.

Brown, L., Branston, M. B., Hamre-Nietupski, S., Johnson, F.. Wilcox. B.. & Gruenewald. L. A rationale for comprehensive longitudinal interactions between severely handicapped students and nonhandicapped students and other citizens. *AAESPH Review*, 1979, *4*(1). 3–14.

Brown, L., Wilcox, B., Sontag, E., Vincent. B., Dodd. N., & Gruenewald. L. Toward the realization of the least restrictive educational environments for severely handicapped students. *AAESPH Review*, 1977, *2*(4), 195–201.

Durksen, G. L. Music for exceptional students. *Focus on Exceptional Children*, 1981. *14*(2). 1–11.

Edgar, E., Spence, W.. & Kenowitz, L. A. Extended school year for the handicapped: Is it working? *The Journal of Special Education*, 1977, *11*(4), 441–448.

Fox, J., Shores, R., Bambara. L., McGill. P., Gunter. P., & Brady, M. Some methodological issues in the analysis and training of young children's social interaction skills. Paper delivered at the Association for Behavior Analysis Conference. Milwaukee. May 1983.

Fredericks, B. Parents/families of persons with severe mental retardation. In D. Bricker. & J. Filler (Eds.), *Severe mental retardation: From theory to practice*. Reston, VA: Council for Exceptional Children, in press. (a)

Fredericks, B. Community based vocational training for severely handicapped youth. *Counterpoint*. In press. (b)

Fredericks, H. D., & The Staff of the Teaching Research Infant and Child Center. *A data based classroom for the moderately and severely handicapped* (4th ed.). Monmouth, OR: Instructional Development Corporation, 1982.

Fredericks, H. D., & The Staff of the Teaching Research Infant and Child Center. *A data based classroom for moderately and severely handicapped secondary students*. Monmouth. OR: Teaching Research Publications, 1983.

Fristoe, M., & Lloyd, L. L. Signs used in manual communication training with persons having severe communication impairment. *AAESPH Review*, 1979 *4*(4), 364–373.

Gage, M., Fredericks, H., Baldwin, V., Grove, D., & Moore, W. *Group homes for developmentally disabled children*. Monmouth. OR: Instructional Development Corporation, 1977.

Goetz, L., Schuler, A., & Sailor. W. Teaching functional speech to the severely handicapped: Current issues. *Journal of Autism and Developmental Disorders*, 1979, *9*(4), 325–343.

Gunter, P., & Brady, M. Increasing the practitioner's utilization of research: A dilemma in regular and special education, *Education*. 1984, *105*(1), 92–98.

Guralnick, M. J. Integrated preschools as educational and therapeutical environments: Concept designs and analysis. In M. J. Guralnick (Ed.), *Early intervention and the integration of handicapped and nonhandicapped children*. Baltimore: University Park Press, 1978.

Hamre-Nietupski, S., & Nietupski, J. Integral involvement of severely handicapped students within regular public schools. *The Journal of the Association for the Severely Handicapped,* 1981, 6(2), 30–39.

Karnes, M., & Cleveland, L. Efficacy studies in early childhood special education. *Journal of the Division for Early Childhood,* 1981, 4, 22.

Larsen, L., Goodman, L., & Glean, R. Issues in the implementation of extended school year programs for handicapped students. *Exceptional Children,* 1981, 47(4), 256–263.

Leonard, J. 180 day barrier: Issues and concerns. *Exceptional Children,* 1981, 47(4), 246–253.

Makuch, G. J. Year-round special education and related services: A state director's perspective. *Exceptional Children,* 1981, 47(4), 272–275.

Peck, C. A., & Semmel, M. I. Identifying the least restrictive environment (LRE) for children with severe handicaps: Toward an empirical analysis. *The Journal of the Association for the Severely Handicapped,* 1982, 7(1), 56–63.

Sowers, J., Lunderwold, D., Swonson, M., & Budd, C. *Competitive employment training for mentally retarded adults – A systematic approach.* Eugene, OR: Center on Human Development, University of Oregon, 1980.

Stainback, W., & Stainback, S. A review of research on interactions between severely handicapped and nonhandicapped students. *The Journal of the Association for the Severely Handicapped,* 1981, 6(3), 23–29.

Stainback, W., & Stainback, S. The need for research on training nonhandicapped students to interact with severely retarded students. *Education and Training of the Mentally Retarded,* 1982, 17(1), 12–16.

Stotland, J. F., & Mancuso, E. U.S. court appeals decision regarding Armstrong vs. Kline: The 180 day rule. *Exceptional Children,* 1981, 47(4), 266–270.

Templeman, D., Gage, M., & Fredericks, H. Cost effectiveness of the group home. *The Journal of the Association of the Severely Handicapped,* 1982, 6(4), 11–16.

Thompson, Z., & Rainforth, B. A functional fine motor program for the severely and profoundly retarded. In R. York & E. Edgar (Eds.), *Teaching the severely handicapped* (vol. IV). Columbus, OH: Special Press, 1979.

Turnbull, A., & Turnbull, R. (Issue Eds.). Parent participation in the education of exceptional children. *Exceptional Education Quarterly,* 1981, 3.

Wehman, P. *Competitive employment – new horizons for severely disabled individuals.* Baltimore: Paul H. Brookes, 1981.

Wilcox, B., & Bellamy, G. T. *Design of high school programs for severely handicapped students.* Baltimore: Paul H. Brookes, 1982.

Wolery, M. *Parents as teachers of pre-school children.* Seattle, WA: WESTAR, 1980.

CHAPTER 15

WHY AREN'T RESEARCH RESULTS IN PRACTICE?

MICHAEL P. BRADY, PHIL GUNTER, CYNTHIA A. LANGFORD

Ivory towers and front-line trenches—the labels alone suggest encampments that will not meet, much less cooperate. Yet this analogy is often used to describe the puzzling relationship between researchers and practitioners. While many researchers view practitioners as the prime beneficiaries of research (Ausubel, 1969; Drew & Buchanan, 1979; Fife, 1979; Krathwohl, 1977; Prehm, 1976), there is ample information to suggest that practitioners are among the strongest critics (Ausubel, 1969; Baer, Wolf, & Risley, 1968; Drew & Buchanan, 1979; Prehm, 1976). The move for accountability that was spurred by P. L. 94-142, ICF/MR regulations, and ACMR/DD accreditation has intensified the practitioner's need for a technology that is clinically significant and yields replicable results. While practitioners may be actively seeking assistance (Bain & Groseclose, 1979), that assistance typically is not identified as "research." Drew and Buchanan (1979) suggested that the statement, "I do not read or use research because none of it is relevant or practical in the real world" (p. 52) summarizes practitioners' opinions about the utility of research in practice.

Contrasted with practitioners' pessimism about the utility of research is the researcher's optimism. Lovaas (1982) exemplified this optimism in his

Michael P. Brady is a Special Education Research Fellow and a Ph.D. candidate at George Peabody College of Vanderbilt University. His current interests and publications include legal issues related to integration, community based education models, handicapped children's social development, applications of instructional technology and applied behavior analysis in special education, and cross-cultural aspects of disability and habilitation. He has worked in school, district, and state education agencies in the U.S. and abroad, and is a member of The Association for Retarded Citizens and the Association for Persons with Severe Handicaps.

Phil Gunter is currently the Coordinator of Exceptional Student Services, Lee County Schools, Fort Myers, Florida. He received his Ph.D. from George Peabody College of Vanderbilt University. He has been a classroom instructor of behavior disordered and severely and moderately handicapped children and adolescents, coordinator of a vocational training grant for mild and moderately handicapped students, and a school administrator. His current research involves control of stereotypic behaviors of persons with severe handicaps and methodological issues of social validation research.

Cynthia A. Langford received her Ph.D. in Special Education from George Peabody College of Vanderbilt University. She is the Director of Independent Living Programs with Volunteers of America in New Orleans, LA. Her research interests include the application of applied behavior analysis strategies with handicapped persons in teaching, vocational, and residential settings. She was formerly with the National Media Production Project for Severely Handicapped Students.

recent critique on research involving self-injurious behavior. He noted that while numerous individuals continue to display this potentially life threatening behavior, "a comprehensive implementation of what we already know about decreasing self-injury would probably reduce instances of such behavior by at least one half; which points to a gross deficiency in dissemination of our techniques and findings" (p. 122). If research and progress are to become more closely linked in education, the barriers that separate research and practice must be identified and examined. To do so, this chapter will focus on the following topics: (a) What is educational research?; (b) What roles do dissemination, service delivery patterns, and environmental contingencies play in implementing research findings?; and (c) What can be done to expedite the implementation of clinically significant research results?

What is Educational Research?

Education has a rich history of borrowing research from allied disciplines such as psychology, sociology, and management. This diversity has both contributed to the richness of the field as well as generated some confusion about the definition and purpose of educational research. Research as defined by Leedy (1974) is a "systematic quest for undiscovered truth" (p. 9). Leedy referred to this type of research as scientific research with the purpose of theory development. He further suggested that the role of theory based research is to explain or predict phenomena. If one were to agree with either of these interpretations, there would seem to be a good deal of validity of Fife's (1979) comment that "most research is reported as if it were going to be read and used only by other researchers" (p. 189) to further the development of theory. From this very narrow view of research, there also would be some justification to Kerlinger's (1977) observation that there is little direct connection between educational research and educational practice.

Shaver (1979) suggested that applied educational research (i.e., research that would provide for more immediate practical use of its results) provides important information to the profession. Applied research was defined by Gay (1976) as research that examined practical problems and posed potential solutions for the practitioner. Baer et al. (1968) stressed that the uniqueness of applied behavioral research was both its utility and the social importance of the problem being studied. It should be stressed, however, that even applied research may have limited *clinical* value. Without such a distinction, some researchers do not consider applied research to be research at all: "It is engineering or technology although the techniques of scientists may be used" (Kerlinger, 1977, p. 4). Kerlinger further pointed out that this demand for research to have immediate payoff has had a "devastating effect on research in education" (p. 6). There are, of course, multiple audiences for research results. Some research reports have a great deal of utility for researchers and little applicability in clinical practice. Others may have great interest for practitioners but be virtually unknown to researchers pursuing a wiley phenomenon.

Obviously, there is much controversy about the definition or purpose of research in education. However, since this chapter is concerned with strategies for implementing research in day-to-day instructional practice, educational research will be defined as empirical studies with clinical significance. Unfortunately, even when research is limited to only those studies with direct application to practice, there remains a startling under-utilization of research findings.

Current Attempts to Implement Research Findings

The literature that addresses the under-utilization of research in practice follows three major themes: inadequate or inappropriate modes of dissemination, inadequate teacher preparation, and contingencies in natural environments that prevent implementation. Each of these topics will be discussed in the first section of this chapter with potential solutions proposed in the following section.

Dissemination of Research

Most practitioners enter the field with little interest in research journals. The majority of research disseminated via journal articles is not reported in a form that is readily understood by practitioners. Furthermore, implications for practice often are not practical or even apparent. Consequently, practitioners seldom read these resources and the gap between research findings and the application of these findings in practical settings grows greater than might be necessary. This position was supported by Sparling and Gallagher (1971) when they noted that journal articles might be "the least effective form of communication known to man" (p. 25). However, most research dissemination to date has been via professional journals (Sparling & Gallagher, 1971). Dissemination of these journals has been high, but the "effectiveness of journal information . . . hovers around zero" (p. 25). It has become apparent that the mere transmitting of unmodified research will not result in quick changes in educational practice.

Beyond journal articles, the traditional means of disseminating research findings to teachers has been by developing a theory from research investigations, producing a product or curriculum from the theory, and then disseminating that product (Prehm, 1976). The development of curricula or products has become a primary educational dissemination vehicle for many researchers. Product development typically has taken years to complete and has contributed to what Bain and Groseclose (1979) referred to as the "dissemination dilemma." "The essence of the dissemination dilemma is that there appears to be much excellent research that never finds its way to America's classrooms at a time when the majority of classroom teachers are honestly seeking assistance" (Bain & Groseclose, 1979, p. 101). Prehm (1976) specifically targeted education of handicapped students when he expressed concern about dissemination practices. He noted that the lack of efficient, rapid, and comprehensive systems for dissemination was a major impediment to the application of special education research findings.

Prehm (1976) further pointed out that the primary alternative method for disseminating the results of research and development efforts has been the ERIC Document Reproduction Service. Unfortunately, this system has suffered the same slowness as the product development and dissemination model. User fees, brevity of information, and its inaccessibility have further hindered ERIC's usefulness for many teachers. Thus there is a clear need for alternative dissemination models for delivery of information to teachers in an efficient, cost effective manner.

Teacher Training

Krathwohl (1977) identified students, teachers, and school administrators as the "ultimate benefactors of education research" (p. 9). These benefactors ought to be among researchers' strongest supporters. Unfortunately, as mentioned earlier, they tend to be among the critics. Rather than promoting empirical investigations of performance in education, teachers have become members of a public that Baer et al. (1968) referred to as a "scientifically skeptical audience." Educators' pessimistic views of research were characterized similarly by Ausubel (1969):

> It should be noted at the outset that there is both little general acceptance of the need for educational research and little appreciation of the relevance of such research for the improvement of education. A tradition of research does not exist in education as it does, for example, in medicine or in engineering where both professionals and consumers commonly agree that research and progress are almost synonymous (p. 6).

In addition to dissemination problems, barriers to the implementation of research findings also might be viewed as a function of inadequate professional preparation. That is, research may fail to get into practice quickly because educators have not been trained or "socialized" to conduct or use it. Teacher training programs generally fail to promote research skills and attitudes favorable to the creation of a "research consciousness" (Clifford,

1973). This inability to analyze or use research among educators is weakened
further once teachers adapt to their particular job roles (Clifford. 1973:
Drew & Buchanan, 1979). "The professional socialization of educators with
regard to research seems to be very different than psychology, for example.
where research is a routine and on-going activity" (Drew & Buchanan. p. 50).

Drew and Buchanan further suggested that few colleges of education were
characterized as research centers or producers of quality scholarship. The
individuals educated in these programs reflect this training deficit in their
careers. In those colleges of education in which research is conducted. the
research is often far removed from student and teacher performance. and
instead focuses on standardized test construction, personal characteristics
of teachers, or educators' opinions of professional issues. This contrasts
significantly with the performance oriented research training advocated for
special educators (Lewis & Blackhurst, 1983; Rousseau, Shores. Hasselbring.
& Cunningham, 1984).

Environmental Contingencies

> Even if dissemination difficulties and teacher training problems were solved.
> there remain constraints to implementing research in the natural environment.
> Most of the academic literature in the field leaves one with the impression
> that implementation of an effective behavior modification program is a
> straightforward, trouble-free affair, and that all one really requires for suc-
> cess is an understanding of learning theory and the techniques of behavior
> analysis. . . . This, however, is clearly not the case. . . . In natural settings. the
> behavior modifier faces a variety of problems that do not relate directly to
> theoretical issues in behavior modification and that are either nonexistent or
> relatively inconspicuous in the laboratory or special research situation.
> where the investigator has almost complete control over the contingencies of
> reinforcement. (Reppucci & Sanders, 1974, p. 650).

Reppucci and Sanders identified specific barriers to implementing behavioral
technology in natural environments. Three that reduce the practitioner's
control over the environment and serve as barriers to implementing research in practice will be discussed in this chapter: (a) political pressure,
(b) competition between services/goals, and (c) limited resources.

Political pressure. Practitioners may find that incorporating research in
classroom instruction is difficult or impossible for essentially political reasons.
While classroom instruction is a central concern of practitioners, practitioners operate within a larger environment: "the community." Education,
more than medicine or engineering, is directly regulated and funded by the
community. Practitioners frequently must lobby not only for resources, but
also for permission to operate in particular ways. While most researchers

have little interest in the vagueries of community politics, practitioners may well need to become skilled in effective lobbying to achieve their objectives. For example, despite the empirical evidence of the efficacy of behavioral techniques such as time out and contingency contracting, many school systems do not support their use. To some the techniques may seem harsh, or inhumane. Such perceptions or experiences may prompt communities to forbid the use of specific techniques despite research that supports their efficacy and fail safes that prevent further misuse. Unfortunately, service delivery systems that do not support the use of empirically validated interventions may adopt eclectic treatment models that are incompatible with implementing research findings and that prevent analysis of the system's efficacy.

Competition between services. In addition to community politics, competition between departments or services within the practitioner's organization may inhibit implementation of research. While interdisciplinary team meetings mandated by P. L. 94-142 have increased the exchange of information between educators and professionals from other disciplines, it is not clear that simply exchanging information has led to increased cooperation. Team members may have devised goals that compete with the interventions planned by other members of the interdisciplinary team. Determining the intervention that will prevail may center around discussions of the relative merits of the various service areas (e.g., "behavior modification" vs. "recreation") rather than how research should guide a particular course of action. Even if the team agrees upon a course of action, they may not be able to implement the intervention because "transportation" or the "business office" cannot or will not change their operating procedures to accommodate unusual or atypical circumstances.

Limited resources. Both research and practice are limited by scarce resources, but in practice the scarcity is perhaps more desperate and less obvious. Practice differs from research not only in the availability, but in the flow of fiscal resources. The difference in the way monies follow work has a strong impact on an organization's ability to implement research. For example, to conduct funded research in a particular area, the researcher must demonstrate to the funding agent that human resources with specialized training are available. If the researcher or the research institution is not able to demonstrate that people with the necessary training are available, the work is not funded and typically does not proceed. In service settings, however, the work must proceed with or without the necessary resources. The practitioner's lack of training in behavioral principles, for example, does not prevent an autistic child from entering the practitioner's classroom. The child, or more typically many children, are assigned to a therapeutic area whether or not the staff is adequately trained.

For both practitioners and researchers, fiscal resources are controlled by the focus of the work. Practitioners are funded to work directly with students. As mentioned earlier, direct service is not now imbued with a research ethic—from either practitioners or funding agents. Thus, activities associated with research (e.g., literature reviews, conference attendance, purchase of journals or "exotic" equipment) are viewed as ancillary rather than central tasks, and funds for ancillary tasks are limited or nonexistent. Indeed, practitioners may find their budgets so slim that items as basic as reinforcers must be privately purchased. Moreover, critical support services (e.g., substantial professional libraries, clerical support) are not available to the majority of practitioners. Since the practitioner may already be bearing the expense of acquiring materials needed in day-to-day instruction, more costly materials (e.g., ERIC computer services, cost of photocopying, computers, miniature cassette recorders, and interlibrary loan materials) may be personally prohibitive.

These examples of environmental constraints to implementing research profoundly impact practitioners' ability and willingness to use research strategies and findings. Far from "trouble free," implementing research is too often troublesome and punishing. Implementing research must become rewarding if there is to be any substantial change in current practice.

Implementing Research Findings and Strategies

Fife (1979) suggested that researchers might help to ameliorate the underutilization problem by expanding existing notions of who are consumers of research. Prior to publishing research findings, researchers should determine: (a) the audience, (b) their educational backgrounds, and (c) their current needs. Fife further emphasized that the population in greatest need of research implications was not other researchers but practitioners. In the remainder of this chapter, we will examine alternative avenues for considering and using educational research strategies and findings. Implementation of such strategies or combinations of strategies could significantly reduce the current gap between research and practice.

Synthesizing Research Results

The need for research findings to undergo intermediary, transition steps before practitioners can use the results has been expressed by numerous educators (Carmichael & Vogel, 1978; Hemphill, 1972; Sparling & Gallagher, 1971). Sparling and Gallagher emphasized the growing need for "special mechanisms" to assist in communication between researchers and practitioners. To date, these special mechanisms have included classroom-based personnel roles such as consulting teachers (Christie, McKenzie, & Burdett, 1972; Nevin, Paolucci-Whitcomb, Duncan, & Thibodeau, 1982); educational synthesizers (Bricker, 1976); individualized education program (IEP) managers (Brady, 1983; Brady & Gunter, in press); and nationally distributed print material such as the "putting research to work" column in TASH Newsletters (see Liberty, 1984, for an example).

Sparling and Gallagher (1971) recommended that a research synthesizer, a person who could make practical suggestions out of recent research, could best communicate current findings to practitioners. They suggested that the idea of the research synthesizer had been criticized by many researchers whose concern has been maintaining validity in this synthesizing/reporting process. Yet researchers have relied heavily on integrative research reviews to keep abreast of the expanse of research information within their fields (Cooper, 1982). Cooper referred to the functions of a research reviewer in much the same way as Sparling and Gallagher (1971) referred to the functions of the synthesizer. Cooper's concern about maintaining the validity of the reviewer's reports led to his proposal of the following five criteria for interpretive reviews: (a) problem formulation, (b) data collection, (c) evaluation of data points, (d) data analysis and interpretation, and (e) presentation of results.

These criteria also would apply to a research synthesizer's report. A specially trained synthesizer would rewrite, in a brief format, study procedures and results which would be readable, relevant, and replicable by those practitioners whose primary responsibilities are instructional. If these brief instructional ideas, drawn from current research, were found to be beneficial by practitioners, their interest in other relevant research might increase.

Disseminating Synthesized Research

An improved system of synthesizing and disseminating research findings could provide solutions to several of the restraints identified by Fife (1979) for the practitioner not using journal-reported research. Fife identified these restraints as:

1. Researchers' language often has been esoteric; sophisticated statistical analyses also have added to the confusion.
2. The length of articles has been unmanageable for many practitioners.
3. There has been a problem of readily identifying what research has been done in specific areas.

If the practitioner received research information with these variables adjusted, we expect that there would be a substantial increase in classroom applications of research findings.

With this condensation of research into a more usable form, there is still a solution needed for the problem of disseminating the information to practitioners. As stated earlier, the ERIC service has not been readily accessible to all practitioners, and traditional development and dissemination methods have been extremely slow. These authors propose a direct delivery of synthesized research to practitioners. This might be accomplished by state or local education agency use of their teacher certification rosters as mailing lists. The process might work as follows: A teacher of a student who exhibits self-injurious behavior might report a need for technical assistance and information. The appropriate education agency would then mail out a two-page report of four synthesized, recent research articles which would be applicable to the reported instructional need. A report would be mailed directly to the instructor each month. The instructor would provide feedback regarding the appropriateness of the report, the utility of the recommendations based on student performance, and the need for subsequent information. As a result, the instructor would not need to search through all of the available literature, identify potentially useful articles, and evaluate possible teaching implications. This process would help eliminate Fife's (1979) concern that the practitioner was unable to identify research resources quickly and efficiently.

Teachers as Clinical Researchers

Even substantial changes in reporting and dissemination techniques may not ensure improvements in classroom practice. Several authors have recommended that teachers and teacher educators take a more active role in educational research to improve classroom practice (Hall, Cristler, Cranston, & Tucker, 1970; Nevin et al., 1982; Shores, 1979; Shores, Burney, & Wiegerink, 1976). That role has included the use of behavior analytic strategies and single subject designs as teacher competencies (Hall et al., 1970; Kerr, Shores, & Stowitschek, 1978; Shores, 1972, 1979; Snell & Smith, 1983). For example, Nevin et al. (1982) proposed that consulting teachers could, and often do, conduct practical and publishable research.

Various combinations of these recommendations, as well as improvements in dissemination, may be necessary before practitioners use research skills on a regular basis. However, to better understand research reports and to conduct classroom research, teachers need to develop research competencies in either their preservice or inservice training (Lewis & Blackhurst, 1983).

Lewis and Blackhurst (1983) recommended that competence in classroom research could be grouped into three general training areas: (a) research content (e.g., results of empirical studies in assessment and instruction); (b) research process (e.g., measurement, sampling, design); and (c) application (e.g., carrying out an empirically based instructional program). Given the low incidence and heterogeneous nature of many exceptional populations and the responsibility of special educators to improve the performance of *individual* students, single subject designs will make up a large part of a teacher's research training. Strain, McConnell, and Cordisco (1983) noted the conceptual compatibility between special education practices and single subject research designs. Specifically, both effective teachers and single subject researchers must know how to specify target behaviors clearly and directly observe student behavior.

The identification of the actual research competencies necessary for teachers is crucial. Lewis and Blackhurst (1983) proposed that training programs distinguish between consumption (to interpret research) and production (to conduct classroom research) competencies. Kerr et al. (1978) identified research competencies embedded in the regular competency based teacher education (CBTE) program. The present authors propose that such competencies are crucial for teachers and should be considered generic to any CBTE program (see Brady, Conroy, & Langford, 1984).

Some Environmental Contingencies of Teacher Performance

The information presented thus far in this chapter has explored obstacles that prevent research utilization and development by the practitioner. Yet, all dimensions of a performance problem must be explored in order to find a solution (see Mager & Pipe, 1970). A dimension yet to be explored concerns the motivation of teachers to perform in an accountable manner, that is, to provide empirically based instructional programs. While several punishers are readily identified, there are few rewards for teachers who use empirically based instructional programs. For example, Mager and Pipe noted that "raises and promotions (for teachers) are based exclusively on the number of months served ... There is little or no attempt to tie these rewards to the quantity and quality of student performance" (p. 67).

Shores (1979) noted that the evaluation of teacher competence and teacher education programs ultimately must examine student performance. The contention of these authors is that most teachers are concerned with the quality of student performance and will use information presented to them to enhance that performance. Moreover, the authors suggest that by investigating the contingencies which may promote teachers' use of research skills and increasing the productivity of teachers in this area, school systems may find a direct correlation between teachers' interest in and utilization of research and improved teacher and student performance.

In 1943, Maslow presented a need hierarchy theory of motivation for human behavior. This hierarchy was modified by Porter (1961) into a tool to assess how well the needs of professionals were being met: the Need Satisfaction Questionnaire. Using this questionnaire, Trusty and Sergiovanni (1966) found that teachers' greatest need deficiencies were in satisfying "esteem" and "self-actualization" needs. That is, motivators that professional educators lacked were respect by others, recognition, creativity, achievement, etc. Other needs such as friendship, belonging, and physiological needs of this group were satisfied.

It is our opinion that the dissemination of *teachers'* empirical classroom findings may be at least one way for teachers to gain professional recognition. This is supported in part by reports of teachers who have published their findings (see Nevin et al., 1982). Administrative systems would do well to investigate means to provide teachers the opportunity and support services to engage in research and dissemination activities (i.e., conference presentations, publications, and professional consultation).

Conclusions

We hope that the development of new dissemination models, new strategies for training teachers as consumers and disseminators of research, and an increased focus on the environmental contingencies of teacher performance will increase the probability of research utilization by practitioners. Increased utilization of research also will decrease the time gap between applied research and its application in clinical settings. The ultimate value of such practices will be improvements in student performance, a goal toward which both researchers and practitioners strive. However, we are convinced that this will not take place without a more global understanding of the driving and restraining forces of the professional educators' engagement in these activities, and a strong commitment at all administrative levels to the ideal that *teachers who are informed by the literature are better teachers.**

REFERENCES

Ausubel, D. P. The nature of educational research. In W. J. Gephart & R. B. Ingle (Eds.), *Educational research: Selected readings.* Columbus, OH: Charles E. Merrill, 1969.

Baer, D. M., Wolf, M. M., & Risley, T. R. Some current dimensions of applied behavior analysis. *Journal of Applied Behavior Analysis,* 1968, *1,* 91–97.

*Parts of this chapter are adapted from Gunter, P., & Brady, M. P. Increasing the practitioner's utilization of research: A dilemma in special education and regular education. *Education.* 1984 *105*(1) 92–98. Reprinted with permission.

Preparation of this chapter was partially supported by Grant No. 029 DH 30070 from the U.S. Department of Education, Special Education Programs.

Bain, H. P., & Groseclose, J. R. The dissemination dilemma and a plan for uniting disseminators and practitioners. *Phi Delta Kappan,* 1979, *61,* 101–103.

Brady, M. P. Rural special education teacher training: Issues in the Pacific Basic Territories. *Teacher Education and Special Education,* 1983, *6*(1), 71–76.

Brady, M. P., Conroy, M., & Langford, C. A. Current issues and practices affecting the development of noncategorical programs for students and teachers. *Teacher Education and Special Education,* 1984, *7*(1), 20–26.

Brady, M. P., & Gunter, P. IEP managers: A model for special education inservice training in rural school systems. *The Rural Educator,* in press.

Bricker, D. D. Educational synthesizer. In M. A. Thomas (Ed.), *Hey! Don't forget about me!* Reston, VA: Council for Exceptional Children, 1976.

Carmichael, L., & Vogel, P. Research into practice. *Journal of Physical Education and Recreation,* 1978, *49,* 29–30.

Christie, L., McKenzie, H., & Burdett, C. The consulting teacher approach to special education: Inservice training for regular classroom teachers. *Focus on Exceptional Children,* 1972, *4,* 1–18.

Clifford, G. J. A history of the impact of research on teaching. In R. M. W. Travers (Ed.), *Second handbook of research and teaching.* Chicago: Rand McNally, 1973.

Cooper, H. M. Scientific guidelines for conducting integrative research reviews. *Review of Educational Research,* 1982, *52*(2), 291–302.

Drew, C. J., & Buchanan, M. L. Research on teacher education. *Teacher Education and Special Education,* 1979, *2*(2), 50–55.

Fife, J. D. Improving the use of higher education research. *Research in Higher Education,* 1979, *10*(2), 189–192.

Gay, L. R. *Educational research.* Columbus, OH: Charles E. Merrill, 1976.

Hall, R. V., Cristler, B., Cranston, D., & Tucker, B. Teachers and parents as researchers using multiple baseline designs. *Journal of Applied Behavior Analysis,* 1970, *3,* 247–255.

Hemphill, J. K. Educational development. In B. C. Porter (Ed.), *The Oregon studies: Research, development, diffusion, evaluation* (Vol. II, part 1). Monmouth, OR: Teaching Research, 1972.

Kerlinger, F. N. The influence of research on educational practice. *Educational Researcher,* 1977, *6*(8), 5–12.

Kerr, M. M., Shores, R. E., & Stowitschek, J. J. Peabody's field-based special education program: A model for evaluating competency based training. In C. M. Nelson (Ed.), *Field-based teacher training: Application in special education.* Minneapolis: Department of Psychoeducational Studies, University of Minnesota, 1978.

Krathwohl, D. Improving educational research and development. *Educational Researcher,* 1977, *6*(4), 8–14.

Leedy, P. D. *Practical research.* New York: MacMillan, 1974.

Lewis, R. B., & Blackhurst, A. E. Special education practitioners as consumers and producers of research: A hierarchy of competencies. *Exceptional Education Quarterly,* 1983, *4*(3), 8–17.

Liberty, K. A. Putting research to work for you. *The Association for Persons with Severe Handicaps Newsletters,* 1984, *10*(5), 8.

Lovaas, O. I. Comments on self-destructive behaviors. *Analysis and Intervention in Developmental Disabilities,* 1982, *2,* 115–124.

Mager, R. F., & Pipe, R. *Analyzing performance problems.* Belmont, CA: Fearon Pitman Publishers, 1970.

Maslow, A. H. A theory of human behavior. *Psychological Review,* 1943, *50,* 370–396.

Nevin, A., Paolucci-Whitcomb, P., Duncan, D., & Thibodeau, L. A. The consulting teacher as a clinical researcher. *Teacher Education and Special Education,* 1982, *5*(4), 19–29.

Porter, L. W. A study of perceived need satisfactions in bottom and middle management jobs. *Journal of Applied Psychology,* 1961. *45,* 1–10.

Prehm, H. J. Special education research: Retrospect and prospect. *Exceptional Children.* 1976. *43,* 10–19.

Reppucci, N. D., & Sanders, J. T. Social psychology of behavior modification: Problems of implementation in natural settings. *American Psychologist.* 1974, *29,* 649–660.

Rousseau, M., Shores, R. E., Hasselbring, T. S., & Cunningham, J. J. Training researchers in special education. *Teacher Education and Special Education,* 1984, *7*(2), 75–81.

Shaver, J. P. The productivity of educational research and the applied-basic research distinction. *Educational Researcher,* 1979, *8*(1), 3–9.

Shores, R. E. What behavior research says to the classroom teacher: An interview with Richard E. Shores. *Teaching Exceptional Children,* 1972. *4*(4), 192–199.

Shores, R. E. Evaluation and research. *Teacher Education and Special Education,* 1979, *2*(3), 68–71.

Shores, R. E., Burney, J. D., & Wiergerink, R. Teacher training in special education: A review of research. In L. Mann & D. A. Sabatino (Eds.), *The third review of special education.* New York: Grune & Stratton, 1976.

Snell, M. E., & Smith, D. D. Developing the IEP: Selecting and assessing skills. In M. E. Snell (Ed.), *Systematic instruction of the moderately and severely handicapped* (2nd ed.). Columbus. OH: Charles E. Merrill, 1983.

Sparling, J. J., & Gallagher, J. J. The need to communicate. In J. J. Sparling, & J. J. Gallagher (Eds.), *Research direction for the 70's in child development.* Chapel Hill, NC: Frank Porter Graham Child Development Center, 1971.

Strain, P. S., McConnell, S., & Cordisco, L. Special educators as single subject researchers. *Exceptional Education Quarterly,* 1983, *4*(3), 40–51.

Trusty, F. M., & Sergiovanni, T. J. Perceived need deficiencies of teachers and administrators: A proposal for restructuring teacher roles. *Educational Administration Quarterly.* 1966. *2*. 168–180.

CHAPTER 16

THE NEXT 30 YEARS IN SPECIAL EDUCATION

M. Stephen Lilly

My task in this chapter is to anticipate the next 30 years in special education. Most responsible professionals would undoubtedly consider this a most formidable (in fact, virtually impossible) task. While admitting that what I just said is true (that is, the task is impossible), I am nonetheless not intimidated. Had I been asked to preview the next five years or next ten years in special education, I would have been somewhat more concerned. However, to use a football analogy, the quarterback who faces a third-and-thirty situation feels little pressure, for no one in the stands expects him (or her) to make a first down from that distance. On the other hand, third-and-five or third-and-ten is possible, and the pressure to succeed is therefore greater. Like the quarterback in the long yardage situation, I am not really expected to be right in what I predict, only reasonable, which in special education provides a great deal of latitude. And almost certainly, when it's time to open the capsule and read the predictions 30 years from now, this paper will be long forgotten and I will be spared the opportunity to say, "I told you so."

My first need in preparing this chapter was to achieve some perspective on how long 30 years really is. Thirty years from now is the year 2012, 12 years into a century that we have not yet begun to imagine. Consider with me these facts about the next 30 years:

- If you were to invest $1,000 today, at 10% interest compounded annually, in 30 years, you would have $17,649. I gave up trying to figure how much you would have if the interest were compounded daily.
- In 30 years, Gary Coleman will be old enough to be a grandfather.
- Thirty years from now, I will be retired and not very sympathetic to

*M. Stephen Lilly was Professor of Special Education and Associate Dean for Graduate Programs, College of Education, University of Illinois at Urbana-Champaign when this chapter was written. He is presently Dean of the College of Education at Washington State University. He has previously held positions at the University of Oregon, Bureau of Education for the Handicapped in the U.S. Office of Education, and the University of Minnesota-Duluth. He has published articles in several education journals on a wide variety of topics related to special education, has edited an introductory special education text, and is co-author of a book on mainstreaming for regular educators. His recent work has focused on policy analysis and relationships between regular and special education.

younger people complaining that my benefits are coming out of their
hides.

- In 30 years, Dandy Don Meredith will be in his seventies and
  contemplating new meaning to the lyrics, "Turn out the lights, the
  party's over."
- If you are making $30,000 right now and receive a 7% salary increase for
  the next 30 years, your salary in 2012 will be $228,367. Your salary *increment*
  during the 30th year will be $14,940. I won't burst your balloon by telling
  you how much a dozen eggs will cost in 30 years.

By now, I'm convinced that 30 years is an awfully long time, and I hope
you are as well. For at this point, I plan to declare impossible the *prediction*
of events that far into the future, and abandon prediction as a goal of the
chapter. Rather than talking about *what will happen,* I will stress *what I would
like to see happen,* given the history and current status of special education in
the United States. I would like to share with you my hopes and dreams for
our field, knowing full well that my hopes are another person's fears.

To begin with, let me share a few assumptions regarding education,
special education, and individuals whom we call "handicapped." These
assumptions are implicit in my "hopes for 2012." The most salient of these
assumptions are:

1. By and large, people are capable of far more than we first imagined:
   and the history of education unfolds as a gradual expansion of our
   expectations for others, both teachers *and* students.
2. There is a dignity in difference and in the inevitable variation among
   individuals. Even differences which result in limitations in functioning
   should be celebrated, not hidden or pitied.
3. Nonhandicapped individuals are capable of far more toleration and
   valuing of individual differences than we sometimes give ourselves
   credit for, and systems of community/school support for handicapped
   individuals do not have to be "bought" or "bartered."
4. We as special educators have been guilty of overlabeling and mislabeling,
   calling individuals handicapped who are not and creating artificial
   and rigid "differences" between so-called handicapped and nonhandicapped individuals.
5. Change is good, continual change is better, and only by continually
   questioning what we do and why we do it can we stay alive intellectually *and* politically.

With these assumptions in mind, let us now delve into my hopes for the next
30 years. There are 14 statements I will make, and obviously I must limit my
remarks on each and save more detailed analysis for other times and other
forums.

Integrated Schools

I hope that in 30 years there are no segregated schools to be found for students who are handicapped or gifted. Segregated special schools are, in my view, a relic of a time when we had a felt need to demonstrate the "uniqueness" of special education and our political savvy as special educators. As the story goes, we were given inadequate space or no space at all for special education programs in regular school buildings, so we set out to remedy the problem by finding our own space or building our own buildings. However, this was done without serious consideration of the consequences for children who would be educated in those buildings. In many communities today, we have moderately, severely, and multiply handicapped students going through their entire school careers with little or no school contact with nonhandicapped individuals. Just as significantly, the non-handicapped individuals in such segregated school settings do not have adequate opportunity to learn about, get to know and be friends with moderately and severely handicapped youngsters. Little wonder that as adults, the general public seems to be less than optimally accepting of their handicapped peers.

Major changes have come about in the last several years with regard to special schooling for the handicapped. We now have entire states and innumerable school districts around the country with *no* segregated special schools. In 1978, the President's Committee on Mental Retardation concluded that "the regular public school building is the proper setting for school-age mentally retarded students" (President's Committee on Mental Retardation, 1978, p. 73). After visiting 11 communities with integrated school programs for severely handicapped students, Taylor (1982) concluded that the notion that some children are so disabled as to require segregated special school placement is a "myth." Likewise, many residential schools for children with sensory handicaps have such low numbers of students in attendance that their futures are in jeopardy. Public school districts now routinely offer special education programs for students with sensory and physical handicaps, either independently or in cooperation with each other.

Unfortunately, the area of the gifted seems to be heading in the direction of more arrangements for separate schooling. Just a few years ago, the state of North Carolina entered a program for establishing special residential schools for students with special talents in science and mathematics. The demand for admittance to established special schools for the gifted seems to have no end. While it is sometimes seen as "unpatriotic" to criticize special education for our most able and talented citizens, the principles regarding education in the least restrictive environment apply to gifted students. I worry about increasingly separate educational provisions for the gifted. As I stated earlier, my vision for the future contains, as an ideal, *no* special schools for any subgroups of students, whether they be handicapped, poor, minority, or unusually able or talented.

Challenging Curricula

I hope that in 30 years our curriculum for moderately, severely and multiply handicapped students is considerably more challenging than it is today. It is not at all unusual today to walk into special schools or classrooms for the moderately or severely handicapped and find 12-year-old students stacking blocks or doing childish puzzles, or 18-year-old students aimlessly sanding random pieces of wood or sorting unimportant objects. While we are *serving* virtually all children of school age, we are neither *educating* nor *training* some of them. In the view of many professionals in this area, the lack of quality in educational programs stems from an overemphasis on developmental approaches to learning which are not suited to the learning rate of more severely handicapped populations of students (Snell & Renzaglia, 1980). Such a developmental approach leads to use of teaching techniques which are not age appropriate (Wilcox, 1979) and to classroom development of nonfunctional skills.

Our educational time with severely handicapped students is far too precious to spend on less than the most important tasks. Development of curriculum for severely handicapped students must be based on analysis of the requirements of adult living environments, rather than study of normal growth and development (York & Williams, 1977) and instruction must be functional, practical, and community based. Hopefully, the future will see more and more emphasis on development of skills in moderately and severely handicapped individuals which will allow them to take their place as contributing adult members of the community.

Deinstitutionalization

I hope that in the year 2012, we will have no large (or small) residential institutions for individuals who are called mentally retarded or emotionally disturbed. I will deal only briefly with this hope; it is well documented that we *know* the alternatives to institutionalization and the task now is to work toward their widespread and effective implementation (Novak & Heal, 1980). We have not stopped the steady growth of institutional living arrangements for the mentally retarded, and for the past 10–15 years, the trend has been in the opposite direction. However, three current dangers exist:

transinstitutionalization, inappropriate service settings, and the lack of community support services.

Transinstitutionalization

Many individuals are being "transinstitutionalized," moved from a large institution to settings with fewer residents but which still isolate and overprotect people from the community (Galloway, 1981). While some "group homes" are excellent, others continue to restrict personal freedoms such as independent life choices and ownership of personal clothes and property, and retain many undesirable elements of institutional life. Location is only one element in determining restrictiveness of life settings; community based residences which retain dependence-producing characteristics of residential institutions will not have the desired effect of normalizing the life experience of those who are being "rescued" from institutions.

Inappropriate Service Settings

In many places, we seem to accept the assumption that residential institutions are appropriate for some individuals, due to the "uniqueness" and severity of their problems. Galloway (1981) has pointed this out as a drawback to the concept of continuum of services, and has provided the following analysis:

- "The concept of a 'continuum of services' translates too quickly into a continuum of existing facility and program types, ordered from most to least segregative.
- Once that translation is rooted, it follows that for every point on the continuum, there must be a group of people who—because of their shared characteristics—'fit' that facility or program type. (We will identify, for example, group home-type clients and state institution-type clients.)
- Once located along the service continuum, one will be required to learn his or her way out of that point and into the next, less segregative, facility or program. (You will hear increasing discussion of behavioral 'exit criteria' for movement along the continuum.)
- Finally, one's prognosis for full participation as valued members of the community will be determined by his or her present location along the service continuum . . .

If these seeds of perversion take root, we will have succeeded in constructing yet another elaborate bureaucratic machine for trapping people in a handicapped world—one now called a 'continuum of services' " (p. 32).

Community Support Systems

Community support systems, both financial and human, are often not available to assure that deinstitutionalization results in the real goal of community integration. For moderately and severely handicapped individuals to be fully integrated in the life of the community as adults, extraordinary support and advocacy systems are necessary. Persons in all walks of life and a wide variety of service occupations must be willing and prepared to serve as advocates for handicapped individuals in a broad range of social settings. We have taken great strides toward deinstitutionalization, and only recently have begun to face up to the significant challenges of *community integration.* Quality of life for many handicapped adults will depend on our success in these endeavors.

In 1966, in *Christmas in Purgatory,* Blatt and Kaplan provided a description of a "good" institution in contrast to the atrocious conditions pictured in the standard institutional settings. This, along with other forces, led to a period of legal and political efforts to produce institutional reform. By 1981, Blatt had concluded that institutions will always produce dependence and incompetence, and called for closure of all institutions. I pray that by 2012, we will have not only closed institutions, but also welcomed their residents into the mainstream of community life.

Competitive Employment

I hope that by the year 2012, the vast majority of moderately and severely handicapped adults will be working in competitive employment situations. Sheltered workshops are an anachronism, albeit a living anachronism, in the 1980s. They provide jobs for the vast majority of moderately and severely handicapped adults, while making it virtually impossible for employees to enjoy independent or semi-independent community living (Wehman, Hill, & Koehler, 1979). Perhaps most ironic is the fact that in many sheltered workshops the most able workers, those with the best chance of "going it alone," are kept in sheltered employment because their productivity "carries" other less proficient workers.

Over the past several years, models for preparing moderately and severely handicapped adults for competitive employment have emerged and have been implemented in Washington, Illinois, Virginia, Wisconsin, and other states. Outcomes of such projects indicate that many moderately or severely handicapped individuals can, with proper training, work in competitive employment settings earning minimum wage or better. In a study of the cost-benefit of competitive employment training, Schneider, Martin, and Rusch

(1981) demonstrated that an individual in competitive employment earns far more over a 10-year period than the cost of training, placement, and follow-up services. Sheltered workshop earnings lag consistently behind training and maintenance costs. I do not contend that all moderately and severely handicapped individuals can succeed in competitive employment. However, many can, and we must give them the opportunity and support to do so. Hopefully, in 30 years, no textbook in mental retardation can appear on the market in which the only chapter on adult services is entitled "Sheltered Employment."

Specializing Regular Education

I hope that by 2012, what we now call "special education for the mildly handicapped" will be relatively indistinguishable from supportive services offered through regular education. Further, I hope that many of us will consider ourselves "regular educators."

This topic is far too broad and complex to cover here; for a more thorough treatment, I refer the reader to a paper entitled "Divestiture in Special Education" which I delivered to the Statespersons' Roundtable at the Council for Exceptional Children Convention in Houston in April, 1982. For a quick summary, I contend in that paper that special education has been in a continually expansive mode for the past 80 years. During this time, three "new" categories of exceptionality emerged: educable mental retardation, behavior disorders, and learning disabilities. Essentially, these three categories consisted of students who had problems of academic learning and/or social behavior in regular classrooms, were referred for special help, and were labeled handicapped and incorporated into the special education system. While special education thus grew, opportunities for supportive services through regular education diminished, as remedial programs were phased out in favor of emerging special education programs. Thus, in many school districts, we have become the "only game in town" for students and teachers who need help. Unfortunately, students must be labeled handicapped to receive remedial services in school.

One need only look at the array of students in programs for the learning disabled and educable mentally retarded to realize that we have come too far in this regard. We cannot hope to "rescue" all of the students who might have difficulty in the regular curriculum, nor can we demonstrate that past rescue efforts have been markedly successful. We have mislabeled and misclassified children in the name of providing help. We have ignored others who need the exact same kind of help but who do not qualify, largely due to resource limitations rather than clear and defensible definitions of the limits of our population. We must strive to break down the barriers we have built between regular and special education. We must admit that in many of our "special education" diagnostic and instructional approaches. "the emperor has no clothes." We must strive to make regular education as good as it can possibly be for as many children as possible. We must become. once again, regular educators. I am convinced this will happen over the next 30 years, and I hope that special educators are willing participants. as opposed to "protectors of hard-won turf."

Establishing a Professional Identity

I hope that 30 years from now, we have enough faith and pride in ourselves as professional educators that we no longer need to emulate the diagnostic and prescriptive models used by medical practitioners. It has always been a matter of curiosity to me that in building our models of professional practice in special education, we have followed the lead of physicians, not other educators. While the complexity and seeming certainty of our diagnostic procedures rival that of the medical world, many special educators do not know the basic readings and seminal works on individualization of instruction. While we strive in many places to bring children to campus to form a "clinical setting" for teacher education, we are largely unaware of the research on teacher behavior and classroom processes which has taken place in regular education. Special educators in both public schools and universities have been notoriously "aloof" from the professional activities of their regular education peers.

In my view, it is critical that we begin to view ourselves first and foremost as *educators* and that we take ownership and pride in the profession of education. We must join with others in celebrating, improving, and selling public education. We must make our primary allegiance with our true peers. As a by-product, we will know more about public education than we know right now. I am convinced that as we know more, we will serve children better and will feel less compelled to mimic the medical model. We will offer better service as a result. Perhaps we will be there in 30 years.

Competency Testing

I hope in 30 years, we are no longer confusing competency with test taking, for either students or teachers. I am convinced that some day we will look back and laugh at the naivete associated with the "competency testing" craze we are currently undergoing. The tragedy is that by the time we have the benefit of hindsight, many students will have been unwisely retained or denied diplomas, and some otherwise talented would-be teachers will have been denied employment.

I believe, with others, that we must be committed to accurate assessment of the outcomes of our educational efforts. What I do not believe is that we can do it very well, or are apt to be able to do it well in the foreseeable future. Further, I am convinced that current assessment systems for both students *and* prospective teachers are so simplistic that basing major life decisions on their results (decisions such as retention, graduation, or entry into the profession) borders on the criminal. Current assessment systems are informative, but no act of a state legislature can make them better than they are. We can assess student skills for the purpose of making educational program decisions. We can assess literacy of teaching candidates at the time of admission to teacher education. What we cannot do is replace professional judgment in the process of retention and graduation of students, or certification of teachers. If the judgment factor is replaced or minimized, then our professional stature is damaged.

Educational Advocacy

In 2012, I hope we all see ourselves as advocates for children, not advocates for buildings, services, or instructional arrangements. In 1980, Paula Smith and I published an article describing special education as a social movement. In that article, we pointed out that successful social movements tend to "conservatize," to draw in the flanks and protect what has been "won." I am afraid that I see rampant "status-quoism" in special education, particularly since the passage of P.L. 94-142 in 1975. While it is important to protect what has been gained for children, it is critical that we not become "reality bound" in our conceptualization and delivery of services.

Over the past few years, I have been involved with several parents seeking less segregated school placements for their children. Specifically, they have been advocating for special class arrangements in regular school buildings as opposed to special school settings. Likewise, I have worked with teachers and school administrators in seeking declassification and regular class placements for students who had been labeled mildly handicapped. In virtually all of these cases, the individuals most adamantly opposed to change were special educators. In the first set of cases, special education administrators have defended their special school arrangements even against the contrary wishes of parents. In the second set of cases, special education teachers have argued that their students are dependent on them and cannot succeed without them. In both cases, I have encountered unquestioning ardent allegiance to special education models which are of dubious value in the mid-1980s.

Fiscal Conservatism

I see two primary sources for conservative tendencies among special educators today. The first is fiscal and relates to the budgetary constraints being faced by public education nationally, at the state level, and in most localities. For several years, education has been dealing with the dilemma of needing to do more with less money, and we have passed the point of paring budgets without appreciably affecting programs. We are being forced to *do* less, and worthwhile educational experiences for children are being eliminated in one school district after another. Further, all of this reduction is occurring in the face of tremendous public pressure to improve the quality of education. As the budget knife cuts into the meat of educational programs, it is all too natural for special interest groups to guard their programs jealously. In such times, objective program analysis becomes more difficult. Many special educators would argue that criticism or admission of weakness in special education programs only makes them more vulnerable than other school programs in the budget cutting process. In other words, even if we know we have problems to be solved, admitting them will only weaken our political posture at a time when we are in intense competition for limited financial resources. There are two questionable assumptions underlying this argument: competition for funds and critical self-evaluation.

Competitive funding. I hold that in many instances, special educators build walls of competition in seeking to maintain special education funding levels, walls which will hinder communication and cooperation with regular educators for years to come. A case in point is our response to federal block grants for education as initially prepared in 1981 by the Reagan administration. The response of most special educators at the time was an expression of outrage regarding inclusion of *special education* funds in the block grants. The outcome was that these funds were withdrawn and retained at the federal level. We did not, however, join with educators in fighting for other monies to be taken out of the block grants. As a result, many important federal education programs have been decimated through inclusion in uncontrolled block grants to states. I contend that we were too narrow in our interests, to the point of being self-serving, and that analogous scenarios are taking place weekly at the state and local levels.

Self-evaluation. Others do not see our problems. For many years, special education grew and flourished without scrutiny. We seem to assume that if we do not admit our problems and weaknesses as a field, others will not notice them. While that might have been true at one time, it no longer is the case. Increasingly, our referral and placement practices are being called into question by regular educators and advocacy organizations. In my view, those who would propose that we "tread softly around our problems" in these times of budgetary uncertainities ignore the fact that our most questionable practices are under attack not only from within, but from outside as well. Issues surrounding identification and placement practices for students labeled LD, BD, and EMR, segregated services for moderately and severely handicapped persons, relationships between regular and special education, and "expansionism" in special education are topics of debate among *all* educators. Our best "political" posture is open and honest discussion of these issues with all educators, not blind allegiance to past practice.

"Protectionism"

The second source for conversative tendencies among some special educators is straightforward and somewhat resistant to change. Some of us have bought our own rhetoric of the past 50 years and are convinced that "the problem is in the child." We are convinced that children must be identified and served according to longstanding principles of special education. This view posits a strong "protectionist" role for special education: programs for severely handicapped must isolate students from regular school settings to protect children from the risk of failure and difficult social situations; programs for the mildly handicapped must save students from the frustrations and shortcomings of the regular education environment. Most of special education was built on the premise that regular education was not serving a specified group of children well. Many special educators have trouble accepting one central tenet of mainstreaming: the worth, value, and strength of the regular school experience. In sum, we have accepted our own arguments that we are "special" and that we are doing something for children which no one else can do. This belief persists in the face of mounting argument and evidence to the contrary. In the final analysis, when faced with the necessity of *proving* that we are really special, we are all the more hesitant to enter into constructive criticism of either our basic philosophical tenets or our mode of operation.

It will be a professional tragedy and a fiscal debacle over the next 30 years if special educators dig in their heels and resist progress. We must continually ask what is best for children based on current thinking and new knowledge in the field. Our job is to serve children, not to serve the system we have created. I hope we do a better job of this than we have done in the last few years.

Reducing Legal Involvements

I hope that over the next 30 years, the "legal mentality" in special education decreases. First let me state what I do *not* mean by this statement. I am not calling for a decrease in the number of lawsuits seeking redress for injustice, though I certainly hope the climate and lack of appropriate services and programs which have led to such lawsuits is improved. Nor am I favoring limitations on the right of parents to seek legal remedies when all administrative remedies have been exhausted.

The legal mentality to which I refer is exhibited by school administrators and is in reaction to the increasingly explicit legal bases for offering special education services. The most unfortunate example of this is the prevailing view of due process hearings as I see them operationalized in school districts and states. Due process hearings were initially ordered by the courts as *extralegal*, administrative procedures designed to mediate differences between parents and education agencies and to bring about the *most appropriate* educational decision for the student. As due process hearings are currently conducted, nothing could be further from the truth. In most hearings, both sides bring their lawyers. The school district typically argues not that their proposed program is best, but that it is *legal*. Appropriateness has become less of an issue in today's hearings than legality. This is a most unfortunate development, for once again, no one is necessarily asking what is best for the child. We need progress on this issue, and it will come only as we develop a standard of reasonableness in the relationship between schools and parents.

Parents as Partners

I hope that in the next 30 years, parents are finally recognized as full partners in the education process. Recognizing parents as full partners does not amount to granting them ultimate wisdom in educational decisions. Obviously, some parents will be wrong in what they want for their children, just as some school personnel make decisions on a basis of other than the educational needs of the child. What is necessary is that parents no longer be treated like second-class citizens. I know parents of handicapped children who have been to more special education conferences and done more reading in the field during the last few years than virtually any administrator or teacher in the school district, and yet whose ideas are rejected out of hand because they do not come from a "professional." On the other hand, I know of school programs in which parents are treated as equal partners, where their ideas are sought and valued. The result is a progressive, exciting school program. The basic issue, I believe, is openness to new ideas and to change. Where that openness exists, parental input is valued rather than ignored. The districts and the states which do not exhibit such openness will not, in my view, fare well over the next several years.

Teacher Training

I hope that 30 years from now, there will be less distinction between regular and special education in our colleges and universities. While I am not yet ready to call for phasing out of departments of special education, I am somewhat closer than I was several years ago. I do believe it is critical that special educators in colleges and universities form more and stronger collaborative relationships with colleagues in content areas in elementary, secondary, and vocational education. Our future depends, in part, on an increased understanding of special education by regular educators, *as well as a new emphasis on special educators understanding and working in the regular education system.* If I take the long view (say, 30 years), I do see increased administrative and programmatic consolidation of special education with other units in colleges of education.

The Dean's Grants have had a major impact on special education in colleges and universities. This impact can best be observed by examining the results of annual conferences of the American Association of Colleges for Teacher Education, an organization in which the primary active participants are deans of colleges of education. Several years ago, it was hard to find anything about special education on the conference program, and it was rare to find two or more deans talking about special education in their lobby conversations. Today, the situation is drastically different. Special education is no longer a "let it run itself" operation in many colleges of education. More and more deans are taking an active interest in special education in their colleges. This is a most significant and positive step in terms of bringing us more into the mainstream of professional education.

Future Research

In 30 years, I hope special education is not so rigidly empirical in its orientation toward educational research. We are, in fact, an empirical lot. We talk and act as though the future will be derived from the datum, and accumulation of bits of data will tell an increasingly complex story about children, teachers and systems. The more I see our data, and attempts to accumulate it to something meaningful, the more I am convinced that research and scholarship go far beyond reliable observation, measurement, recording, and analysis of data. The big (indeed, the real) picture lies somewhere beyond our numbers. To the surprise of many special educators, there are research methodologies which are designed to capture at least a larger part of the picture than our purely empirical methods will net.

For the past 16 months, as part of my position as Associate Dean for Graduate Programs, I have reviewed every dissertation submitted to the Graduate College by students in the College of Education. I cannot describe what an enriching, educational experience this has been for me. I have become thoroughly engrossed in and impressed by dissertations using historical research methodology, philosophical methodology, case study methodology, and naturalistic methodology, to name only a few. The richness of some of these accounts makes some empirical research pale in comparison. I am not calling for a moratorium on empirical research; I have great respect for our best researchers in special education. What I am calling for, and what I hope we see over the next 30 years, is increased respect for all types of research and scholarship in special education. Jim Kauffman (1981) has written recently that

> perhaps what (special education) needs more than anything else today is its philosophers—special educators who are capable of understanding special education in its historical and contemporary social and cultural contexts, articulating a coherent set of relevant premises about the education of exceptional children in our society, and elaborating the implications of various courses of action" (p. vii).

If such scholars are to emerge in special education, we must value their contributions as equal to those of the empirical researchers in our field.

"Double-Loop Learning"

I hope that between now and 2012, we are all "double-loop-learners." I recently ran across a book called *Reasoning, Learning, and Action* by Chris Argyris (1982). This book introduced me to a notion which summarizes my view of and hopes for special education nicely. Argyris distinguishes between single-loop-learners and double-loop-learners in the following way:

> Individuals or organizations who achieve their intentions or correct an error without re-examining their underlying values may be said to be single-loop-learning. They are acting like a thermostat that corrects error (the room is too hot or cold) without questioning its program (why am I set at 68 degrees?). If the thermostat did question its setting or why it should be measuring heat at all, that would require re-examining the underlying program. This is called double-loop-learning (pp. xi–xii).

Earlier in this chapter, I cited an article by Paula Smith and myself dealing with special education as a social movement. In our conclusion, we stated that "the dynamic nature of special education will be maintained only if we resist the conservative tendencies which are unavoidably present in our current situation" (Lilly & Smith, 1980, p. 11). My most fervent hope for special education in the next 30 years is that we find the will and the way to be double-loop-learners in all we do, to systematically examine and modify the underlying theories and assumptions on which we work.

Concluding Statement

Finally, I hope that in 30 years, we are all here to say, "my gosh, what a 30 years that was." Just think, in 30 years, we will all gather again (sporting our salaries in excess of $200,000!), and we will be the ones who look back on the last 60 years in special education. And some unsuspecting soul will be asked to look at the "next 60 years." Whoever that person is, I urge him or her to share the best hopes and dreams for the field. It is fun, and it is bound to stir up some discussion.*

REFERENCES

Argyris, C. *Reasoning, learning, and action.* San Francisco: Jossey-Bass, 1982.

Blatt, B. *In and out of mental retardation.* Baltimore: University Park Press, 1981.

Blatt, B., & Kaplan, F. *Christmas in purgatory.* Boston: Allyn & Bacon, 1966.

Galloway, C. The "continuum" and need for caution. *Education Unlimited,* 1981, *3*(3), 32–34.

Kauffman, J. M. From the editor. *Exceptional Education Quarterly,* 1981, *2*(2), vii.

Lilly, M. S. *Divestiture in special education.* Paper presented at Statespersons' Roundtable, Council for Exceptional Children Convention, Houston, April 1982.

Lilly, M. S., & Smith, P. Special education as a social movement. *Education Unlimited,* 1980, *2*(3), 7–11.

President's Committee on Mental Retardation. *Mental retardation: The leading edge.* Washington, D.C., 1978.

Novak, A. R., & Heal, L. R. (Eds.). *Integration of developmentally disabled individuals into the community.* Baltimore: Paul H. Brookes, 1980.

Schneider, K. E., Martin, J. E., & Rusch, F. R. Are we sacrificing quality: Cost versus benefits of sheltered and nonsheltered vocational training programs. *Counterpoint,* November 1981, *1*, 28.

Snell, M. E., & Renzaglia, A. Characteristics of services for the severely handicapped. *Education Unlimited,* 1980, *2*(1), 55–60.

Taylor, S. J. Making integration work: Strategies for educating students with severe disabilities in regular schools. *Counterpoint,* May/June 1982, *1*, 30.

Wehman, P., Hill, J. W., & Koehler, F. Helping severely handicapped persons enter competitive employment. *AAESPH Review,* 1979, *4*, 274–290.

Wilcox, B. Severe/profound handicapping conditions: Administrative considerations. In M. S. Lilly (Ed.), *Children with exceptional needs: A survey of special education.* New York: Holt, Rinehart & Winston, 1979.

---

*This chapter was originally prepared for the Peabody Symposium and Celebration, George Peabody College of Vanderbilt, November 1982. We appreciate the author's revisions for inclusion in this text.

York, R., & Williams, W. Curricula and ongoing assessment for individualized programming in the classroom. In R. York, P. Thorpe, & R. Minisi (Eds.), *Education of the severely and profoundly handicapped people.* Hightstown, NJ: Northeast Regional Resource Center. 1977.

Subject Index

311